W9-AGU-266

DATE DUE

~~APR 1 4 1999~~	
~~OCT 2 8 2000~~	
████████	

MUSIC OF
LATIN AMERICA

Da Capo Press Music Reprint Series

GENERAL EDITOR
FREDERICK FREEDMAN
VASSAR COLLEGE

MUSIC OF
LATIN AMERICA

By Nicolas Slonimsky

New Foreword and Addenda by the Author

DA CAPO PRESS • NEW YORK • 1972

Library of Congress Cataloging in Publication Data

Slonimsky, Nicolas, 1894-
  Music of Latin America.

  (Da Capo Press music reprint series)
  1. Music—Latin America. 2. Musicians, Latin
American. I. Title.
ML199.S55   1972   781.7′8   69-11288
ISBN 0-306-71188-5

This Da Capo Press edition of *Music of Latin America* is an un-
abridged republication of the third printing, revised, published in
New York in 1949. It incorporates a new foreword and addenda
prepared by the author, and is reprinted by special arrangement with
Thomas Y. Crowell Company.

Published by Da Capo Press, Inc.
A Subsidiary of Plenum Publishing Corporation
227 West 17th Street, New York, New York 10011

Manufactured in the United States of America

Foreword: 1972

To revise or not to revise? That is the question that has confronted many literary explorers contemplating the products of their labors performed at an earlier, more innocent age. The natural impulse is to scrap the whole tray of print and start anew, taking advantage of accumulated personal wisdom and the flow of available information. But what about the point of view? Should that be changed in deference to altered conditions?

The perusal of my book thirty years after my Latin American tour of exploration convinces me that revision through elimination and supplementation would serve no purpose. Little touches of literary and musical technicolor could be removed antiseptically with a sterilized brush, leaving no stains, but such an operation would not satisfy readers who seek an entirely different outlook. On the other hand, a drastic revision may disappoint those who want to gain an impression of musical affairs in Latin America as seen by an enthusiastic observer to whom the scene appeared in the fullness of exotic colors.

Exoticism — that was the crux of the trouble. No nation, no group of people, no individual likes to be regarded as an exotic object. Such repugnance is understandable if exoticism connotes condescension. But the Latin American scene evoked in me a sense of wonderment, profound curiosity, and excitement of discovery. Surely, there was admiration, and even humility.

Upon reflection, I have decided not to add new names in this reprint, not to bring up-to-date the list of works of Latin American composers already included in the book, and to limit additions to obituary data and a few corrections of dates of birth. The descriptions of the national musical cultures of the twenty Latin American republics covered in my book are still valid. No fundamental changes could have occurred in the period of thirty years.

What did change was the stylistic direction of Latin American composers of the new generation, and that change was momentous. The folkloric effervescence of Latin American music, its melodic and rhythmic ebullition, suddenly fell out of fashion. Many young Latin Americans received grants and subsidies to study abroad, particularly in the United States. As often happens in cultural exchanges, the more urbanized trends displaced the ingenuous ones. Some sort of Gresham's law entered here, and the colorful product of a spontaneous talent was exchanged for the common coin of international musical technology. Following the universal trend, Latin American composers came to regard national folkloric references as irrelevant to the times. Just as adolescent Americans of European national extractions feel reluctant to use the language of their parents, many young Latin American composers, having tasted the intellectual wine of avant-garde techniques, abandoned their national allegiance in favor of more refined, more scientific cosmopolitan trends.

The balance between the gains and losses in this process of socio-musical entropy is difficult to evaluate. Composers of the older generation exuded nationalistic fervor; they launched militant slogans — Brasilidade, Mexicanismo, Chilenidad — and urged their followers to express the spirit of their nations in rousing melodies and rhythms rooted in folklore. Their music was their national passport; one could name its country of origin by examining the scores. The titles themselves proudly announced the national derivation. Not so with the composers of the new Latin American avant-garde. Most of the titles attached to their compositions are abstractions or designations of classical form. The predominant influences of the educated Latin American composers at the turn of the twentieth century were Wagner and Richard Strauss; the next generation was nurtured by French impressionism; Stravinsky was the lodestone of younger Latin American musicians. Romanticism, impressionism, and primitivism were all compatible with native resources, but a profound change came with the advent of the international avant-garde as the source of inspiration of the Latin American youth. It became impossible to discover the nationality of composers who exploited such universal techniques.

Some self-conscious scholars protest that my search for ethnic resources was misdirected. Music is an international language, they assert, and a composer, whether he comes from Patagonia or Massachusetts, reflects his regional image of music as a universal art. Others maintain that any piece of music written by a citizen of a certain country becomes, ipso facto, an eponymous product of that country. But this theory disregards the loss of collective originality and the concomitant increase of stylistic entropy inherent in the abdication of national art. Even when a Latin American composer exploits ethnic resources, native melorhythms become morphologically or topologically altered, resulting in a coded message which can be deciphered only by obtaining the key to these latter-day enigma variations. There is no denying a high degree of sophistication and technical proficiency in the musical scores of new Latin American composers. They no longer wear a musical poncho, no longer celebrate a melorhythmic afternoon siesta. Such exotic dalliance, translated into musical terms, is repugnant to a sophisticated Latin American. But what is wrong with local color? The great Russian national school of music effloresced in multicolored hues, throbbing with authentic Russian melorhythms. Stravinsky emerged from this rich heritage, of which the score of his *Firebird* is an example. But he plucked off the flaming plumes of the fabulous bird, took out the florid cadenzas, eliminated supernumerary harps and tinkling celestas, and presented to the public an austere ornithological abridgment of his score. Still, conductors and the audience prefer the old opulent edition. Color won out.

We witness a similar condition in the new esthetics of Latin American music: off with melorhythmic feathers, down with ethnical flummery! But it is still the gorgeous flamboyance of the dancing tunes and bewitching rhythms that fascinate student and performer alike.

But isn't there plenty of color in the Latin American musical avant-garde? Doesn't the introduction of electronic techniques and aleatory progressions create new resources for jungle-like sound, with tropical birds singing in ear-splitting shrillness on the threshold of ultrasonic frequencies? Doesn't the rhythmic exuberance of the amplified percussion in ultramodern Latin American scores unfold a hyperexotic panorama of typical Latin Americanism? Undoubtedly. But the means employed to achieve these effects tend to become universalized. Nevertheless, perhaps serialism, electronic sound, and aleatory devices will be absorbed into the melorhythmic tissue of new Latin American music, and national cultures will emerge again and give rise to a new Brasilidade, a new Chilenidad, a new Mexicanismo.

To recapitulate: A whole generation of Latin American composers has arisen since the first publication of my book in 1945. As a result, the "density of composers" per area and per population (a statistic which I blandly offered on page 37 of my book, to the great dismay and indignation of some readers, but to the delectation of others) has increased considerably. Composers already included in the book have written a number of new significant works; some have radically changed their style of composition, abandoning their pristine ethnic sources of inspiration and embracing the novel methodology of the international avant-garde. But to take note of these new accessions, a fundamental revision of the book would have been necessary, sacrificing the aroma of the original book, period piece though it may be. This is how the musical panorama of Latin America unfolded before my eyes and ears thirty years ago, and these impressions, some of them highly personal, and the body of solid information that the book contains, seem to me worth preserving. This is the raison d'être of the 1972 reprint.

Nicolas Slonimsky
March 1972

MUSIC OF
LATIN AMERICA

MUSIC OF LATIN AMERICA

Nicolas Slonimsky

ILLUSTRATED WITH
PHOTOGRAPHS

THOMAS Y. CROWELL COMPANY
NEW YORK

MANUFACTURED IN THE UNITED STATES OF AMERICA
BY THE VAIL-BALLOU PRESS, BINGHAMTON, NEW YORK

Contents

CONTENTS

Preface to the Third Printing

IN THIS new printing I have made no attempt to revise or radically revaluate the presentation of Latin American music given in the original edition of 1945. Recent deaths of Latin American musicians have been noted; minor alterations have been made here and there; details have been fixed in the light of new information, some of factual importance (such as the documentary evidence that Villa-Lobos was born in 1887 and not in 1881), some trivial (such as the fact that the Chilean composer Alfonso Leng is a paradontist, and not an orthodontist by profession).

The surprising thing is that no major errors have been pointed out by critics. To be sure, there was plenty of sharp opposition to the book, some reviewers, in both Americas, rising to a considerable pitch of verbal vehemence. But this vehemence of expression was seldom accompanied by a list of demonstrable errors. The disagreement was in the interpretation of the musical scene. Do Latin American governments give help and encouragement to creative musicians? I say, yes. The critics cry: no, the public honors to composers and the cash rewards are just a façade to cover up the official indifference to art. Is the music publishing industry a prospering business in the Latin American republics? I say, yes, considering the size and population. The critics say: ridiculous, a lot of good music remains unpublished. Does Sr. So-and-So merit inclusion as a representative native composer? I say, yes, give him the benefit of the doubt—and five lines in the book. The sarcastic critic counters with the remark: "According to Mr. Slonimsky, a composer is a person who can put recognizable notes on the music staff." Yet, some of the youngsters among Latin American musicians whom I included on faith, have fully justified their promise. Two or three of them have since made quite a stir in the music world as composers and conductors, and not only in their native lands, but in the Estados Unidos as well!

My brief travelogue in the first section of the book caused the lifting of many a dignified eyebrow. A North American librarian referred to me as "Baron von Münchausen Slonimsky," but conceded that "if you take his book with a grain of humor, as, of course, it was intended, you will find out something about music in the lands to the South of us." A Cuban writer likened me to Don Quixote: "There occurred a quixotic episode," he reminisces, "similar to the one related in Chapter II of Part I of *Don Quixote*. An itinerant knife-sharpener began to play his mouth organ. Suddenly, Slonimsky got excited and nearly jumped out of the car in his eagerness to get hold of the man. During the ride, he kept singing the tune repeating with emotion: 'This is the Mixolydian scale of the Greeks.' " Another reviewer pitied my gullibility: the knife-sharpener's panpipe, he asserted, was no native instrument, but a commercial product on sale at the Woolworth stores in Havana!

Sometimes opinion widely diverged even on the pages of a single publication. Thus, the *Saturday Review of Literature* published an article in its issue of November 3, 1945, describing my Latin American impressions as "Slonimsky in Wonderland," and blasting my book as "superficial, inaccurate, and unreliable." But another reviewer in the same journal, in the issue of January 26, 1946, set down my book as "a rare combination of accuracy, good judgment, and humor"!

Latin Americans themselves greeted the book with the friendly welcome of a cultured host towards a well-meaning if somewhat naive tourist. But there were also gratifying expressions of true appreciation of my effort. Wrote the octogenarian dean of Argentine composers, Alberto Williams: "Su obra representa una labor inmensa. Usted ha bebido en las fuentes, ha leido las obras y ha escuchado lo popular y lo academico."

The most flattering tribute came in the form of a translation of my book published in Buenos Aires as *La Musica de America Latina,* in 1947. The edition was magnificently put out, with my geo-musical map serving as end papers. The translation was extremely conscientious, with all my flights of fancy rendered into beautifully sonorous Spanish vocables. Alas, the admirable translator fell into an etymological trap by titling my chapter on Artless Folklore, *Folklore Inartistico!* Fortunately, the contents of the chapter belie the gratuitous negative of the Spanish heading.

With all its faults, the book is still the only comprehensive account of Latin American music, its native elements, its composers, its local color. The successive printings demonstrate that the book satisfies a continued demand. What more can an aspiring author, venturing into a new field, ask of the reading public?

Acknowledgment

To my friends in the twenty republics of Latin America goes my gratitude for contributing the factual data without which this book could not have been written. Their names appear all over these pages in the form of quotations from their writings, credit lines under musical illustrations, and musical autographs. I also want to thank Arthur Cohn for checking up on dates and titles of orchestral scores by Latin American composers in the Fleisher Collection in Philadelphia. Translations from foreign books in various languages are my own.

N. S.

Venient annis saecula seris
Quibus Oceanus vincula rerum
Laxet et ingens pateat tellus,
Thetisque novos detegat orbes,
Nec sit terris ultima Thule.

[Seneca]

A Pan American Fishing Trip

ONE hundred and twenty-eight years ago, the Government of the United States sent a mission to South America, on the frigate *Congress,* with the purpose of collecting information on the state of the neighboring continent. The secretary of the mission was H. M. Brackenridge, who subsequently played a part behind the scenes in the drama of the Monroe Doctrine. In his account of the voyage, published in 1819, he wrote: "The study of South American affairs has not yet become fashionable; persons who possess the most minute acquaintance with the different countries of Europe have scarcely given themselves the trouble to become familiar with the mere geographical outlines of our great Southern Continent. . . . What is wanted at present is not so much a work embracing the necessary information on the subject of South America generally as one that should create a desire to be informed."

Since Brackenridge's time, many a weighty volume has been published dealing with geography, politics, and economics of South America, Central America, and the West Indies, the parts of the world which are commonly referred to under the collective name of Latin America. But in the domain of the arts, and more particularly of music, Latin America remains largely a *terra incognita.*

To find out what is what and who is who in the music of Latin America, I undertook a journey using a swifter conveyance than Brackenridge's frigate—the airplane. I discovered a veritable El Dorado of music, and this book embodies my findings. In my quest of musical treasure, I was greatly helped by my Latin American friends. But not all were of one mind as to how I should treat the subject in my book. José Castañeda, the Guatemalan musician who excels in fiery journalism, admonished me earnestly in an article entitled *La Pesca Panamericanista* (Pan-

I

American Fishing Trip), published in *El Liberal Progresista* of Guatemala City, January 17, 1942. He wrote:

A restless temperament, an explorer by nature, Slonimsky has always sought the sources of the musical unknown. It is logical, therefore, that he should be wandering in our lands in search of a Pan American adventure. It is possible that, pestered by musicians avid for publicity, he should yield and carry away an all too numerous collection of musical works, or what pass for such. The danger for Slonimsky lies in his amiable nature, in his inability to reject bluntly the impostor who unashamedly submits manuscripts to him for inclusion in his programs or in the book he is writing. Let us hope that this is a transitory peril. Back in Boston, in the cultural atmosphere of the learned Northern city, he will recover his critical faculties, and will again become the Slonimsky we know, a critic of fine sensibility, of alert judgment, with no consideration for mediocrity. His book should be something more than a congealed catalogue. Something more than mere statistics. It should give the candid and bold view of one who has seen us at close range.

In the meantime, let Slonimsky ponder the gravity of his undertaking. All over the Americas, his book will be received with warm attention, but also in a critical spirit. Pan American fishing should be done with a rod, and not with a net. How gratifying it would be to find evidence, on the pages of his future book, that the author has jettisoned the ballast of mediocre production, and rejected all compromises! We cannot expect anything else from Nicolas Slonimsky, the subtle annotator of modern music.

I am now back in Boston, breathing the cultural air of the "learned Northern city," but I am still unconvinced that Castañeda's rod is the proper instrument for a factual survey. And now that my book is here, there are found in it all sorts of fish, multi-colored tropical fish cavorting in the southern sun, and common ordinary fish that will hardly excite the palate of an ichthyological gourmet. But here they are, all assembled between covers, and—who knows?—some of them may yet spawn significant caviar, which even the fastidious Castañeda will find stimulating.

On my Pan-American tour, I gave a lecture-recital in each country, featuring modern music, including compositions by native musicians. My appearances in the countries I visited were presented under the auspices of local cultural organizations, official, semi-official, and private.* The

* Among these were *Escola Nacional* and *Conservatorio Brasileiro* in Rio de Janeiro; *Conservatorio Dramatico e Musical* in S. Paulo, Brazil; *Grupo Renovación*, and *Amigos del Arte* in Buenos Aires; *Instituto de Bellas Artes* at the University of Chile in Santiago; *Instituto Cultural Peruano Norte-Americano* in Lima; *Radio Nacional* in Quito, Ecuador; *Conservatorio Nacional* of Panama; *Asociación de Cultura Musical* in San

subject of my lecture-recitals was modern music in all its ramifications, including such matters as polytonality, neo-classicism and expressionism. Most of my talks were broadcast. I should very much like to know the psychological reaction of a dweller of the Ecuadorean Andes, or of the Indians in Nicaragua, to the *Klavierstück, Opus 33a* of Schoenberg, which I included in all my programs as a classical example of the twelve-tone technique.

I spoke extemporaneously, in Spanish, albeit unorthodox as to grammar and word usage. In Brazil I took a long shot at Portuguese, with the aid of makeshift linguistic formulas which I had devised for the purpose of converting Spanish words into Portuguese. The children of Oscar Lorenzo Fernandez, the Brazilian composer, drilled me in Portuguese pronunciation; they could not understand my difficulties. It was so simple, so natural to them to speak in Portuguese.

At the end of my lecture, Oscar Lorenzo Fernandez had a surprise for me. Solemnly, he tendered me a diploma which conferred on me the title of Professor Honorario of the *Conservatorio Brasileiro de Musica,* of which he is the Director. I felt it incumbent upon me to say a few words in reply, but here my Portuguese broke down, and I had to let my last sentence go unfinished. But on the whole, my linguistic venture was successful. The morning paper *Correio da Manhã* wrote that my Portuguese was "perfeitamente compreensivel," and even abounding in "deliciosos humorismos."

When I repeated my lecture in São Paulo, a lady came to the green room and complimented me on my Portuguese. "It sounded exactly like Mario de Andrade," she observed. The commendation was double-edged, however, for Mario de Andrade, who was also present at my lecture, is known as the James Joyce of Brazilian literature and takes considerable liberties with syntax.

The musical tourist in Latin America is constantly amazed by the attention which the local press pays to concert life, often featuring musical events on the front page. When I played in Panama City, in a joint recital with the Panamanian violinist, Alfredo de Saint Malo, one newspaper devoted a special editorial to our concert, which concluded with these words: "And to think that these two artists, with their souls engrossed in the sacred art of music, tread the same pavement which serves us in

---

José, Costa Rica; University of Managua, Nicaragua; Secretariat of Public Instruction of El Salvador; *Conservatorio Nacional* in Guatemala City; and the University of Mexico.

our daily tasks!" Incidentally, the Panama concert netted us one hundred and sixty-eight dollars, a gratifying return, considering that we played a modern program, including the first local performance of Stravinsky's *Duo Concertant*.

Chief executives of Latin American republics often take a personal interest in musical events. During the presidency of the now exiled General Jorge Ubico of Guatemala, it was necessary to secure a permit from him for each concert by a foreign artist. To my telegraphic request for such a permit, I received a prompt reply, which I translate: I THANK YOU FOR YOUR FINE ATTENTIONS AND AM GRATIFIED THAT YOU REGARD WITH APPROBATION THE STATE OF MUSIC IN GUATEMALA. I SALUTE YOU. JORGE UBICO.

In San Salvador, the capital of the smallest Central American republic, El Salvador, four hundred people attended my concert. This would be proportionate to thirty-two thousand people turning up at Madison Square Garden to hear a talk on sinusoidal vibrations proffered by a gentleman speaking in Basic English, embellished with international polysyllables. The principal newspaper of San Salvador, *El Diario Latino*, devoted four columns of space to the review of my concert, which is proportionate to thirty-six columns of print in a weekday issue of *The New York Times*.

About halfway through my talk, a middle-aged man, clad in khaki, entered the hall and sat inconspicuously among the audience. I heard someone whisper: *"El Señor Presidente!"* It was General Maximiliano Hernández Martínez, at that time Dictator-President of the republic of El Salvador. He was late because, as he explained to me afterwards, he had been detained at a cabinet meeting. (El Salvador had just declared war on the Axis powers.) The Dictator-President was a music lover, and used to play the drums in a military band, but I felt it was fortunate that he arrived after I had finished the Schoenberg *Klavierstück*. Atonal music does not usually agree with absolute rulers. He applauded heartily when I played some piano pieces by three Salvadorean composers, who were also present at the concert.

In Nicaragua, the newspapers took the opportunity to express their admiration for the military achievements of the country of my birth, Russia, and greeted me with exuberant headlines on the front page:

You come to Managua, oh Nicolas Slonimsky, at the time when the soul of Russia flies on the heroic wings of liberty in

DEFENSE OF THE ALERT SPIRIT OF DEMOCRACY— YOU BRING US A
MESSAGE OF IMMORTAL RUSSIA, THE RUSSIA OF THE ARTS, AND A
REFLECTION OF THE EPICAL ACCOMPLISHMENT OF A NATION THAT
KNOWS HOW TO PROTECT THE INTEGRITY OF HER SACRED SOIL—
BE WELCOME, OH NICOLAS SLONIMSKY!

In Cuba a music critic called me "un verdadero Rey de la Batuta," and
since then I sign letters to my Cuban friends, "Affectionately yours,
King of the Baton." Another Havana critic, outraged by my ultra-modern
programs, said I was "loco," and accused me of playing a practical joke on
the Cuban public. I had conducted *Ionization* by Edgar Varèse, scored
for instruments of percussion, friction, and sibilation, as well as Schoenberg's twelve-tone piece, *Accompaniment to a Cinema Picture*.

Latin American journalists have learned from their Yankee colleagues
the fine art of sensational reporting. In Rio de Janeiro, an evening paper
published an interview with me, and the headline, right over my picture, read: "There Are No Musicians in South America." I was horrified
when I saw it, but was somewhat reassured by the opening paragraph of
the story, which explained: "This is what the dictionaries say, but
Slonimsky believes otherwise."

In São Paulo, Brazil's second largest city, I told the reporter of the
Diario da Noite how greatly impressed I was by Villa-Lobos' ingenious
Bachianas Brasileiras, which interpret Bach as part of Brazilian folklore.
In the Chorale of the fourth suite from *Bachianas Brasileiras*, there is a
recurring pedal note on a high B flat which, so Villa-Lobos explained, is
the exact reproduction of the cry of a jungle bird, the Araponga. I also
mentioned to the reporter that I had never seen the Araponga, but should
like to do so if there were one in captivity.

The story appeared in the *Diario da Noite* under this heading:

CAME TO BRAZIL TO SEE ARAPONGA

Yankee Composer Introduced Today to the Bird
That Inspired the B Flat of the Bachianas Brasileiras

In vivid Portuguese prose, the reporter described my visit to the bird
shop (he even gave the exact address) and my reaction to the Araponga.
It was, of course, all pure fiction. I never saw the Araponga and am still
without definite confirmation as to whether it actually emits a high B
flat.

Villa-Lobos has many another trick up his inventive sleeve. He has, for instance, perfected a method whereby he can extract melodies from pictures. He calls it "millimetrization." He traces the contours of the picture on graph paper, and then plots the melody, a semitone to a square of the graph in the vertical direction, and an eighth-note to a horizontal unit. Thus an ascending curve in the picture results in a melody going up, and a descending line produces a falling musical phrase. An undulating landscape is reflected in a florid cantilena. Villa-Lobos has in this manner transcribed the melody of the New York sky line, using a panoramic photograph supplied by an American steamship company. He harmonized and orchestrated it, and on his visit to the United States in 1945, conducted the piece as a gesture of good will at his radio debut in New York City.

Not all pictorial material is suitable for millimetrization. When a lady asked Villa-Lobos to set to music the X-ray picture of her heart, he politely declined, explaining that her heart was musically uninteresting. He graciously agreed to write down the melody of my wife, my child and myself at the breakfast table, from a photograph I gave him in Rio de Janeiro. He spent over two hours on it, and I can testify to the honesty of his effort. If the result is uninspiring, it is through no fault of Villa-Lobos. It must be that my family is simply not musicogenic.

TRIBULATIONS OF A MUSIC COLLECTOR

One of the principal objectives of my tour was to gather orchestral manuscripts of Latin American composers for the Fleisher Collection in the Free Library of Philadelphia, founded by Philadelphia's Edwin A. Fleisher. The scores were to be copied by the WPA Music Copying Project working in cooperation with the Fleisher Collection, under the supervision of Arthur Cohn, the accomplished and scholarly American musician, who is himself a composer. In March 1943, the WPA came to an end, and the task of copying the scores was assumed by the Fleisher Collection on a grant from the City of Philadelphia, with Arthur Cohn as Director of the Collection.

I had imagined that the Latins would leap at a chance of having their works preserved in so respectable a repository. Before long, I knew differently. I found that I had to wheedle and cajole them into surrendering their manuscripts, and all too often my blandishments proved to no avail. The musicians explained their reluctance to cooperate by an unhappy previous experience with "Yankee promises." Two or three composers had lost their scores in the United States under strange circumstances. Humberto Allende, the pioneer Chilean modernist, gave the original score of his *Escenas Campesinas* to the Chilean Ambassador to take to Washington, and it vanished without trace on the way. Allende had to rewrite the score from memory, which, however, proved not without benefit, for in the meantime his technique of orchestration had improved so greatly that he was able to turn out a much more competent piece of work. Another tale of woe was told to me by the Chilean composer René Amengual, whose music was unaccountably mislaid on the premises of the Guggenheim Foundation in New York, never to be recovered.

Accidents, also, have been responsible for the loss of manuscripts. Prospero Bisquertt of Chile lost one of his orchestral manuscripts when, on June 7, 1927, a train was wrecked in the Andes between Santiago and Buenos Aires, with the resultant destruction of the mails which carried Bisquertt's score. In 1936, José María Castro of Argentina forwarded the score and parts of his *Concerto Grosso* to Prague, for a performance at the International Festival there. To gain time, he sent the music by transatlantic airmail. The plane went down in mid-Atlantic, and all the mail was lost.

I did not, of course, carry all the music on the plane with me, but dispatched a number of manuscripts ahead by post. My experiences with the postal clerks in Latin American cities were nearly as horrible as a plane accident. I shall never forget the agonizing hours in the central post office of Mexico City, when, laden with the collected works of the Mexican composer, Arnulfo Miramontes, I tried to persuade the Señorita in charge to accept the music for shipping. She claimed I had too much postage on the packages, and that it was against the rules to accept foreign parcel post with excess postage. I finally had to summon the chief of the parcel post division in order to get the shipment through. On top of all this, my Mexican scores were held in Laredo, Texas, for customs examination, and it took the Fleisher librarians several months to rescue the music.

In my Pan-American fishing net I drew in a number of manuscripts by Latin American composers now dead. In this task I was helped by the families of the composers. The son of Ernesto Drangosch of Argentina lent me his father's orchestral scores. From the daughter of Barrozo Netto, the Brazilian composer of flavorsome salon music, I received the orchestral compositions he left at his death in 1941. The daughter of Alberto Nepomuceno, the pioneer of Brazilian modern music, helped me to secure his unpublished works for orchestra. This daughter, incidentally, was an extraordinary person in her own right. Although born with only the left arm, she studied the piano and became well known as a one-armed pianist.

A very important part of my catch was a set of orchestral manuscripts by that extraordinary genius, Silvestre Revueltas, the Mexican, who lived his forty years of life like a character in a Parisian novel, dividing his time between composition, leftist politics, and the drinking of Mexican *tequila*, a beverage which American tourists call *to-kill-ya*, so murderous is its impact. Weakened by alcohol, Revueltas' bulky body succumbed to an attack of pneumonia on the night of October 4, 1940, as his ballet *El Renacuajo Paseador* was having its first performance at the *Palacio de Bellas Artes*. After his death, his musical manuscripts were lovingly collected by his sister, and thus preserved for the future.

As to music by living composers, I applied the method of search and seizure on the premises. I recall many a profitable afternoon in Buenos Aires, at the spacious residential home of the octogenarian composer of nine symphonies, Alberto Williams; at the cottage of the gray-haired author of the celebrated *Estrellita*, Manuel Ponce, in Chapultepec; in the tower studio of the formidable Carlos Chavez, in a suburban section of Mexico City; in the modern apartment of the urbane Brazilian composer, Francisco Mignone in Rio de Janeiro; at the pleasant little villa of Humberto Allende of Chile, filled with Indian drums and seven-foot long fifes, along with modernistic sculptures of Allende's daughter, Tegualda, named for an Araucanian goddess; at the house of María de Baratta in San Salvador, where she has assembled a veritable museum of Aztec pottery; at the residence of Luis A. Delgadillo in Managua, Nicaragua, with street-level windows through which a wide-eyed audience of street urchins watched a private concert; and in the Panama studio of Alfredo de Saint-Malo, where I had the shock of my life when the upright piano all but disintegrated into dust as I stepped on the pedals— the termites having been at work there ahead of me; and in the dentist's office of affable Alfonso Leng, the Chilean composer of romantically inspired music and also a prominent Santiago paradontist, thanks to whose friendly ministrations I had an urgent job expertly done on a bothersome molar.

One of the most exciting experiences on my tour was the meeting with João Gomes de Araujo, the Brazilian author of *Maria Petrovna*, an opera on a Russian subject with an Italian libretto. João Gomes de Araujo was born in the year 1846. Taking it for granted that he was no longer living, I had written, in advance of my visit, to the Conservatory of São Paulo (where Gomes de Araujo used to teach), inquiring as to the exact date of his death. Fancy my surprise when, in reply, I received a cordial missive from the ancient man himself, in which he wrote, in quaint English: "It is a fact that I was born on the fifth of August, 1846, but in spite of this being quite a long existence, I should say that I am still healthy and fit for anything." With the letter, he sent me a musical manuscript, written in a shaky hand, and dedicated to me.

Later on, when I arrived in São Paulo, my first thought was whether João Gomes de Araujo was alive. He was, and he came unassisted to see me at my hotel. He wore no glasses, and I observed that he had a fine complement of natural teeth. I paid a visit to him at his own home, where he introduced me to his aged children and middle-aged grandchildren. It was my fervent hope that he might live to see his hundredth anniversary, August 5, 1946, but shortly afterwards I received word that the venerable musician had succumbed; he died in São Paulo on September 8, 1942.

All told, I brought with me for the Fleisher Collection over three hundred orchestral scores. There were among these manuscripts compositions of all dimensions, from a short *Gavotte* by Manuel Ponce, written at the age of fourteen, to huge symphonic edifices such as *Chôros No. 11* by Villa-Lobos, or the industrial ballet *Mekhano* by the Argentine composer-conductor, Juan José Castro. There were compositions in conventional style, and there were also ultra-modern elucubrations, including music in quarter-tones. Numerically, Mexico yielded the richest harvest. My good friend, the German-Spanish-Mexican musicologist Otto Mayer-Serra, excoriated me for carrying away so much stuff. He wrote in *Revista Musical Mexicana* on June 7, 1942: "When Nicolas Slonimsky left Mexico, he took with him over a hundred orchestral manuscripts. From his lexicographical viewpoint, this constitutes a veritable triumph. But when we examine these works from an esthetic angle, we find that fully 40 per cent are nothing more than conservatory exercises; and 40 per cent, though technically adequate, are conventional in form and style. Some 20 per cent, perhaps as little as 10 per cent, represent the product of real composers, musicians who have something worthwhile to communicate."

In private conversation, Otto Mayer-Serra used a more picturesque language. He called my musical haul *basura*, garbage, or worse, *basura de basura*, garbage of garbage. By obvious inference, I was a musical garbage collector.

Otto's nose was, however, far less sensitive to the *basura* of the past, provided it was well petrified. Rummaging in a second-hand book shop in Mexico City, I came across a stack of manuscripts by one Hermann Roessler, which I purchased for the sum of six Mexican pesos. From the inscriptions on the music, I gathered that Roessler was a German musician who came to Mexico City with the Emperor Maximilian. The successive dedications of his compositions, first to the exalted personages of the Imperial Court of Mexico, then to the victorious generals of the Revolution, and lastly to the Inspector of a School for Señoritas, told the melancholy decline of Roessler's fortunes. Some of his piano pieces were printed editions. I particularly relished the cover design for two Nocturnes entitled respectively *For Mama's Birthday* and *For Papa's Birthday*, showing a well-behaved female child performing at the piano, while a dignified Papa, ornamented with a Vandyke beard, stands by contentedly, with an adoring Mama reposing her coiffured head on his shoulder. Roessler's music was *basura* of the first water, but Otto Mayer-Serra was fascinated by its bland naïveté. He was genuinely grateful to me when I presented the whole collection of Roessleriana to him as a token of intermusicological solidarity.

ELUSIVE EDITIONS

Music publishing is a prolific business in Latin America. There is a tremendous and varied output of published music. However, it is not always easy to collect the fruits of this cornucopia. There is a word in the Spanish language that I have come to abhor: it is *agotado*, exhausted, or out of stock. It greeted me everywhere, from Brazil to Costa Rica, from Cuba to Chile. It seemed to me that the mysteriously unavailable music could not possibly be of interest to more than a handful of people like myself, bent on the discovery of obscure bibliographical material. How had such esoteric editions become exhausted? Were they actually sold out, or only lost in the shuffle? How many people, for instance, could be interested in purchasing lithographed excerpts from an Italianate opera by the late Peruvian composer, Valle-Riestra? Yet I could not get any copies in Lima, and had to beg one from a friend of the Valle-Riestra family.

On the eve of my departure from Buenos Aires I found out that the full score of an orchestral overture by the late Argentine composer, Celestino Piaggio, was published by the National Culture Committee of Argentina, and was available gratis to anyone with cultural intentions. There was no way of knowing that the Piaggio Overture had been published, because copies were not distributed commercially and not included in any local music catalogues. I sped to the Committee, and got my copies at the last moment.

Similarly unobtainable through regular channels was an excellent album of Brazilian music for piano, voice, and violin, published by the University of Rio de Janeiro in 1937 under the title *Musique Brésilienne Moderne*. Free copies of this collection were given away to visitors to the Brazilian Pavilion at the New York World's Fair, but none leaked out to the music stores either in Brazil or the United States. In fact, when I inquired about *Musique Brésilienne Moderne* in the largest music store in Rio de Janeiro, I was met with a puzzled glance, and was told there was no such album in existence. It took me some time to trace the publication to its source, which proved to be the *Escola Nacional de Musica*, which sponsored my concert. By sheer chance, I stumbled upon a stack of copies in the Director's room, and claimed a few copies as my rightful share according to the law of "finders keepers." Looking around for more hidden treasure, I unearthed, in the editorial offices of the *Revista Brasileira de Musica* in the same building, a practically virgin deposit of printed scores of Nepomuceno's *Symphony in G,* which had been regarded as *agotado*.

In the end, I had collected something like a quarter of a ton of printed Latin American music, including popular songs and salon pieces. I turned over my duplicates and some single copies to the Boston Public Library, where the music is now available for study in the Music Department, presided over by the cooperative and scholarly Richard G. Appel.

Hard as it is to hunt down Latin American printed editions, it is even more difficult for Latin American musicians to get hold of music by American composers. As a result, the Latin American conception of who's who in music in the United States is almost as grotesque as the popular notion in this country that all Latin American music consists of Tangos and Rumbas. In a supposedly authoritative article in the June, 1938, issue of the *Revista Brasileira de Musica,* the following are named as representative American composers: Victor Harris, Soward (*sic*) Brockway, Arthur Bird, Harry Rowe Scheley, Henry Holden Huss, and Tom Dobson. The latter is described as "occupying a unique place in the musical world of North America being the composer of a number of inspired songs, as well as a pianist, and singer of refined taste." Among American women composers, the author cites Senhora Philip Hale!!

The most active music publishing houses of Latin America are in Argentina and Brazil. The branch of the Italian Ricordi Company in Buenos Aires has a rich and varied catalogue of music in all forms, including operas, orchestral scores, and chamber works by Argentine composers, and also some Chilean and Uruguayan compositions. Other music publishers in Argentina are Carlos Lottermoser in Buenos Aires, Romano in Rosario, and Grignola in Tucumán. The composer-members of the progressive *Grupo Renovación* in Buenos Aires have printed at their own expense some of their piano pieces and songs. Alberto Williams maintains a publishing enterprise named *La Quena* (the *Quena* is the ancient flute of the Incas), under whose imprint he has published virtually the entire catalogue of his symphonic and instrumental music, as well as piano pieces and songs by his daughter Irma.

In Brazil, the largest music publishers are the Arthur Napoleão company and the Brazilian Ricordi branch. Together with lesser firms, Carlos Wehrs, Miranda, Vitale, and others, they have published thousands of Brazilian compositions, mostly for piano and voice, but also some in larger forms.

The most idealistic music publisher of Latin America is beyond doubt Francisco Curt Lange of Montevideo, a German student of philosophy, architecture, literature, and music, who settled in Uruguay in 1923, quickly mastered the language, and launched a movement which he called *Americanismo Musical,* designed to link and integrate musical research in the Americas. The organ of *Americanismo Musical* is the mastodontic *Boletín Latino-Americano de Música,* issued once every two or three years, which contains a staggering amount of material on Latin American folklore and various aspects of native music. The publication of each issue of Lange's "bulletins" is made possible by his extraordinary perseverance, a sort of musicological fanaticism that overcomes the insurmountable and breaks down the stone walls of public indifference. In the words of a brochure published in Bogotá in 1938 on the occasion of Lange's visit there, "one must possess a will of iron to organize the publication and distribution of the *Boletín,* to raise the necessary money, and to maintain the enormous correspondence." Lange's correspondence is, indeed, measured in astronomic figures. The latest letter I have received from him bears the number 13,953.

Not satisfied with his already varied program of activities, Lange undertook in 1940 the formation of an Inter-American Cooperative of Composers, with the object of publishing Latin American music of the noncommercial type. The composers pay one half of the printing expenses, and the royalties, if any, go towards the publication of new works. This arrangement aroused the ire of Otto Mayer-Serra, who wrote in *Revista Musical Mexicana:* "When apprised of this condition, the composers whom I have approached were indignant. We thought that the time when a musician had to labor exclusively *ad maiorem Dei gloriam* was definitely past." But is it not better to work for the greater glory of God without material reward than to sulk forever in the outer darkness of unpublished obscurity?

Outside Argentina and Brazil, there are few music publishing establishments. In Chile, the Faculty of Fine Arts of the University of Chile has issued piano pieces and songs by the Chilean composers Domingo Santa Cruz, Carlos Isamitt, Prospero Bisquertt, Alfonso Leng, Samuel Negrete, Jorge Urrutia Blondel, Alfonso Letelier, Acario Cotapos, Humberto Allende, his brother Adolfo Allende, and some others. Unfortunately, these editions, too, belong to the *agotado* category.

In Peru, the Carlos Brandes Co. has printed some Peruvian music and has also taken over the representation of the small Parisian establishment, *A la Flûte de Pan,* which had issued several Peruvian compositions. In Mexico, the first of Wagner & Levien has in its catalogue the early music of Chavez and a large number of piano pieces and songs of Manuel Ponce, most of which are now out of print.

Orchestral scores, chamber music, and other works by Carlos Pedrell (nephew of the Spanish scholar Felipe Pedrell) and Alfonso Broqua of Uruguay, who spent practically all their lives in France, have been published in Paris. Some composition by Villa-Lobos, Humberto Allende, and Alejandro García Caturla of Cuba have also been issued by Paris music firms. These editions are available in the larger American music libraries.

In recent years, American music publishers have made a determined effort to satisfy public interest in serious Latin-American music. The Associated Music Publishers have taken over music by Villa-Lobos, Camargo Guarnieri, Oscar Lorenzo Fernandez, and José Siqueira of Brazil. The G. Schirmer Company has issued a collection of piano pieces by twelve modern Latin-American composers, *The Album of Latin American Art Music for Piano.* The quarterly *New Music* has for years included compositions of the modern type by Latin-American composers such as Caturla of Cuba, Juan Carlos Paz of Argentina, and Domingo Santa Cruz of Chile. In October, 1942, *New Music* put out a special issue of Brazilian piano music which I obtained for publication from the composers themselves, including "millimetrizations" of the New York sky line and of a Brazilian mountain chain by Villa-Lobos.

The Music Division of the Pan American Union in Washington, under the enlightened directorship of the Mexican-born American music scholar, Charles Seeger, has issued several informative brochures on Latin-American music, among which the most comprehensive is *Music in Latin America*, compiled by Charles Seeger. A very valuable publication of the Pan American Union is the annotated list *Recordings of Latin American Songs and Dances*, compiled by the Spanish musician, Gustavo Duran. The booklet contains much more than the title indicates, and is in fact a detailed glossary of Latin American dance forms.

The most satisfyingly complete bibliography of Latin American music is now available in *A Guide to Latin American Music* compiled by the Havana-born American music scholar Gilbert Chase, and published in 1945 at the U.S. Government Printing Office. This supplements the previous bibliographical lists compiled by Gilbert Chase, *A Partial List of Latin American Music Obtainable in the United States* and *Bibliography of Latin American Music*, both issued in 1942. A helpful bibliography is also contained in the mimeographed brochure, *The Music of Latin America*, compiled by Benjamin Grosbayne and published in 1943 by the Brooklyn College Press in the series *Outline of Lectures, Notes and References*.

Eleanor Hague pioneered with her slender but sensitively written volume, *Latin American Music, Past and Present*, published in 1934 by the Fine Arts Press in Santa Ana, California. But the author herself makes no claim as to the accuracy of the scant information given in the book.

In 1947, the knowledgeable Otto Mayer-Serra put out a resplendent two-volume encyclopedia, *Musica y Musicos de Latinoamerica*, published in Mexico City by Atlante Co. These two volumes aggregating 1134 pages, printed on glossy paper and illustrated with hundreds of portraits and musical examples, is a paragon of Latin American book manufacture. Otto Mayer-Serra did a capital job of compiling information on native musicians, dances, songs, and national music history.

In Argentina, Carlos Vega whose complete title of office is Technician of the Folklore Section of the Faculty of Philosophy and Letters at the Institute of Argentine Literature, is the author of the novel index of musical patterns, *Fraseologia Musical*, and of two basic volumes on Argentine folk music, *Danzas y Canciones Argentinas* (1936) and *Panorama de la Música Popular Argentina* (1944).

The most complete account of Brazilian music is found in the second enlarged edition (1942) of *Historia da Musica Brasileira* by Renato Almeida. Brazilian songs and dances are analyzed in *Estudos de Folclore* (1934) by the late Brazilian folklorist Luciano Gallet.

There are two good histories of Mexican music, one by Miguel Galindo (1933), and the other by Gabriel Saldivar (1934). The modern period of Mexican music is intelligently outlined in *Panorama de la Música Mexicana* (1941) by Otto Mayer-Serra. Several treatises on the musical folklore of Mexico have been published, notably *El Folklore Musical de las Ciudades* (1930) by Rubén M. Campos, and *El Folklore y la Música Mexicana* (1928), by the same author.

On the occasion of the quadricentennial of Santiago in 1941, the University of Chile published the first history of Chilean music, *Los Origenes del Arte Musical en Chile* by Eugenio Pereira Salas. Later, the University of Chile issued a collection of essays on native folklore, with musical examples, under the title *Chile*.

Cuban music is analyzed by the late Emilio Grenet in his preface to the collection of eighty Cuban songs, *Música Popular Cubana*,* published in 1939 under the auspices of the Secretariat of Agriculture of Cuba, and printed by the Southern Music Publishing Company; but this is available neither from the sponsor nor from the printer. Equally unobtainable are three little volumes of Costa Rican songs and dances published by the government in San José between 1929 and 1935. For Panama there is an excellent treatise, *Tradiciones y Cantares de Panama* by Narciso Garay, the country's foremost musician, who left art for politics and was at one time foreign minister of Panama. The folklore of Guatemala is discussed in detail by Jesús Castillo, the native "ethnophonist," as he likes to call himself, in the little brochure *La Música Maya-Quiché* (1941).

The principal source book of Peruvian music remains the French tome, *La Musique des Incas et ses Survivances* by d'Harcourt, published in Paris in 1926. Rodolfo Barbacci, the Argentine-born musicologist now

---

* Grenet lost his right arm and leg when attacked in swimming by a shark. He recovered and continued his studies, dying in 1939 from an appendectomy.

living in Lima, has completed a gigantic survey of Peruvian music (over one thousand typewritten pages), but there is no likelihood of its ever being published.

Bolivian folk music is authoritatively analyzed in the preface to a three-volume collection, *Aires Nacionales de Bolivia* by Teófilo Vargas, printed for the author in 1940–1941, and obtainable from him in his native town of Cochabamba. Information on Ecuador's music is found in an excellent paper by the Ecuadorian composer Segundo Luis Moreno, published in the centennial edition, *El Ecuador en Cien Años de Independencia* (1930).

Folk music of Colombia is outlined in *Folklore Colombiano* (1942) by the Colombian scholar and composer Emirto de Lima; and the cause of Venezuelan music is ably presented in the brochure *Contribución al Estudio de la Música en Venezuela* (1939) by José Antonio Calcaño.

Documentation on the historical antecedents of Uruguay's musical culture is given in Lauro Ayestarán's important work, *Historia de la Música en El Uruguay*, the first volume of which, covering the colonial period, was published in 1945.

In Paraguay, Juan Carlos Moreno González, the country's leading musician, who has been active as a composer and a pedagogue despite his tragic handicap (he lost both legs in a street car accident at the age of thirteen), has prepared a paper on Paraguay's folk music.

Surprisingly flourishing is the science of native musicology in the Dominican Republic. *Folklore Musical Dominicano* (1939) by Flerida de Nolasco, and *Del Areito de Anacaona al Poema Folklórico* (1942) by the country's leading musician and composer, Enrique de Marchena, present a panoramic survey of the field.

The voodoo music of the Negro Republic of Haiti has been the theme of fiction and drama. There is an excellent book on the subject in English, *Haiti Singing* by Harold Courlander (1939).*

Even tiny El Salvador has its musical historiographer, Rafael González Sol, the author of the handy little pamphlet, *Historia del Arte de la Música en El Salvador*, published in San Salvador in 1940.

Very little information is available on the subject of musical culture in Honduras and Nicaragua. Musical life in Costa Rica is described in the 1942 issue of *Educación*, published in San José by the Association of School Supervisors.

There are numerous music magazines published all over the continent,

---

* The University of North Carolina Press, Chapel Hill.

and the islands. These magazines are excellently printed, on good paper, and they carry pictorial and musical illustrations. But after a fine start, they usually begin to falter, appear at irregular intervals, sometimes vanish from sight altogether and then reappear in new shapes and sizes. Thus the sprightly Havana publication, *Musicalia*, founded in 1927 by Antonio and María de Quevedo, after a few years in limbo emerged in 1943 in a somewhat reduced form. The *Revista Brasileira de Musica*, a fine magazine modeled after the Parisian *Revue Musicale*, has appeared sporadically since 1932, with such lapses that it is difficult to specify whether it is a quarterly, annual, or biennial publication. The Mexican magazine, *Revista Musical Mexicana*, launched in 1942 as a fortnightly went on bravely until 1944, but then began to wilt and finally gave up the ghost. A handsomely printed Mexican music quarterly, *Nuestra Musica* made its auspicious appearance in 1945, under the editorship of Rodolfo Halffter, and as of 1949 was still in healthy bloom. The *Eco Musical* of Buenos Aires joined the limbo of defunct music magazines after several years of spasmodic existence. The Ricordi Co. in Buenos Aires used to publish a fairly substantial music periodical, *La Revista Musical*, but it folded up in 1930. Alberto William published a music magazine, *La Quena*, in the 1920's. A modern music magazine, *Pauta* (the word means the music staff), was published for a few months in Buenos Aires in 1939. The *Revista Musical Argentina*, which used to be published by Rodolfo Barbacci in Buenos Aires, is also a thing of the past. When Barbacci moved to Lima, he undertook the publication of an informative eight-page leaflet, *Revista Musical Peruana*.*

A Brazilian magazine of modern music, *Musica Viva*, launched by the German refugee composer of atonal music Hans Koellreutter in 1940, led a life of suspended animation until 1943, when it fluttered and gave up the ghost. An illustrated music magazine, *Resenha Musical*, has appeared, off and on, in São Paulo since 1940.

In Chile, musical periodic literature blossomed forth after years of in-

---

* Barbacci was forced to discontinue the publication in July, 1945, and issued the following printed communication: "Persons and musical organizations criticized in the last two issues of the *Revista Musical Peruana*, being unable to refute the incontrovertible accusations therein contained, and fearing the publication of even more energetic articles in future issues, have resorted to the 'democratic' procedure of petitioning the proper authorities to suspend the publication of the *Revista Musical Peruana*. As a result, the publication has been temporarily discontinued. In its place is substituted a leaflet, *America Musical*, set in type and printed manually by the editor, until the advent of better times for liberty of thought."

activity in 1945, when an impressive little bi-monthly, *Revista Musical Chilena,* was launched by the Instituto de Extensión Musical. It still maintained a steady pace of regular publication in 1949. But Pablo Garrido's *Vida Musical,* also started in 1945, did not last beyond a few issues.

The *Orquesta Sinfónica Nacional* of Bogotá, Colombia, issued, in 1941 and 1942, monthly leaflets entitled simply *Música.* In Costa Rica, a few issues of the magazine *Revista Musical* appeared in 1941. In Ecuador, a single issue of *Pentagrama* (the word means the five-line music staff) was published some years ago. In August, 1943, the National Conservatory of Panama began issuing a monthly publication, *Armonía,* edited by Luis A. Delgadillo, the Nicaraguan composer who had joined the faculty of the Panama Conservatory. In Guatemala the *Asociación Musical Juvenil* began publication in 1945 of a periodical, *Música,* serving chiefly the interests of young musicians.

Among Latin-American music journals, the *Torpedero Musical* of Buenos Aires is in a class by itself. As the title indicates, the *Torpedero* specializes in musical sniping. It publishes fantastic stories, attacking everything and everybody in Argentina, even its own contributors, as in the case of Argentina's modern composer, Juan Carlos Paz. The *Torpedero* accused him of authoring an article about himself, and of having induced one Hector Gallac, a member of the editorial board of the selfsame *Torpedero,* to publish it under his, Gallac's name, in the *Boletín Latino-Americano de Música.* Needless to say, the insinuation is without factual foundation.

The general tone of musical journalism in Latin America is highly emotional. Personalities explode; names are called. Private conversations and private letters are apt to bob up in print, much to the discomfiture of the persons concerned. For instance, Rodolfo Barbacci prints in his book, *Anecdotas Musicales,* the following story: "When the composer and conductor Nicolas Slonimsky was in Lima in 1941, he looked over some music by the Peruvian composer (here transparent initials of the composer are given). Spotting a curious passage in the music, Slonimsky inquired of the composer: 'How is it that you have an E double-sharp in a piece with a key-signature in flats?' He added, 'I've never seen an E double-sharp in any piece of music.' To this the composer replied: 'Oh, that is a mere detail. The note may be taken out altogether.' " The story is true, but it put me in Dutch with the composer in question.

Composers and Society

THE creative musician occupies an exalted place in the social fabric of the Latin-American countries. He is the pride of the nation. He serves his country by enhancing its cultural prestige. And he is given wholehearted support by the government. Every Latin-American republic has a Department of Fine Arts, which regulates, promotes, and finances musical activities, maintains conservatories and symphony orchestras, sponsors publications of music, distributes prizes and medals for musical works, and establishes traveling fellowships for talented musicians. All these attentions are lavished on the deserving artists and composers with great pomp and ostentation, such as no other country, with the possible exception of Russia, displays towards native talent. Thus, the popular Cuban composer Ernesto Lecuona received a gold medal in appreciation of his services to native arts, in a special ceremony, held in a large theater in Havana, on February 22, 1943, and broadcast over the government radio.

Foreign musicians, too, are often given medals and diplomas of appreciation. The Italian nineteenth-century musician Juan Aberle, who settled in Central America, received from the government of Guatemala a medal inscribed: "To the Prince of Central American Music." After Aberle's death, the medal went to the Salvadorean composer Jesús Alas, who in his turn intends to bequeath it to the most deserving musician of El Salvador.

Posthumous honors are rendered to the particularly distinguished musicians. The ashes of Teresa Carreño, the Venezuelan pianist, who died in New York in 1917, were transported to Caracas with solemn ceremony and reinterred there on February 15, 1938. The body of Jaime Nunó, author of the Mexican National Anthem, was disinterred from his grave in Buffalo, where he died in 1908, and transferred for reburial in Mexico City in November 1942, in an official ceremony. In 1943, the Mexican Government paid to the American descendants of Nunó the sum of 368 pesos, in payment of a long overdue bill for copying expenses the composer had incurred in 1854.

Competitions for the best musical works are usually held on important anniversaries. Thus on the occasion of the centennial of the Dominican

Republic in February 1944, the Secretariat of the Education of Fine Arts announced a competition for native works in the field of literature, music, and painting, with the following prizes (in American dollars, the official currency of the Dominican Republic): $1,000 for a symphony in four movements; $600 for a cantata for chorus and orchestra; $500 for a symphonic poem for large orchestra; $200 for a *Merengue* (Dominican national dance form); $500 for a collection of no fewer than twenty-five folk songs.

Four symphonies, four symphonic poems, and four cantatas were submitted for the contest, not a bad crop for a republic which occupies but a portion of a Caribbean island!

In Cuba, the Ministry of Education announced, in October, 1942, a competition for a symphonic work, a choral composition, a piece for military band in the folklore manner, and an original song in the popular vein, with prizes of 1,000, 500, 300, and 200 Cuban pesos.

In Buenos Aires, I was present at the distribution of prizes, impressively staged in the hall of one of the largest theaters, with press representatives and photographers in attendance. The major prize winners for musical works were Arturo Luzzatti, who received 5,000 Argentine pesos for an oratorio; Jacobo Ficher, who got 3,500 pesos for his *Third Symphony;* and Alberto Ginastera, who was awarded 3,500 pesos for a ballet in the native vein. In addition, a number of lesser prizes and fellowships for travel and study were given for the best works in the small forms and for folkloric research. The prizes were awarded without regard to the commercial possibilities of the works submitted. There was also an encouraging evidence of impartiality as to race and country of origin: Luzzatti is an Italian, and Jacobo Ficher is a Russian Jew. The money value of the prizes was very high in relation to the cost of living. (The Argentine peso is worth 25¢ in American money.)

The 400th anniversary of the foundation of Santiago in November, 1941, was the occasion for a Music Festival, including a contest for the best works by Chilean composers. The prizes, albeit in depreciated Chilean currency (the Chilean peso was worth about 3¢ at the time), were generous: 1. Prize of Honor, for the best work in large forms, 25,000 pesos; 2. Two prizes, 15,000 and 10,000 pesos, for an opera, an oratorio, a cantata, or a ballet; 3. Two prizes, 15,000 and 10,000 pesos, for symphonic works; 4. Five prizes, ranging from 5,000 to 15,000 pesos, for chamber music; 5. Three prizes, of 10,000 pesos, 6,000 pesos, and 4,000 pesos, for a collection of original songs in the native manner; 6. Two prizes, 3,000 and 2,000 pesos, for vocal compositions suitable for schools; 7. A prize of 5,000 pesos for a collection of popular songs, workers' songs, sport songs, and the like.

The jury was composed of three foreign musicians: Oscar Lorenzo Fernandez, who was conducting concerts in Santiago at the time; Honorio Siccardi, an Argentinian, who flew from Buenos Aires for the occasion; and the American composer Aaron Copland, who was touring South America as a musical ambassador of good will.

So numerous were the prizes that the jury awarded one virtually to every musician who sent in a piece. Among the prize-winning works were compositions in all genres: music by modernists such as Santa Cruz, Humberto Allende, Carlos Isamitt, and René Amengual; by romanticists, such as Prospero Bisquertt, Samuel Negrete, and Alfonso Letelier; and by academic musicians such as Enrique Soro.

The Prize of Honor went to Domingo Santa Cruz for his *Cantata de los Rios de Chile,* a monumental work in three "madrigals," as the composer designated the movements. After the jury's decision was made public, an extraordinary thing happened. The Committee for the Fourth Centennial published a statement in the press declaring the award of the Prize of Honor null and void, on the ground that "Señor Santa Cruz, being a personal friend of Messrs. Oscar Lorenzo Fernandez and Honorio Siccardi, and being furthermore instrumental, in his capacity as Dean of the Faculty of Fine Arts, in extending the invitation to them to come to Chile, had no moral right to submit his music to the judgment of these gentlemen."

As a matter of fact, Domingo Santa Cruz had never met Siccardi before, and as he told me later, had to look up a photograph of Siccardi in one of my illustrated articles on South American composers in order to identify him at the airport (which was easy, in view of Siccardi's conspicuously bald occiput). Ironically enough, Aaron Copland, who was a friend, had voted in favor of not awarding the honor prize to anyone.

There was a loud outcry against the Committee's action. In a public statement, Santa Cruz demanded from the Committee of the Fourth Centennial a repudiation of its decision, threatening to challenge the chairman of the Committee, whom he described as a "miserable poetaster," to an encounter on the field of honor, "como caballeros." But the Committee stuck to its legal right of final decision, and when the prizes were distributed at a special ceremony at the *Teatro Municipal* in Santiago, Domingo Santa Cruz was not among those called to receive a diploma and a check.

TEACHING, PLAYING, AND SINGING

Saint-Saëns, who visited Argentina in 1916, called Buenos Aires "Conservatoriopolis." It is true that there is hardly a block of houses in the Argentinian capital city which does not shelter a music school, with a proud plaque proclaiming *"Conservatorio."* But Buenos Aires is not an exceptional case. Music education is rampant in Latin America, and conservatories dot the map.

To take a typical musical nation, the Republic of Colombia has eleven state-supported conservatories, in Bogotá, Cali, Medellín, Barranquilla, Manizales, Popayán, Santa Marta, Pato, Cucuta, Bucaramanga, and Ibaqué. Oddly enough, the Conservatory in the port town of Cali, which is not a musical center, is the best-equipped, not only in Colombia, but in all Latin America. It is housed in a modern building with spacious studios, which was erected at a cost of $175,000. It owes its existence entirely to the energy and shrewdness of its founder and director, the Colombian pianist-composer Antonio María Valencia, who elicited the necessary funds from a culturally minded administration. By contrast, the Conservatory of Bogotá, the capital, occupies a dilapidated colonial building, sadly lacking in facilities. Its studios open on the central patio, and when classes are held simultaneously there is a horrendous polytonal confusion.

The oldest Latin-American conservatory is the *Escola Nacional de Musica* in Rio de Janeiro, which celebrated its hundredth anniversary in 1941. The most progressive Conservatory is undoubtedly the *Conservatorio Nacional* of Mexico. Carlos Chavez, who was its director from 1928 to 1934 (he received his appointment at the age of twenty-eight), introduced a revolutionary method of instruction, dispensing with textbooks and teaching his pupils to compose in all styles, with particular attention given to national Mexican melos and rhythms. After Chavez left the Conservatory, his ideas and progressive policies were continued and expanded.

Every sizable city in Latin America has its own symphony orchestra or a military band. It is the policy of these orchestras to champion native talent. Twenty-three works by Uruguayan composers were given by the Montevideo symphony orchestra, the OSSODRE, during four seasons,

1931–1934. The *Orquesta Sinfónica* of Santiago, Chile, presented, during the five seasons, 1931–1936, twenty-three works by nine Chilean composers. In the first five years of its existence, 1938–1943, the *Orquesta Sinfónica Nacional de Lima* gave performances of forty-four compositions by sixteen Peruvians. The *Orquesta Filarmónica de Habana* gave during its first decade, 1924–1934, virtually all the orchestral works by the Cuban modernists Caturla and Roldán, and eight compositions in the Cuban style by the Spanish conductor-composer Pedro Sanjuan, who had directed the orchestra for several years. At one of my concerts with the Havana Philharmonic, I featured the first local performance of Gershwin's *Cuban Overture*, based on the rhythms of the Rumba and the Conga.

The *Orquesta Sinfónica de Mexico*, under the energetic direction of its founder, Carlos Chavez, presented, in sixteen seasons, 1928–1943, seventy works by thirty-one Mexican composers. The inaugural concert of the symphony orchestra in Ciudad Trujillo, capital of the Dominican Republic, on October 23, 1941, consisted entirely of works by eight native composers.

The frequency of performances of native works by Latin American orchestras is the more impressive when taken in proportion to the total number of creative musicians in the country, allowing the greatest latitude of professional qualifications. For instance, by the most generous count, there are twenty-one practicing composers in Peru, and of these, sixteen have been represented in the programs of the *Orquesta Sinfónica Nacional de Lima*.

Conductors for local orchestras are more often than not recruited among native musicians. Armando Carvajal, a Chilean violinist, is the permanent conductor of the *Orquesta Sinfónica de Santiago*. Amadeo Roldán, the late Cuban musician, began as a violinist in the Havana Philharmonic and became its conductor, a post he occupied until his death in 1939. Other native conductors are Juan José Castro and his older brother José María Castro of Argentina; Guillermo Espinosa, the conductor of the *Orquesta Sinfónica Nacional* in Bogotá, Colombia; Emilio Sojo, who conducts the *Orquesta Venezuela* in Caracas; José María Velasco Maidana, the director of the *Orquesta Nacional* in La Paz, Bolivia; Carlos Chavez, the conductor of the *Orquesta Sinfónica de Mexico*; Herbert de Castro, the leader of the Panama orchestra.

Among the foreign conductors active in Latin America are Casal Chapí, a Spanish refugee who is the conductor of the orchestra in Ciudad Trujillo; Lamberto Baldi, an Italian, who leads the OSSODRE orchestra in Montevideo; Theodore Buchwald, an Austrian, who directs the *Orquesta Sinfónica de Lima*; and Eugene Szenkar, the well-known Hungarian conductor, who is now in charge of the *Orquestra Brasileira* in Rio de Janeiro. Erich Kleiber, the German conductor, divides his time among the orchestras of Santiago, Lima, Mexico, and Havana. His Beethoven cycles are famous.

The wages of orchestral musicians in Latin America are much lower than those of their colleagues in the United States, even taking into account the low currency in relation to the dollar. As a consequence, most Latin-American musicians eke out their subsistence by playing in restaurants and cafés. This in turn leads to insecure attendance at rehearsals and even at concerts. Eugene Szenkar once suffered a heart attack when the oboe player failed to show up at a concert of the *Orquestra Brasileira,* and the incident was reported in the press.

When I conducted the Havana Philharmonic in 1933, I announced my rehearsals one hour ahead of the actual time. I called the advanced hour *Hora Cubana,* and the real time *Hora Americana.* But still the Cubans were late!

Latin America possesses well-organized choral societies, of which the *Orfeon Lamas* in Caracas, Venezuela, enjoys great renown. The largest choral ensemble is the Brazilian school children's chorus, numbering several thousand boys and girls, with Villa-Lobos as conductor. Each year, on Brazil's Independence Day, September 7, this chorus, which Villa-Lobos with his love for neologisms calls *"Orpheonic Concentration,"* gives a gala performance at the great stadium in Rio de Janeiro. Villa-Lobos stations himself atop a specially constructed platform fifty feet high and directs the chorus, not with an ordinary conductor's baton, but with flags of national colors. Before the beginning of each concert, Villa-Lobos "tunes up" the children by making them sing a six-part canon in thirds, resulting in a chord of the eleventh, with the following words:

Bondade
Realidade
Amisade
Sinceridade
Igualidade
Lealdade

These words, meaning respectively, goodness, reality, amity, sincerity, equality, and loyalty, form an acrostic, spelling BRASIL, which is the proper orthography in the Portuguese language.

Opera is universally popular in Latin America, but only two opera houses maintain regular seasons, the *Teatro Colón* (which means, of course, Columbus Theater) in Buenos Aires, and the *Teatro Municipal* in Rio de Janeiro. Pursuing a protective national policy, the *Teatro Colón* has produced numerous native operas and ballets. However, few of these remain in the repertoire, the maximum number of performances of an opera by an Argentine composer being twenty-five. A list of operas presented at the *Teatro Colón* during the first quarter of a century of its existence is given in the de luxe volume *El Arte Lírico en el Teatro Colón, 1908–1933.*

Italian traditions dominate the opera in Latin America. The performances are usually in Italian, and the principal singers are usually Italians as well. Native composers are apt to use Italian libretti, even when the subject of the opera relates to indigenous history and legend. The first significant operatic work by a Latin-American composer was *Il Guarany*, by Carlos Gomes, the Brazilian Verdi. The story of the opera is taken from a novel of Indian life by José Alencar, a pioneer of the national school of Brazilian literature. Characteristically, Gomes read this novel not in the original, but in an Italian translation, while he lived in Milan. His opera is Italian in its musical idiom, as well as in the language of the libretto, and it was first produced in Italy.

The opera *Malazarte*, by the contemporary Brazilian composer Oscar Lorenzo Fernandez, was originally written to a Portuguese libretto by the late Brazilian poet, Graça Aranha. The story deals with the legendary master of black magic named Malazarte (from *malas artes*, evil arts), and the action takes place in colonial Brazil. When the production was announced for September, 1941, and the rehearsals began, it became increasingly clear that the singers, the majority of them Italians, could not cope with the text in the vernacular, and the libretto had to be hurriedly translated into the language of all opera singers, Italian.

However, efforts are being made by the nationalist group of Brazilian writers and intellectuals to make Brazilian art truly Brazilian, especially with regard to the use of the Portuguese language. The *Congresso da Lingua Nacional Cantada*, which assembled in São Paulo in 1937, urged Brazilian composers to use Portuguese texts for their vocal compositions. A government decree of January 26, 1937, read in part: "All musical programs given in playhouses, concert halls, and theaters in Brazil shall include compositions by Brazilian composers."

Radio broadcasting in Latin America contributes greatly to the musical education of the people. There are special radio orchestras, of which the best is the *Orquesta Sinfónica del Servicio Oficial de Difusión Radio Electrica,* or OSSODRE, in Montevideo, Uruguay. The best-equipped radio station in Central America is *La Voz de Guatemala.* In Mexico there are one hundred and forty-nine long-wave and thirteen short-wave radio stations. There are one hundred and eleven radio stations in Colombia. One of them, *La Voz del Chocó,* is in the jungle. The Indians no longer need their giant drums to carry messages to neighboring villages. They can use radio!

Phonograph recordings of popular music are made in every Latin-American country, but the recording of serious music is handicapped by an inadequate technical apparatus. Some of the best recordings of native music made in Argentina and Brazil have been taken over by American phonograph companies. Among American recordings of Latin-American music, made in the United States, there are Victor albums of symphonic music by Villa-Lobos and Chavez. I made records of pieces by Argentine, Brazilian, Chilean, Colombian, Peruvian, and Uruguayan composers, in an album called *South American Chamber Music,* issued by the Columbia Phonograph Company.

MUSICIANS OF ALL RACES

Reviewing the new edition of a music dictionary, Philip Hale once wrote: "In the making of dictionaries there is no such thing as plenary inspiration." But in the life of a musical lexicographer, there are moments when little else but plenary inspiration is of any use. Collating biographical data on Latin-American composers, I have stumbled upon numerous discrepancies of vital chronology, not all of them accidental. Take, for instance, the question of the birth date of Villa-Lobos. Riemann's dictionary gives 1890; *Who's Who in Latin America* gives 1884. Villa-Lobos himself hesitates; in the calendar of his life published in 1941 in the Brazilian magazine *Musica Viva,* he marks 1888 as the year of his birth, but during his tour of the United States in the spring of 1945, he gave the date of his birth as 1886. On the other hand, Burle Marx, the Brazilian musician who knew the Villa-Lobos family intimately, states categorically, in an article published in the October 1939 issue of *Modern Music,* that Villa-Lobos was born in 1881. I made a diligent search in the birth registries of the Church of St. José in Rio de Janeiro in which Villa-Lobos is supposed to have been baptized, but found nothing.*

The year of birth of Carlos Chavez is given in the dictionaries as 1899, but Jesús Romero, the Mexican musicologist who has compiled the Latin-American supplement for the *Diccionario Ilustrado de Música*, published in Spain in 1930, sets the date one year back, to 1898. Romero knew Chavez as a youth, and claims that his date is the right one. However, in the absence of documentary evidence, I retain the date as given by Chavez himself, which is 1899.

The Mexican composer Rafael Tello gave me the date of his birth as September 5, 1872. But in the scrap book he showed me, I found a clipping from a newspaper *Patria* of September 8, 1883, which contains a review of Tello's appearance as a child pianist, giving his age as thirteen, which places his birth in 1870, and not in 1872.

The year of birth of Acario Cotapos, the Chilean modernist, is given as 1886 in the program of the International Guild of Composers in New York, when one of his works was performed there in 1923. But Cotapos himself gives his birth year as 1889.

Even special biographical essays cannot be relied upon for chronological data. The *Revista Brasileira de Musica* has published two biographical sketches of the late Brazilian composer Leopoldo Miguez, one of which gives his dates of birth and death as September 7, 1850, and September 6. 1902; while the other gives September 7, 1852, and July 6, 1902.

The problem of Spanish patronymics is a vexatious one. The mother's family name is usually added at the end, but is not regarded as a true last name. Thus, the name of the mother of Domingo Santa Cruz is Wilson (she is a descendant of one of the numerous Irishmen who played an important part in Chile's revolution), and his full name is Domingo Santa Cruz Wilson. But he should be listed in the dictionaries under his father's name, which is Santa Cruz. The early piano pieces of Carlos Chavez are published under his full name, Carlos Chavez Ramirez. Ramirez is his mother's family name. It sometimes happens, however, that the mother's name is retained rather than the patronymic, par-

* Apparently, I did not dig deep enough, for according to an article by Lisa Peppercorn, entitled *The History of Villa-Lobos' Birthdate* (*Monthly Musical Record* of London, July 1948) a Brazilian music historian located the entry in the same Church of St. José, and located the registry proving that Villa-Lobos was born on March 5, 1887. Since then, I have confirmed this date from the files of the Colegio Pedro II in Rio de Janeiro, which Villa-Lobos attended as a child. I had the pleasure of announcing my findings to Villa-Lobos himself when I saw him in Paris in the spring 1949.

ticularly if the latter is very common. For instance, Alejandro García Caturla used his mother's name Caturla in preference to García, which is a common name in Cuba.

Portuguese names present no such difficulties, because the father's name is generally used as last name. The spelling of Brazilian names of Spanish origin varies, as there is a tendency to dispense with unnecessary double consonants. Thus Villa-Lobos often signs his name Vila-Lobos, which precludes the mispronunciation in the Spanish way, *Viya-Lobos,* or in the Argentine manner, where the double *l* is sounded like *z* in *azure,* resulting in the impossible pronunciation *Vizha-Lobos.* Middle names exist in Brazilian usage, but are often omitted. Camargo Guarnieri was given the middle name Mozart, but he avoids using it in order not to suggest invidious comparisons.

There is also the matter of accents. Strictly speaking, the name Chavez should have an accent on the first syllable, but the American usage dispenses with it. The name Fernandez in Spanish has an acute accent on the second syllable; however Oscar Lorenzo Fernandez, being a Brazilian, does not use the acute accent but occasionally puts on a circumflex.

In the dictionary section of the book I indicate, whenever possible, the racial origin of each composer. Carlos Chavez is half Indian, on his mother's side. The young Mexican musicians Daniel Ayala and Blas Galindo are Mayan Indians. The late Peruvian composers Teodoro Valcárcel and Daniel Alomias Robles were of Indian descent. María de Baratta of El Salvador is the granddaughter of the last Indian chief of the Lenca tribe.

The father of Alberto Nepomuceno, the pioneer of Brazilian music, was the natural son of an Indian woman and a Brazilian landowner. He was named after Saint Nepomuk, on whose day he was born. Nepomuk is the national Saint of Bohemia, hence the Slavic sound of Nepomuceno's name.

Negro musicians are prominent in the West Indies and in Brazil. The Haitian composer Ludovic Lamothe has been called a "Black Chopin." Assis Republicano, who is Professor of Composition at the *Escola Nacional de Musica* in Rio de Janeiro, is a Negro. Amadeo Roldán was a mulatto born in Paris of Cuban parents. Other Latin-American composers are of Spanish, Italian, Portuguese, German, and French extraction. Most musicians of Italian origin live in the large cities of the Atlantic coast. Francisco Mignone of Brazil, Luis Gianneo, Honorio Siccardi, Nicolas Lamuraglia, Pedro Quaratino, Gilardo Gilardi of Argentina, and

Eduardo Fabini of Uruguay are native-born, but of Italian parentage. Camargo Guarnieri is half Italian and half Brazilian. Among the naturalized Italian-born musicians who settled in Latin-American countries are Arturo Luzzatti, Pascual de Rogatis, and the late Gaetano Troiani of Argentina; Benone Calcavecchia of Uruguay; and the late Vicente Stea of Peru. André Sas, born in Paris, is a naturalized Peruvian citizen; he now prefers to sign his name in the Spanish way, Andrés Sás. Alfonso Leng of Chile is half German and half English. His maternal aunt Carmela Mackenna, a composer in her own right, is the descendant of a famous general of the Chilean Revolution, who was Irish. The grandfather of Alberto Williams was an Englishman. Walter Stubbs of Peru is also of British extraction. Two Russian-Jewish musicians, Jacobo Ficher of Argentina and Jacobo Kostakowsky of Mexico, are naturalized citizens.

After the fall of Loyalist Spain, a number of Spanish composers sought refuge in Latin America. Rodolfo Halffter, himself half German on his father's side, is now in Mexico. Julian Bautista has settled in Buenos Aires. Casal Chapí, the grandson of the famous Spanish composer of light opera Ruperto Chapí, is now active in Ciudad Trujillo, in the Dominican Republic. Jaime Pahissa, the Catalan modernist, left Spain before the outbreak of the civil war and settled in Argentina, as did a Spanish musician of the older generation, Alberto Villalba-Muñoz, who now conducts a conservatory in Jujuy, Argentina. The great Manuel de Falla left Spain in 1939 and settled in Córdoba, Argentina, where he died in 1946.

Quite a few among Latin American musicians have other professions besides music. Alfonso Leng is a prominent dentist in Santiago. José Castañeda, he of the vitriolic pen, is Chief of the Passport Division at the Ministry of Foreign Affairs in Guatemala. Alejandro García Caturla, the stormy Cuban modernist, was a district judge in his native town of Remedios, where he was tragically shot and killed on November 12, 1940, by a criminal whose case he had under advisement. Domingo Santa Cruz is a lawyer. Carlos Isamitt, the Chilean musician who specializes in Araucanian folklore, is a painter. The Peruvian composer Francisco González Gamarra has designed pictorial postage stamps for the government. Guillermo Uribe-Holguin, the foremost musician of Colombia, is a coffee grower.

Often, Latin-American musicians are given appointments in the diplomatic service. Ernesto Lecuona, the Cuban composer of popular Rumbas, has served as an attaché in the Cuban legation in Washington. José Asunción Flores, the originator of the native dance *Guarania*, is a member of the Paraguayan legation in Buenos Aires. Jaime Ovalle, the Brazilian composer of jungle-like incantations, is a customs officer.

The record number of occupations is enjoyed by the Colombian musician Emirto de Lima. The complete list of his titles, given in his book on Colombian folklore, takes up two pages. Here are some: Consul of Honduras in Barranquilla, Envoy Extraordinary of the Republic of Liberia, Doctor of Music of the Andhra University of Vizianagaram, Great Dignitary of the Order of Charlemagne, Holder of the medal of the Society *La Chanson au Sanatorium* of France, Holder of an award of the *Société pour Actes de Courage* of Belgium, Honorary Professor of the Music School in Zacatecas, Mexico, Member Correspondent of the Young Men's Literary Club of Monrovia, Permanent Delegate of the *Société Parisienne de Sauvetage.*

MUSIC IN ALL STYLES

There is a great diversity of style among Latin-American composers, ranging from the academic to the ultra-modern. Free from the inhibitions imposed on European and North American composers by considerations of economics and musical politics, and unimpeded by conventional professional training, the most original among Latin-American composers create their own style, often improvisatory in character, and amazingly unlike any European-inspired type of harmony, melody, or rhythm.

Villa-Lobos is such a composer. He experiments with music unmindful of the preceding evolution of music history. His instrumental writing is often tricky and requires acrobatic technique. Once Villa-Lobos put a non-existent low *A* in the bassoon part. When the player pointed it out to him, Villa-Lobos remarked cheerfully: "All right. Stick a roll of paper into the tube, and that will give you the extra note."

In his early days, Carlos Chavez used to write music which was harsh and unmellow. When I conducted his chamber orchestra piece *Energía* at one of my Pan American concerts in Paris, André Coeuroy described Chavez as *"un Mexicain cruel et raffiné qui cloue les sonorités au poteau de torture, pendant qu'il danse alentour une danse du scalp."* Paul Dambly observed: *"Chavez bannit sans pitié mais non sans grandeur le sourire et la grace de la musique."*

Scientific and mechanistic subjects have a great attraction for Latin-American modernists. In one of his whimsical moments, Silvestre Revueltas wrote a piece entitled *8 x Radio.* "To solve this algebraic equation," he explained in a mocking program note, "requires profound knowledge of mathematics." However, the title denotes nothing more abstruse than "Eight by Radio," for the piece is an octet, and was written for a radio performance by an ensemble of eight players.

Daniel Ayala of Mexico, a Maya Indian, has written a piece called *Radiogram*, imitating the Morse code. Francisco Casabona, Director of the Conservatory of São Paulo, composed *An Einstein Fable*, but its harmonic style is quite Euclidean. Julio Mata of Costa Rica is the author of a *Suite Abstracta*. Luis Sandi of Mexico disarms potential critics by calling one of his orchestral works *Suite Banale*.

The ultra-modernistic and communistic José Pomar of Mexico avers that his interest in music was activated by his boyhood experiment with a tomcat, which, when pulled by the tail, emitted meows of different pitch and duration. It is not the first time that cats have provided musical inspiration. I have in my possession a lithograph printed by Schirmer in New York in 1869, which shows an orchestra in a state of savage frenzy, the violins sawing away for all they are worth, the bells ringing, and the drummer perforating the bass drum with his skull. In the percussion section there are seven cats, marked A, B, C, D, E, F, and G, with a musician standing behind and pulling their tails through the holes in a wooden partition. The conductor is suspended in mid-air, frantically beating time with both arms and feet. On the conductor's stand, the score reads: "Fr. Liszt." Another score is thrown down at his feet, near the podium. It is inscribed: "Wagner. Not to be played much till 1995." Such was the cartoonist's idea of Wagner's music!

Atonal music has its converts in Latin America, but they are few. Juan Carlos Paz of Argentina has passed through four evolutionary styles of atonal music. The young Brazilian violinist, Claudio Santoro, composes exclusively in the twelve-tone technique. The German-Brazilian musician Hans Koellreutter also uses the system of composition in twelve tones. Acario Cotapos, the Chilean modernist, devised a system in which a thematic phrase consisting of different notes serves as a melodic and harmonic basis for the entire composition.

The musical leftists of Latin America are usually active in leftist politics as well. Carlos Chavez expressed his political predilections in such works as *Sinfonia Proletaria*, the vocal score of which is illustrated with anti-capitalist pictures by the Mexican painter Diego Rivera. Silvestre Revueltas took part on the cultural front in the Loyalist Government during the Spanish Civil War, and wrote a symphonic dedication *Homenaje a Federico García Lorca,* in memory of the Spanish poet murdered by the Fascists. The Chilean musician Pablo Garrido was once arrested as a Bolshevik.

The impressionist school of composition has numerous followers in Latin-American nations traditionally connected with the culture and the arts of France. Villa-Lobos picked up some points of impressionist esthetics during his sojourn in Paris. Camargo Guarnieri, of a later generation, leans towards the more austere style of Gallic neoclassicism. Oscar Lorenzo Fernandez and Francisco Mignone may be characterized as romantic impressionists, somewhat in the Italian tradition. José Siqueira, also a Brazilian composer, seasons his natural rhapsodic style with impressionistic spice.

When Manuel Ponce went to Paris in his early forties, he changed his style of composition in the direction of greater emphasis on color. His symphonic music, most of which was produced after his stay in Paris, clearly shows the influence of impressionism. Candelario Huizar, one of the most significant composers of Mexico, adds a touch of Debussyan and Ravelesque harmonies to his profoundly nativistic music. The same may be said of another Mexican, José Rolón, who studied in Paris. Guillermo Uribe-Holguin of Colombia attended the class of Vincent d'Indy at the *Schola Cantorum* in Paris, and his music, though Colombian in thematic material, follows the technique of French impressionism.

The late Carlos Pedrell of Uruguay, who spent his mature years in Paris, is to all effects and purposes a French composer with a Latin-American background. Alfonso Broqua, also of Uruguay, is equally French in his musical esthetics.

Several Latin-American composers who do not follow the French impressionist code have nonetheless adopted some characteristically Debussyan procedures in their music. Thus Alberto Williams, who is a devoted disciple of César Franck (he calls his own pupils "musical grandchildren of César Franck"), makes use of the shibboleth of early impressionism, the whole-tone scale, virtually in every one of his nine symphonies. Humberto Allende (who had received a complimentary letter from Debussy congratulating him on his Cello Concerto) illustrates the fall from the horse in his symphonic poem, *Escenas Campesinas,* by a cascade of chromatically descending augmented triads. Prospero Bisquertt of Chile applies whole-tone progressions as intervallic variants of native-inspired themes. Eduardo Fabini of Uruguay splashes whole-tone scales all over the harp parts of his symphonic poems, which glorify the tropical landscape.

Romantic and rhapsodic modes of expression have a natural appeal to Latin-American musicians. Alfonso Leng of Chile writes music in a brooding quasi-Russian manner. The exultant melos of Jacobo Ficher's symphonies is cast in a neo-romantic mold. Another Latin-American Russian, Jacobo Kostakowsky of Mexico, hardens Tchaikovskian harmonies with the cement of dissonant counterpoint. An isolated figure in Mexican music is Alfonso de Elias, whose lyrical talent is virtually unaffected by contemporary music.

The romantic composers of Argentina lean towards a broad operatic style of composition even in purely symphonic music. Constantino Gaito orchestrates his ballet scores with a sure hand, in bright Italianate color. Pascual de Rogatis, Felipe Boero, Florio Ugarte, Athos Palma, and Raúl Espoile write operas, often on native subjects, but with the application of Italian stage technique. In his symphonic suite, *Escenas Argentinas*, Lopez Buchardo contrives a brilliant kaleidoscope of native rhythms.

The advanced type of Argentine music is cultivated by the *Grupo Renovación*, a vanguard group founded in 1929, whose principal members are Jacobo Ficher, Honorio Siccardi, José María Castro, his young brother, Washington Castro, and Roberto García Morillo. Close to the *Grupo Renovación* in his musical esthetics is the young Alberto Ginastera, whose lyrically expressive talent places him high among creative musicians of his country.

The dominant figure of modern music in Chile is Domingo Santa Cruz, "the Chilean Hindemith," as he has been dubbed, who writes in a finely delineated contrapuntal style. The young generation of Chilean composers follow him in forming their modern Chilean school of composition, in which native themes are treated as germinal material in absolute musical forms.

One of the most uncompromising modernists was Alejandro García Caturla, the Cuban composer who studied in Paris, but never accepted the necessity of formal organization in free composition. He transferred to the music staff his musical impressions of the Afro-Cuban jungle, rich in colorful variety of sounds and noises. The mulatto composer Amadeo Roldán also cultivated Afro-Cuban folklore in his music. After the death of Roldán, and then that of Caturla, young musicians of Cuba veered away from the native Cuban vein and turned to neoclassicism. Several of them have recently banded together in a society named *Grupo de*

Renovación Musical, probably in emulation of the *Grupo Renovación* of Buenos Aires, with José Ardévol, a Spanish musician settled in Havana, as their principal mentor.

A curious blend of primitivism and formalism is the ballet *Nahualismo* by María de Baratta of Salvador. The story is derived from the primitivistic cosmogony of the Nahua people of Central America, and the score is subtitled *Diabolus in Musica,* for the thematic material is based on the interval of the tritone, the devil of the medieval musicians.

By far the most extraordinary and revolutionary theory of composition evolved in Latin America is *Sonido 13,* the Thirteenth Sound, promulgated by the Mexican-Indian musician, Julian Carrillo. He studied music in Leipzig, wrote academic overtures, and then suddenly plunged into the uncharted seas of microtones. The name Thirteenth Sound symbolizes the realm of intervals smaller than a semitone, thus lying beyond the twelve chromatic degrees. Carrillo's theory presupposes any number of such microtones, but he limits himself in actual composition to quarter-tones, eighth-tones, and sixteenth-tones.

The symbolic number 13 bobs up everywhere in Carrillo's writings and his social activities. He is the honorary chairman of the Pro-Carrillo Committee of Thirteen. His magazine *Sonido 13,* of which only a few numbers were issued some years ago, was published on the thirteenth day of each month. In the first issue, Carrillo published a grandiloquent manifesto bristling with exclamation points (and in Spanish exclamation points precede, as well as follow, each sentence): "¡The art of music has hitherto possessed only two modes! ¡This slavery lasted until the twentieth century after Christ! ¡This great problem remained unsolved until the publication of my Theory of the Thirteenth Sound! ¡The Thirteenth Sound is the point of departure for a new musical generation which will revolutionize the art of music!"

The dedication of Carrillo's book *Génesis de la Revolución Musical del Sonido 13,* published in 1940, is worth quoting in full: "To the memory of the Greek, Terpander, who, six centuries before Christ, conquered Sounds VI and VII, and to that of a Roman musician, who, in the eleventh century of our era, conquered Sound VIII, this book is dedicated by the Mexican, Julian Carrillo, who, in 1895, experimentally achieved Sound XIII, with which he closed the cycle of conquests of sound and opened the portals of musical infinity."

If indeed Carrillo "experimentally achieved Sound XIII" in 1895, then he holds clear priority over the European pioneers of quarter-tone music, none of whom began their experiments before the turn of the century.

Apart from original compositions for microtones, Carrillo has made transcriptions of Bach and Beethoven in quarter-tones, in which the octave is shrunk to the tritone, and other intervals are similarly halved. For his music, Carrillo has evolved a special system of notation; he has also constructed the Carrillophone, on which microtonal compositions may be played. According to Carrillo's own computations, the complete edition of his Theory of the Thirteenth Sound includes 1,193,556,232 chords, filling 14,315 volumes of 500 pages each. No publisher has as yet offered him a contract.

Among other musical inventors in Latin America, the names of the Paraguayan-born Angel Menchaca (1855–1924) and of the Colombian Diego Fallon (1834–1905) merit notice. Menchaca constructed a sloping piano keyboard, enabling the pianist to perform chromatic *glissando* passages. Fallon proposed a syllabic music notation in which vowels indicate metrical divisions, and consonants the degrees of the scale. Thus, the C major arpeggio in quarter-notes is transcribed in Fallon's notation by the vocable *Bayamb*.

The question now arises, which of these Latin-American musicians should be listed in a biographical dictionary, so as to sin neither on the side of charity nor on the side of exclusivity. The local critics render a pessimistic judgment on the state of music in their countries. Arturo Briceno of Venezuela declares: "In the field of art Venezuela is the most unfortunate of South American nations." Gustavo Santos, Director of the Department of Fine Arts in Colombia, proclaims: "We are a nation without music, if not an unmusical nation." Luis A. Delgadillo of Nicaragua writes: "It is painful to confess that nobody except myself takes music seriously in Nicaragua. I am a Don Quixote of music, fighting in a vacuum." Rafael Coello Ramos, Inspector General of Music in the Republic of Honduras, concludes his survey of native music with this melancholy pronouncement: "It is no exaggeration to say that music in Honduras is like a person in a state of coma." And Pablo Garrido of Chile writes a pamphlet with the significant title, *Tragedia del Músico Chileno*.

It was left to a German-born Americanist, Francisco Curt Lange, to inspire confidence among Latin-American musicians. "It is a Latin-American habit," he wrote in the statement of aims and purposes of *Americanismo Musical*, "to belittle the native achievements, and to dismiss with a gesture of specious candor not only the positive values already gained, but even the potentialities of cultural achievements."

It is clear that a high standard of selectivity cannot be pursued in the account of a young art as yet in its first century of evolution. What if geographers and natural scientists should confine themselves to the description of picturesque terrain and attractive vegetation, excluding from their survey the more modest specimens of native flora? The *South American Handbook* * describes a stretch of land along the Pacific coast, from Arica to Copiapó, as "sandy desert, utterly rainless, a land of merciless sunshine and forbidding mountains devoid of vegetation." Still, the geographers have placed this infertile desert on their maps. T. Harper Goodspeed in his book, *Plant Hunters in the Andes*,† tells of the prolonged search for a rare tobacco plant named *Nicotiana Cordifolia,* "a rather scraggly shrub, possessing a nasty odor and unpleasant taste." But this "scraggly shrub" was worth more to him than a thousand aromatic blossoms of the tropics.

In the spirit of frivolous profundity, I drew up a formula expressing the necessary requirements for a musician to be put on a geo-musical map. I called it a "Formula for Musicological Eligibility." Quantity as well as quality are factors in my formula. Did not Dr. Samuel Johnson himself recognize the value of a purely numerical achievement? Said he to Boswell, commenting on a contemporary poetaster: "To be sure, he is a tree that cannot produce good fruit; he only bears crabs. But, sir, a tree which produces a great many crabs is better than a tree which produces only a few."

In alloting space in a music dictionary, composers of music in larger forms should naturally receive preferential treatment. Other things being equal, a symphony is a more impressive achievement than a piano sonata, and an opera merits more attention than a ballad. Let us assign an arbitrary numerical coefficient to each musical form, expressing approximately their relative values. Let us take a song with piano accompaniment as a musicological unit. Let us rate a piano piece as worth five songs (always regarding quality as a constant), a piece of chamber music equal to twenty-five songs, a symphony to fifty songs, and an opera to one hundred songs.

Popularity and mass appeal should also be taken into consideration as positive factors. Thekla Badarczewska, the Polish girl who wrote that

* Edited by Howell Davies, Trade and Travel Publications, London, 1941.
† Farrar & Rinehart, 1941.

perennial of the drawing-room, *A Maiden's Prayer,* was no female Chopin, but her name is rightfully preserved in music dictionaries. The composers of national anthems are in almost every case musical amateurs, but their names, too, are placed alongside those of real musicians.

The more primitive the cultural state, the more important looms even a mediocre talent. Therefore lexicographical eligibility ought to be measured in the inverse ratio to the state of local culture. Let P stand for popularity and Q for quality. The "Formula for Musicological Eligibility" will then appear as follows:

$$\text{Eligibility} = PQ \,(100 \times \text{Opera} + 50 \times \text{Symphony} + 25 \times \text{Chamber Music} + 5 \times \text{Piano} + 1 \times \text{Song}) \div \text{Musiculture}$$

The following table gives the number of composers by country who are included in my biographical panorama. The density of composers, per area and per population, is also indicated.

Country	Number of Composers	Composers per Population	Composers per Area in Square Miles
Argentina	60	1/220,000	1/18,000
Brazil	41	1/1,100,000	1/80,000
Mexico	33	1/600,000	1/23,000
Peru	22	1/320,000	1/22,000
Dominican Republic	22	1/75,000	1/880
Chile	20	1/250,000	1/14,000
Cuba	15	1/280,000	1/3,000
Uruguay	12	1/180,000	1/6,000
Guatemala	12	1/275,000	1/4,000
Colombia	10	1/800,000	1/44,000
Costa Rica	7	1/90,000	1/3,300
Panama	7	1/80,000	1/5,000
Bolivia	6	1/575,000	1/70,000
Venezuela	5	1/700,000	1/70,000
El Salvador	4	1/450,000	1/3,300
Honduras	4	1/250,000	1/11,000
Ecuador	3	1/1,000,000	1/60,000
Paraguay	3	1/350,000	1/56,000
Haiti	3	1/900,000	1/3,600
Nicaragua	1	1/1,380,000	1/57,000
ALL COUNTRIES	290	1/443,000	1/15,000

Apart from the problem of lexicographical eligibility, there exists, of course, the factor of availability of information. Although I used a liberal net in hauling my fish, it is quite possible that some, if not the big ones, got away. I am reasonably sure, however, that none did in the Dominican Republic, where I had the assistance of José G. Ramirez-Peralta, the Dominican musician, now resident in New York City. He has supplied me with a list of every Dominican Tom, Dick, and Harry, complete with their biographical data and samples of their music.

Artless Folklore

IT IS a paradox of spontaneous creative force that folk music should be, by definition, an anonymous art, originated by simple men and women without learning, and yet attaining the most perfect musical expression of the nation's collective soul. Leon Mera, writing in the preface to the collection of Ecuador's folklore, *Antología Ecuatoriana,* observes: "These peasants have no idea who Rossini or Mozart was, but they create their own melodies with astounding ease." The very old or blind men are often the best interpreters of native art. Juan Alvarez, writing in the 1909 issue of the Argentine publication, *Revista de Derecho, Historia y Letras,* calls the blind singers "keepers of the native tradition." The *Hymn to the Sun,* one of the noblest Inca airs, was preserved thanks to the memory of a 117-year-old Indian named José Mateo Sánchez, who had spent all his life in a remote village in the Andes. Daniel Alomias Robles, the late Peruvian collector of folklore, wrote down the music of the Hymn from the lips of this ancient. He gives a vivid description of the man: "Despite his advanced age, the muscular body of this Indian enabled him to walk erect with the martial gait of a soldier, for indeed he had served in the War of Liberation in 1824. The Indians, as a race, are reserved and uncommunicative. But when the spirit moves them, they grow eloquent. One day Sánchez invited me to go hunting. Later, having regaled me with a splendid heron he had shot that morning, he said to me: 'You will now hear the hymn we sing to the Sun.' And he intoned this mystical chant, saved from oblivion in the silent memory of an ancient Indian."

Carlos Vega, who has spent years traveling in the mountains and plains of South America, collecting and recording the ancient folklore of the Indians, exclaims: *"Cuando agoniza un anciano analfabeto, parece que se quema una biblioteca."* (When an illiterate oldster expires, it seems a library is burning.)

Not all folk songs are collective creations. Melodies composed by individual authors may become folk songs when they attain the simplicity and perfection of spontaneous art. The universally popular *Estrellita* was written by the Mexican composer Manuel Ponce, and was published in 1914. Ponce was abroad at the time. When he came back to Mexico, he found that his melody had become famous. Ironically enough, *Estrellita* has not earned its creator any money, for an irregularity in the copyright registry has permitted the publishers to reprint it without paying royalties.

When Villa-Lobos was asked: "What is folklore?" he replied, "I am folklore!" Elaborating, he added: "A truly creative musician is capable of producing, from his own imagination, melodies that are more authentic than folklore itself."

These words are substantiated not only in the genuinely folk-like music of Villa-Lobos himself. Guillermo Uribe-Holguin of Colombia has expressed the innermost spirit of native folklore in his *Trozos en el Sentimiento Popular,* of which he has written over three hundred. Camargo Guarnieri of Brazil never resorts to literal quotations from folk songs, but writes original melodies whose inflections and rhythms are intensely Brazilian. Carlos Chavez reinvents folk-like melodies in the Mexican manner by dint of intimate absorption of Indian melos. Carlos Isamitt of Chile, on the other hand, prefers to use original songs of the Araucanian Indians as the themes of his delicate instrumental evocations. In his *Trio Brasileiro,* Oscar Lorenzo Fernandez makes use of four authentic Brazilian melodies and five original inventions.

What are the characteristics of a folkloric style? Carlos Vega offers the following observations, writing in a preface to the collection, *Puneñas* (melodies of the *Puna,* high plateau) compiled by Isabel Aretz-Thiele, Vega's assistant in the Cabinet of Native Musicology at the Argentine Museum of Natural Sciences: "The musical style of a people is a language, which must be learned in childhood, as natives do. Those who have not received such early training must achieve fluency in the musical idiom in the same way as in language study, by learning grammar. When a composer has acquired perfect understanding of the melo-rhythmic patterns corresponding to individual words in a language, when he has learned to build these patterns into sentences, and is able to construct them correctly, then, and only then, will he have mastered the new language."

The songs of the people are generally monodic, devoid of the undertones of an implied harmony. The problem arises, what type of harmonic setting is congenial to the inner spirit of a folk song? In other words, what are the practical rules of a perfect stylization?

Humberto Allende writes: "The stylizer of folk songs should not attempt to imitate the popular creation, but should rather strive to re-create the spirit of these songs. He should set his melody in attractive harmonies, within an established musical form." But by what yardstick can we judge the "attractiveness" of these specially arranged harmonies? A style attractive to one musician may be utterly repugnant to another. The ultimate criterion is the degree of natural fusion, musical osmosis, that is attained between a linear melo-rhythmic phrase and a system of applied harmony. In rare instances this musical osmosis is effected with such inevitableness that the melody, rhythm, and harmony become one. The harmonic setting of Russian songs by Moussorgsky, of Polish dances by Chopin, of Norwegian modes by Grieg, are examples. I have proposed the term *"Musical Syncretism"* to describe this fusion of a folk-inspired rhythmic melody and applied harmony. The acceptance of such a term would fill a definite lacuna in musical esthetics.

Urban folklore, as well as the folklore of the countryside, offers material for creative composition. Humberto Allende has written an orchestral suite, *La Voz de las Calles,* which features the musical cries of Santiago's street vendors, the *pregones.* Fructuoso Vianna of Brazil takes the singsong of the coconut-drink peddler in Rio de Janeiro as a theme for one of his Ravelesque *Miniatures* for piano. Domingo Santa Cruz interpolates the imitation of the Chilean policeman's whistle in his orchestral *Madrigals.*

In Havana, the symphony of pushcart tenors is particularly rich and varied. The *fiorituras* that a Havana knife-sharpener performed on his mouth harmonica reminded me of the neo-Grecian modes of Debussy's *Flûte de Pan* from *Chansons de Bilitis.* I noted down the tune.

The Call of a Havana Knife-Sharpener

Beggars, too, resort to music to attract attention. In Mexico City, every morning one could watch a blind beggar sitting on the sidewalk opposite the *Palacio de Bellas Artes,* with an array of old shoe-polish tins arranged in a semicircle about him. Upon these tins he played Mexican airs, using a harmony in consecutive thirds or sixths, and unerringly striking the proper notes with his two wooden mallets.

GUITARS, FLUTES, AND DRUMS

The aboriginal musical instruments of Latin America are flutes and drums; but it is the Spanish guitar that is the heart of popular music from Patagonia to the Rio Grande. An Uruguayan legend tells of the birth of the guitar. A lonely Gaucho of the pampas, unable to find a soulmate, seeks advice from a sage of the land, and receives from him "a piece of wood, shaped like a beautiful woman's body, from whose breasts the Gaucho moulds poetic ballads, while his left hand caresses her shapely neck."

The etymology of the word guitar is clear. It comes from the Greek κιθάρα and the Latin *cithara.* It is cognate with the word *zither.* Ricardo Muñoz, in his exhaustive monograph, *Historia de la Guitara,* states, without corroboration, that the word guitar comes from *guiterna,* and is of Arabic origin.

Several distinct types of guitars are in use in different Latin American countries. The Cuban *Tres* is, as the name implies, a guitar with only three strings. The *Cuatro* is a four-string guitar. The *Tiple* is a guitar without the lower strings (*Tiple* means treble, and the register of a *Tiple* guitar is high). The name *Charango* is used in some countries to mean a simple home-made guitar. The Brazilian "carnival guitar" is called *Violão.*

Rafael Adame, Professor of the Guitar at the National Conservatory of Mexico, is the author of the first Concerto for Guitar and Orchestra. The full artistic and musical possibilities of the guitar as a solo instrument are demonstrated in Manuel Ponce's Concerto, which has been widely performed by the famous guitarist Segovia.

The style of native music is often affected by the harmony inherent in the tuning of the guitar. Narciso Garay complains that Panama's folk music is circumscribed by the "guitar harmony of six-four chords." In reply to my question: "What is your harmonic style?" an amateur composer from Honduras wrote: "I use chords that I can find on my guitar."

The harp is another European instrument that was imported into Latin America at an early date and acquired an extraordinary popularity. Primitive harps are manufactured by village Indians, and many are adept in harp playing. Violins, clarinets, and other orchestral instruments were established in Latin America in the eighteenth century.

The most popular wind instruments in Latin America are vertical flutes, which are made of bamboo reed or of baked clay. There are also V-shaped twin flutes with a single mouthpiece, and a great variety of panpipes. In Bolivia, there is in existence a triple panpipe with reeds arranged in rows like typewriter keys, and the range of these triple panpipes is often extended to a complete chromatic scale.

A very curious native instrument is the nose flute peculiar to the Indians of the Amazon River basin. It is made in the shape of a disk and has perforations. The player holds the disk close to the nostrils and blows. The Boston Museum of Fine Arts has in its possession a golden object manufactured by the Quimbaya Indians of Colombia, which represents a human figure blowing into a twin nose flute.

The group of percussion instruments of Latin America is particularly abundant and varied. There are in use among the Indians drums made of burned-out tree trunks, such as the *Teponaxtle* in Mexico and the *Trocano* in Brazil. Fruit shells are used for scrapers, made by notching the surface of the dried gourd, or for shakers, made by filling the shells with hard pellets or pebbles. Clapping of hands, stamping on the ground, tapping a wooden surface with long reeds, all these noises are used in native music accompanying the Indian dances. The Catuquinarú Indians of central Brazil construct elaborate "earth drums" by digging a hole in the ground and placing in it a hollow trunk of a palm tree, which is filled with rubber, powdered mica, and fragments of animal bones, and which serves as a resonator when stamped upon during the dance.

The sizes and shapes of the aboriginal instruments of Latin America vary from the minuscule to the gigantic. The longest instrument is the Chilean *Trutruca*, a reed pipe reaching the length of two meters. The largest panpipe is the Bolivian *Bajón*, which is made of spiraled tree bark cemented by baked clay.

The loudest native instruments are the jungle drums of Brazil and Paraguay. The softest percussion instrument is the picturesquely named *Culo-en-tierra* (buttocks-in-the-ground) used by the Indians of Venezuela. The sound of the Patagonian musical bow is so faint that it cannot be heard two steps away. It is made of a piece of horse's rib, strung with a horse hair, and rubbed with a condor feather. The bow is held by the player close to his mouth, so that the oral cavity serves as a resonator. The whole story of musical bows is fascinatingly told, in English, in Henry Balfour's monograph, *The Natural History of the Musical Bows* (Oxford, 1899). Need it be added that these primitive bows have nothing to do with violin bows?

The most complete manual of Latin-American musical instruments is published, surprisingly enough, not in South America, but in Sweden. It is a richly illustrated volume of 453 pages, *Musical and Other Sound Instruments of the South American Indians* by Karl Gustav Izikowitz, published in English in Volume V (1936) of *Kungliga Vetenskapsoch Vitterhets-Samhället.*

It must be borne in mind that the same instrument may be known under different names in different countries. Thus the common Indian panpipe is called *Antara* in Peru, *Capador* in Colombia, *Rondador* in Ecuador, and *Sicus* in Bolivia. Some native writers refer to all panpipes under the generic name *Zampoña*, a Spanish word which is probably a corruption of *Sinfonia*. But in Spain the *Zampoña* is a bagpipe, not a panpipe.

Native authorities themselves disagree on the proper nomenclature of indigenous instruments. Thus the late Teodoro Valcárcel of Peru has in the score of his Inca ballet *Suray-Surita* a drum with one membrane, called *Tynia*, and one with two membranes, called *Wankar*. But an authoritative article in the January, 1943, issue of the periodical *Peruanidad* uses the names of the two instruments as synonyms, "the *Tynia* or *Wankar*."

According to the classification of the late Luciano Gallet, the Brazilian instrument *Ganzá* is a hollow cylindrical gourd with a notched surface rubbed with a stick to make a rasping noise, and he publishes a photograph of the *Ganzá* in his book, *Estudos de Folclore*. He also gives a description of the popular Brazilian *Chocalho*, which is a large rattle. But in the footnote to a musical example in the same book, Gallet says, "*Ganzá*, the same as *Chocalho*." It seems that the two names are used interchangeably in the region of Bahia, where the local name for a notched rasp is not *Ganzá*, but *Amelé*, which in its turn, means a shaker elsewhere in Brazil.

Narciso Garay, in his excellent book, *Tradiciones y Cantares de Panama*, describes the local shaker as "a calabash filled with dried seeds, similar to the Cuban *Güiro*." But in Cuba the *Güiro* is a scraper, not a shaker, which latter is universally known as the *Maracas*.

Great divergence exists among native authors in the orthography of names of indigenous instruments. For instance, the Mexican high drum *Huehuetl* is spelled *Wewetl* by d'Harcourt in *La Musique des Incas et ses Survivances*. Both the spelling *Huankar* and *Wankar* are used for the Peruvian drum. The aboriginal Indian flute, the *Quena*, is sometimes spelled *Kena*. The curious orthography *Qquena* is also found in some sources. The South American jungle drum, the *Bututú*, appears in a variety of forms, *Pototó*, *Butotó*, *Fututú*, and in fact every conceivable combination of the consonants P, B, and F, with the vowels O and U.

Latin-American composers make use of native instruments in their symphonic music for the sake of local color. Villa-Lobos includes a battery of Brazilian percussion in his formidable *Chôros No. 11*. In the score of his *Sinfonia India*, Chavez has a part for the Mexican water drum, *Jicara de agua*, which consists of an inverted gourd half-submerged in a basin of water. In his Afro-Cuban ballet, *La Rebambaramba*, Amadeo Roldán provides six separate groups of percussion, and there is a solo for the Cuban *Maracas*. In one of his *Rítmicas*, Roldán features the *Quijada del Burro* (jawbone of an ass), which is shaken in the air, or struck with the fist, or rubbed with a stick on the teeth in a sort of asinodental *glissando*.

The natives hold performers on the drums in high esteem. In the interior of Panama, a virtuoso on the *Repicador* (a small drum) enjoys fame similar to that of a fine pianist or violinist in large cities. The Cuban poet Alejo Carpentier, in his article *La Música Cubana en estos 20 Últimos Años*, published in the bulletin *Conservatorio* of March, 1944, cites the slogan of the Afro-Cuban school of musicians: "*¡Abajo la lira! ¡Viva el Bongo!*" Down with the Lyre! Long live the *Bongo*!

European composers have, upon occasion, included native Latin-American instruments in their orchestral compositions. Prokofiev uses the

Maracas in his cantata *Alexander Nevsky,* which glorifies the victory of a thirteenth-century Russian warrior over the Teutonic knights, and certainly has no connection with anything Cuban. Edgar Varèse lists several Cuban percussion instruments in the score of *Ionization:* the *Maracas,* the *Güiro,* a pair of *Claves* (hardwood bars, held in a cupped hand for resonance, and struck together), and the *Bongos* (small twin drums held on the knees and tapped with the fingers). The score of Stravinsky's *Sacre du Printemps* contains a part for the *Güiro,* which makes a scratch just before the final dash of the piccolo in the *Danse Sacrale.* The scratch is usually overlooked by the conductor and the players, possibly because the *Güiro* is designated, in French, by the word *râpe* (rasp) whose meaning may not be immediately clear.

VOICES OF THE JUNGLE

All sorts of materials of mineral, vegetable, and animal origin are used by the natives of Latin America for the construction of their primitive instruments. Jaguar claws, deer hoofs, and specially treated inflated eyes of tigers are among the objects which serve as percussion in the South American jungle. The Peruvians employ llama skulls for drums. Mexican native dancers wear on their ankles bunches of dried butterfly cocoons which they shake with a whirring noise.

Even human bones are, or at least were, used by the Indians for the making of flutes and drums. In a book by John Constance Davis, Esq., published in London in 1805 under the engaging title, *Letters from Paraguay Writ. en by a Gentleman of Liberal Education and Considerable Property Who, Having Been Disappointed in his Hopes for Happiness With a Beloved Female, to Relieve the Distress of his Mind Resolved to Travel,* the author relates a gruesome tale: "Paraguay is a nation of wild roving Indians, who have sworn everlasting hatred to the Spaniards, as a proof of which I was shown a musical instrument, somewhat resembling the pipes of Pan, made out of the bones of one of the missionaries they sacrificed among them some years ago."

The ancient Mexicans made use of human skulls for drums, and femur bones for ratchets. In the Department of Anthropology at the National Museum of Mexico there are several specimens of notched human femurs, which are rubbed with a piece of bone to produce a rasping sound. Reproductions of these human rasps are found in the monumental dissertation on pre-Cortez Mexican music, *Instrumental Precortesiano* by Daniel Castañeda and Vicente Mendoza, published in 1933. The National

Museum of Rio de Janeiro has a trophy trumpet which consists of a long tube ending with a human skull.

An amazing tale of musical necrophilia is related in the chronicles of eighteenth-century Peru. A native musician named Camporreal fell in love with an Indian girl, who died. Stricken with grief, Camporreal secretly removed the girl's tibia bone and fashioned it into a vertical flute. When the sense of bereavement overcame him, he would take out the relic flute and play upon it a melancholy *Yaravi.*

Because primitive musical instruments are used in the native religious rites, they are often regarded as sacred objects. Theodor Koch-Gruenberg, in his book *Zwei Jahre Unter den Indianern,* gives a graphic description of the secret *Yurupari* ritual observed by the Indians of the Amazon basin: "In the middle of the night I heard mysterious music resembling a church organ, which was interrupted from time to time by outbursts of savage howling. Two youths who were standing watch at the door of my hut motioned me away when I attempted to go out, but I succeeded in leaving the hut despite their objections. I saw six native boys standing in the village square and blowing into musical instruments of different shapes and sizes. Four of these instruments were vertical flutes, and two were trumpets made of tree bark, wound in spirals and held fast by wooden hoops. It was these trumpets that emitted the eerie bellowing I heard during the night . . ."

The *Yurupari* trumpets were believed by the natives to possess magic powers protecting young boys against feminine seduction, and for this reason no woman was allowed to see the trumpets lest the spell be broken. The taboo was apparently lifted when travelers and explorers invaded the region. Recently, photographs have even been taken of the sacred objects.

Similarly taboo was the thunder stick of the Bororó Indians in Brazil, for it was supposed to exercise evil power over small children. The thunder stick is a wooden rattle swung in the air by a rope, and it is found among the Indians of North America as well.*

The aborigines usually personify their flutes and drums, attributing to them the masculine or feminine gender. Thus the *Maracas* is feminine

---

* A description of the world's "strangest instruments that could be found" is contained in chapter XI of Oscar Wilde's novel *The Picture of Dorian Gray,* where he speaks of the exotic tastes and hobbies of the hero. In Dorian Gray's collection there are "mysterious *Yuruparis* of the Rio Negro Indians, that women are not allowed to look at," "painted gourds filled with pebbles that rattled when they were shaken," and other instruments of South and Central America.

and the *Güiro* masculine. Narciso Garay tells us that the Cuna Indians of Panama possess two species of the flute *Tolo*, a male specimen with one hole, and a female flute with four holes.

The social and political importance of primitive musical instruments is underlined by the fact that large drums are used in the jungle for communication among the neighboring villages. The eighteenth-century traveler Joseph Gumilla reports in *Orinoco Ilustrado*, published in Madrid in 1745, that during the Indian wars in Venezuela, the natives made use of a jungle drum that carried messages to a distance of twenty-two kilometers. The Cuban Government at one time banned the large Afro-Cuban drum, the *Conga*, because of the resurgence of what was termed "primitivismo" among the Negro population of the island. The ominous beat of the jungle drum provides much of the dramatic effect in O'Neill's play, *Emperor Jones*, which tells the story of a Pullman porter who became the ruler of a Caribbean island.

The practice of jungle telegraphy is not confined to the New World. It is of ancient use among the natives of Central Africa. Dr. Albert Irwin Good, writing in the September 1943 issue of *Natural History*, cites messages commonly transmitted by African signal drums: "Person he not go in house, but outside," or "You shall die by witchcraft tonight."

During the early centuries after the conquest of South America, the ecclesiastical authorities tried in vain to suppress the native drums and flutes, which were regarded as accouterments of pagan ritual. A seventeenth-century Jesuit missionary in Peru proudly reported to his superiors that he had personally destroyed 605 large and 3418 small drums and flutes in the Peruvian villáges. In 1614, the Archbishop of Lima ordered the confiscation and destruction of all Indian musical instruments in his bishopric. Those found in possession of the forbidden objects were punished by receiving three hundred lashes in the public square, and then led through the streets on the back of a llama.

Despite this persecution, native music survived, and eventually found its way into community life, and even into the Church itself. In a quaint little book, *Three Vassar Girls in South America*, published in 1870 in New York, there is a picture showing the performance of a Mass held in a Bolivian church, with an Indian boy playing the gigantic *Sicus* pan-pipe, to the accompaniment of an organ.

Christianity and religious primitivism are combined in a curious palimpsest in the festivals and street parades celebrated in Latin-American towns and villages. The Afro-Brazilian *Macumba* is a complex body of primitive ritual, accompanied by collective dances and magic incantations. The basic African cosmogony is fused in the *Macumba* rites with the Indian elements, and over these is superimposed Christian lore, personified by popular saints. The *Voodoo* ritual of Haiti is a vast system of magical practices, in which primitive music is an integral part. The Afro-Cuban festival *Náñiga* is similar in many respects to the *Macumba* and the *Voodoo* rituals, with which it has a common African ancestry. During the *Náñiga*, singing, dancing, and the beating of the drums go on for days, until the participants expend the last drop of dynamic energy. In Nicaragua, the mystery play, *Güegüence*, celebrated on St. Jerome's day, combines elements of Christian and Indian folklore. Almost entirely Christian in its derivation is the festive play *Historia de Moros y Cristianos*, as it is performed in El Salvador. It portrays in pantomime and dialogue the struggle against the infidels during the Crusades.

Religious hymns, too, often comprise native elements. José Pacífico Jorge, a missionary at Ayacucho, Peru, published in 1924 a collection of religious songs, *Melodias Religiosas en Quechua*, in which both Latin and the Quechua language are used, with Inca chants and Gregorian melodies sung in alternation.

The influence of Christianity on the Indian folklore of Latin America is seen in the names of native dances, such as the *Sanjuanito* of Ecuador, named after St. John. Christmas carols are popular in Latin American countries under local names, *Adoración* in Bolivia, *Gualichadas* in Peru, and the *Esquinazo* (literally, corner song) in Chile. Christmas itself is known under different names. It is *Posadas* in Mexico, *Pascuas* in Colombia, and *Navidad* in Argentina. It is *Dia de Natal* in Brazil.

The sumptuous and gay Carnivals of Latin America also reflect the two elements, Christian and pagan, European and native. In his book, *Rio*,* Hugh Gibson, former Ambassador of the United States to Brazil, gives a word picture of the colorful Rio Carnival:

There is one thing that gives dash to the Carnival of Rio—the Carnival songs. Every year, there is a fresh supply. Not a rehash of familiar tunes, but something which is different from last year's songs . . . Nearly every day as you drive through the town, you see, more or less vaguely, the straggling mass of wretched-looking shanties clinging to the bare rock of the Morro do Salgueiro. Here is a little independent Negro kingdom, which leads a life of its own. Every shanty has its musician—even if he has nothing better than a cigar box on which to beat out a rhythm. About New Year's Day, things begin

* Copyright 1937 by Doubleday, Doran and Company, Inc.

to warm up, climatically and musically. People in Rio begin to wonder what they are going to dance to for four successive days and nights. So they get up parties to go up on the Morro and find out. The song writers go up and listen. If they find a promising song, they buy it, words and music, and put it in form for publication.

Huge floats with sculptured symbolic figures of saints and clowns are paraded on the streets at Latin-American carnivals. Until recently, the dominating figure of the Rio Carnival was Zé Pereira, a large fellow with a big drum. He has now been replaced by Momo, the King of the Carnival. Villa-Lobos makes Momo the subject of his composition for piano and orchestra, *Momoprecoce*, a precocious *Momo*, which is to say, child Carnival King. (Villa-Lobos telescopes two words, *Momo* and *precoce*, into one, as he does in his oratorio *Vidapura*, which looks like an Indian name until it is split into its component parts, *Vida Pura*, pure life; and in his redoubtable *Rudepoema*, which means, of course, a Rude Poem.)

Other days of the calendar than Carnival days are occasions for public parades and street dances. On St. John's Eve, Brazilian young men and girls launch balloons made of light cloth and paper propelled by hot air generated by a piece of burning wax underneath the bag. They follow the balloons merrily singing:

> *Cae, cae, balão! Cae, cae, balão!*
> *Na rua do Sabão,*
> *Não cae, não, não cae, não, não cae!*
> *Cae aqui na minha mão!*

CAE, CAE, BALÃO!

The words mean: "Fall, fall, balloon, but not in Soap Street. Fall here, in my hand." The melody of the Balloon Song is nearly a century old. It is included in the interesting little book *Folklore Brésilien*, by Santa Anna Nery, published in Paris in 1889. The game behind the custom of chasing the balloons is that young men or women lucky enough to catch the balloon are assured of success in love. The practice was, however, banned by the authorities when forest fires were started by run-away balloons. Several Brazilian composers have written variations on this tune, and I wrote a set, too, under the title *My Toy Balloon.*

The basic scale of pre-Columbian music is the pentatonic. This is, of course, the five-note scale represented (approximately) by the five black keys of the piano keyboard. If the tonic is placed on F sharp, the scale is in major; if on D sharp, in minor. Thus, pre-Columbian melodies may be adjusted to our system of major and minor keys, and André Sas of Peru makes the logical deduction that ancient Peruvian chants should be harmonized in a major key, or its relative minor.

If the theory that the Incas are of Mongolian origin and came from Asia has any foundation, the pentatonic scale would emerge as the basis of both Oriental and American music. But even this theory would not account for the use of the pentatonic in Scotland. It is much more likely that the selection of not more than five different tones in folk music was dictated by the necessity of clear recognition of pitch, with wide intervals between the essential sounds. An anthropological hypothesis also suggests itself, as the five tones of the primitive scale correspond to the five fingers of the human hand.

A great number of authentic Indian melodies are cast in the pentatonic scale. After the conquest, the Indian scale was supplemented by two passing tones, thus completing the heptatonic scale of our major and minor keys. In his essay on Ecuadorian music, Segundo Luis Moreno cites two variants of the indigenous melody *El Abago.* In its original form there are only five different tones, and the accompaniment is provided by rhythmic drum beats. When the melody was adapted for singing by the Spaniards, the scale was extended to a complete minor key, and the melody was harmonized by major and minor triads.

D'Harcourt distinguishes three evolutionary phases in Latin-American folk music: (1) pure Indian melos in the pentatonic scale; (2) the so-called "mestization" of the Indian scale, resulting in a "mestizo" scale identical with the European major or minor; (3) "mestization of mestization," consisting in a further elaboration of the scale by means of grace notes and chromatic ornamentation.

While the pentatonic scale is dominant in the ancient Indian music of South America, it is not the only scale that was used. The structure of the

"El Abago," Indian Melody of the Andes, in Its Original Pentatonic Form

The Same Melody Extended to a Complete Minor Scale and Harmonized
(*Segundo Luis Moreno*)

wind instruments of the Nazca culture of Peru, which flourished in the second century of our era, indicates that chromatic, and possibly ultrachromatic, tones were known to the Indians. And to this day, the Araucanian Indians of the extreme South use scales of narrow intervals. The National Museum of Costa Rica possesses an ocarina with six apertures, capable of producing eighteen chromatic tones.

The purest form of pentatonic Indian music was practiced in the nations where the present Indian population is numerous, that is in Peru, Bolivia, Ecuador, Mexico, and Central America. Negro influence is very strong in the dance music of the West Indies and northern Brazil. The urban folklore of Brazil possesses an inexplicable yet unmistakable affinity with Russian popular music of the Gypsy song type. In the spirit of fun, I wrote a piece in which I combined Russian and Brazilian melo-rhythmic elements and called the synthetic product *Modinha Russo-Brasileira* (*Modinha* is a Brazilian sentimental song, usually in a minor key). My Brazilian friends swore that the thing was Brazilian to the core, while to a Russian my *Modinha* sounds like an old-fashioned Russian Gypsy song.

The ancient Greek modes were classified according to the presumed quality and character of each mode, expressing fortitude or weakness, courage or effeminacy. Similar characterizations of indigenous folk music of South and Central America have been offered by native writers. Luis Segundo Moreno explains the predominance of minor keys in Ecuadorian music by the bleakness of the landscape:

> The absence of seasons weakens the stimulus towards progress. The great altitude makes respiration difficult, especially in the early hours of the afternoon when the rays of the sun beat down perpendicularly, engendering the sense of lassitude. As the dweller of the Sierra contemplates the vastness of the scene, a feeling of infinite solitude pervades him, and fills him with profound melancholy . . . That is why the aborigines of the Andes have adopted, no doubt by instinct, the minor mode, the wistful, monotonous, plaintive chant . . . This minor key is the natural product of the geographic conditions.

The Chilean composer Carlos Isamitt finds, independently from Luis Segundo Moreno, that the mountainous country where the Araucanian Indians live leaves the imprint of melancholy in their folk songs. I was told that phonograph records of Araucanian chants, made by Chilean ethnologists, are not let out of the country in order not to create the impression abroad that the Araucanians are an unhappy and oppressed race.

Victor Andrade, the Bolivian writer, finds to the contrary that the rarefied air of the mountains tends to create an invigorating effect on man and music. He writes in his article *La Música, Voz de la Tierra*, published in the Bolivian magazine *Kollasuyo:* "The songs of the mountains are generally cast in the major keys, responding to the invigorating air of the sacred lake Titicaca, while the music of the lowlands is impregnated with the nostalgia of the minor mode, reflecting the melancholy spirit of the landscape."

María de Baratta writes: "Topography influences the character of the race as well as the musical soul of the nation. Central America, geographically and historically considered, is situated in the most favorable position. In its coastal areas, and in the mountains, there is a racial concentration of custom, idiom, and art. The song of the birds, the rush of the wind, the murmur of the waters, the roar of nature, all these elements combine to create the sonorous treasure of native music."

Jesús Castillo of Guatemala contends that the Indians of Central America have been influenced in their folk songs by the amazingly vocal and musically articulate native bird, the Cenzontle, of the thrush family, which sings melodies based on the major arpeggio. He cites examples of these bird melodies which he had noted down from a Cenzontles in captivity, and compares them to the tunes of popular Indian songs and dances, proving, to his satisfaction, that the Indians use the musical "technique of the birds."

Tunes of the Guatemalan Bird, the Cenzontle (*Castillo*)

The primitive chants of pre-Columbian Indians are not always monodic. There is evidence that singing in groups, with the employment of some sort of prearranged harmony, was widely practiced in some regions of South America. The *Memby* flutes of the Guarany Indians were built in different sizes calculated to produce perfect fifths and octaves when played together. Playing in fifths and octaves is also common among the Indians of Colombia.

The American librarian, J. M. Coopersmith, who has spent some time doing musical research in the Dominican Republic, maintains that the Indians there sing antiphonal chants dating back to the thirteenth century. Antiphonal singing, or improvisation in dialogue, is indeed encountered in widely separated corners of the earth, and in different eras of history. The Gauchos of Argentina perform such improvisations professionally for entertainment. These minstrels of the pampas are called *Payadores,* and their singing dialogues *Payas,* or *Contrapunto* (without allusion, of course, to counterpoint in the sense of a technique of composition). In the *Contrapunto,* the contestants propound questions which are answered in song and verse, "point counter point." In Venezuela the practice is known as *Porfías,* and in Brazil *Desafío* (literally, challenge).

European forms acclimatized in Latin America acquire the unmistakable native accent. Thus the Viennese Waltz becomes *Vals Tropical.* Incidentally, one Latin-American Waltz, *Sobre las Olas* (Over the Waves), by the Mexican composer Juventino Rosas, has become a universal favorite. The *Schottische,* a round dance in the character of a slow Polka, has evolved under the tropical skies into a slightly syncopated Latin-American air, unrecognizably spelled *Chotis.*

The Paraguayan Polka is a combination of three-four and two-four time. The Spanish *Bolero* is in three-four time, but its Cuban counterpart is in two-four. The Brazilian *Marcha* is not the military March of the German type, but a carnival dance resembling a one-step. The Foxtrot, too, acquires a native inflection when transplanted into Latin America. Some music publishers in Ecuador have issued native dances under the subtitle *Foxtrot Incaico.* Carlos Valderrama, the Peruvian composer of light music, names his dances *Paso Inca* and *Inca Step.* This desire to imitate the product of Western sophistication reaches the peak of absurdity in the title of a Brazilian salon dance, *Quadrilla Sifilitica!*

The melo-rhythmic components of Latin-American songs and dances are of threefold extraction, Indian, Negro and European. The Indians contribute the basic pentatonic pattern, the Colonial European influence is expressed in the extension of the scale and the addition of chord harmony, and the Negroes add chromatic elaboration.

In meter and rhythm, the Indians adhere to short phrases, with long pauses, and a monotonous drum beat for accompaniment. The Colonial rhythms are prevalently Spanish, and are typified by the dual meter of three-four and six-eight, resulting in characteristic cross-rhythms in the middle of the measure. The Negro influence brings syncopation within an almost unchanged two-four time. To summarize:

Melos
{
Aboriginal pentatonic melody ....Indian
Extension to the seven-tone scale ....Colonial European
Chromatic elaboration ....Negro
}

Rhythm
{
Aboriginal rhythmic monotony ....Indian
Dual meter of 6/8 and 3/4 ....Colonial European
Syncopated 2/4 time ....Negro
}

A MAP OF SONGS AND DANCES

In the language of the Quechua Indians, the same word *Taqui* means either dancing or singing. This duality of function is characteristic of all Latin-American folk music. Any native dance is sung, and any air may be danced. The names of identical song-dances, however, vary from region to region. Thus, the Chilean national dance, the *Zamacueca* or *Cueca*, became known in other South American countries as the *Cueca Chilena*, or simply *Chilena*. During the war between Peru and Chile in 1879–1883, the Peruvians changed the name *Chilena* to *Marinera* in order to avoid mentioning the enemy country, and also to honor the Peruvian Navy. The entire history of the Chilean *Cueca* is told in excellent detail in *Biografía de la Cueca* by Pablo Garrido, published in Santiago in 1943.

The etymology of most Latin-American dance names is not easy to trace. The Argentine dance, *El Triunfo*, is said to have originated after the repulse of the British invasion in Rio de la Plata, early in the nineteenth century, but this derivation is not corroborated by historic evidence. The temptation to invent plausible etymologies leads to such absurd theories as, for instance, the proposed derivation of the Peruvian *Yaraví* from the muezzin's invocation *Ya Rabi*, heard in Moorish mosques. The ascertainable truth is that when the Conquistadores heard a slow and melancholy song, called in the native language *Yaravi*, they changed it, by assonance, to *Arabicus*, which led some theorists to conclude that the song was of Arabic or Moorish origin.

The most celebrated Argentine dance, the Tango, has been given a respectable but entirely spurious pedigree in Webster's Dictionary: "Argentine Sp., dance, fiesta, fr. Sp. *tango* a gypsy festival, dance, music, fr. *tangir* to play (an instrument), touch, fr. L. *tangere*. See TANGENT." With all due respect, the Tango has nothing to do with Latin or with tangents. The word is of Negro origin, and was formed as an imitation of the drum beat, with a slight accent on the second syllable, *Tangó*. The origin of the Tango is further clarified in the important treatise, *Cosas de Negros* by Vicente Rossi, published in 1926 in Córdoba, Argentina.

The dances and songs of Argentina, other than the Tango, are of clear Spanish extraction, as shown by the names *Bailecito, Cuando, Gato, Estilo, Firmeza*, and *Ranchera*. Carlos Vega gives detailed information on Argentine dances in an excellent series, *Bailes Tradicionales Argentinos*, which he published in 1944.

Musically, the Tango is an isotope of the *Habanera*, with which it has a common rhythmic figure. The history of the *Habanera* itself can be traced, surprisingly enough, to the Country Dance of seventeenth-century England. The English Country Dance became the *Contredanse* in France, and this in turn was called *Contradanza* in Spain, or later, simply *Danza*. When imported by the Spaniards into Cuba, it became the *Danza Habanera*, that is, the dance of Havana, and then was reintroduced into Spain as *Habanera*. During the Spanish-American War, a popular dance called *Habanera del Café* appeared, which was the prototype of the Tango. The whole genealogy is presented in the following chronological table:

> Country Dance, England 1650
> Contredanse, France 1700
> Contradanza, Spain 1750
> Danza, Spain 1800
> Danza Habanera, Cuba 1825
> Habanera 1850
> Habanera del Café 1900
> Tango 1910

The most famous *Habanera* is the one from *Carmen*. Contrary to general belief, it was not written by Bizet, but borrowed by him from a song

Natives of Bolivia playing on the gigantic panpipes, *bajones*

A Peruvian figurine representing a flute player, made of the thighbone of a llama. Markings may be rudimentary music notations. Early Chimu period (c. 200 B.C.).

An Ecuadorian Indian playing the rondador (panpipe), and another playing the harp

A blind beggar in Mexico City playing native airs on shoe-polish tins

called *El Areglito* by the Spanish composer Sebastian Yradier, which was published in Madrid about 1840 with the subtitle *Chanson Havanaise*.

For some unaccountable reason, music publishers in France, England, and the United States persist in putting a spurious *tilde* over the *n* in *Habanera*, making it *Habañera*. The Funk and Wagnalls Dictionary compounds the offense by giving the phonetic transcription of the word as *Habanyera*.

It is interesting to observe that the names of Brazilian and Cuban dances of Negro origin are, like the Tango, mostly two-syllable words, *Conga, Rumba, Jôngo, Lundú, Samba*, strongly suggesting onomatopoeia. The *Rumba* became popular in the United States in 1929. In the same year, the Brazilian *Samba* was demonstrated at the Society of Dancing Teachers in New York, which legislates on choreographical matters.

The latest Latin American dance hit is the ancient Mexican air, the *Bamba*, which was taken up in a modernized fast tempo by the society in Mexico City in 1945, and later spread to the United States.

One of the most successful Brazilian dances of the older generation was the *Maxixe*. It is suggested, not too seriously, by Mario de Andrade in his *Ensaio sobre Musica Brasileira* that the name comes from that of an actual person, a Senhor Maxixe.

Darius Milhaud, who was an attaché at the French Embassy in Brazil during the first World War, wrote a suite of Brazilian impressions entitled *Saudades do Brasil*. *Saudades* means a nostalgic memory, and is not the name of a native dance form. *Carioca* means an inhabitant of Rio de Janeiro, and the dance of that name stands for the *Samba carioca*, that is, a *Samba* played and danced in the accepted style of Rio de Janeiro.

In rare instances, inventive efforts of individual musicians have resulted in the creation of a new dance form. Villa-Lobos has extended the scope of the Brazilian dance *Chôros* to a pan-Brazilian synthesis of native folklore, a *"Brasilofonia,"* as he has described his concept. José Asunción Flores, the Paraguayan musician, has launched a popular dance in the spirit of the Guarany Indians and named the product *Guaranía*. It took root in Paraguay and has become an acknowledged native form. Not so lucky was the Dominican composer, Juan Francisco García, who originated a native rhapsody called *Sambumbia* (the word is applied to a plate of cold cuts, vegetables, and corn), which, however, remained an individual creation, without popular following.

The musical ballads called *Corridos* play a very important part in

Latin American musical life. The words are often topical and relate to political events. It has been suggested that the word *Corrido* is derived from *correr*, to run, because the singer had to run for his life when caught in the process of reciting a subversive ditty. *Corridos* are particularly popular in Mexico, with its seething political life. Numerous topical *Corridos* are found in the collection *Romance y Corrido* by Vicente T. Mendoza, published in 1939 in Mexico City.

The lyrics of Latin-American popular songs of the commercial type are chiefly concerned with love and passion. Frances A. Wright, Assistant Professor at the University of California, has examined two thousand popular Latin-American airs, and found that every one of them contained the words *el amor* and *la luna*.

The *Calypso* songs of Trinidad, sung in a curious brand of English, often quite uninhibited in vocabulary, have acquired a sudden popularity in recent years. Other islands of the West Indies have contributed songs of their own. In Jamaica, the most popular native dance is the *Mento*, which resembles a *Rumba* played in slow tempo. The French islands of St. Lucia and Martinique have produced the *Béguine*, made famous by Cole Porter's tune *Begin the Béguine*. The French word *béguin* means flirtation.

Although Puerto Rico is a part of the United States, it is culturally connected with the Latin-American world through common Spanish-American ties. Several distinctive airs have originated in Puerto Rico, among them the *Plena*, which is a topical ballad similar to the Mexican *Corrido*; and two song-dances in the Spanish manner, *Seis* (that is, "Six," from a six-string guitar) and *Mariandá*.

The choreography of Latin-American dances varies greatly according to region and time. However, it is possible to indicate the principal types of choreographic figures, described in such terms as amorous dances, in which the partners hold each other closely, handkerchief dances, in which the partners, dancing apart from each other, wave handkerchiefs, and so on. Ten principal categories may thus be established. They are (1) Amorous dances, such as the *Rumba*, *Merengue*, and the *Tango*; (2) Handkerchief dances: *Bailecito*, *Marinera*, *Sanjuanito*, *Zamacueca*; (3) Finger-snapping dances: *Gato*, *Chacarera*, *Jarana*; (4) Street dances: *Chôros*, *Guaracha*, *Guajira*; (5) Pursuit dances: *Firmeza*, *Escondido*, *Bambuco*, *Jarabe*; (6) Square dances: *Pericón*, *Punto*, *Mejorana*; (7) Rustic dances: *Ranchera*, *Pasillo*, *Joropo*; (8) Ritual dances: *Jôngo*, *Macumba*;

Dance Map of Latin America

(9) Carnival dances: *Samba, Conga;* (10) Topical ballads, such as the *Corrido.*

To illustrate the geographic distribution of native songs and dances, I drew up a "geo-musical" map of Latin America. The names of the dances are placed as nearly as cartographically possible in their natural habitat. The *Zamacueca* fits neatly into the long and narrow ribbon of Chile. The *Tango* is found in the vicinity of Buenos Aires, and the *Habanera* is placed near Havana. The *Rumba,* which originated in the underbelly of the island of Cuba populated by Negroes, is affixed there. The *Pasillo,* which is popular both in Colombia and Venezuela, straddles the two countries. Tiny Panama has three distinct national dance forms, the *Mejorana,* the *Tamborito,* and the *Punto.* I fitted the *Son Guatemalteco* as best I could into the Cartesian oval of Guatemala. The Mexican dances and ballads, the *Huapango,* the *Jarabe,* the *Corrido,* are scattered in Mexico proper, while the *Jarana,* which is a regional dance of Yucatán, is tucked away in that peninsula. I have given the *Pericón* to Uruguay, because it was in Montevideo that the *Pericón* was revived after long years of desuetude. The vast spaces of Argentina and Brazil afforded me the opportunity to populate them liberally with dance names. However, in order not to clutter up the map, I have left out obsolete or narrowly regional dances.*

THE LASCIVIOUS TANGO

In the Social History of Fads, the appearance of the Tango on the world stage is an exciting chapter. An exotic product of the slums of Buenos Aires, the Tango was first revealed to the world in the "Review of 1911," produced in New York. But it was not until the early months of 1914, on the eve of World War I, that the Tango skyrocketed to fame. All at once, everybody was either dancing it or talking about it. The press of both hemispheres devoted columns to the discussion of the new craze. Gloomy commentators saw in the popularity of the Tango a sign of moral decadence. Royalty, clergy, and society were unanimous in damning the dance from Argentina. The Kaiser of Germany, the King of Italy, the Queen of England, and the Pope, were all quoted in the newspapers as

* That my map is geo-musically accurate is proved to my satisfaction by its reproduction (from my article in the *Christian Science Monitor* of May 8, 1943) in the collection *Chile,* published late in 1943 by the University of Chile in Santiago. No credit was given to me by the editors and cartographers of *Chile,* and I hereby hasten to establish my priority of invention lest it be insinuated that I got the idea of the map in this book from that reproduction of my own brainchild.

having expressed their abhorrence. An article in the British magazine, *The Gentlewoman*, described the Tango as "the dance of moral death, the creation and manifestation of barbarism." Father Bernard Vaughan of London warned of dangers lurking at social gatherings known as "Tango teas." "It is not what happens at a Tango tea that so much matters," he pointed out, "as what happens after it. I have been too long with human nature not to know that, like a powder magazine, it had better be kept as far as possible fireproof."

The Church denounced the Tango in vigorous terms. The Bishop of Verdun urged all families "to combat the Tango which is a powerful dissolvent of French morality." The Archbishop of Lyons declared: "This abominable dance kills virtue, and gives rein to every appetite." On January 9th, 1914, the Archbishop of Paris proclaimed: "We condemn the dance of foreign origin known as the Tango, which by its lascivious nature offends morality. Christians ought not in conscience to take part in it. Confessors must in the administration of the sacrament of penance enforce these orders."

The Archbishop's proclamation had an unexpected sequel, when a New York dancing teacher, one Stilson, sued the Paris dignitary for $20,000, claiming that as a consequence of the ban he lost pupils. Later, Stilson reduced the amount of his suit to $4,000. The newspapers failed to mention the ultimate outcome of Stilson's action.

In Boston, Cardinal O'Connell looked at the Tango and commented gravely: "If this Tango-dancing female is the new woman, then God spare us from any further development of the abnormal creature." In New York, Rabbi Wise said: "If one were to enter a New York ballroom after a ten years' absence, one would be struck dumb and speechless with disgust at the degeneration which has come to pass."

On March 2, 1914, the Bible Conference, held in Atlanta, Georgia, heard Dr. Campbell Morgan, who declared that the Tango is a reversion to the ape, and a confirmation of the Darwin theory.

On July 16, 1914, the Mississippi Pearl Button Company filed an injunction against the river steamboat line, claiming that the playing of the Tango on the ship's calliope organ distracted the girls working in the factory of the Company, causing a serious drop in the production of pearl buttons.

Social phenomena attending the rise of the Tango were many and varied. On January 4, 1914, *The New York Times* reported in a feature article:

Since the Tango became popular, an extraordinary number of dark-skinned young men have appeared in New York as teachers of the Argentinian dance, and who claim to have come from South of the Rio de la Plata. Doubting Thomases assert that the arrival of these dusky young Tangoists dates from the first of recent Mexican revolutions, and unmask them as refugees from the other side of the Rio Grande.

A new criminal profession, that of the "Tango Pirates," invaded New York City in 1915. *The New York Times* of May 30, 1915, carried these headlines:

TANGO PIRATES INFEST BROADWAY

Afternoon Dances Develop a New Kind of Parasite Whose
Victims Are the Unguarded Daughters of the Rich

The story recounted how "young fellows wearing a silk hat, tilted at an angle of forty-five degrees, cutaway coats and spats" took advantage of the pleasure-seeking New York females. "They never spend money on the girls. The girls pay for everything, for the lunches, drinks, motor cars, etc. All these Tango pirates are victims of the drug habit. They often teach the girls to take cocaine. The Tango pirate does not try to seduce these rich girls; he just wants their money."

The importation of the Tango into Imperial Japan was, in some unfathomable manner, a follow-up of an illicit love affair between a scion of New York society and a married woman, and involved a global chase after the couple by a famous correspondent. The correspondent could not persuade the scion to leave the lady of his choice. The couple took to appearing as Tango-dancers, and the Tango became the rage of Japan.

Guglielmo Ferrero, the great Italian sociologist, commented sagely upon the Tango:

The ease with which these frivolous dances spread among all classes of people should not lead us to unwarranted pessimistic deductions. Possibly, at an earlier period of history, the popularity of the Tango would not have been so rapid and so universal, and its devotees would not have been so numerous. But they might have gone beyond the Tango on the road to evil.

The medical properties of the Tango came under discussion when Dr. Boehme of New York City announced, in April 1914, the appearance of a new disease, the Tango foot, which he described as being akin to such occupational ailments as housemaid's knee, miner's elbow, and weaver's bottom.

A letter to the editor of *The New York Times*, published in the issue of February 18, 1914, told of curative powers of the Tango:

Abbut three years ago I began to suffer severely with indigestion. My physician warned me of the danger of the frequent acute attacks. I dieted and followed all instructions; the only result was that I was a nuisance to myself and friends, and retained the ailment. About Christmas time in 1913, I decided to abandon doctors, and began to learn the Tango and other new dances. Within two weeks practically all symptoms of indigestion left me. When the evening's dance was over, I would eat a sandwich and retire to a sound dreamless sleep. At the present time, I can eat anything, even the proverbial cobblestones.

Visitors in Argentina are, as a rule, enchanted and captivated by the Tango as it is danced in its land of birth. Waldo Frank rhapsodized after attending a Tango in Buenos Aires:

Violins, harmonicas, flutes, weave the Tango music, interminable as the generations, pulsant, monotonous, delicious as the play of sex . . . The Tango is the profoundest folk dance in the world . . . The choric genius of three supremely plastic races—Negro, Indian, Spaniard—has produced it.

The Argentine literati are inclined to spurn the Tango. Leonidas Barletta, the leading Argentine poet of the vanguard, poured invective upon invective on this most celebrated product of Argentine folklore. He wrote in the Buenos Aires journal *Disonancias:*

The Tango is a jeremiad of the effeminate man, the tardy awakening of a woman unconscious of her femininity. It is the music of degenerates who refuse to don the proletarian clothes, whose greasy-haired women leave factories for prostitution. . . . The Tango is unhealthy. The sensuality that pervades it is that of inhibition, timidity and fear. The music of other nations is frankly sensual, ingenuously sexual. In the Tango, the sensuality is deceptive, artificially created.

At the peak of anti-Tango agitation in 1914, the Argentine Ambassador in Paris made a formal declaration that "the Tango is a dance peculiar to the houses of ill fame in Buenos Aires, and is never cultivated at respectable gatherings."

In July 1943, the Argentine government launched a campaign for the "purification of national art," which action included the revision of suggestive lyrics of popular Tangos. Thus a Tango entitled *Tal vez será mi alcohol* was denatured to *Tal vez será tu voz.*

The Tango received its *coup de grâce* from the Russians, when the *Proletarian Musician*, the mouthpiece of the since defunct Russian Association of Proletarian Musicians, described it as "the dance of impotent men."

Is Latin America Latin?

THREE racial elements make up the fabric of Latin-American culture: Indian, Colonial European, and Negro. White natives are commonly called *Criollos*, Creoles. Often the adjective Creole is added to the title of a European dance or song acclimatized in Latin America, as for instance *Barcarola Criolla*. The offspring of an Indian and a Creole are *Mestizos*, and in Central America, *Ladinos*. In Brazil, a cross between the Portuguese and the Indian produces the *Mameluco*. A half-Indian, half-Negro is a *Cafuso* in Brazil, and a *Zambo* in Spanish America.

In view of this racial diversity, is it proper to call the South Americans, the Central Americans, and the natives of the West Indies, indiscriminately, Latin Americans? The question is the subject of a lively debate. Dr. Rafael Belaunde, former Peruvian ambassador to Chile, declared, in a statement to the American press made in September 1942, that the term Latin America is false, for it implies a non-existent spiritual tie with Italy. As a substitute, he suggested the name Hispanic America, which would, according to Dr. Belaunde, also apply to Portuguese America, inasmuch as in Roman times Hispania was the designation for the entire Iberian Peninsula, including modern Portugal.

In a letter to *Time* Magazine of November 24, 1941, a reader reported the query of an Argentine intellectual: "Why do your papers call us Latin Americans? Don't they know that every one of us resents that? We are Central or South Americans, not Latin Americans."

However, the term Latin America has the support of one of the most articulate exponents of Pan Americanism, Luis Quintanilla, whose brilliant book on Inter-American affairs is entitled *A Latin American Speaks.*

Haya de la Torre, the Peruvian intellectual and founder of the *Alianza Revolucionaria Americana,* is in favor of the name Indo-America, pointing out that Indians are the only true Americans. Other writers of the same school of thought have suggested Amerindia. But many Latin-American Indians reject the racial claims of the Indian birthright. The late Honduran poet, Rómulo Durón, expresses this desire to renounce the pre-Columbian past in favor of the Latin-American present. *"No tenemos mitotes; bailamos Vals o Danza"* (We have no more rustic airs; we dance the Waltz or the *Danza*), he writes, and concludes: "Although Indian blood runs in my veins, I feel, think, and love as though I were Spanish. *No Soy Indo-Hispano; Hispano-Indiano soy!"*

In discussing native music, Latin-American writers often apply the terms Ibero-American and Hispano-American. Francisco Curt Lange calls his unique magazine *Boletín Latino-Americano de Música.* But Otto Mayer-Serra entitles his sixty-page essay on native music in the *Enciclopedia de la Música,* published in Mexico in 1943, *Panorama de la Música Hispano-Americana.* The Festival of Music presented in Bogotá in 1938 was announced as the *Festival Ibero-Americano.*

With the rising consciousness of national culture, the Latin Americans of the twenty republics prefer to speak of the quality of being Mexican, Chilean, Peruvian, and so on, in place of a vague Latin Americanism. The terms *Mexicanismo, Chilenidad, Peruanidad, Brasilidade, Centro-Americanismo* (comprising the closely related cultures of the six Central American republics) are used more and more often in native literature. The combined quality of race and nation is suggested by the concept of *Afro-Cubanismo.* The description of Haitian culture as *Afro-Latin* has been proposed by a native writer.

By a further extension of the concept of a nation, all elements, including later European immigrants, are regarded as national. Thus, Mario de Andrade declares: "Brazilian music is national in its entirety, whatever ethnological basis may underlie it . . . The criterion of Brazilian music should be not dialectical, but social."

Carlos Chavez writes: "The music of the Indians is Mexican music; and also Mexican is the art of Spanish extraction. It is fit and proper to regard as Mexican even the native operas in the Italian style, or the German-inspired Mexican symphonies. Naturally, the state of being Mexican does not qualify an art product esthetically. Only when Mexican music attains artistic quality does it become true national art."

In keeping with these sentiments, the National Anthems of the twenty republics of Latin America are regarded by native musicians as part of national folklore. Yet most of these hymns are artificial compositions in an indifferent Italian or Germanic manner, written by some immigrant musician. Thus the National Anthem of Colombia was composed by an Italian tenor who was stranded in Bogotá after the failure of his opera company. The Chilean Anthem is the work of a Spaniard who had never set foot on Chilean soil. This Anthem superseded the original Chilean patriotic song by a native musician, a preference that aroused considerable resentment among Chilean patriots. The Mexican National Anthem was the composition of a Spanish musician who eventually settled in the United States and taught music in Buffalo. Juan Aberle, the Italian musician who lived in Central America, was the author of the National Anthem of El Salvador. Panama's Anthem was originally a school song composed by a Spanish resident musician, and entitled *Himno Istmeño*. After Panama's separation from Colombia, the *Isthmus Hymn* became the National Anthem of the new republic. The Cuban National Anthem was composed spontaneously by a local band leader when the liberating forces entered the village of Guanabacoa during the Cuban War of Independence.

The Uruguayan Anthem was improvised by a native amateur musician and won the honor of becoming the National Hymn through a contest. It is entirely Italian in its melody and in fact closely resembles the Gondoliers' Chorus from Donizetti's opera *Lucrezia Borgia*. The Argentine Anthem was written by a music teacher in Buenos Aires. It, too, sounds like an aria from an old Italian opera. The Argentine Anthem is also the longest of all Latin American patriotic songs.

The music of the original Brazilian Hymn of Independence was composed, according to irrefutable evidence, by the "Constitutional Emperor and Perpetual Defender of Brazil," Dom Pedro I, upon the declaration of independence from Portugal on September 7, 1822. After the abdication of Dom Pedro in 1831, a new patriotic hymn was composed by a professional musician, Francisco Manuel da Silva, and became the present National Anthem of Brazil.

The oldest Latin-American Anthem is the "Venezuelan Marseillaise," *Gloria al Bravo Pueblo*, composed during the War of Revolution by Juan Landaeta. Incidentally, the composition of the Anthem is often ascribed to Teresa Carreño, the famous "Valkyrie of the Piano," who was of Venezuelan birth. She did write a festival hymn for the Bolivar Centennial, but not the "Venezuelan Marseillaise."

The National Anthem of Costa Rica came to be written under curious circumstances. When, in 1853, the envoys of Great Britain and the United States arrived in San José, the capital, the President of the young republic, desiring to impress the foreign dignitaries, resolved to have a national hymn played at their reception. Since there was none in existence, he ordered one Manuel María Gutiérrez, reputed to be the best musician in the country, to write such a song. But Gutiérrez balked, saying that he knew very little about writing music. The President then caused him to be thrown into jail, and the poor man was kept there until he managed to set down on paper a plausibly playable tune.

LANDMARKS AND HISTORY

Musical culture in Latin America is actually more ancient than in North America. The first music school in the New World was established in Texoco, Mexico, in 1524, by Pedro de Gante, a Franciscan missionary. He was also the first to teach the natives to sing hymns and use Gregorian musical notation. The first book with music published in the Western Hemisphere was an *Ordinarium* printed in Mexico in 1556, one hundred and forty-two years before the first book containing musical notation was published in North America. An important historical landmark was the publication in Mexico in 1604 of a folio volume, *Liber quo IV Passiones Christi Domini Continentur*. It contained original Passion music, eight Lamentations, and a Jeremiad, composed by Juan Navarro. This Navarro has been unwarrantedly identified in music dictionaries with the sixteenth-century Spanish musician of the same name. Gilbert Chase has cleared up the matter in his article, "Juan Navarro Hispalensis and Juan Navarro Gaditanus," published in the April 1945 issue of *The Musical Quarterly*.

One of the important pioneers of ecclesiastical music in Latin America was the famous Italian composer and organist Domenico Zipoli. He died in Córdoba, Argentina, on January 2, 1726, a date established by documentary evidence in the monograph by Lauro Ayestarán, *Domenico Zipoli, El Gran Compositor y Organista Romano*, published in 1941 in Montevideo, Uruguay.

The first Mass celebrated in the New World was given in Santo Domingo in 1512. The first native-born composer of the Western Hemisphere was Cristóbal de Llerana, who flourished in Santo Domingo in the second half of the sixteenth century. The first song to words in an Indian dialect was an *Ave Maria* in the Nahuatl language, set to music by Hernando Franco in Mexico circa 1575. Here are the first two lines of this *Ave Maria:*

> *In ilhuicac cihuapille tenantzin dios in titotepantlahtohcatzin*
> *Mahuel tehuatzin topan xinotlahtolti in titlahtlacoanime.*

The first revelation of the existence of native music in Latin America was the collective dance that Queen Anacaona staged for the benefit of the Spanish Governor on the island of Santo Domingo in the year 1520. Gonzalo Fernandez Oviedo, the official historiographer of Christopher Columbus, describes the event in his chronicle, *La Historia Natural y General de las Indias:*

> On this island, the only record of the arts are songs called *Areitos,* which are transmitted from generation to generation. At one time, when Nicolas de Ovando ruled the island, Anacaona, the wife of a local chief, sang an *Areito* for the Governor, and three hundred maidens took part in the dance, all of whom were the king's progeny, and all marriageable; for he did not wish married men or women to sing *Areitos.*

The exact nature and form of the pre-Columbian *Areito* is difficult to establish. An example of the *Areito* is found in *Cuba Primitiva* by Bachiller y Morales, published in Havana, Cuba, in 1883. But this melody is obviously a procrustean adaptation in the nineteenth-century European form, and could not be even remotely connected with the tune that the good Indian Queen sang for the Spanish Governor of Santo Domingo.

The classical *Chaconne* is said by some authorities to be of New World origin. According to this theory, the *Chaconne* was popular in Mexico during the sixteenth century, and was known under the name *Chacona mulata* or *Indiana amulatada.* Its Mexican version was a wild and savage dance, quite different from the stately and measured air made familiar by the works of the classics. There is, of course, no evidence for or against the theory of Mexican origin of the *Chaconne,* and the derivation of the word itself is obscure.

How unreliable are the accounts of native music by early travelers in Latin America, is demonstrated by Carlos Vega, who has painstakingly perused the old books of exploration in search of pertinent data. He has discovered that too often an ostensibly first-hand report on native dancing and singing proves to be an undisguised borrowing from an earlier account, with considerable geographic mutation in the process. Thus an

Englishman, Anthony Helm, writes in 1806: "At Montevideo, a lively and very lascivious dance is much practiced; it is called *Calenda,* and the Negroes, as well as the Mulattoes, whose constitutions are sanguine, are excessively fond of it." This turns out to be a literal translation of a passage from *Histoire d'un Voyage* by Antonio Joseph Pernetty, published in 1763. Pernetty's account, in its turn, is taken from another French travel book, *Histoire Générale des Voyages,* published in 1746–1761, with this difference, that the locale of the report is placed in Santo Domingo rather than Montevideo. But this is not the rock bottom of the tale, which is found in a still earlier volume, *Nouveaux Voyages,* published in 1724!

An apparently authentic account of a song festival in Chile is given by Frézier, a reputable French writer who traveled to South America early in the eighteenth century. His book was published in an English translation in 1724, under the somewhat extensive title: *A Voyage to the South Sea and Along the Coast of Chili and Peru in the Years 1712, 1713, and 1714, Particularly Describing the Genius and Constitution of the Inhabitants As Well Indians as Spaniards, Their Customs and Manners, Their Natural History, Mines, Commodities, Traffick With Europe, etc.*

There being adorn'd with Feathers of Ostriches, Flamencos and other Birds of sprightly Colours, stuck round their Caps, they fell to singing to the Sound of two instruments made of a Piece of Wood, with only one Hole bored through it; blowing in which, either stronger or more gently, they form'd a Sound more or less sharp or flat. They kept Measure alternately with a Trumpet made of a Bull's Horn, fastened to the End of a long Cane, the Mouth of which had a Pipe, that sounds like a Trumpet. They fill'd up this Symphony with some Strokes of a Drum, whose heavy and doleful Sound was answerable enough to their Mien; which in the Height of their Exclamations had nothing in it that was gay. I observ'd them attentively on the Stage, and did not, during the whole Festival, see one smiling Countenance among them.

The author goes on to comment on the native dances and instruments:

The *Zapateo,* a Dance of Peru and Chili, is as common with them as the Minuet is in France; they call it the *Zapateo,* because they alternately strike with the Heel and the Toes, taking some Steps. By this Piece of Musick may be discern'd what a barren Taste they have in touching the Harp, the Guitarre, and the Bandola, which are almost the only instruments used in that Country. The two last are of the Species of Guitarras, but the Bandola has a much sharper and louder Sound.

Robert Semple, who traveled in Venezuela early in the nineteenth century, does not conceal his dislike of the Indian songs. He reports his findings in a book published in London in 1812 under the title *Sketch of the Present State of Caracas: Including a Journey from Caracas Through La Victoria and Valencia to Puerto Cabello.*

Some of the Indians amused themselves by blowing into a species of flute, if it can be so called, without doubt one of the rudest ever sounded by the human breath. The sound was like that of the wind sighing in the forests, or among rocks; sometimes rising almost to a scream, and then dying away into a whisper. This alternate rise and fall constituted the whole of the music. It seemed to afford infinite satisfaction to those for whose ears it was designed; they listened in silence, and when the performers reached the height of screaming, all eyes were turned towards us to see if we were not yet touched by such masterpieces of melody.

F. Hassaurek, who was the United States minister in Ecuador in the middle of the nineteenth century, records his impressions of the Negro dances in *Four Years Among Spanish Americans*, published in New York in 1868:

The main part of the orchestra consists of the voices of the women and children. Clapping their hands continually, they sing a great variety of songs. In musical talent and taste, these Negroes are infinitely superior to the Indians. Their melodies are neither so monotonous nor so lifeless as those of the aborigines. On the contrary, they are varied and fiery, and full of exciting vigor. Their dance is not the slow measured step of the Indians, but is peculiar to the Ethiopians . . . The fellow who beats the drum never stops. When he is treated to a cup of rum, someone of the company presents it to his lips, and he swallows it while his hands continue to beat the drum. Perspiration pours down his face, but he has no time to wipe it off.

To the Europeans of the sixteenth and seventeenth centuries, America was the land of wonders, natural and supernatural. Kircher's *Musurgia Universalis*, published in 1650, contains a drawing of an indigenous American animal, *pigritia* (sloth), attributing to it the ability to sing a diatonic hexachord (the notes accompany the drawing). Kircher adds significantly: "Whatever music may exist in the Americas, is doubtless derived from the miraculous vocal scale of this animal."

One of the most precious souvenirs I brought with me from my "Pan-American Fishing Trip" is a Peruvian figurine, carved from the thighbone of a llama, and representing a musician, or a priest, playing on a vertical flute. The statuette dates back to the early Chimu civilization, about the second century B.C., and it may well be one of the earliest specimens of musical sculpture in pre-Columbian America. There is on it a curious lettering, a linear tracery that suggests notation. Are these strange markings nothing more than dyed cracks in the bone structure? Or do they correspond to the melody of some ancient Indian chant? Are they primitive musical symbols? ¿*Quién sabe?*

* * *

The course of evolution of Latin American music, from the dawn of continental civilization to the present times, is summarized in the following paragraphs:

PRE-COLUMBIAN CULTURES (before 1492). Primitive musical instincts expressed in singing and rhythmic stamping. Manufacture of drums made of hollow tree trunks and covered with animal skins; scratchers made of notched fruit shells; and shakers, or gourds with dry seed inside. Production of vertical flutes and panpipes made of baked clay, and sometimes of animal and even human bones. Formation of the pentatonic scale, possibly of chironomic origin, symbolizing the five digits of the hand.

EARLY CENTURIES OF THE CONQUEST (1492–1750). The first native festival heard by Europeans, given by Queen Anacaona in Santo Domingo in 1520. Church music carried by the Jesuits to the natives of South America. Determined efforts of colonial authorities to suppress indigenous music, with forcible destruction of drums and other Indian instruments. Gradual amalgamation of native and European rhythms and melodies into new distinctive Latin-American forms. Extension of the pentatonic scale to the heptatonic, symmetrization of musical phrases, and introduction of traditional European harmony into popular music of Latin America. Infusion of African rhythms consequent upon the importation of Negro slaves.

FORMATION OF NATIONAL CULTURES (1750–1900). Foundation of conservatories and music schools. Immigration of Italian and other foreign musicians to South America. Composition of national anthems, after the War of Independence.

MODERN ERA OF LATIN AMERICAN MUSIC (1900–1950). Establishment of opera houses in the principal centers. Organization of symphonic ensembles under the direction of native and foreign musicians. Foundation of music publishing firms. Government subsidies for musical education. Music festivals and prize contests for composers. Emergence of native creative composers who combine in their music a deep racial and national consciousness with modern technique. Inclusion of Latin America into the commonwealth of universal musical culture on equal terms with the great schools of composition of Europe and North America.

LA CHACARERA

EL GATO

Argentina

De su lumbre divina
Triunfante y de ambiciosos respetada,
Libre, rica, tranquila, organizada,
Ya brilla la República Argentina.

[JUAN CRUZ VARELA]

¿Te llamas la Argentina?   —¡La Argentina!
¿Cual es el nombre de tu madre?   —¡Gloria!

[R. J. PAYRO]

The name Argentina is the Latin equivalent of the Spanish word La Plata, silver, as the region was known during colonial times. Argentina is the second largest South American nation, and numbers thirteen and a half million inhabitants. Buenos Aires, the capital, is the largest South American city, with a population of two and a half million.

The arts, the poetry, and the music of Argentina are connected in the popular mind with the picturesque figure of the Gaucho, the roving creole of the Pampas, the minstrel horseman, ever ready to burst into song. The word Gaucho may have come from *vaquero*, cowboy, or it may be an adaptation of the Indian Araucanian word *Guacho*, meaning orphan.

The best singers among the Gauchos formed a clan of *Payadores*, who supplied entertainment at the inns and were rewarded for their singing. Arturo Torres-Rioseco in his book *The Epic of Latin American Literature* * gives an illuminating account of the songs of the Gaucho:

In his songs or Payadas, the Gaucho used a very picturesque style, full of objective images and metaphors, and he sang his verses in a voice warm with pathos and emotion. He employed eight-syllable quatrains, the old ballad form, and his language was the sixteenth-century Spanish spoken by the conquerors and

* Oxford University Press, New York, 1942.

73

kept intact in certain isolated regions. Possibly the most interesting form of the Payada was the one called the *Contrapunto*, which was performed in the following manner: Two Gauchos would sit on the skulls of oxen, tuning their guitars, while bystanders stood around them in a circle and urged them with yells and applause into a singing match. Then one singer would challenge the other to explain, for instance, the origin of time and space; the second singer would improvise half a dozen stanzas and end by asking a question in his turn. In this way they often passed hours, sometimes days, in a sport that was a real tournament of wit, to the great delight of the spectators.

This art of the Gaucho, the wonderful *Contrapunto*, is now but a part of the national legend. In the world of the airplane and radio, the Gaucho is no longer a solitary figure, alone with nature and his poetic soul. His songs are now composed for him by professional poets, and the music he strums on his guitar is that of the latest hit from Buenos Aires.

The origin of a great number of Argentine songs and dances is ascribed, rightly or wrongly, to the Gaucho. These are the sentimental *Vidalita*, the prancing *Gato*, the lively *Pericón*, the picaresque *Escondido*, the leisurely *Ranchera*, the melancholy *Estilo*. . . . In his monumental work *Danzas y Canciones Argentinas*, Carlos Vega cites no fewer than 130 Argentine songs and dances, and yet qualifies the list as "presumably incomplete." Arturo C. Schianca, in *Historia de la Música Argentina*, gives a detailed description of 38 dances and 14 songs. Such is the wealth and abundance of native folk music in Argentina.

Each of these numerous songs and dances possesses a strong individuality of rhythmic and formal structure. Yet, all of them fall into a larger melorhythmic category which is unmistakably Argentine. The prevailing meter of Argentine folk music is a dual time-signature of three-four and six-eight, the latter often evolving into syncopated duple time. The titles usually derive from the repetition of a certain word in the verse. Thus, *Vidala*, or *Vidalita*, is a word repeated at the end of each refrain. Incidentally, the word is a hybrid, for its root, *Vida*, is Spanish, while the suffix *la* is a Quechua Indian diminutive. The *Vidala* is most often written in triple meter, three-four or three-eight, whereas the *Vidalita* is usually in six-eight time.

The *Estilo* is a nostalgic song inspired by the vastness of the landscape. It consists of two parts, the first in slow two-four or four-four time, the second in lively three-four or six-eight time. The *Gato* (which means "cat") is a country dance performed by two couples. In rhythm it resembles a very rapid waltz, in steady quarter-notes. A very popular form of the *Gato* is the *Gato con Relaciones,* that is, "Gato with Stories." The stories are of diversified content, amorous, philosophical, political. The dance called *Escondido* (literally, hidden, for in it the female partner hides from the male) belongs to the *Gato* type rhythmically and choreographically.

Several Argentine airs, long obsolete, have been revived by native composers in suites of dances modeled after the classical European suite. Among these airs, the best known are the *Cielito* (literally "little heaven," from the repetition of the word at the end of the refrain), and the *Cuando* (from the refrain in which the lover asks "¿Cuando?" meaning "When?"). The *Cielito* is in waltz time, while the *Cuando* resembles a minuet. Other airs that are now being revived are the *Media Caña* (literally "semicircular molding," from the dance figure in which the partners perform a semicircle), and the *Triunfo* ("triumph").

One of the most original airs of Argentina is the *Pericón,* which fell into desuetude, then was revived in Montevideo, and finally returned to Argentina by way of Uruguay. It is in triple time, in rapid tempo, and in a steady rhythm of even notes. A well-known humorous song, *Remedio* (in which the singer offers a remedy for the anguish of love), is of the *Pericón* type.

Other dances of Argentina, directly or indirectly associated with the Gaucho tradition, are the *Firmeza* ("firmness"), a lively air in six-eight time; the *Ranchera* (a ranch dance), which is a mazurka with the accompanying figure in six-eight time; the *Chacarera* (from *chacra,* farm), which is practically identical with the *Ranchera;* and the *Chamamé,* an air in three-four time, probably of Indian origin, with an unusual rhythm consisting of a group of triplets, followed by two groups of duplets, in three-four time.

Several Peruvian and Chilean dances have been acclimatized in Argentina. The *Refalosa* (or, more correctly, *Resbalosa*)· is an old dance of Peruvian origin, which became fashionable in Buenos Aires in the nineteenth century. It is in moderate six-eight time.

The Chilean *Zamacueca* (or as it was formerly called, *Zambacueca*) has generated in Argentina two different dance forms, the *Zamba* and the *Cueca.* The *Zamba* is a rather slow air in six-eight time, popular in northern Argentina, and the *Cueca,* sometimes called *Cueca Chilena,* or simply *Chilena,* is a lively and syncopated dance in three-four time.

Carlos Vega offers an interesting theory regarding the migration of folk songs from Peru to Argentina. He writes: "Spain communicated with its South American colonies through Lima, via Panama. The manner of dress, customs, dances, and music of the period flourished in the Lima salons. But already in 1700 there was formed a nucleus of a more ancient stock, that of native music. As a consequence, Spanish music underwent the process of Peruvianization. Soon, all South America became similarly Peruvianized. The picaresque dances of Argentina, which we call indigenous, are in reality an importation from Peru, and have come first by way of Bolivia, and then through Chile."

Vega describes the second phase of the process as the "Argentinization" of South America: "The revolution of 1810 opened the gates of Buenos Aires to Paris, London, and, to a lesser extent, New York. Social life in Buenos Aires about 1816–1818 rivaled that of the most elegant world capitals. Argentina adopted the colonial dances and made them her own. Later, these Argentine dances reached Peru, by way of Bolivia. A focal point was thus created in Buenos Aires, and soon a partial Argentinization of South America took place."

A penetrating analysis of the Gaucho music of Argentina is found in a little-known monograph, *Origenes de la Música Argentina*, by Juan Alvarez, published in the 1909 number of the *Revista de Derecho, Historia y Letras*. He writes:

There is no set rule by which we can tell which music belongs to the Gaucho, and which does not. The *Gato* seems unmistakably genuine; yet it is often embellished with variations in the form of a waltz or a polka. The difficulty is increased by the fact that there are fewer and fewer people in the country who are familiar with native music. Many Argentines live and die without having ever heard a *Gato*, without suspecting that the *Chacarera*, the *Triunfo*, the *Firmeza*, are products of our indigenous art . . . True, this music often possesses elements alien to it. There exists, for instance, a dance called the *Minuet Federal*. Obviously, it is a European Minuet, "federalized" for the occasion. For alongside Argentine popular music, there exists also official music, adopted and made native by decree. Examples of such official music are: the National Anthem by Blas Parera, which used to be called *Marcha de la Patria*, although there is nothing of a march in this music; the *Canción Patriotica* by Esteban de Lucca; the *Himno de los Restauradores* by Rivera Indarte; the *Marcha Triunfal* by Artigas.

But despite the embellishments and additions, there is something in our music that makes it, if not always, then nearly always, unmistakably native. A *Gato*, embellished with variations in the form of a waltz, is still a *Gato*. Our music may have come from a different ethnic group, but it has now acquired definite characteristics of this particular region of South America. To question the authenticity of this music is about as sensible as to deny the Spanish language the right to exist because the vocables that make it up are similar to the words of another language . . . In this we follow the dictum of the founding fathers of the Republic, namely that our nation fuses into one race the energies of all men desiring to live on Argentine soil.

Among urban airs of Argentina, the *Milonga* is the most important for the development of native music. It was originated as a song of the lower social strata of Buenos Aires, and held its popularity until the turn of the century, when it was absorbed by the *Tango*. But the name *Milonga* has remained, hyphenated with the *Tango*. Both the *Tango* and the *Milonga* retain the characteristic swinging rhythm that first appears in the *Habanera*.

The Argentine airs as sung and played around Cuyo, on the Chilean border, possess a rhythmic distinction and a lyrical quality that set them apart as a special type of regional folklore. Alberto Rodriguez has published an important collection of traditional dances and songs of Cuyo entitled *Cancionero Cuyano* (Buenos Aires, 1938).

Although there are few Negroes left in Argentina, African rhythms have profoundly affected Argentine popular music. Juan Alvarez writes: "African music has left among us traces thicker than blood. Now that there are almost no Negroes in the country, the *Zamba*, the *Milonga*, the *Tango* have developed into the most aggressive type of native music."

Vicente Rossi, in his informative book, *Cosas de Negros* (Córdoba, 1926), also supports the view that Negro music is a basic influence in Argentine folk songs.

C. J. Videla-Rivero, in an article published in the Bulletin of·the Pan American Union, credits the Negro slaves with influencing the Gaucho songs:

The plaintiveness of the Negro found an echo in the sadness of the Gaucho, and thus Argentine music was born . . . The *Fandango* was the first materialization of the Negro-Gaucho psychological crossing . . . From the rural districts it stole into the social affairs of the city's lower classes, and stealthily made its way to the middle-class homes, where it was danced behind drawn blinds. It was ready to assault the drawing rooms of the aristocracy when Juan José Peralta, Archbishop of Buenos Aires, dealt it a death blow. Under pain of excommunication for those who dared to disobey, the Archbishop banned the *Fandango* on July 30, 1743.

The history of *música culta*, or "educated music" in Argentina, begins with the Jesuits. A seventeenth-century Belgian Jesuit, Luis Berger, was the first to teach the Indians to play the guitar and the lute. The Italian

Examples of Rhythmical Patterns of Some Argentine Dances and Airs, as Employed in Free Stylization by Argentine Composers

musician Domenico Zipoli, whose name occupies an important place in the general history of music, was also one of the Jesuit missionaries in South America. Other European musicians, all of them members of the Jesuit order, active in the part of South America which is now Argentina, were a Flemish priest, Juan Vaseo, and the Germans Anton Sepp, Martin Schmidt, Johann Messner, and Florian Baucke.

Secular music was not encouraged by the Jesuits. There is a record of an action brought against a Spanish army officer who, in the year 1650, was accused of offending religious propriety, for "after the church services, he went to a wedding and sang to the accompaniment of a guitar."

In the nineteenth century, Buenos Aires became a musical center on a par with the cities of North America. Several Italian opera companies visited Argentina early in the nineteenth century. The first opera on an indigenous subject was *La Indigena,* produced in Buenos Aires in 1862. A performance of Gounod's opera *Faust* inspired the Argentine poet Estanislao Campo to write a Gaucho version of the story. The result was an epic in verse, entitled *Fausto,* which still retains its popularity in Argentine literature.

Argentina was the first South American country to adopt a new National Anthem. It was the *Marcha Patriotica* by Blas Parera, which was sanctioned by the General Constituent Assembly of Argentina on May 11, 1813. In his handbook, *Music of the New World,* compiled for the broadcast series of the Inter-American University of the Air, Gilbert Chase describes the progress of this first patriotic song of an independent South America in the following paragraph:

The Argentines in the army of General San Martín, liberator of Peru and Chile, carried Parera's *Marcha Patriotica* to those countries. It is recorded that in an impressive public ceremony at Santiago de Chile in 1818, San Martín himself, preceded by a fanfare of bugles, electrified the crowds by singing the Argentine anthem in his powerful bass voice. San Martín, in fact, was very partial to music. He made his regimental bands rehearse daily so as to insure a high standard of execution.

The names of Amancio Alcorta (1805–1862), Juan Pedro Esnaola (1808–1878), and Juan Bautista Alberdi (1810–1884) are prominent among Argentine musicians of the nineteenth century. Alberto Williams, who edited the Anthology of Argentinian Composers, writes in the brief preface to the first volume, *Los Precursores,* containing selected compositions by these three pioneers:

These composers cultivated music as amateurs. In their music there is noted the influence of Bellini and Rossini. Our musical nationalism appeared in 1890. It was inspired by popular elements, and inaugurated a genuinely Argentine art.

Alberto Williams (who incidentally is a grandson of one of the three "precursors," Amancio Alcorta) is probably the first thoroughly educated Argentine musician who has consistently cultivated native forms in his music. He studied with César Franck, and founded, in 1893, a chain of Conservatories and music schools in Argentina. Following his lead, literally hundreds of private music teachers set up schools in Argentina. One cannot pass a city block in Buenos Aires without encountering an *academia de música* or a *conservatorio*.

The twentieth century has brought about an extraordinary expansion of musical activities in Argentina, in creative composition, education, opera and concert activities, music publishing, and musicology. Popular music has in the meantime reached the dimensions of a major industry: some composers of Tangos have amassed a small fortune from their royalties. The 1941 list of members of the *Sociedad Argentina de Autores y Compositores de Música* contains 3500 names of composers of serious and popular music. There are several large publishing houses in Buenos Aires and other Argentine cities. The Ricordi firm alone has a catalogue of publications of native music, including orchestral scores and opera, which rivals great music publishing firms in Europe and the United States.

The *Teatro Colón*, established in Buenos Aires on May 25, 1908, is one of the world's most illustrious opera houses. It has presented famous singers in a large repertoire of classical, romantic, and modern operas, as well as numerous operas and ballets by Argentine composers.

The orchestra of the *Teatro Colón* is probably the best in South America, and may be favorably compared to major American orchestras. Another Buenos Aires orchestra, the *Orquesta Filarmónica de la Asociación del Profesorado Orquestal*, established in 1894, gives regular performances of symphonic works. Large symphony orchestras exist also in Rosario, Tucumán, and other Argentine towns. Among the best known native conductors are Juan José Castro, who conducts the orchestra of the *Teatro Colón;* his brother José María Castro, conductor of the *Asociación del Profesorado Orquestal;* and José Francisco Berrini, who directs the *Asociación Sinfónica* in Rosario.

The cause of modern music in Argentina is promoted by the *Grupo Renovación*, established on October 22, 1929. The declared aims of the group are "to discuss compositions of its members; to perform and to publish their best works; to arrange performances of native music abroad; and to discuss publicly the general subject of music, with the intention of contributing to the progress of musical culture." The original members of the *Grupo Renovación* were the Castro brothers, Gilardo Gilardi, Juan Carlos Paz, and Jacobo Ficher, a naturalized Russian musician. Juan José Castro and Gilardi withdrew in 1932, and Honorio Siccardi joined the *Grupo Renovación* in the same year. In 1936, Juan Carlos Paz left the group and founded his own series of concerts, *Conciertos de la Nueva Música*, devoted to the cause of ultra-modern music.

Both the *Grupo Renovación* and the *Conciertos de la Nueva Música* present their concerts in the large hall of the *Teatro del Pueblo* in Buenos Aires. The *Teatro del Pueblo* is managed by a cooperative theatrical company, which specializes in modern drama, and the concerts are arranged at the smallest cost, so that the price of admission is kept down to one-half peso. The *Grupo Renovación* gives as many as fifteen concerts during each season, which lasts through the Argentine winter from March to November.

In the field of musical science, Argentina is well ahead of its sister republics. As a part of the Argentine Museum of Natural Sciences, there is in Buenos Aires a Section of Indigenous Musicology, headed by Carlos Vega, who has painstakingly collected thousands of folk melodies of Argentina and adjacent countries and has classified his findings in a formidable catalogue of motives and rhythms. He is also the editor of a monumental series *Fraseología Musical*, which proposes to establish a basic classification of rhythmo-melodic entities.

The range of creative composition in Argentina varies from ultra-conservatism and academism to the ultra-modern tendencies. The Italian influence is profound in Argentine opera and ballet, and most of the native theatrical works produced at the *Colón* reflect this influence. The folkloric tendency, and the desire to utilize native songs as a basis for symphonic and other works is manifested among the younger generation. But there exists also a strong anti-folkloric tendency. The *Grupo Renovación* is the bulwark of this opposition to integral folklorism. The group behind the *Conciertos de la Nueva Música*, led by Juan Carlos Paz, composer of atonal music, goes even farther towards the ideal of absolute music, without nationalistic connotations, and constitutes the extreme musical left wing in Argentina.

MUSICIANS OF ARGENTINA

Julian AGUIRRE (1868–1924), the romantic composer, was taken to Madrid when four years old, in 1872; he studied music at the Madrid Conservatory. He returned to Buenos Aires in 1889, and dedicated himself to teaching and composing. While not a master of technique, Aguirre possessed a genuine feeling for native melos and folklore. His symphonic suite *De Mi Pais* was performed in Buenos Aires on September 9, 1910. Ansermet has orchestrated Aguirre's dances, *Huella* and *Gato*, and he conducted them in Buenos Aires on April 6, 1930. The score was published by Ricordi, who has also published Aguirre's piano pieces, *Aires Criollos*, *Aires Nacionales*, and several songs. The scores of Aguirre's orchestral dances (in both the Ansermet arrangement and the original) and *De Mi Pais* are in the Fleisher Collection in Philadelphia.

José ANDRÉ (1881–1944) was a composer of songs and piano pieces, occasionally flavored with native rhythms. He was active primarily as a pedagogue and wrote a number of compositions for schools.

Isabel ARETZ-THIELE, the composer and specialist in folklore, was born in Buenos Aires in 1909. Her orchestral suite *Puneñas* (songs of the *Puna*, the Andean plateau) is characterized by Carlos Vega as "the finest specimen of the Inca style, pentatonic in melody and harmony." The piano reduction of *Puneñas* and three songs in native manner, *Cueca*, *Vidala*, and *Triunfo*, are published by Ricordi.

Julian BAUTISTA (1901——) is a Spanish composer resident in Buenos Aires. He studied at the Madrid Conservatory, began to compose at an early age, and rapidly gained recognition as one of the most brilliant musicians of new Spain. After the fall of the Spanish Republic, he crossed the border, on foot, to France. He emigrated to Argentina in May, 1940, and settled in Buenos Aires. Bautista has written a ballet, *Juerga* (1929); a one-act opera, *Interior; Three Japanese Preludes* for orchestra; *Suite all'Antica* for string orchestra; two string quartets; piano music; and songs. His style of writing is terse and compact, with diatonic harmonies enhanced by added tones. His instrumentation stresses colorism in a neoimpressionist manner. The score of the *Suite all'Antica*, published in Barcelona in a limited edition in 1938, is in the Fleisher Collection in Philadelphia. Also published is his album of piano pieces, *Colores*.

Arturo BERUTTI (1862–1938) was born and died in San Juan. He studied music with his father. In 1883 he went to Germany, where he took courses at the Leipzig Conservatory, and later traveled in France and Italy. While in Europe he wrote two orchestral works on native themes: an overture, *Los Andes,* and a *Sinfonia Argentina.* His operas, *Vendetta, Evangelina, Tarass Bulba, Pampa, Yupanki, Khrisse, Horrida Nox,* and *Los Heroes,* follow the Italian operatic style. *Pampa, Horrida Nox* (from the time of the dictatorship of President Rosas in Argentina), and *Los Heroes* were inspired by events of Argentine history. *Los Heroes* was performed at the *Teatro Colón* on August 23, 1919.

Pablo BERUTTI (1866–1916), a brother of Arturo Berutti, studied at the Leipzig Conservatory, and upon returning to Argentina founded a music school in Buenos Aires. He wrote an opera on a South American subject, *Cochabamba,* which remains unperformed.

Felipe BOERO (1884——) studied with Pablo Berutti, and later (1912–1914) at the Paris Conservatory. Upon his return to Argentina, he devoted his energies to teaching and operatic compositions. Of his operas, the following were performed at the *Teatro Colón: Tucumán* (June 29, 1918); *Ariana y Dionisios* (August 5, 1920); *Raquela* (June 25, 1923); *Las Bacantes* (September 19, 1925); *El Matrero* (July 12, 1929); and *Siripo* (June 8, 1937). The vocal score of *El Matrero* has been published by Ricordi, as well as numerous songs and piano pieces. Boero's music, even that of native inspiration, is Italianate and undistinguished in style.

Carlos Lopez BUCHARDO (1881–1948) studied in Buenos Aires, and later went to Paris, where he took lessons with Albert Roussel. Upon his return to Argentina, he was appointed director of the National Conservatory of Music in Buenos Aires. In his compositions, Buchardo cultivates native themes. His *Escenas Argentinas* for orchestra, consisting of four movements characteristic of the Argentine scene—*Campera, Dia de Fiesta, El Arroyo,* and *Baile y Gauchos*—first performed in Buenos Aires on August 12, 1922, by Weingartner, is one of the most brilliant native works in its genre. His opera, *El Sueño de Alma,* was produced at the *Teatro Colón* on August 4, 1914. The score of *Escenas Argentinas,* two albums of songs, and piano pieces have been published by Ricordi.

Manuel Gomez CARRILLO (1883——) is a composer who, from the beginning of his musical career, was interested in native folklore. In his own words, he "strove to serve the cause of Argentine music, by accumulating folkloric material, and integrating it in established musical forms." Of his orchestral scores, *Rapsodia Santagueña,* reflecting the spirit of

Liszt's rhapsodies, is based on the motives of Carrillo's native province of Santiago. It was first performed in Paris on February 15, 1924. The orchestral score of *Rapsodia Santagueña* is in the Fleisher Collection in Philadelphia, and a piano reduction is published by Ricordi. Carrillo's *Fiesta Criolla*, for large orchestra, was performed by the *Asociación Sinfónica* in Rosario, on July 8, 1941. The piano score is published by Ricordi. Carrillo's daughter, María Inés Gomez Carrillo, born in Buenos Aires on April 2, 1919, is a talented pianist. She has also published some piano pieces and songs.

Enrique M. Casella (1891——) is an Argentine composer who was born in Montevideo, Uruguay. In 1907 he went to Europe, where he studied violin and composition. He returned to South America in 1914, and settled in Tucumán, where he founded a Musical Institute. Casella has written several operas on native subjects, of which *Corimayo* was produced at the *Teatro Colón* on September 20, 1926. In his opera *Chasca*, performed in Tucumán on August 28, 1939, he introduced a theatrical innovation by placing the orchestra, divided into three sections, behind the scenery. Among Casella's symphonic works are *Suite Incaica*, performed in Tucumán on August 6, 1925, and *Nahuel-Huapi*, conducted by the composer in Buenos Aires on April 14, 1929. He has also written two string quartets, a Violin Sonata, piano pieces, and songs. The piano score of *Suite Incaica, Norteñas* (five pieces in a style of northern Argentine folk music) for piano, and songs have been published by Ricordi.

José María Castro (1892——), composer and conductor, is the brother of Juan José and Washington Castro. He studied composition and violoncello. In 1931 he was engaged as conductor of the *Asociación del Profesorado Orquestal* in Buenos Aires. In 1933 he became conductor of the Municipal Band of Buenos Aires. He is a founding member of the *Grupo Renovación*. As composer, José María Castro cultivates a style close to neoclassicism. His most effective orchestral work is a Concerto Grosso, first performed by the composer in Buenos Aires on June 11, 1933, in which he clothes the classical form in modern harmonies. However, his *Overture for a Comic Opera*, performed by the composer in Buenos Aires on November 9, 1936, is entirely classical in treatment. His Concerto for Piano and Orchestra, performed in Buenos Aires on November 17, 1941, is light and transparent. His *Sonata de Primavera* (1941) for piano reflects romantic concepts. In the ballet *Georgia*, produced at the *Teatro Colón* on June 2, 1939, under the composer's direction, Castro employs a modernistic idiom, abounding in strident, dissonant harmonies. The score and parts of the Concerto Grosso, and of an early Piano Sonata, are published by the *Grupo Renovación,* and several of Castro's songs are published by Ricordi. The orchestral scores of *Georgia,* the Piano Concerto, the *Overture,* and the Concerto Grosso are in the Fleisher Collection in Philadelphia. His four piano pieces are included in the album *Latin-American Art Music for the Piano* (Schirmer, 1942).

Juan José CASTRO (1895——), best known as a composer, is the brother of José María and Washington Castro. He studied piano and violin, and also composition. In 1914 he received a government stipend to go to Europe for further study. He spent five years in Paris, where he took lessons with Vincent d'Indy. Upon his return to Buenos Aires, he founded a quintet, in which he played the first violin and his brother José María played the cello. In 1928, he organized a chamber orchestra, *Renascimiento,* and in 1930 was engaged as a conductor at the *Teatro Colón.* Since then, he has conducted orchestras in the principal Latin American republics. In 1942 he made a tour of the United States. In October, 1943, Castro was temporarily removed from his post as conductor of the *Teatro Colón* by the reactionary clique in the government, as a result of his signing a manifesto urging the realignment of Argentina with the cause of democracy.

As composer, Juan José Castro is both versatile and prolific. He has written music in all genres, except opera. The style of his early compositions is marked by a certain rhapsodism, which he later abandoned in favor of a more terse and compact manner of writing. Parallel with this transition, Castro adopted a pronounced polyphonic idiom, as contrasted with the surcharged harmonic style of his first period. His earliest work was a Violin Sonata (1914); then followed a Violoncello Sonata (1916); a Piano Sonata (1917); and a Trio for violin, clarinet, and piano (1919). His first work for orchestra was a symphonic poem entitled *Dans le Jardin des Morts,* an effective piece of program music, in the French style. It was performed for the first time by the *Asociación del Profesorado Orquestal* in Buenos Aires on October 5, 1924. Another symphonic poem, *A Una Madre,* performed in Buenos Aires by the Colón Orchestra, on October 27, 1925, is marked by a considerable inspissation of the harmonic idiom, with some polytonal effects. The third symphonic poem, *La Chellah,* performed by the *Asociación del Profesorado Orquestal* in Buenos Aires on September 10, 1927, shows the influence of Russian colorism. The second cycle of Castro's creative evolution com-

prises compositions in classically defined forms: *Suite Breve*, first per-·
formed by Castro's chamber orchestra on May 11, 1929; *Suite Infantil*
(Children's Suite), performed by Castro and the *Asociación del Profesorado Orquestal* in Buenos Aires on August 24, 1929; *Three Symphonic Pieces*, performed on July 26, 1930, by the *Asociación del Profesorado Orquestal*, Ansermet conducting, and also presented at the
London Festival of Contemporary Music in 1931; and *Sinfonía*, performed by the Colón Orchestra, under the direction of Ansermet, on
July 22, 1931. The harmonic and melodic texture in these works is marked
by considerable chromaticism, often approaching atonality, particularly
in the *Sinfonía*. In his orchestral works written after 1931, Castro shows
an interest in cultivating native themes. To the category of native-inspired
works belong two symphonies: *Sinfonía Argentina* (conducted by Castro
with the Colón Orchestra on November 29, 1936), and *Sinfonía de los
Campos* (performed by the Colón Orchestra, Kleiber conducting, on October 29, 1939). The latter is in six atmospheric movements, with solo passages for the oboe, English horn, French horn, and trumpet. The *Sinfonía Bíblica*, a lengthy work, first conducted by the composer at the
Teatro Colón on November 15, 1932, is an excursion into the domain
of religious music. Among Castro's theatrical works the most significant
is the ballet *Mekhano*, composed in 1934, and produced under the direction of the composer at the *Teatro Colón* on July 17, 1937. This, as the
title indicates, is the glorification of the mechanical man, and the music
follows the model established in similar works by European composers.
There is a relentless rhythmic drive, virtually in unaltered duple meter,
with an overabundance of special instrumental effects. The choreography
of the ballet features a dance of the hammer, the injection of the vital fluid
into the veins of the mechanical men (to the accompaniment of whole-tone
progressions), and a dance of seduction.

In nontheatrical music, Castro continues to cultivate a neoclassical,
modernistically economical style, of which his piano Toccata (1940) and
Concerto for Piano and Orchestra (1941) are the most successful examples. Castro has written little for the voice. Among his recent vocal
compositions are six songs to the text of García Lorca, and *Tres Cantos
Negros*. The orchestral score of *Sinfonía Argentina* is published by Ricordi; nine orchestral works by Castro are in the Fleisher Collection in
Philadelphia. Castro's piano piece, *Danza Guerrera*, is included in the
supplement to Volume I of the *Boletín Latino-Americano de Música*,
and two short pieces for piano are published by C. Fischer.

Sergio de Castro (1922———) is one of the youngest of Argentina's composers. At the age of ten, he was taken to Montevideo, where he studied with Guido Santórsola. He returned to Buenos Aires in 1942. He has written some piano music and songs, in an unassumingly romantic vein. Two of his songs are published by the *Editorial Cooperativa* in Montevideo.

Washington Castro (1909———) is the youngest of the Castro brothers. He studied violoncello with his brother José María, and composition with Siccardi. Later he went to Paris, where he continued his musical education. Upon his return to Argentina, he taught violoncello at the Municipal Conservatory of Buenos Aires. He has written a Piano Sonata, a piano Suite, and cello pieces. The score of his *Festive Overture* for chamber orchestra is in the Fleisher Collection in Philadelphia.

Pedro Valenti Costa (1905———) studied with Gilardi, and has written mostly choral music, some of which reflects native melos and rhythms.

Ernesto Drangosch, the composer, was born in Buenos Aires in 1882 and died there in 1925. He studied piano and composition with Alberto Williams and Julian Aguirre in Buenos Aires, and later with Bruch and Humperdinck in Berlin. He returned to Buenos Aires in 1905, and dedicated himself to composition and to teaching. He composed a suite for string orchestra, *Sueños de un Baile* (1906), a Concerto for Piano and Orchestra (1912), and an orchestral overture of native inspiration, *Obertura Criolla*, which latter was performed in Buenos Aires by Felix Weingartner on September 24, 1920. The score and parts of the *Obertura Criolla* were published in 1939 by the National Culture Committee in Buenos Aires. Also published are Drangosch's Violin Sonata, several groups of songs, and a number of piano compositions, among them a *Fantasia Quasi Sonata*, seven characteristic pieces, six concert Etudes, and dances in the native manner. Most of these editions are, however, out of print. The scores of Drangosch's Piano Concerto, symphonic suite, and the *Obertura Criolla* are in the Fleisher Collection in Philadelphia.

Emilio Dublanc (1911———) studied piano and composition at the National Conservatory in Buenos Aires. After graduation he settled in Mendoza, where he teaches piano. He has written a piano Suite, a Violin Sonata, songs, and a short cantata on a Christmas subject.

Raúl Espoile (1888———) studied voice, and on November 21, 1922, gave a recital of his own songs in Buenos Aires. In March, 1925, he was appointed inspector of music in the public schools of Argentina. Espoile has written two operas in an Italian manner, but with native subjects. *Frenos,* a symbolic opera in four acts portraying an Argentine Faust, in which one scene is set in a biological laboratory, was produced at the *Teatro Colón* on June 19, 1928. His second opera, *La Ciudad Roja,* was produced on July 17, 1936. He also wrote a symphonic suite, *En la Paz de los Campos,* which was presented by the *Asociación del Profesorado Orquestal* in Buenos Aires on August 27, 1927, and a symphonic poem, *Kuntur* (1941). Ricordi has published a considerable number of Espoile's songs, many vocal compositions for school use, and two arias from *La Ciudad Roja.* The score of the orchestral suite from *Frenos* is in the Fleisher Collection.

Arnaldo D'ESPOSITO (1897–1945) studied music with Gaito, Drangosch, and Palma. In 1928 he was appointed assistant conductor of the *Teatro Colón* in Buenos Aires. He composed two ballets, in an Italianate style, seasoned with some modernistic harmonies, which have been performed at the *Teatro Colón: Rapsodia del Tango* (February 2, 1934) and *Cuento de Abril* (June 21, 1940). His one-act opera, *Lin-Calel,* was produced at the *Teatro Colón* on August 12, 1941. His Concerto for Piano and Orchestra was performed in Buenos Aires on May 13, 1943.

Juan A. García ESTRADA (1895——) studied jurisprudence in Buenos Aires, and composition in Paris, where he took lessons with Jacques Ibert. Upon his return to Argentina, he was appointed a justice of the peace, and virtually abandoned his musical career. Estrada has written a Suite of symphonic dances, three movements of which were performed in Paris on February 28, 1929. His *Elegy* and *Prelude* for orchestra were performed by the *Asociación del Profesorado Musical* in Buenos Aires on July 2, 1927. The scores of three of his symphonic numbers are in the Fleisher Collection in Philadelphia. Estrada has also written piano pieces and songs, in a conventional harmonic style.

Jacobo FICHER (1896——), a prolific composer, is a naturalized Argentine; he was born in Odessa, Russia. He studied violin and composition at the Leningrad Conservatory, and graduated in 1917. In 1923 he emigrated to Argentina, and settled in Buenos Aires. He played violin in theater orchestras in Argentina, and at the same time began to compose. In 1928 he submitted the score of his symphonic work *Heroic Poem* to a contest of the Leningrad Philharmonic Orchestra, and it received the first prize. In 1937 he received a Coolidge prize of $500 for his second

Covers of Latin American compositions

Marimba player of Guatemala (a wooden toy)

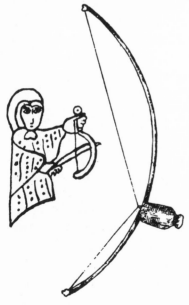

Primitive musical bows of Patagonia
(left) and of Central America (right)

Nasal flute

String Quartet. His Third Symphony was awarded a prize of the National Culture Committee in Buenos Aires in 1941. Ficher is a founding member of the *Grupo Renovación*, and he is also active as an orchestral conductor. His early music is inspired by Hebrew melos, while his later compositions reflect a Russian influence. Apart from three Argentine dances for piano composed in 1943, Ficher has made no attempts to write in a native South American vein.

Ficher has written three symphonies. The first, scored for chamber orchestra, was first performed by the *Asociación del Profesorado Orquestal*, in Buenos Aires, on December 8, 1932, under the composer's direction. The Second Symphony was written in 1933, under the impact of the Nazi campaign against the Jews. It is emotional and rhapsodic in essence, with Hebraic thematic undertones. It was conducted by the composer in Buenos Aires on October 23, 1939. The Third Symphony, in four classical movements, comes close to the symphonic tradition of Mahler and the Russians. The following symphonic compositions by Ficher have been performed in Buenos Aires: *Two Poems from Tagore* (December 23, 1928); *Sulamith* (July 20, 1929); *Ouverture Pathétique* (May 17, 1930); and *Three Symphonic Pieces after the Talmud* (September 16, 1934). Ficher has also written a Violin Concerto (1942), performed under the composer's direction in Buenos Aires on July 17, 1944. He is the author of a ballet, *Los Invitados* (1933). Ficher has written a great deal of chamber music, which includes two string quartets, a Violin Sonata, a Sonatina for Flute and Piano, and a Sonatina for Clarinet and Piano; Sonata for Viola, Flute, and Piano; Sonata for Oboe and Piano (performed on August 6, 1942, at the Festival of the International Society for Contemporary Music, held in California); and Sonatina for Trumpet, Saxophone, and Piano (published by *New Music*). Ficher's *Three Preludes* for piano are published by the *Grupo de Renovación*, and a song, *Palabras a Mama*, is printed by Ricordi. This song is included in the Columbia album of *South American Chamber Music*. Ficher's *Valse* and *Humoresque* for piano are published by Carl Fischer, and *Six Animal Fables* by Axelrod. The Fleisher Collection in Philadelphia has the scores of Ficher's three symphonies, the Violin Concerto, an early symphonic suite, the symphonic poem *Sulamith*, *Two Poems from Tagore* for chamber orchestra, *Three Symphonic Pieces after the Talmud*, and *Los Invitados*.

Constantino GAITO (1878–1945) showed musical talent at an early age, and was sent to Naples to study. He traveled in Europe, and in 1901 returned to Buenos Aires, where he founded a Conservatory of Music bearing his name. Since 1903 he has taught music in the public schools of Argentina. As a composer, Gaito's predilection is for the opera and ballet. He writes in a style patterned after the Italian school of modern theater music, and employing a large orchestra, with emphasis on coloristic effects. Most of Gaito's music is based on Argentine folklore, and his stylizations of Argentine dance rhythms are effectively contrived. The following ballets and operas by Gaito were produced at the *Teatro Colón: Petronio* (September 2, 1919), *Flor de Nieve* (August 3, 1922), *Ollantay* (July 23, 1926), *La Flor de Irupé* (July 17, 1929), *Lazaro* (November 1, 1929), and *Sangre de las Guitarras* (August 17, 1932). His symphonic poem, *El Ombú,* was performed at the *Teatro Colón* on October 29, 1925, and *Danzas Fantasticas* for orchestra was performed on March 30, 1930. Gaito is also the author of an oratorio, *San Francisco Solano,* produced at the *Teatro Colón* on November 13, 1940. In this oratorio, based on the subject of Christian proselytism in Argentina, Gaito combines Gregorian modal melodies with native folklore. The harmonic idiom is complex, including polytonal usages. Ricordi has published a number of Gaito's works, among them the Second String Quartet, six *Danzas Americanas* for piano, a piano version of *Danzas Fantasticas,* and excerpts from the operas *Ollantay* and *Sangre de las Guitarras.* The orchestral score of *El Ombú* is in the Fleisher Collection in Philadelphia.

Luis GIANNEO (1897———) studied music with Gaito and Drangosch. In 1923 he settled in Tucumán, where he teaches and conducts concerts of the *Asociación Sinfónica.* From 1932 to 1944 he was a member of the *Grupo Renovación.* As a composer, Gianneo cultivates native folklore; his harmonic treatment is basically tonal, with little elaboration. He has written a symphonic poem *Turay-Turay* (first performed by the *Asociación del Profesorado Orquestal* in Buenos Aires on September 21, 1929), *El Tarco en Flor* (conducted by the composer with the *Asociación del Profesorado Orquestal* on September 6, 1931), and a violin concerto named *Concierto Aymará,* based on themes of the Aymará Indians. In 1942 this concerto was awarded second prize at the contest for the best violin concerto by a Latin American composer, organized under the auspices of the Fleisher Collection in Philadelphia. The concerto was performed in Buenos Aires on April 13, 1944. Gianneo's *Sinfonietta,* written in homage to Haydn, was performed in Buenos Aires on September 20, 1943. Gianneo has written a great many songs, piano pieces, and some chamber music. In addition, he has written music for children, of which

Música para Niños, an album of ten effectively stylized airs and dances in native manner, for piano, has been published. Also published are his *Pampeana y Coplas* for piano, conceived in the Gaucho style of Argentine melodies, and some teaching manuals. The scores of Gianneo's *Obertura para una Comedia Infantil* and *Concierto Aymará* are included in the Fleisher Collection.

José GIL, Spanish-born (1886), went to Argentina as a child. He studied with Alberto Williams, and after graduation dedicated himself to composition and teaching. He is professor of harmony and counterpoint at the National Conservatory in Buenos Aires. Gil has written some chamber music, couched in a traditionally academic style. In the native manner, he has composed *Danzas Argentinas* for piano and string quartet.

Gilardo GILARDI (1889——) studied in Buenos Aires with Pablo Berutti, and began to compose at an early age. His predilection lies in vocal and theater music. His opera *Ilse,* produced at the *Teatro Colón* on July 13, 1923, was not retained in the repertoire. More successful was his second opera, *La Leyenda de Urutaú,* on the native legend from the early years of the conquest, in which he follows the Wagnerian principle of leitmotivs. It was produced at the *Teatro Colón* on October 25, 1934, with considerable acclaim. For the orchestra, Gilardi has written a suite of Argentine airs in four movements, of which the *Preludio* and *Chacarera* were performed by the *Asociación del Profesorado Orquestal* in Buenos Aires on July 12, 1930, and *Firmeza* and *Noviando* by the same organization on May 10, 1931. His orchestral score, *Evocación Quichua,* originally written for a quartet of lutes, was performed by the radio orchestra in Buenos Aires on July 9, 1941. Gilardi was a founding member of the *Grupo Renovación,* in 1929, but withdrew from that organization in 1932. His harmonic idiom has little that is original or modern, and the merit of his music lies in the capable stylization of native melodies and rhythms. His violin sonata, titled *Sonata Popular Argentina,* and first performed in Buenos Aires on April 1, 1939, exemplifies his devotion to folklore. Only a few songs and piano pieces by Gilardi are published. The orchestral scores of *Evocación Quichua* and *Noviando* are in the Fleisher Collection in Philadelphia.

Alberto GINASTERA (1916——), an outstanding composer of the young generation in Argentina, studied music with Athos Palma at the National Conservatory in Buenos Aires, graduating with honors in 1938. Ginastera began to compose at an early age, adopting a style economical in means but highly concentrated in effect. In his music, Ginastera cultivates folklore, not as coloristic material, but as a thematic background for composition in established forms. At the age of twenty, he wrote a ballet, *Panambí*, based on an Indian legend. A suite from this ballet was performed on November 27, 1937, by the Colón Orchestra, under the direction of Juan José Castro, and the ballet in its entirety was produced at the *Teatro Colón* on July 12, 1940. Ginastera's *Concierto Argentino* for piano and orchestra was performed on July 18, 1941, by the SODRE Orchestra in Montevideo. His *Sinfonía Porteña* (*Porteña* is the adjective of the port of Buenos Aires) was performed by the Colón Orchestra, on May 12, 1942. Ginastera has also written a ballet, *Impresiones de la Puna* for flute and string quartet, in three brief movements—*Quena, Canción,* and *Danza*—published by the *Editorial Cooperativa Interamericana* in 1942; *Cantos del Tucumán* for soprano, flute, violin, harp, and two drums; a Psalm for chorus and orchestra; a Sonatina for Harp; piano pieces and songs. His three *Piezas Infantiles* are included in the album *Latin-American Art Music for the Piano,* published by Schirmer in 1942. *Danzas Argentinas* for piano is published by Durand in Paris; *Tres Piezas* for piano, representing stylizations of native airs, and a song, *Canción al Arbol del Olvido,* in tango rhythm, are published by Ricordi. In 1943, Ginastera received a Guggenheim fellowship in the United States. The orchestral scores of *Panambí* and the *Concierto Argentino* are in the Fleisher Collection in Philadelphia.

Guillermo GRAETZER (1914———) is Austrian born; he studied in Berlin with Hindemith. In 1939 he went to Argentina, and settled in Buenos Aires. Graetzer has written a symphony, a Rhapsody for Violin and Orchestra, and a piece entitled *Music for an Ensemble of Amateurs.* His lugubrious *Danza de la Muerte y la Niña* was performed in Buenos Aires on October 18, 1943. His three toccatas for piano have been published by the *Editorial Cooperativa Interamericana* in Montevideo.

Pascual GRISOLIA (1904———) studied composition with Athos Palma. Grisolia has written a symphonic poem, *La Tarde* (1938), a Piano Sonata, and songs.

Carlos GUASTAVINO, a composer of the young Argentine school, was born in Santa Fé in 1914. He studied chemical engineering and piano in his home town, and later went to Buenos Aires where he took lessons in composition. Guastavino cultivates mainly vocal music, and has written some sixty songs of the *Lied* type, with definite folkloric flavor. He has also composed a *Sinfonía Argentina* on native themes, a ballet on a subject from colonial times in Argentina, and piano music. Twenty of his songs, a Sonatina, and Argentine airs for piano are published by Ricordi.

Hector IGLESIAS VILLOUD (1913——) studied composition in Buenos Aires, with Constantino Gaito. In 1939, Iglesias Villoud received a fellowship from the National Culture Committee of Argentina for travel in South American countries. As a composer, Iglesias Villoud cultivates the folkloric element exclusively, in symphonic works as well as in minor compositions. His ballet *Amancay*, on an Indian legend, was produced at the *Teatro Colón* on November 20, 1937, and another ballet, *El Malón*, on June 16, 1943. His *Danzas Argentinas* for orchestra were performed by the *Asociación Sinfónica* in Rosario, on November 24, 1940. He has also written a one-act opera, *La Noche Colonial;* a symphonic poem, *Leyenda del Lago Andino* (based on the ancient legends of Lake Titicaca in the Andes); and *Escenas Indoamericanas*. The score of his ballet *Amancay* is in the Fleisher Collection in Philadelphia.

Nicolas LAMURAGLIA (1896——) studied composition with Athos Palma. He has written a symphonic poem, *El Jardinero* (after Tagore), which was performed in Buenos Aires on July 4, 1938; a Suite for piano and string orchestra, first performed in Buenos Aires on September 16, 1940; piano pieces and songs. The score of the Suite is in the Fleisher Collection in Philadelphia. Lamuraglia writes in a romantic vein, without striving for modernism, and with no recourse to native themes.

Arturo LUZZATTI (1875——), Italian-born and naturalized in Argentina, is active in Buenos Aires as a teacher and composer. As composer, Luzzatti follows the Italian romantic school. He has written, for orchestra, *Le Jardin Voluptueux* (performed in Buenos Aires on September 4, 1927), *Eros*, and *Orientale*. Luzzatti's oratorio, *Solomon*, received first prize of the National Cultural Committee in October, 1941. It was performed in Buenos Aires on May 30, 1942. He has also written two operas, *Aphrodita* and *Atala*, and a ballet, *Judith;* he conducted the ballet on August 18, 1938, at the *Teatro Colón* in Buenos Aires. The manuscript of *Le Jardin Voluptueux* is in the Fleisher Collection in Philadelphia.

Juan Bautista MASSA (1885—1938) began composing at an early age, and wrote prolifically, often using native themes in his music. The style of his writing is determined by the influence of Italian opera. He was particularly successful in choral composition. For many years he was conductor of the Argentine Choral Society in Rosario. Among his works are the operas *Zoraide* (first performed at the *Teatro Colón* on May 15, 1909), *L'Evaso* (produced in Rosario on June 23, 1922), *La Magdalena* (produced at the *Teatro Colón* on November 9, 1929); a ballet, *El Cometa* (*Teatro Colón*, November 8, 1932); three operettas, *Esmeralda* (1903), *Triunfo del Corazón* (1910), *La Eterna Historia* (1911); also chamber music, piano pieces, and songs. His symphonic poem *La Muerte del Inca* (Death of the Inca), based on Indian themes, was performed under the composer's direction at the *Teatro Colón* on October 15, 1932. He also wrote two Argentine Suites for orchestra, of which the first has been published by Ricordi. The score of *La Muerte del Inca* is in the Fleisher Collection in Philadelphia. A detailed monograph on Massa by Francisco Curt Lange is published in Volume IV of the *Boletín Latino-Americano de Música*.

Angel MENCHACA was a musical theorist; he was born in Asunción, Paraguay, in 1855 and died in Buenos Aires in 1924. He developed a system of notation, and a special piano keyboard which he called Continuous Keyboard, on which the black keys slope down. His theories attracted some attention in America and in Europe. He summarized his views in a brochure, *Sistema Teórico-Gráfico de la Música*, published in 1914, and now out of print.

Roberto García MORILLO (1911——) studied piano and composition with Aguirre, Juan José Castro, Gaito, and others. From 1927 to 1929 he lived in Paris. Upon his return to Buenos Aires, Morillo dedicated himself to composition and music criticism. His early works disclose a strong Scriabin influence, while his later style comes closer to Stravinsky. Morillo's music is determined by purely acoustical constructions, and is entirely devoid of folkloristic associations. He has written an overture for piano and small orchestra, *Bersaerks*, first performed by the composer with the Ensemble of the *Conservatorio Nacional*, on December 29, 1932; a *Poem* for symphony orchestra, performed in Buenos Aires on October 30, 1936; a Piano Concerto, first performed at the *Teatro Colón*, on November 7, 1940; a musical suite inspired by Goya's pictures, *Las Pinturas Negras de Goya*, scored for piano, violin, cello, flute, clarinet, and bassoon, and first performed at the University of Montevideo, Uruguay, on May 27, 1940; a Quartet for piano, violin, cello, and clarinet, performed in Buenos Aires on June 9, 1937; *The Fall of the House of Usher*, after Poe; and a ballet, *Harrild*. Morillo's piano suite, *Conjuros*, is published by the *Editorial Interamericana* in Montevideo; his early *Tres Piezas* for piano are published by Ricordi; and a piano piece, *Canción Triste y Danza Alegre*, is included in the album *Latin-American Art Music for the Piano* (Schirmer, 1942). The orchestral scores of Morillo's Piano Concerto and *Poem* will be found in the Fleisher Collection in Philadelphia.

Emilio NAPOLITANO (1907——) studied the violin and in 1922 joined the orchestra of the *Teatro Colón*. He also took lessons in composition with Gaito and Ugarte. His first work, a Sonata for Violin and Piano, was performed in Buenos Aires on September 25, 1936. He has written several songs, in the native manner, of which a *Lullaby*, and an air, *Picaflor*, are published by Ricordi.

José de NITO (1887–1945) went to Italy in 1901, and studied at the Conservatory of Naples. Returning to Argentina in 1909, he founded, in Rosario, the Beethoven Conservatory of Music. Between 1921 and 1928 he again traveled in Europe. As a composer, Nito has published several children's pieces and some songs in the native manner.

Jaime PAHISSA, a Spanish composer living in Argentina, was born in Barcelona in 1880. Largely an autodidact, he pursued from the very first a quest for the new in music. He is also one of the first composers who cultivated a nationalist Catalan style, selecting texts in the Catalan language for his songs and taking part in the revival of the musical folklore of Catalonia. On November 15, 1906, Pahissa presented in Barcelona a concert of his symphonic and chamber music. His orchestral work, *El Cami* (The Path), was performed in Barcelona on March 21, 1909; his symphonic poem, *Nit de Somnis* (Night of Dreams), on April 30, 1920; and *Sinfonietta* on November 3, 1921. On October 12, 1925, his most original score, *Monodia*, was performed in Barcelona. It is written exclusively in unisons and octaves, sustaining interest only by changes of register, orchestral color, and rhythm. Pahissa follows a diametrically opposite line of invention in his *Suite Intertonal*, which was performed in Barcelona on October 24, 1926. In this work he contrasts the integral dissonant counterpoint of the first, second, and fourth movements with the classical harmony of the third movement. Pahissa has also written several operas: *Gala Placida* (produced in Barcelona on January 15, 1913), *La Morisca* (produced on February 15, 1919), *Marianela* (produced on March 31, 1923), and *La Princesa Margarita* (produced on February 8, 1928). The scores of *El Cami, Suite Intertonal, Monodia*, and *Sinfonietta* are published, and copies are in the Fleisher Collection in Philadelphia. Also published, but out of print, are Pahissa's Trio, Violin Sonata, songs, and piano pieces (in the latter Pahissa uses interesting chromatic tone-clusters). A very comprehensive nine-page account of Pahissa's career is found in the second volume of the *Diccionario de la Música,* published in Barcelona in 1930. In 1935, Pahissa settled in Buenos Aires, where he is teaching composition and piano.

Athos PALMA (1891——) went to Europe in 1904 and studied music in Italy and France. Returning to Argentina in 1909, he devoted himself to composition and teaching. He has written a one-act opera, *Nazdah,* on a subject of ancient India, which was produced at the *Teatro Colón* on June 19, 1924; a symphonic poem, *Los Hijos del Sol,* based on an Inca legend and employing the pentatonic scale, performed at the *Teatro Colón* on November 10, 1928; and an impressionistic symphonic poem, *Jardines,* performed on May 4, 1930, by the *Asociación del Profesorado Orquestal* in Buenos Aires. He has also written a ballet, *Accia,* a Piano Sonata, and songs. Palma's style of composition derives its effectiveness from rich harmonies, somewhat in the modern Italian manner. There is an influence of Debussy in his songs *La Escuela de las Flores,* which are published by Ricordi. Also published are Palma's harmonizations of indigenous songs, *Canciones Salteñas.* The orchestral score of *Los Hijos del Sol* is in the Fleisher Collection.

Hector PANIZZA (1875——) was born in Buenos Aires and later studied piano and composition at the Conservatory of Milan, Italy. He has devoted himself principally to operatic conducting, and toured widely in Europe and America. Panizza's own music, entirely academic in texture, is distinguished by a certain mastery of composition. He has written a cantata, *Il Fidanzato del Mare,* performed in Buenos Aires on August 15, 1897; an opera, *Medio Evo Latino,* produced in Buenos Aires, with Toscanini conducting, on July 21, 1901; and an opera, *Aurora,* directed by the composer in Buenos Aires, on September 6, 1908. After a long period of time, during which Panizza composed little, he wrote a new opera, *Bizancio,* which was produced at the *Teatro Colón* on July 25, 1939, under the composer's direction. Panizza's *Reverie* for violin and piano, a song, *Chanson Galante,* and an aria from *Medio Evo Latino* are published by Ricordi.

Juan Carlos PAZ (1897——) studied composition with Gaito. From his earliest ventures in composition, Paz followed modernistic trends. He was one of the founders of the *Grupo Renovación,* a modern music society of Buenos Aires, established in 1929. In 1936, Paz left the *Grupo Renovación* and founded an association named *Conciertos de la Nueva Música*, which presents concerts of new music. As a composer, Paz has undergone several changes of style. The first period (1920–1927), characterized by neoclassical polyphony, comprises nine ballads and two sonatas for piano, and *Canto de Navidad* for orchestra. The second period (1927–1934), marked by atonal melodic idiom and polytonal harmony, includes *Movimiento Sinfónico* for orchestra, incidental music to Ibsen's play *Julian the Emperor, Polytonal Variations, Three Jazz Movements, Three Inventions* for piano, Sonatina for Clarinet and Piano, Sonatina for Flute and Clarinet (performed on June 15, 1933, at the International Festival of Contemporary Music in Amsterdam), Sonatina for Oboe and Bassoon, and Overture for twelve solo instruments. The third period (1934–1944) is signalized by the adoption of the twelve-tone system of composition. To it belong *Passacaglia* for orchestra (performed on June 25, 1937, at the Paris Festival of Contemporary Music); four *Composiciones en los 12 Tonos* for various instruments; ten piano pieces on a twelve-tone theme; Quartet for violin, clarinet, saxophone, and bass clarinet; and the Third Piano Sonata. In the last few years, Paz has introduced some modifications into the twelve-tone technique.

Paz is strongly opposed to folkloric ideas in music, and in a series of articles in the press has sharply criticized the nationalistic trends among Argentine musicians. The only piece of descriptive music he ever wrote is *Pampeana*, for piano, published by C. Fischer. His *Jazz Movements* and *Inventions* for piano are published by the *Grupo Renovación*. The third of the *Composiciones en los 12 Tonos*, for clarinet and piano, is published by *New Music*. Ten *Piano Pieces on a Twelve-Tone Theme* are published in the music supplement to Volume IV of the *Boletín Latino-Americano de Música*. The Second Ballad for piano is included in the album *Latin-American Art Music for the Piano* (Schirmer, 1942). The scores of *Passacaglia*, Overture for twelve solo instruments, *Movimiento Sinfónico*, and a suite from *Julian the Emperor* are in the Fleisher Collection in Philadelphia. A comprehensive essay on the music of Paz, by Francisco Curt Lange, is published in Volume IV of the *Boletín Latino-Americano de Música*. An analysis of Paz's compositions, *La Obra Musical de Juan Carlos Paz*, by Hector J. Gallac, is included in Volume I of the *Boletín Latino-Americano de Música*.

Julio PERCEVAL, the Belgian-Argentine musician, was born in Brussels in 1903. He studied piano and organ at the Brussels Conservatory. Upon graduation, he went to Argentina and was naturalized there in 1930. Perceval has written a String Quartet, a Piano Sonata, a Violin Sonata, a Violoncello Sonata, piano pieces, and several compositions for the organ. Perceval's harmonic idiom is marked by considerable dissonance. His *Danza* on an Argentine theme is included in the music supplement to Volume IV of the *Boletín Latino-Americano de Música*.

Celestino PIAGGIO (1886–1931) studied piano and composition with Alberto Williams and Julian Aguirre. In 1908 he was given a government fellowship for further study in Europe. He took lessons with Vincent d'Indy in Paris, and in 1914 went to Bucharest, Rumania, where he conducted orchestral concerts and gave piano recitals. He remained in Rumania until 1921, and then returned to Buenos Aires, where he taught at the National Conservatory of Music. Piaggio wrote little music, all in a classical manner without reference to Argentine folklore. His Overture in C minor, composed in 1914, and entirely academic in texture, was performed in Buenos Aires by the *Sociedad Argentina de Conciertos Sinfónicos* on September 9, 1919. The full score of this Overture was published in 1939 by the *Comisión Nacional de Cultura*.

Alfredo PINTO (1891——), the Italian-Argentine composer, studied piano and composition at the Conservatory of Naples. He went to Argentina in 1915, and gave numerous piano recitals. He began to compose seriously in 1929, and wrote a number of atmospheric pieces for orchestra, in an unassuming romantic vein. Of these, the following were performed by the *Asociación del Profesorado Orquestal* in Buenos Aires: *Nostalgias* (August 3, 1929), *Eros* (May 31, 1930); *Contrastes* (August 28, 1932), *Comentario a un Canto dannunziano* (after d'Annunzio, performed on October 7, 1934), and *Popular Italian Suite* (October 5, 1936). Pinto has also written an opera on Argentine themes, *El Gualicho*, produced at the *Teatro Colón* on November 17, 1940. For a brief interval in 1935, Pinto was a member of the *Grupo Renovación*. The score of his short symphonic piece, *Eros*, is in the Fleisher Collection in Philadelphia.

Pascual QUARATINO (1904——) went to Italy in 1920, where he entered the Conservatory of Naples. Upon his return to Buenos Aires in 1928, Quaratino was engaged as assistant conductor at the *Teatro Colón*, and at the same time continued to compose. He has written a Suite for harp and string orchestra (performed in Buenos Aires on March 26, 1933); an orchestral dance, *El Rastreador* (performed in Buenos Aires on October 14, 1940); and a number of piano pieces and songs, all of them in the native vein. Quaratino's *Lamento Indio, Tres Canciones Argentinas, Pampeana, Siesta, El Flechazo* for voice and piano, *Rapsodia Argentina,* and *Tres Piezas Argentinas* for piano are published by Ricordi.

Antonio de RACO (1915——) is one of the younger Argentine composers. He studied piano and composition at the National Conservatory in Buenos Aires. He writes in a neoclassical manner, mostly chamber music and songs.

Pascual de ROGATIS, the Italian-born Argentine composer, was born in 1881, and went to Buenos Aires as a child. He studied violin and composition at the National Conservatory of Buenos Aires. Three operas by Rogatis have been performed at the *Teatro Colón: Anfione e Zeto* (July 18, 1915), *Huemac* (July 22, 1916), and *La Novia del Hereje* (The Heretic's Bride, performed on June 13, 1935). The first of these operas is on a classical subject, the second is based on a Mexican legend, and the third is derived from the colonial era. The harmonic idiom employed by Rogatis is that of the modern Italian opera, with some Wagnerian overtones. In 1910, Rogatis wrote a symphonic poem, *Zupay,* which is one of the earliest examples of an orchestral work employing the native rhythms of Argentina. His later symphonic work, *Atipac,* performed in Buenos Aires on April 7, 1929, continues in the native tradition. A collection of five songs by Rogatis, *Canciones Argentinas,* and some piano pieces have been published. The Argentine writer Ricardo Rojas summarized Rogatis' place in native music in these words: "His harmony is perhaps European, and so is his orchestra; but the origin, the idea, and the function of his melodic invention belong to Argentina."

Luis R. SAMMARTINO (1890——) studied piano and composition, and for many years acted as accompanist and operatic coach in Buenos Aires. He has composed symphonic music, piano pieces, and songs. His orchestral Suite in four programmatic movements was performed on October 7, 1923, by the *Asociación del Profesorado Orquestal* in Buenos Aires. Most of his works are couched in the traditional European idiom. His *Zamba* for piano is published by Ricordi.

Arturo C. SCHIANCA (1889——), the musicologist and composer, is the author of the informative book, *Historia de la Música Argentina,* and of numerous dances and songs in the native style.

Alfredo SCHIUMA (1885——) has written several operas, in a competent Italianate manner, of which the following were produced at the

Teatro Colón: Amy Robsar (April 24, 1920), *La Sirocchia* (April 23, 1922), *Tabaré* (August 6, 1925), and *La Infanta* (August 12, 1941). The opera *Tabaré* deals with Indian life in the early centuries after the conquest. The following of Schiuma's symphonic works were performed by the *Asociación del Profesorado Orquestal: Symphony in F* (June 15, 1928), *Pitunga* (March 31, 1929), and *Los Incas* (April 26, 1931). The score of *Pitunga* is available in the Fleisher Collection.

Honorio SICCARDI (1897——) studied music in Buenos Aires with Pablo Berutti, and later in Italy with Malipiero. Since 1932, he has been a member of the *Grupo Renovación*. Siccardi writes in a highly concentrated contrapuntal style, often tensely dissonant in texture, and his instrumental treatment stresses contrasting colors. He has written a cantata, *Prometheus; Títeres* (Puppets) for various heterophonous instrumental combinations; two symphonic poems after the Argentine epic, *Martín Fierro;* a Violin Concerto; a Suite for clarinet and piano; a String Quartet, and songs. Two of Siccardi's piano pieces are included in the music supplement to Volume IV of the *Boletín Latino-Americano de Música*. The score of *Títeres* and the Violin Concerto are in the Fleisher Collection in Philadelphia.

Lorenzo SPENA (1874——), Italian-Argentine musician, settled in Buenos Aires in 1901, and in 1907 founded the Clementi Conservatory of Music. He has written six operas, and also symphonic and chamber music, in a competent but conventional style.

Carlos SUFFERN (1905——) studied music in Buenos Aires with Athos Palma and Constantino Gaito. He began to compose at an early age, and adopted in his compositions an economic and compact manner of writing, while his harmonies are impressionistic. His predilection lies in miniature forms. In his Piano Sonata, in one movement, he introduces elements of all four movements of the classical sonata. He has written a *Dialogue* for violin and piano, a piano Quintet, a piano Quartet, a suite of instrumental and vocal pieces, *Juegos Rústicos*. His piano piece *Nostalgia* is published in the music supplement to Volume IV of the *Boletín Latino-Americano de Música,* and his *Danza* is included in the album *Latin-American Art Music for the Piano* (Schirmer, 1942).

Celia TORRA (1889——) was born in Concepción, Uruguay, and went to Buenos Aires at an early age. There she studied with Alberto Williams. In 1909 she went to Europe, where she studied the violin. Returning to

Buenos Aires in 1921, she dedicated herself to teaching and choral conducting. Celia Torra has written several orchestral works on native themes, a Piano Sonata, songs, and choral compositions. She conducted the first performance of her suite in three movements, *En Piragua* (In a Canoe), *Cortejo* (Cortege), and *Fiesta Indigena* (Native Festival) with the *Orquesta Sinfónica Femenina* in Buenos Aires, on November 28, 1937. The score of the suite is included in the Fleisher Collection in Philadelphia.

José TORRE BERTUCCI (1888——) studied music with Alberto Williams. Since 1922 he has taught composition at the *Conservatorio Nacional* of Buenos Aires. Torre Bertucci composed mostly for piano and voice, in a European manner, without reference to native folklore.

Gaetano TROIANI (1873–1942), the Italian-Argentine composer, was born in Chieti, Italy, and died in Buenos Aires. He studied piano and composition in Naples. In 1898 he emigrated to Argentina, and settled in Buenos Aires, where he devoted himself to teaching and composition. He has written for orchestra, for piano, and for voice, employing an agreeable melodic style of composition. His *Children's Scenes* for orchestra were performed by Weingartner at the *Teatro Colón* on August 18, 1922, and the score is published by Ricordi. Also published are his two Argentine dances, *Estilo* and *Cueca*, for string orchestra, and *Ritmos Argentinos* for piano.

Florio M. UGARTE (1884——) was born in Buenos Aires and, as a young man, studied in Paris. Upon his return to Argentina in 1913, he taught music privately, and from 1924 at the National Conservatory in Buenos Aires. He was, until 1943, the musical director of the *Teatro Colón*. Ugarte composed prolifically, for orchestra, for the theater, and for instruments. He has written the following symphonic suites and symphonic poems: *Paisajes de Estio* (1912), *Escenas Infantiles* (1915), *Entre las Montañas* (1922), *De mi Tierra* (1923), and *La Rebelión del Agua* (1931). His one-act fairy tale, *Saika*, was produced at the *Teatro Colón*, on July 21, 1920. The orchestral score of *Rebelión del Agua* is in the Fleisher Collection in Philadelphia. Ricordi has published the piano reduction of the symphonic poem *De mi Tierra*, and also Ugarte's manual of harmony.

Alberto VILLALBA-MUÑOZ, a Spanish composer resident in Argentina, was born in Valladolid in 1878. Three of his brothers were also musicians of distinction. As a boy, Villalba-Muñoz entered the Augustinian Order.

In 1906 he went to Lima, Peru. There he abandoned the Order, and married his pupil, a pianist. With her, he settled in Jujuy, Argentina, and became director of the Clementi Conservatory of Music. Villalba-Muñoz has composed a symphonic poem, *Los Andes*, a Requiem, and a number of piano pieces and songs. The piano reduction of his ballet, *Leyènda del Zorro del Rio Xingu*, based on ancient Inca legends, is published by Ricordi.

Alberto WILLIAMS, the oldest composer, was born in Buenos Aires in 1862. His paternal grandfather was Benjamin Williams of Exeter, England, and his maternal grandfather was Amancio Alcorta, one of the pioneers of Argentine music. Williams began to play the piano and to compose at the age of eight. In 1882 he was given a government scholarship for study in Europe. He took lessons in piano with Mathias, a pupil of Chopin, and in composition with César Franck. Throughout his career, Williams cherished the memory of his association with Franck, and liked to call his own pupils "musical grandchildren of Franck." Williams returned to Argentina in December, 1889, and in 1893 founded the Conservatory bearing his name. Numerous branches of the Conservatory were subsequently opened all over Argentina, and laid the foundation of a considerable fortune. Part of his income Williams diverted to his music publishing enterprise, *La Quena*. Under the imprint of *La Quena*, in association with German and French music publishers, Williams has published virtually the complete edition of his compositions—full orchestral scores, chamber music, piano pieces and songs—112 opus numbers in all. Alberto Williams is the most prolific composer of the continent; he has written nine symphonies, two symphonic poems, two overtures, four orchestral suites, three suites of Argentine dances for string orchestra, ten poems for piano, *Sonata Argentina* for piano, thirteen collections of Airs of the Pampas, two Argentine suites for piano, seven collections of children's piano pieces, sixteen waltzes, four mazurkas, 165 miscellaneous character pieces for piano, three violin sonatas, a Flute Sonata, a Violoncello Sonata, a piano Trio, and numerous songs. Besides, Williams is the author of textbooks of elementary theory of music, harmony, counterpoint, solfeggio, and musical calligraphy. Williams is also a poet. One volume of his lyric poems and a volume of reflections upon music, *Pensamientos Sobre la Música*, were published in 1941. The texts of Williams' vocal compositions are generally his own, and his songs are all written in Spanish.

In his early compositions Williams followed the German model of romantic music, and later, the precepts of César Franck, particularly in chamber music. About 1890, Williams composed his first piece in the native Argentine manner, *El Rancho Abandonado* for piano, in which he stylized the melodic airs of the Gauchos. Subsequently, Williams wrote a number of concert pieces in the form of native dances, *Milongas*, *Hueyas*, *Vidalitas*, *Gatos*, *Cielitos*. His poems and suites for piano are often illustrations of the Argentine landscape, from tropical scenes—as in the *Poema de la Selva Primaveral*—to the Antarctic—as in *Poema Antartico*, and *Poema Fueguino*, the latter depicting Tierra del Fuego.

The harmonic idiom of Williams' music undergoes a considerable change about 1910, when he adds to the Franckian resources the entire vocabulary of French Impressionism: parallel chord progressions, employment of consecutive fifths, extensive use of pedal points, passages in unresolved seconds, and superposition of tonalities. Episodes in whole-tone scales are constantly encountered in Williams' symphonic and piano works. Pictorial and descriptive titles are assigned to symphonies and piano pieces, and each movement of the symphonies also bears a programmatic subtitle. The First Symphony (1907) has no descriptive title. Symphony No. 2 is entitled *La Bruja de las Montañas* (Witch of the Mountains); No. 3, *La Selva Sagrada* (Sacred Forest); No. 4, *El Ataja-Caminos* (Night Bird); No. 5, *El Corazón de la Muñeca* (Heart of a Doll); No. 6, *La Muerte del Cometa* (Death of the Comet); No. 7, *Eterno Reposo* (Eternal Repose); No. 8, *La Esfinge* (The Sphinx); No. 9, *Los Batracios* (The Frogs). Each symphony is prefaced with an original poem, with a title corresponding to that of the symphony itself.

The first four symphonies follow the classical model of four movements. The form of the Fifth, Sixth, Seventh, Eighth, and Ninth symphonies is unusual in that the middle movement of each is ternary, and contains a slow movement, a scherzo, and the recapitulation of the slow movement. The First and Second symphonies were performed in Buenos Aires, under the composer's direction, on November 25, 1907, and September 9, 1910, respectively. The following symphonies were performed in Buenos Aires, conducted by José Gil: No. 3 (December 8, 1934), No. 4 (December 15, 1935), No. 5 (November 29, 1936), and Nos. 6 and 7 at a concert on the occasion of Williams' seventy-fifth birthday, given on November 26, 1937.

Williams' facility has not diminished with age. At seventy-six, he completed his Ninth Symphony in two and a half months, between January 10 and March 26, 1939.

Seven of Williams' symphonies and some other works are in the Fleisher Collection in Philadelphia. In 1942, on his eightieth birthday, two dedicatory volumes were published: Z. R. Lacoigne's *Alberto Williams, Músico Argentino* and *Homenajes a Alberto Williams*. A detailed *catalogue raisonné* of his works was issued in 1946. See also N. Slonimsky's article "Alberto Williams, the Father of Argentinian Music" in *Musical America* of January 10, 1942.

Williams' daughter, Irma, also composes. Her piano pieces and songs have been published by *La Quena*. She imitates the style of her father.

Bolivia

> ¡Bolivia! ¡La heredera del gigante!
> [OLEGARIO V. ANDRADE]
>
> ¡Viva sí, viva Bolivia!
> ¡Caramba la boliviana
> Que tiene tanta salera!
> ¡Caramba la boliviana
> Que tiene amor verdadero!
> [TEÓFILO VARGAS]

Bolivia is often called the Switzerland of South America, for, like Switzerland, it is landlocked and is traversed by mighty mountain ranges. Bolivia is situated between the Equator and the Tropic of Capricorn. The climate varies with the altitude. La Paz, the capital, lies at an altitude of 11,910 ft. The population of Bolivia is three and a half million, the majority of which is composed of Indians and Mestizos.

The character of national music, as of all national expression, is to some extent determined by the geography and the climate of the country. The case of Bolivia demonstrates this point. The highlands with their bleak landscape, as well as the thinness of the air, are apt to induce dejection and melancholy; these characteristics are reflected in the music of the inhabitants. In contrast, the popular songs of the Bolivian valleys are characterized by rhythmic variety and color. The dance movements of the Indians of the highlands are slow and measured, whereas those of the inhabitants of the valleys are rapid and full of abandon.

The Indian music of Bolivia is based on the pentatonic scale. With the advent of the conquistadores, this scale was extended to seven tones.

Teófilo Vargas, in the preface to his three-volume collection *Aires Nacionales de Bolivia,* describes the mutual influence of the Indians and the Spanish: "The natives listened to the Spanish melodies, and the Spanish musicians, attracted by the originality of Incaic chants, assimilated native melos, even to the point of including native chants in church singing. The ecclesiastics, in their desire to make propaganda for their faith by all possible means, took advantage of the tremendous power exercised by the art of music, and encouraged the natives to sing religious hymns using Incaic modalities in church."

Bolivian Pentatonic Melody (*Vargas*)

The native art of Bolivia is expressed in its purest form in the songs which bear the generic name of *Aire Indio.* The *Aire Indio* is not confined to any specific meter or scale, and consists of short motives, with pauses between phrases. Often, an original Indian song or dancing tune is taken up by popular musicians and adapted to suit modern tastes. Thus, the *Huaiño,* a typical air of the Andean foothills, was originally a funeral procession of the Quechua Indians, but as it is performed today by village musicians it comes close to the American one-step. It is in two-four time and is played in a lively tempo. Other Bolivian dances of the *Huaiño* type are the *Cacharpaya* (the word means "to say good-bye" in the language of the Quechua Indians) and the *Pasacalle* (not to be confused with the classical form of the Passacaglia). The *Trote* (from *Trot,* or *Foxtrot*) is a modern dance of the pseudo-American category.

Many native dances of Bolivia bear descriptive titles, or are named after the province where they are most popular. Yet these dances of different names may all be essentially similar in character, usually of the *Huaiño* type. Thus, there is a one-step called the *Pala-pala* (which means "a crow" in Quechua). A pantomime of the bullfight is called by the Quechua word *Huacatocori.* The dance *Meçapaqueña* is named after the province of Meçapaca. There is also the *Kaluyo,* which is a tap dance.

Also a Bolivian phenomenon, the hybrid Spanish-Indian religious chant, similar to Christmas carols, and called *Adoración*, is of especial interest.

One of the most popular native dances of non-Bolivian origin is the Chilean *Cueca*, or, as it is sometimes called, *Chilena*. But while the Chilean *Cueca* is cast invariably in a major key, its Bolivian counterpart is often in the minor. Out of the twenty *Cuecas* included in the collection *Música Nacional Boliviana* by the Bolivian composer Simeón Roncal, eight are in a minor key. Each *Cueca* has an introduction of a few bars. The *Cueca* proper consists of two sections, the second being more lively than the first. The meter is usually six-eight combined with three-four, as in the Chilean *Cueca*, the Colombian *Pasillo* and other dances of Spanish origin.

The melancholy *Yaravi* of Peru is also sung in Bolivia. Teófilo Vargas describes the Bolivian *Yaravi* in these words: "The *Yaravi* is a romantic *lied*, a soliloquy of the soul of the Indian and of the white native, oppressed by the brutalities of Spanish despotism, by the unrest and agitation of the republican period, and by the solitary existence created by our geographical isolation. Some might say: 'Why should we inflict upon the world our sorrows, our distresses?' But what people, having thrown off but recently the chains of slavery under the tyranny of a foreign government, would sing the joy of life?"

Bolivia possesses a number of distinctive indigenous instruments, of purely Indian origin and of pre-Columbian antiquity. The most remarkable of these are the gigantic panpipes, *Sicus* and *Bajones*. Antonio González Bravo, the Bolivian music scholar, gives this information on the nature of the instruments: "The *Sicu*, or *Syrinx Aymará*, is made up of a series of tubes of sugar cane, closed on one end. The *Sicu* is played vertically, by holding the lower lip and blowing at the open end of the tube. The *Bajón* is composed of tubes made of palm-tree leaves overlaying the reed tubes inside. It combines the characteristics of the *Sicu* and of the *Kkepa*, the pre-Columbian trumpet. The *Bajón* is played by placing both lips on the edge of the reed which serves as a mouthpiece, as in modern brass instruments. The *Sicu* is often as long as one meter and twenty centimeters, and the *Bajón* may be two meters long."

Bolivian twin flutes, which are two vertical flutes, V-shaped, with a single mouthpiece where the two reeds join, come in four sizes, and are called *Taica, Mahalta, Licu*, or *Chuli*.

Other Bolivian instruments are listed in the preface to *Aires Nacionales de Bolivia* by Teófilo Vargas. They are: the *Pututú*, which is a bull horn, having a cornet mouthpiece, and which serves as a war trumpet of the rebellious mountain folks, or as a postillion's horn; the *Erque*, which is made of thick, hollow cane; the *Charca*, a sort of primitive wind instrument; the *Senka Tankara*, the *Pinquillo*, and the *Quena* which are flutes of various sizes; and a variety of panpipes. Of the latter, the paired panpipes are the most interesting. They are called *Sicuris* or *Laquitas*, and their scales overlap, so that by playing the first note on one panpipe, and then the first on the other, the second on the first, and the second on the other, etc., a complete diatonic scale is obtained. There are in existence *Sicuris* arranged in triple or even quadruple rows, somewhat in the manner of organ manuals, and capable of performing a chromatic scale.

An ingenious method of "tuning" Bolivian flutes and panpipes is achieved by dropping sand in the tubes to adjust the length of the air column.

The progress of *música culta* in Bolivia has been, until recently, rather slow. The first symphonic organization, the *Orquesta Nacional de Conciertos*, was established in La Paz under the auspices of the Ministry of Fine Arts, and the Bolivian composer José María Velasco Maidana was appointed conductor. The inaugural concert took place on March 14, 1940. The Orchestra makes it a matter of policy to promote Bolivian music, and performs native compositions on nearly all its programs.

MUSICIANS OF BOLIVIA

Eduardo CABA (1890——) of Spanish-Italian parentage, studied music with his mother, and in 1926 went to Buenos Aires to complete his education. He remained in Buenos Aires until 1943, when he returned to Bolivia. In his music, Caba cultivates the Indian folklore of his country. In this style were conceived his ballet *Kollana*, a pantomime *Potosi*, *Quena* for flute and orchestra, eighteen *Indian Airs* for piano. *Leyenda Keshua* for piano is included in the music supplement to Volume IV of the *Boletín Latino-Americano de Música*.

Antonio GONZÁLEZ BRAVO (1885——), the composer and educator, represents one of the major cultural forces in Bolivian music. As a pedagogue, he has introduced the Dalcroze method into Bolivian schools. At the same time he stresses the study of native Indian folklore. He is the author of numerous choral compositions for children. His *Trova a la Virgen de Copacabana* for female chorus and orchestra was performed in La Paz on April 1, 1942.

Simeón RONCAL (1872——), the composer of popular music, studied piano with his father, and played the organ at the Cathedral in Sucre. He has published an important collection for piano, *Música Nacional Boliviana*, comprising twenty original *Cuecas*, in the native vein. Roncal's piano piece entitled *Jazz*, which is also published, is a curious reflection of American popular music.

Teófilo VARGAS, the folkloric composer and music scholar, was born in 1868. He was choirmaster of the Cathedral at Cochabamba from 1892 to 1938, and wrote a Mass, *Niño Dios*, for chorus and orchestra. His piano pieces, *El Huérfano, Suspiros, Idillo*, and *Ecos del Litoral* (a battle piece), have been published by the composer. Vargas has made an important contribution to Bolivian musical folklore in the publication of three volumes under the title *Aires Nacionales de Bolivia* (1940) which contain harmonizations of authentic melodies, as well as original compositions. Vargas admits, however, that his music "makes no claim to scientific knowledge of harmony, and is the product of a desire to prove to foreign nations the existence of Bolivian national music." Vargas' symphonic overture, *La Coronilla*, was performed by the *Orquesta Sinfónica Nacional* of La Paz on October 24, 1942.

José María VELASCO MAIDANA (1899——) is the foremost Bolivian composer. He studied in Buenos Aires, specializing in violin. At the same time, he began composing music based on Bolivian folklore. His major work is the ballet *Amerindia*, designed as a glorification of the "new Indian of tomorrow." Velasco Maidana was invited by the German Ministry of Propaganda to present his ballet in Berlin, and the performance took place on December 6, 1938. When *Amerindia* was performed in La Paz on May 27, 1940, the President of the Republic welcomed it in a special message to the composer as "an event of transcendent significance in the history of Bolivia's artistic culture." Velasco Maidana is the conductor of the *Orquesta Sinfónica Nacional* in La Paz. In 1943 he toured Peru and Mexico, where he presented concerts of Bolivian music. The following works by Velasco Maidana were performed by the La Paz Symphony under his direction: symphonic legend, *Cory Wara* (October 6, 1941); overture, *Los Hijos del Sol* (February 6, 1942); symphonic poem, *Vida de Cóndores* (March 14, 1942); *Los Huacos* (April 22, 1942); *Los Khusillos* and *Cuento Brujo* (April 11, 1943).

Humberto VISCARRA MONJE (1898——) studied at the Conservatory of La Paz, and later in Italy. He is the author of piano pieces in a somewhat academic manner.

Brazil

Bondade
Realidade
Amisade
Sinceridade
Igualidade
Lealdade

BRASIL

[Acrostic by VILLA-LOBOS, used by him
as a motto at the annual choral festival
on Brazil's Independence Day]

Brazil occupies nearly one-half the area of South America, and is larger than the continental territory of the United States. The Amazon River, whose course lies almost entirely in Brazil, is the largest in the world. Brazil touches every South American nation except Ecuador and Chile. Brazil is the only Latin American nation whose language is Portuguese. Its population numbers forty-five million, of which 1,500,000 are Indians, and 3,000,000 Negroes. Brazil's capital, Rio de Janeiro, is a modern city of two million inhabitants.

Brazilian folk music is of great brilliance, warmth, and vivacity. The diversity of the songs,—from the Indian chants and ritual incantations of the descendants of Negro slaves to the Italianized ditties of the coastal towns,—corresponds to the diversity of the natural scene in Brazil's vast lands. The threefold racial origins of Brazilian music relate it to the folklore of Europe, Africa, and primeval America. _
The Indian strain in Brazilian music was strong in early times after the conquest, and is still strong in the remote regions of the Amazon basin. This aboriginal music was based upon three or four notes, rarely reaching the complete range of the pentatonic scale. The rhythm of the Indians of Brazil is monotonous, representing short phrases separated by long holds. The syncopation in Brazilian music comes from the Negro, but this syncopation never approaches the complexity of Afro-Cuban music. For one thing, the down beat is always strong in the great majority of Brazilian popular songs, and the basic rhythm of many Brazilian melodies of Negro origin is a sixteenth-note, an eighth-note, and a

sixteenth-note. The repetition of short and rapid notes is also very common in Afro-Brazilian music. The major mode is predominant in all
Brazilian folk songs. The time-signature is two-four in most Brazilian
dances. The melodic structure of a typical Brazilian air is peculiar in that
it is often built on a sequence.

The analysis of 118 Brazilian songs in the collection *Guia Pratico*, compiled by Villa-Lobos for use in schools, reveals that fully 110 songs are
in a major key; one hundred songs are in duple time. Seventy-one songs
are based on melodic sequences. Only eight songs are in minor; eleven
songs are in three-four time, five songs in six-eight, and one in five-four
time. Only in two songs is the first beat missing. Rhythm in even notes, in
rapid tempo, is very frequent.

Mario de Andrade writes in his *Ensaio Sobre Musica Brasileira:*

> Although Brazilian music has attained an original ethnical expression, its
> sources are of foreign derivation. It is Amerindian in a small percentage, Afri-
> can to a much greater degree, and Portuguese in an overwhelmingly large
> proportion. Besides, there is a Spanish influence, mainly in its Hispano-American
> aspect. . . . The European influence is revealed not only through parlor
> dances such as the Waltz, Polka, Mazurka, and the Schottische, but also in the
> structure of the *Modinha*. . . . Apart from these influences, already absorbed,
> we must consider recent contributions, particularly American jazz. The jazz
> procedures are infiltrating into the *Maxixe,* but, curiously enough, the poly-
> phonic and polyrhythmic devices of jazz do not alter or disfigure the character
> of the music. . . . A Brazilian composer should derive his materials and his
> inspiration from native folklore. This folklore, in its characteristic manifesta-
> tions, reveals the origin of its birth.

Among Brazilian dances and songs, the *Modinha* represents the purest
European strain. The word *Modinha* is the diminutive of *Moda*, and is
directly derived from Portuguese songs of that name. The early *Modinhas*
were greatly influenced by Italian music. Thus, the fifteen songs in the
collection *Modinhas Imperiais* by Mario de Andrade (S. Paulo, 1930),
representing the style of the Brazilian Empire (1822–1889), are little
different from Italian operatic arias. The present-day *Modinhas* are
sentimental in mood, cast mostly in minor keys, and are profusely ornamented with grace notes and appoggiaturas. The harmonic scheme of
the *Modinhas,* with its characteristic modulation into the minor sub-
dominant, enhances the already striking melodic affinity existing between
Brazilian sentimental ballads and Russian popular songs, an affinity that
is astonishing, since there could have been no direct influence.

Moda

Fernandez

RUSSIAN POPULAR SONG

Brazilian and Russian Melodies

Other Brazilian airs closely related to European music are the *Toada,* and perhaps also the *Chula.* The *Toada* is the Portuguese word for the Spanish *Tonada,* and is simply a song in the popular vein. The *Chula,* now rarely heard in Brazil, is a rustic dance, in two-four time, and in a major key.

Brazilian airs and dances reflect Negro rhythms, while the melodic line usually adheres to the standard pattern of a short symmetric period, in a major key and in two-four time. The names of these dances—the *Batuque,* the *Coco,* the *Congada,* the *Jôngo,* the *Lundú,* the *Maracatú,* and many others—are from the African dialects rather than from any European source.

The *Batuque* has been popularized in the concert hall by Oscar Lorenzo Fernandez, whose orchestral dances of that name are frequently performed by orchestras in the United States. The *Batuque,* also known under the name *Batucada,* is the most expressive of Afro-Brazilian airs. It is danced by Negroes in a circle, with much clapping of hands, beating on the drums, and making noise with pieces of iron, glass, and wood. The basic rhythm is common to most Afro-Brazilian dances, centered on a figure of one sixteenth-note, one eighth-note, and one sixteenth-note.

The *Congada* is familiar to music lovers through the brilliant orchestral

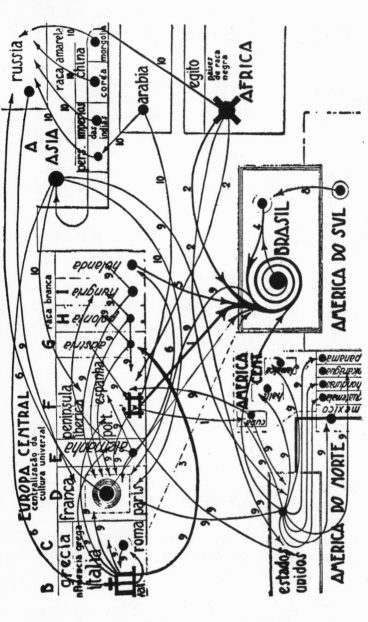

Planispheric Ethnological Graph Showing the Origin of Music in Brazil (*Villa-Lobos*)

Key: *A,* Origin of music; *B, C,* Formation of musical culture; *D,* Concentration and expansion of musical culture; *E,* Germanic musical expression (sobriety and circumspection); *F,* Centralization of Oriental musical expression; *G,* Lively and witty musical expression; *H,* Sentimental and passionate musical expression; *I,* Mixed musical expression in vivid and unexpected colors. 1, Channel of primary importation of foreign civilization; 2, Rhythmic influences; 3, Religious influences; 4, Autochthonous influence of Brazil's aborigines; 5, Channel of importation of Germanic influences; 6, Communication of foreign culture; 7, Influence of social music since 1918; 8, Influence of American Indians; 9, Intercommunication of musical characteristics among individual countries; 10, Communication of characteristic elements in the formation of Oriental music.

version of the dance by Francisco Mignone. The word *Congada* is derived from *Congo*, a religious play of the Brazilian Negroes, celebrated in honor of Our Lady of the Rosary, patron saint of the Negroes. The *Coco* is a dance of the *Batuque* type. As a song, it comes close to the primitive African incantations, and consists of short phrases shouted out rather than sung. The *Jongo* also harks back to Africa. In it, a solo voice is accompanied only by drums, and the syncopation is violent. The *Lundú* is a song-dance in rapid tempo, sung and danced to the accompaniment of guitars. A variation of the *Lundú* is the *Corta-Jaca*, a rhythmic dance in rapid movement. Both the *Lundú* and the *Corta-Jaca* are the prototypes of most Afro-Brazilian dances, and are probably older than the popular *Maxixe* and *Samba*.

There are two clearly differentiated forms of the *Samba*, the rural and the urban. The rural *Samba* is characterized by greater syncopation than the city *Samba*, which latter is less varied in rhythm, and usually adheres to the pattern of a succession of even notes in rapid tempo. In its extremely citified form, the *Samba* appears as the *Samba Carioca*. It is a salon dance, the word *Carioca* denoting Rio de Janeiro.

The *Samba* combines freely with the *Tango*, the *Rumba*, and the *Foxtrot*. In such hybrid forms, the title is hyphenated. The *Samba-Canção* (Samba-Song) is a type of nostalgic Serenade, and quite different in character from the standard *Samba*. The song *Brasil*, popularized in Disney's film *Saludos Amigos*, is a *Samba-Canção*.

So universal is the spread of the *Samba* that virtually all Brazilian airs and dances are now loosely called *Sambas* by Brazilians. In the North, even the dance halls themselves are called *Sambas*. But whatever the various forms of the *Samba*, its three principal characteristics are always present. They are the duple meter, the major key, and lively tempo.

Brazilian Samba (*Villa-Lobos*)

Camargo Guarnieri has given a perfect stylization of the urban *Samba* in his third *Dansa Brasileira*. He and other Brazilian composers have elevated the *Samba* to an art form, as distinctive as any of the European dance forms used in classical music.

The *Maxixe,* which attained immense popularity all over the world in 1910–1915, is of mixed musical parentage. Arthur Ramos, in his *Folclore Negro no Brasil,* speaks of the *Maxixe* as "a Brazilian dance which has borrowed Negro elements from the *Batuque* and incorporated the stylization of Hispano–American and European music." Mario de Andrade writes: "In the *Maxixe* there are reflected in a distorted shape the rhythms of the *Catereté* and other rural dances, deformed lines from the *Emboladas* of the Northeast, and even the rhythms of children's rounds."

The *Oxford Companion to Music* gives the following description of the *Maxixe:* "A rather strenuous Brazilian dance in two-in-a-measure time, which had some European popularity in the early years of the nineteenth century and then reappeared about 1911–1913 in a somewhat different form as the *Tango.*" Apart from the identification of the *Maxixe* with the *Tango,* with which it has little in common except the time-signature, there is in this definition an inaccurate dating. The *Maxixe* did not appear even in Brazil before the last quarter of the nineteenth century; the first mention of the *Maxixe* in Brazil was made in the *Gazeta da Tarde* of January 25, 1884.

One of the most important manifestations of Brazilian musical folklore is the *Chôro.* It does not represent any definite form of composition, but covers a number of Brazilian airs. Originally, the *Chôro* was the name given to an ensemble of instruments, African and European, similar to the jazz band, but antedating the appearance of jazz in the United States. As in jazz, the players of *Chôros* improvise in free and often dissonant counterpoint, which they call *Contracanto.* By metonymy, *Chôros* has come to mean the music played by the *Chôro* ensembles, in plural, *Chôros.* Villa-Lobos has enlarged the meaning of the word *Chôros,* applying it to any composition in the Brazilian manner, from a guitar solo to a symphonic or choral work.

Another type of Brazilian folklore which cannot be reduced to any definite musical form is the *Desafio.* The word means a competition, for in the *Desafio,* two or more singers contend with one another in free improvisation.

A powerful resource of Brazilian music is represented by European folk songs acclimatized in Brazil. These airs experience a sea-change, which alters their European inflection, and makes them truly native in function. The Brazilian Waltz has little in common with its Viennese prototype. It is languorous, and intertwined with grace-notes, appoggiaturas, and chromatic embellishments. The March becomes the *Marcha* or *Marchinha* (little March), which is a lively two-step. The European Polka is Brazilianized into a *Miudinho*. American jazz colors the Brazilian rhythm of a *Ponteio*. The Brazilian *Tango* and the *Tanguinho* (little *Tango*) are much more languid, more sentimental, and more tropical, so to speak, than the Argentine *Tango*. Portuguese airs are similarly incorporated into Brazilian folklore. The *Tirana*, a work song of the Azores, is also naturalized in Brazil, where it approximates the rhythm of a *Samba*. Finally, *Aboios*, which are shepherds' songs, arhythmic and wordless, and *Pregoës*, street vendors' cries, add to the color of Brazil's urban and rural life.

To these dances and airs there may be added a long list of regional variants, not always clearly differentiated, and often representing a familiar *Samba* or a *Batuque* under another name. In the second edition (1942) of Renato Almeida's monumental work, *Historia da Musica Brasileira*, two hundred and seventy-nine pages are devoted to the description of various forms of Brazilian folk music.

Brazilian composers, particularly Villa-Lobos, Fernandez, Mignone, and Guarnieri, have written numerous compositions in the style of native folk songs, and by so doing, have preserved the indigenous Brazilian rhythms in musical literature. Sometimes, the titles of their compositions indicate a mood, a character, or a landscape, rather than a definite musical form. For instance, the *Caboclo*, which is the name of Indian peasants, indicates music of rustic character. The music of the countryside is evoked in Mignone's *Lendas Sertanejas* (Legends of the Country).

Music for children is an integral part of Brazilian folklore. Villa-Lobos has written a number of *Cirandas* (round dances), and, in the diminutive, *Cirandinhas*. *Rodas* are children's marching songs. The well-known song *Cae, Cae, Balão*, which accompanies the game of sending a balloon flying in the air, is a typical example of Brazilian folk music for children.

All these various dance forms, Afro-Brazilian, Amerindian, and Latin European, are represented at the Carnival of Rio, celebrated annually in February. For this occasion the untamed songs of the jungle are polished up and reduced to a singable design. There commercial song hits are made. From the Carnival of Rio, the rest of the Americas learns what the Brazilian jungle sings.

In the meantime, the jungle continues to cultivate its primitive art. The Indians hold the forbidding rites of *Yurupari*. The Brazilian Negroes practice their fetichistic ritual of the *Macumba,* from which stem many Brazilian dances. The *Catereté,* the *Embolada,* the *Maracatú,* the *Chiba,* the *Cururú,* the *Coco de Zambé,* and other dances establish the link between Africa and Brazil. The *Macumba* is also known under the names *Candomblé, Babacué, Catimbo,* and *Pagelança.* The songs of the *Macumba* are often named after the Afro-Brazilian deities, such as *Xango,* the Jupiter of the jungle. Closely connected with the *Macumba* is the *Cucumbi,* an Afro-Brazilian pantomime. The name, often in its diminutive form, *Cucumbizinho,* is used by modern Brazilian composers to designate a lively syncopated dance.

The most interesting feature of Afro-Brazilian folklore is the mixture of jungle elements with Christian symbolism. Such syncretism of cultures is observed in the formation of the *Frevos,* which were derived from Christmas plays introduced by the Jesuits into Brazil in the sixteenth century, and variously known as *Ternos, Ranchos,* or *Blocos.* When these plays were assimilated by the Negro slaves of the interior, they acquired many African characteristics. The music of the *Frevos* is apt to be sharply syncopated. When performed instrumentally, the *Frevos* are usually scored for brass instruments. José Siqueira has written a concert type of *Frevos,* for an ensemble of trumpets and trombones.

Among native Brazilian plays in which the Christian element predominates, the most popular is the trilogy, *Pastoris, Cheganças,* and *Reisados.* The *Pastoris* represent the shepherds' adoration of Christ. The *Cheganças,* or *Cheganças de Marujos* (Arrival of Mariners) are historic dramas picturing the adventures of the great navigators who discovered Brazil. Elaborate pageants depicting the age of discovery are called *Marujadas.* The *Reisados* (the word comes from *Reis,* the Kings) commemorate the pilgrimage of the Magi to Bethlehem. But the concluding act of the *Reisados, Bumba Meu Boi* (My Good Ox), is pagan in origin, and is the glorification of the sacred ox.

Brazilian folk orchestras possess a rich choice of indigenous instruments. Some are native counterparts of European instruments, the *Violão* (guitar), the *Cavaquinha* (mandolin), and the *Rabeca* (violin). But the greatest part of the native orchestra consists of drums, shakers, and scrapers of African origin. There are drums, bearing different names in different regions of Brazil, such as the *Tambú* or *Tambor,* the *Caxambú* (bass-drum), the *Tabaqué* or *Atabaqué* (high drum), the *Trocano* (the jungle drum made out of a hollow tree trunk). Then there are various shakers, the *Chocalho,* sometimes spelled *Xocalho* or *Xucalho,* which is a metal or wooden rattle; the *Maraca,* which is a gourd with dry seeds inside; and the *Chequeré* (also called *Xaqué-Xaqué*), which is a double rattle on a stick. There are rasps or ratchets, of which the most popular is the *Reco-Reco,* a notched wooden cylinder, which is rubbed with a stick; and the *Ganzá,* usually made of a hollowed-out bamboo stick. The *Adufé* or *Pandeiro* is the Brazilian tambourine. The *Adjá* is a conic metal bell, and the *Agogó* is an iron slab, which is struck with a metal stick. An instrument which is used at Carnival shows and called *Cuíca* or *Puíta* is of the animal-roar type. It is usually made of a tin cylinder with a drumhead on one end, and has a gut string rubbed with rosin which extends from the center of the drumhead; it is played by pulling the hand tightly over the string. It emits a sound similar to the grunt of a pig, according to the description of a Brazilian author.

The role of native percussion instruments in the primitive rites of Brazilian Negroes is discussed in the authoritative article *Drums and Drummers in Afro-Brazilian Cult Life* by Melville J. Herskovits, published in *The Musical Quarterly* of July, 1944.

Luciano Gallet (1893–1931), who was one of the first scientific explorers of Brazilian folklore, noted the performance of an Afro-Brazilian village ensemble, which included the voice, the clapping of hands (*Palmas*), the drum *Tambú,* the shaker *Chocalho,* the tambourine *Pandeiro,* and the bass drum, *Caxambú* or *Bombo.* Each instrument has an independent rhythmic figure, resulting in an astonishingly rich polyrythmic design.

Luciano Gallet summarizes the essence of Brazilian music in these words:

Brazilian music was born from the fusion of the elements of Portuguese Latin melos with African rhythms. The conjunction of these elements with the racial contribution of the Indian, the master of the continent, has originated the musical psychology of the people of Brazil. Brazil's musical material, whether introduced by the Portuguese or imported from Africa, is enormously rich in form, melody, and rhythm. The alien materials were modified in the new surroundings, and there emerged new modalities, which are now acquiring shape. This music, rich in flavor, exuberant in sentiment, and full of inner life, begins to attract the attention of foreign music scholars who are coming to Brazil to learn the new art. Within a short period of time, Brazilian music, conscious of its strength, will greatly contribute towards the affirmation of Brazil's vitality.

Polyrhythmy in a Brazilian Folk Ensemble (*Gallet*)

The wealth of Brazilian folk music is matched by a similarly flourishing state of musical culture in Brazil. The Jesuit missionaries were the first to introduce European music, mostly liturgic, into the new territory. Secular music was not long in following. As early as 1747, there were opera performances in Rio de Janeiro, and one of the streets was called *Rua da Opera*. In *Travels in South America During the Years 1819-20-21* (London, 1825), Alexander Caldcleugh writes:

The Opera, which is supported by an annual lottery, and afforded to many some amusement, was not conducted in that way which an European audience would have demanded. No great attention to cleanliness was paid, and it cannot be denied that some of the Venuses of the ballet were not exactly of an European tint; but, in this climate, great allowances must be made, and the first theater in South America must not be too severely criticized. The performances were alternately Portuguese and Italian.

The same author describes the concerts of the Royal Chapel of Music at the Court of the Emperor of Brazil:

In the opinion of most persons, the Royal Chapel afforded the greatest satisfaction to the lovers of music. Similarly arranged to that of Lisbon in former days, no expense was spared to render the performance fully worthy of the subject. Sopranos, as many as fourteen or fifteen, mingled their peculiar voices in the music of Portugallo and the finest church composers, forming, on the whole, a strain of melody duly appreciated by foreigners in particular. Excepting when the court was present, the auditory was principally composed of foreigners and the lowest classes of society.

"Portugallo" was Marcos Portugal, celebrated Portuguese musician, who went to Brazil in 1811, and remained there until his death in 1830. His body was, many years later, transported back to Portugal for burial there.

Another interesting sidelight on the musical life in Brazil early in the nineteenth century is provided by the following advertisement in the *Gazette* of Rio de Janeiro of July 8, 1820:

Whoever wishes to purchase a slave suitable as a coachman, who can play on the Piano and Marimba, and combines with a knowledge of music some acquaintance with the trade of a tailor, may apply at the Apothecary's shop.

Among the names of native Brazilian musicians of the first half of the nineteenth century are Damião Barbosa de Araujo (1778–1856), violinist and composer of religious music; José Reboucas (1789–1843), who was the first Brazilian musician to study in Europe; and José Mauricio Nunes Garcia (1767–1830), mulatto son of a Portuguese colonist and a slave girl. José Mauricio is usually regarded as the father of Brazilian music. His models were Handel and Gluck. He wrote church music, some of which has been published.

The progress of music in Brazil was in no small measure indebted to the Emperor Pedro I, who was himself an amateur composer. An Overture from his opera was performed in Paris in 1832. Pedro I was also the author of the Brazilian Hymn of Independence, which he wrote on September 7, 1822, immediately after he had declared Brazil's independence from Portugal and was proclaimed Constitutional Emperor. A detailed account by a contemporary writer specifies the exact time of the composition of the Hymn, between 5:30 and nine o'clock in the evening of September 7, 1822, which is Brazil's Independence Day. Pedro I is reported to have sung the Hymn, accompanied by a chorus, at a patriotic gathering in São Paulo on the same night.

After the abdication of Pedro I in 1831, a new patriotic song was

written by Francisco Manuel da Silva (1795–1865), an educated musician and composer. This song has become the present National Anthem
of Brazil. The story of the Hymn of Independence and the National
Anthem of Brazil is told in complete detail in the brochure, *Hino da
Independencia e Hino Nacional* by José C. Caldeira (São Paulo, 1941).

Brazilian music came of age with the advent of Carlos Gomes (1836–
1896), the only native composer whose music has become part of the
operatic repertoire all over the world. Gomes also exemplifies the tri-
umph of Italian influence in Brazilian music. His celebrated opera *Il
Guarany* was written to the story by a Brazilian national writer, José
Alencar, who was the James Fenimore Cooper of Brazil, and cultivated
Indian folklore in his novels. Gomes wrote *Il Guarany* to a libretto in
Italian, and the opera was produced in Italy before it was heard in Brazil.

João Gomes de Araujo (1846–1942), whose long life spanned almost
a century, also followed the Italian model in his operatic production. In
fact, so great was the grip of Italian tradition on Brazilian music in the
nineteenth century that Luigi Chiaffarelli, an Italian musician who lived
in Brazil, declared in 1906: "I regard Brazil as a musical province of
Italy."

The first Brazilian opera in the Portuguese language was *A Noite de
São João* (St. John's Eve) by Elias Alvares Lobo (1834–1901), written to a story by José Alencar, the author of *Il Guarany*. In his valuable
and informative brochure *Relação das Operas de Autores Brasileiros* (Rio
de Janeiro, 1938), the Brazilian musicologist Luiz Heitor lists 107 operas
by 59 Brazilian composers. Most of these operas are written to Italian
libretti. Fifty operas have been performed, but none remained in the
active repertoire, with the exception of the operas of Carlos Gomes. The
music of the operas written before 1910 is definitely Italianate. The distinctive Brazilian quality is revealed in the operas of the modern school
of Brazilian composers, Villa-Lobos, Fernandez, Mignone, and a few
others. But although the bust of Villa-Lobos graces the vestibule of the
Rio Opera House, none of his operas has been given. Fernandez's opera
Malazarte, based on a native legend, was performed in 1941 in an Italian
translation of the original Portuguese text by the Brazilian poet Graça
Aranha.

If nineteenth-century Brazil depended on Europe for its music, native
musical activities were nevertheless remarkably developed. One can form
an idea of the popular interest in music from the number of musical organizations, societies, and clubs that flourished in Brazil in the second

Ancient Mexican rattles (sonajas and cascabeles)

Tetzilacatl: ancient Mexican shield
used as a gong

Ancient Mexican
whistling jar

Ancient Mexi-
can whistle

Suribi, ritual
Brazilian
trumpet

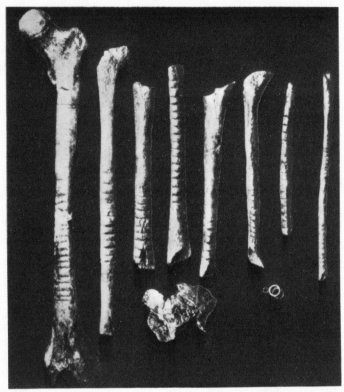

Ancient Mexican musical instruments (omichicahuaztlis)
made of human bones

Brazilian percussion instruments: (left to right) adjá;
chocalho; chequeré; agogó

half of the nineteenth century. In Rio de Janeiro in the 1880's there were the Beethoven Club, Ricardo Wagner Club, Rossini Club, Schubert Club, Weber Club; and in São Paulo flourished the Haydn Club and Mendelssohn Club. There existed also many German and French music societies. Foreign artists frequently visited Brazil. The Portuguese pianist Arthur Napoleão (1843–1925) settled in Brazil and founded there the well-known music publishing firm bearing his name. The Spanish musician José Amat, who settled in Brazil in 1848, was the founder of the Imperial Academy of Music. He published two albums of Brazilian songs, *Mélodies Brésiliennes* and *Les Nuits Brésiliennes*, conceived in the style of early *Modinhas*. In the twentieth century, Darius Milhaud, the French modernist, who served as an attaché at the French Embassy in Rio de Janeiro, composed a suite entitled *Saudades do Brasil* (*Saudades* means nostalgic memories).

Symphonic music in Brazil lagged somewhat behind the brilliant flowering of Brazilian folklore and creative composition. The first important symphonic organization was the *Sociedade de Concertos Sinfonicos,* established in Rio de Janeiro in 1908, and conducted by the Brazilian composer Francisco Braga until his retirement in 1933. Members of this orchestra later joined the orchestra of the Opera House, which has also presented numerous symphonic concerts. A new orchestra, named *Orquestra Sinfonica Brasileira,* was inaugurated in Rio on July 11, 1940, under the direction of the Hungarian conductor Eugen Szenkar. In São Paulo, the *Sociedade de Concertos Sinfonicos* was organized on October 17, 1921.

In the realm of musical education, Brazil possesses excellent conservatories and music schools. Its oldest musical institution is the *Escola Nacional de Musica,* which recently celebrated its hundredth anniversary. It was founded on November 27, 1841, under the directorship of Francisco Manuel da Silva, the composer of the Brazilian National Anthem. The original name was the *Imperial Conservatorio de Musica,* which was changed to the *Instituto Nacional de Musica* after the fall of the Empire, and later to the *Escola Nacional de Musica.* Its present Director is the music educator Antonio Sá Pereira, and its staff includes prominent Brazilian composers. A modern conservatory, named the *Conservatorio Brasileiro de Musica,* was established by Oscar Lorenzo Fernandez in 1940 in Rio de Janeiro. The *Conservatorio Dramatico e Musical* in São Paulo, under the direction of Francisco Casabona, is an important educational center. There are also conservatories and music schools in Porto Alegre, Bahia, and Belem.

A significant development in modern musical education in Brazil was the appointment in 1932 of Villa-Lobos as General Director of Music Education. He has introduced novel methods of musical instruction, particularly in the domain of choral singing. Among the subjects Villa-Lobos includes in the curriculum of Brazilian schools are *Califasia* (the art of fine speech), *Califonia* (the art of fine singing), and "orpheonic effects," which comprise vocalization on consonants, percussive effects, vocal sighs and so on. In an impassioned invocation to St. Cecilia, patron saint of music, read over the radio on November 22, 1939, Villa-Lobos expressed his hopes for the further progress of music in Brazil:

> Divine Protector, who has given to Brazil the gift of music, who has exalted the birds, the rivers, the waterfalls, the winds, and the people of this land into an incomparable symphony whose melodies and harmonies have contributed to the formation of Brazil's soul! Illumine those who cultivate Brazilian music! Encourage the musicians disappointed in their musical life! Enlighten public opinion so as to make the appreciation of Brazilian art possible! Gratify the wish of those who believe music to be of national importance, educating the soul as gymnastics strengthen and develop the body! Lend faith to those who trust that the day will come when music becomes the Sonorous Flag of Universal Peace!

Musicology is being fostered in Brazil as a separate science thanks to the efforts of the pioneers of Brazilian folklore, Luciano Gallet, Luiz Heitor, and Mario de Andrade, who have published collections of Brazilian folk songs. Musical folklore in Brazil is dealt with by Mario de Andrade in his annotated essays, *Ensaio sobre Musica Brasileira* and *Modinhas Imperiais,* both now out of print. As to music history in Brazil, the most complete work is *Historia da Musica Brasileira* by Renato Almeida, of which the second edition appeared in 1942. It is a volume of 507 pages, with 151 musical illustrations. The first volume of *Historia da Musica* by Ulysses Paranhos (1940) includes biographical sketches of modern Brazilian composers. *Storia della Musica nel Brasile* by the Italian musician Vicenzo Cernicchiaro, published in Italy in 1926, is an unsatisfactory compilation, in which nuggets of useful information are sunk in the mire of rambling accounts of concert tours by visiting musicians. Articles on Brazilian music are featured in the foremost music periodical of Brazil, the *Revista Brasileira de Musica.* The cause of Brazilian modernism was championed in the short-lived magazine *Musica Viva*, published in São Paulo from 1940 to 1942.

The precursors of the modern school of Brazilian creative composition were Alexander Levi (1864–1892), Leopoldo Miguez (1850–1902), Henrique Oswald (1852–1931), Glauco Velasquez (1884–1913), and Alberto Nepomuceno (1864–1920). The true pioneer of modern Brazilian music was Alberto Nepomuceno, who composed the first orchestral suite based on Brazilian themes. The present generation of Brazilian composers includes many names already well known outside of Brazil.

MUSICIANS OF BRAZIL

Mario de ANDRADE (1893–1945), a modern poet and Brazilianist, greatly contributed to the development of native folklore collecting by his searching analysis of the rhythmic and melodic structure of Brazilian songs and dances. His publications include *Ensaio sobre Musica Brasileira* (1928) and *Modinhas Imperiais* (1930; dealing with the development of *Modinhas* during the Brazilian Empire). He also edited Gallet's *Estudos de Folclore*.

João Gomes de ARAUJO (1846–1942) died in São Paulo, on September 8, 1942, at the age of ninety-six. He studied music at the Conservatory of Rio de Janeiro, graduating in 1865. In 1884 he went to Italy, where he wrote four operas, *Edmea, Carmosina, Maria Petrovna* (on a Russian subject), and *Helena. Carmosina* was produced in Milan on May 1, 1888, in the presence of Pedro II, Emperor of Brazil. Apart from operas, Araujo wrote, between 1899 and 1925, six Symphonies, two Cantatas, six liturgic Masses, sixty songs, piano pieces, and instrumental compositions. Araujo's style of composition was derived from that of nineteenth-century Italian opera, and he rarely used Brazilian folklore as a source of inspiration. The vocal score of his opera *Maria Petrovna* has been published by Ricordi.

Francisco BRAGA (1868–1945) studied clarinet in Rio de Janeiro, and later took up composition. His first work was a *Fantasie-Ouverture* for orchestra which was performed at the inaugural concert of the Society of Popular Concerts in Rio de Janeiro on January 5, 1887. Upon the proclamation of the Brazilian Republic, Francisco Braga composed a Republican hymn, which earned him a two-year travel fellowship from the government. Braga went to Paris, where he studied with Massenet, whose music influenced Braga's own style of composition profoundly.

He conducted a concert of Brazilian music in Paris, including his own symphonic poem, entitled *Cauchemar* (Nightmare). Later he went to Germany, where he studied Wagner's operas, and composed a symphonic poem on Brazilian themes, *Marabá*. Impressed with the Italian *verismo*, Braga attempted the composition of an opera which would constitute a Brazilian counterpart of *Cavalleria Rusticana*. The result was a one-act opera, *Jupira*, in which an Indian maiden kills her unfaithful lover. The opera was produced in Rio de Janeiro on March 20, 1899, shortly after Braga's return to Brazil. He also composed a four-act opera, *Anita Garibaldi*. From 1908 to 1933, Braga conducted the orchestra of the *Sociedade de Concertos Sinfonicos* in Rio de Janeiro, and presented numerous works by Brazilian composers, as well as the classical repertoire. As a composer, Braga represents the romantic tradition in Brazilian music, with a harmonic idiom in the nineteenth-century manner and some reflections of Wagnerian dramatism. His symphonic poems, all very short, bear descriptive titles, *Paysage, Insomnia, Cauchemar, Crepusculo, Chant d'Automne*. Braga has written numerous liturgical works, including two Masses and a *Te Deum*; chamber music, songs, and piano pieces. His *Hymn of the National Banner* has become an official patriotic song. His piano Trio was published by the University of Rio de Janeiro in 1937, and some songs have been published by Ricordi. The scores of *Marabá, Cauchemar*, and *Paysage* are included in the Fleisher Collection in Philadelphia. A biographical brochure by Tapajos Gomes, *Francisco Braga*, was published in Rio de Janeiro in 1937.

José Vieira BRANDÃO (1911———) is active primarily as a pianist. He studied in Rio de Janeiro, at the *Escola Nacional de Musica*, graduating in 1929. In 1932 he joined Villa-Lobos in organizing choral singing in Brazilian schools. Brandão began to compose in 1935. He has written a number of songs, mostly to texts expressive of Brazilian folklore, and several piano pieces. Ten of his songs are published. Brandão writes in a simple unassuming style without attempts at modernism.

Walter BURLE MARX (1902———), the composer and conductor, is the son of a German-Jewish father and a Brazilian mother. He studied piano at the age of seven with his mother and in 1921 went to Berlin, where he took lessons in composition with Reznicek, and in conducting with Weingartner. In 1925–1926 Burle Marx gave piano recitals in Vienna, Berlin, Paris, and Milan. His first orchestral composition, *Theme, Variations, and Fugue*, was played at Rostock on November 23, 1926. In 1928

Burle Marx returned to Brazil and founded an orchestra named the Philharmonic of Rio de Janeiro. He conducted his *Fantastic Episode*, which is the third movement of his Symphony, at the World's Fair in New York on May 4, 1939, and received great praise in the press. Orchestral scores and parts of *Fantastic Episode*, are available through the Associated Music Publishers.

Agostino CANTÙ is of Italian extraction; he was born in Milan in 1880, and studied at the Conservatory of Milan. His opera *Il Poeta* won a prize at the Sonzogno competition in 1902. Subsequently he was engaged to teach piano at the *Conservatorio Musical* in São Paulo, Brazil, where he settled down as a pedagogue and composer. Cantù has written numerous piano compositions, of which many are derived from Brazilian inspiration, such as *Tres Rapsodias Brasileiras*, *Tres Lendas Brasileiras*, and *Impressões Brasileiras*. Other works are in a general European manner: *Scherzetto*, *Kermesse*, *Cavaliere Arabo*, *Polonaise Fantastique*, etc. Most of these piano pieces have been published by Ricordi.

Dinorá de CARVALHO (1905——) studied piano at the *Conservatorio Musical* in São Paulo, and later with Isidor Philipp in France. She has given many concerts in Brazil. In 1932 she took lessons in composition. Dinorá de Carvalho has written numerous pieces for piano, particularly for children, songs, and *Fantasia Brasileira* for piano and orchestra. She emphasizes native color in her music, and her harmonic style follows some of Debussy's procedures.

Eleazar de CARVALHO (1912——) played the tuba in the Naval Band and studied composition in the *Escola Nacional de Musica* in Rio de Janeiro. His interest lies primarily in theater music. He has written two operas, *A Descoberta do Brasil* (Discovery of Brazil) and *Tiradentes*, both intensely Brazilian in subject matter and musical treatment. Tiradentes (literally, tooth-puller) was the nickname of a Brazilian hero of the Revolution, who was a dentist. The opera was produced on Independence Day, September 7, 1941, at the *Teatro Municipal* in Rio de Janeiro. In 1946, after his debut with the Boston Symphony, Carvalho was known as one of the foremost young conductors of the Americas.

Francisco CASABONA (1894——) went to Italy as a young man, and there studied at the Conservatory of Naples. In Italy he wrote two comic operas, *Godiamo la Vita*, which was produced in Rome on October 6, 1917, and *Principessa dell'Atelier*, produced in Naples on August 20, 1918.

Upon his return to Brazil, he was appointed director of the *Conservatorio Musical* in São Paulo. His symphonic poem *Nero* was performed in São Paulo on January 13, 1924, and his Symphony in D was presented in São Paulo, the composer conducting, on September 1, 1937. He has also written a symphonic poem, *Crepusculo Sertanejo* (Country Twilight); *Noite de São João* (The Eve of St. John) for orchestra; a String Quartet, several choral works and songs; an album of piano pieces, *Suggestions,* one of which is entitled *An Einstein Fable;* a Piano Sonata; a Brazilian suite, *Pindorama,* etc. *Suggestions* and *Pindorama* have been published by Ricordi, and some songs have been published in Italy.

Luiz Cosme, the composer, was born in Porto Alegre in 1908. He studied violin in his native town, and in 1927 went to Cincinnati, where he took lessons in composition. Upon his return to Brazil, he devoted himself to teaching and composing. His music is intensely Brazilian in sentiment, while his harmonic and contrapuntal style is of considerable complexity. He has written a ballet, *Salamanca do Jurau,* based on a native legend. An excerpt from this ballet, arranged for violoncello and piano, has been published by *Musica Viva* (1941). His song *Canção do Tio Barnabé* (Song of Uncle Barnabas) was published in 1943 by the *Editorial Cooperativa Interamericana de Compositores* in Montevideo, and a violin piece, *Mãe d'Agua Chante* (Mother of Waters Sings), is included in the album *Musique Brésilienne Moderne* (Rio de Janeiro, 1937). The Fleisher Collection in Philadelphia has the orchestral score of Cosme's *Oração a Teiniagua* (Oration to Teiniagua).

João Itiberé Da Cunha, the musical journalist and composer, was born in 1870. A man of cosmopolitan culture, he is chiefly known as a commentator on music in the Brazilian daily press. As a composer, he uses the nom de plume Iwan d'Hunac, an anagram of Cunha. His effective piano pieces in a humorous manner, *Danse Plaisante et Sentimentale* and *Marche Humoristique,* have been published by Ricordi. He has also written some dances in the Afro-Brazilian vein.

Ernesto Dos Santos (1891——) is a Negro composer of popular music. He is well known as the author of popular *Sambas,* and also as a band leader. In 1917 he made several appearances in Paris.

Oscar Lorenzo Fernandez (1897–1948) was born in Rio de Janeiro. He studied at the *Instituto Nacional de Musica,* and on November 22, 1923, presented in Rio de Janeiro the first concert of his own works. In 1924 Fernandez received a municipal prize for his second piano trio, entitled *Trio Brasileiro*, which was subsequently performed on April 26, 1925. On November 17, 1925, the orchestra of the *Instituto Nacional de Musica* in Rio de Janeiro performed his orchestral works on Brazilian themes, *Suite Brasileira* and *Suite Sinfónica Sobre Tres Temas Populares*. On November 7, 1926, the same orchestra played his suite in three movements: *Crepusculo Sertanejo* (Twilight in the Country), *Canção na Tarde* (Song in the Afternoon), and *Dansa dos Tangaras*. Fernandez's next important work was the Suite for five wind instruments (flute, oboe, clarinet, bassoon, and horn) in four movements, one of which is a fugue on a folk tune depicting the jungle creature of the popular fancy, *Sacy-Pereré*. This Suite was first performed in Rio de Janeiro on September 20, 1927. Fernandez's children's suite for orchestra, *Visões Infantis*, was performed in Rio de Janeiro on September 26, 1927. On September 2, 1929, Francisco Braga conducted Fernandez's "Amerindian" suite *Imbapára*, scored for a large orchestra. Its themes are partly authentic, partly stylized in the Indian manner, and based on the pentatonic scale. Francisco Braga also conducted the first performance of Fernandez's orchestral suite, *Reisado do Pastoreio*, on August 22, 1930. The suite is in three movements: *Pastoreio* (symbolizing the shepherds' journey to Bethlehem), *Toada* (a nostalgic song), and *Batuque* (an Afro-Brazilian dance). The *Batuque*, with its propulsive rhythm and effective orchestration, has become extremely popular both in Latin America and in the United States. Another *Batuque*, from the opera *Malazarte*, was performed, along with several other excerpts from the opera, on October 21, 1933, in Rio de Janeiro, with the composer conducting. On April 14, 1937, Fernandez's Concerto for Piano and Orchestra was played for the first time in Rio de Janeiro. His ballet on Inca themes, entitled *Amayá*, was produced by the Ballets Russes in Rio de Janeiro, on July 9, 1939. On September 30, 1941, Fernandez conducted the world première of his opera *Malazarte*, produced in the Italian language by the opera company of the *Teatro Municipal* in Rio de Janeiro. The subject of the opera is the legendary figure of Malazarte, the master of evil arts (*malas artes*), and the action unfolds in colonial Brazil. In his opera, Fernandez adopts the system of leading motives, expressing the principal moods rather than the characters of the drama, namely Destiny, Seduction, Love, and Death. The musical material of the opera is Brazilian, the central aria of *Malazarte* being cast in the form of a nostalgic *Modinha*.

Apart from symphonic and operatic composition, Fernandez has written prolifically for instruments. In 1942 he composed a Concerto for

Violin and Orchestra, based on native themes. Over a hundred piano pieces and songs by Fernandez have been published in Brazil by Ricordi, Vitale, Wehrs, and the Casa Mozart. Virtually all of these compositions are in the native vein. His most brilliant piano pieces are *Tres Estudos em Forma de Sonatina*, published by Ricordi (the first of these *Estudos* is reprinted in the album *Musique Brésilienne Moderne*, 1937), *Valsa Suburbana* (a slightly ironic interpretation of a salon waltz, which is also included in *Musique Brésilienne Moderne*), *Moda* (published in the Brazilian issue of *New Music*, October, 1942), and the humorous *Marcha dos Soldadinhos Desafinados* (March of Mistuned Little Soldiers). Among works by Fernandez for chamber music and orchestra, the *Trio Brasileiro* has been published by Ricordi; the score and parts of the Suite for five wind instruments were printed by the University of Rio de Janeiro in 1937, and later reissued by the Associated Music Publishers in New York. The score and parts of *Imbapára* were published by the University of Rio de Janeiro in 1938. The suite *Reisado do Pastoreio* has been published by Ricordi. The score of the *Batuque* from *Malazarte* was issued by *New Music* in 1939. *Imbapára, Batuque, Suite Sinfónica*, the Violin Concerto, the *Himno de la Raza* (The Hymn of the Race, commissioned by the Colombian government in 1939), and the orchestral arrangements of two songs, *A Sombra Suave* and *Nocturno*, are in the Fleisher Collection in Philadelphia. The scherzo from the *Trio Brasileiro* and the song *Samaritana de Floresta* are recorded in the Columbia album *South American Chamber Music*.

Fernandez was one of the most prolific composers of Latin America. Yet he found time for teaching and conducting. He established and directed the *Conservatorio Brasileiro de Musica* in Rio de Janeiro. He was a guest-conductor at the Ibero-American Music Festival in Bogotá in 1938. He died in his sleep on the night of August 25–26, 1948, after conducting a concert of his works in Rio de Janeiro.

A Brazilian music critic has called Fernandez *Brasileirissimo* in appreciation of his devotion to the spirit of native folklore. Fernandez uses both the method of actual quotation of popular songs, and the invention of original melodies in the native vein. Thus, in the *Trio Brasileiro*, three themes are actual folk melodies, and five themes are original. As to Fernandez's harmonic style, it is rich and full, often based on supporting pedal points. The chordal structure does not transgress the limits of enhanced tonality. In his orchestral works, Fernandez rarely resorts to the use of native instruments, preferring to recreate rhythms and sonorities of Brazilian folk music through the accepted medium of European instrumentation.

Agnelo FRANÇA (1875——) is a music educator and composer. He is the author of a textbook on harmony, choral works, and a one-act opera *As Parasitas,* which has not been performed. His *Ave Maria* was published in 1937 by the University of Rio de Janeiro.

Luciano GALLET, the musicologist and composer, was born in Rio de Janeiro in 1893, and died there in 1931. He studied music with Henrique Oswald. From his first steps in composition he became ardently interested in Brazilian folklore. He essayed successfully unusual combinations in chamber music, as in his Suite for viola, clarinet, violin, and percussion, and in another Suite on Afro-Brazilian themes for wood-wind quartet. Villa-Lobos conducted Gallet's *Suite Bucolica* for orchestra on January 20, 1926, in Rio de Janeiro, and Ottorino Respighi, during his Brazilian tour, presented Gallet's *Dansa Brasileira* for orchestra on July 6, 1928. Six of his piano pieces, two violin pieces, two cello pieces, and thirty-one songs have been published. His annotated collection of native songs and dances, *Estudos de Folclore,* was published posthumously in 1934, with an introductory biographical sketch of Gallet written by Mario de Andrade.

Radames GNATTALI (1906——) is of Italian parentage. He received elementary musical instruction from his mother, and later entered the Conservatory of Porto Alegre, where he completed his studies in piano. At the same time he began to compose. He has written two concertos and a Concertino for piano and orchestra, a *Poem* for violin and orchestra, a Suite for small orchestra in five movements in the form of Brazilian airs, and three *Miniatures* for chamber orchestra. For chamber music he has written a Violoncello Sonata, a piano Trio, a String Quartet, and a Concerto for Violin and Piano with the accompaniment of a string quartet. Of his piano works the most important is *Rapsodia Brasileira,* based on four folk themes. Gnattali has also written numerous songs. All of his music is in the native manner, either by actual use of Brazilian folk songs as material or by invention of original themes in the Brazilian manner. Gnattali's *Rapsodia Brasileira* has been published by Ricordi. His *Valsa* for piano is included in the collection *Musique Brésilienne Moderne* (Rio de Janeiro, 1937), and his *Chôro* for piano was published in the Brazilian issue of *New Music* (October, 1942). Gnattali's Second Piano Concerto was performed at the concert of the Chicago Symphony Orchestra on March 11, 1943.

Carlos GOMES, the opera composer of world renown, was born in Campinas, Brazil, in 1836, and died in 1896. His father, who was married four times and had twenty-five children, was a musician, and gave Gomes elementary instruction. At the age of fifteen, Gomes composed simple airs, and at eighteen wrote a Mass. In 1859 he went to Rio de Janeiro, where he entered the Conservatory. His first work to be performed was a cantata, *A Ultima Hora do Calvario*, which was given in Rio de Janeiro on August 16, 1860. In the following year, on September 4, 1861, Gomes' first opera, *A Noite do Castelo* (Night in a Castle), was performed. His second opera, *Joanna de Flandres*, was produced in Rio de Janeiro on September 15, 1863. Both operas were written in an Italian style, and the subjects were taken from the Crusades. In 1864, Gomes received a stipend from the Emperor of Brazil to go to Europe for further study. He settled in Milan, where he took private lessons with Lauro Rossi. In Milan he wrote his first work on a Brazilian subject, the opera *Il Guarany*. It was produced at the Scala Theater in Milan, on March 19, 1870, and received great acclaim. *Il Guarany* was destined to remain the most successful Brazilian opera, and the only one by a South American composer which has been in the active repertoire of opera houses the world over. *Il Guarany* is written to an Italian libretto, after a Brazilian novel by José Alencar, the central figure being an Indian of the Guarany tribe. But despite the Brazilian associations, the opera is Italian in structure and character of music.

After a brief visit to Brazil, where *Il Guarany* was staged in Rio de Janeiro on December 2, 1870, Gomes returned to Italy. His new opera, *Fosca*, on a romantic subject connected with Venetian pirates, was produced at the Scala in Milan on February 16, 1873. In this opera, Gomes introduces the system of leitmotivs, but otherwise the music has nothing Wagnerian in it. The opera *Salvador Rosa*, on a subject from Italian history, was performed in Genoa, Italy, on March 21, 1874. *Maria Tudor* followed, after the drama of Victor Hugo. It was produced at the Scala in Milan on March 27, 1879. In his next opera, *Lo Schiavo*, Gomes selects a Brazilian subject dealing with a romantic union of a nobleman and an Indian slave girl. The opera was produced in Rio de Janeiro on September 27, 1889. Gomes' last opera was *Condor*, with a plot somewhat resembling that of Verdi's *Aïda*, and the action placed in Samarkand. *Condor* was produced in Milan on February 21, 1891. On October 12, 1892, on the occasion of the four-hundredth anniversary of the discovery of America, Gomes' oratorio *Colombo* was presented at the Opera of Rio de Janeiro. Soon afterwards, it was found that Gomes had cancer of the tongue, attributed to an excess of smoking. He died at Belem, Brazil, on September 16, 1896.

In 1936, on the occasion of Gomes' centenary, the Brazilian government organized celebrations in his honor, and two postage stamps with Gomes' portrait and a musical quotation from *Il Guarany* were issued. In 1936, the *Revista Brasileira de Musica* published a voluminous commemorative issue dedicated to Gomes' life and works.

Camargo GUARNIERI (1907———) is a Brazilian modernist. His father was born in Sicily, and was taken to Brazil as an infant. His mother was of an ancient Brazilian family. Guarnieri was one of nine children in the family. He received instruction in the rudiments of music from his father, who was a band flutist. That his father intended Guarnieri to be a musician is manifest from the fact that he gave Guarnieri the middle name of Mozart, which, however, Guarnieri never uses, regarding it as presumptuous. Guarnieri's studies continued at the Conservatory of São Paulo, and in 1938 he was awarded a government fellowship for study in Europe. He took lessons in composition with Charles Koechlin in harmony, counterpoint, and orchestration, and returned to Brazil in 1940. In 1942 he visited the United States, and conducted his works with the Boston Symphony Orchestra, and other American orchestras.

Guarnieri's music is imbued with Brazilian folklore. He shuns actual quotation from popular songs, preferring to re-create the spirit of *Brasilidade* (Brazilianism) in original melodies. As to treatment, Guarnieri has expressed the belief that "Brazilian music ought to be treated polyphonically. The quality of our folk music, of its dynamic force, is such that we should avoid harmonization by chords. . . ." Mario de Andrade has called Guarnieri "the strongest polyphonic composer of Brazil."

Guarnieri has composed prolifically. For the orchestra he has written a symphonic poem, *Curuçá* (the Indian name of Guarnieri's native town of Tieté); a symphonic dance, *Pereréca;* ten *Ponteios* (dances in the rustic manner); three lyrical *Toadas; Dansa Brasileira* (in the rhythm of the *Samba*); *Dansa Selvagem* (Forest Dance); *Encantamento;* and *Abertura Concertante* (Overture Concertante, a composition of a strongly contrapuntal nature, in the neoclassical manner). For chamber orchestra, Guarnieri has written a work for fifteen instruments, *Flor de Tremembé*, which includes in its scoring the native instruments, *chocalho, reco-reco*, and *cuica.*

For the theater, Guarnieri has composed a comic opera in one act,

Pedro Malazarte, after a legend of colonial Brazil, and a "tragic cantata," *A Morte do Aviador*. For voice and orchestra, Guarnieri has written *Tres Dansas* (*Samba, Catereté, Maxixe*), *Desesperança*, and *Tres Poemas*. In addition, he has written three concertos—for piano, for violin, and for violoncello with orchestra. The Violin Concerto was awarded first prize at the contest for the best Latin American composition for violin and orchestra, held in Philadelphia in 1942. For chamber music, Guarnieri has written a piano Trio, a String Quartet, a group of four works under the title of *Chôro* and scored for wind instruments and Brazilian percussion, two violin sonatas, and a Violoncello Sonata. Guarnieri has also written over seventy songs, and fifteen choral works, to texts in Portuguese and in the Afro-Brazilian dialects. His list of piano compositions includes a Toccata, three sonatinas, ten *Ponteios* (also arranged for orchestra), *Dansa Brasileira* and *Dansa Selvagem* (which are the piano transcriptions of orchestral works), five compositions for children, and three waltzes.

The following orchestral works by Guarnieri have been performed: *Curuçá* (São Paulo, July 28, 1930, Villa-Lobos conducting), Concerto for Piano and Orchestra (São Paulo, December 30, 1936, under the composer's direction, with Souza Lima as soloist), *Toada Triste* and *Tres Poemas* (São Paulo, January 12, 1940, composer conducting), *Flor de Tremembé* (Rio de Janeiro, May 27, 1940), *Dansa Brasileira* (São Paulo, March 7, 1941, composer conducting), *Dansa Selvagem* (São Paulo, July 22, 1941, composer conducting), Violin Concerto (Rio de Janeiro, September 20, 1942), and *Abertura Concertante* (São Paulo, June 2, 1943, composer conducting).

The following piano pieces by Guarnieri have been published in Brazil: *Sonatina, Ponteio No. 1*, five children's pieces, *Dansa Brasileira, Dansa Selvagem*. His *Toada Triste* for piano is included in the Schirmer collection *Latin-American Art Music for the Piano* (New York, 1942). The *Valsa* for piano is published in the Brazilian issue of *New Music* (October, 1942). Two of Guarnieri's songs in the Afro-Brazilian vein are included in the album *Musique Brésilienne Moderne* (Rio de Janeiro, 1937). A song, *Macumba*, is printed in the music supplement to Volume I of the *Boletín Latino-Americano de Música*. The Fleisher Collection in Philadelphia has the orchestral scores of the Violin Concerto, three *Ponteios, Dansa Brasileira, Dansa Selvagem, Flor de Tremembé*, and *Abertura Concertante*. The orchestral scores and parts of Guarnieri's *Dansa Brasileira, Flor de Tremembé, Encantamento, Abertura Concertante, Dansa*

Selvagem, Suite Infantil, and the Violin Concerto are available at the Associated Music Publishers, in New York.

Arthur IBERÉ DE LEMOS (1901———) went to London in 1915; he studied violoncello with John Barbirolli and harmony at the Royal Academy of Music. He also studied in Berlin, and still later in Milan. Iberé de Lemos has written mostly in small forms, his most successful compositions being lyric songs of Brazilian inspiration. His harmonization is conventional, and his style derivative. His *Three Pieces* for voice and piano, *Momentos Liricos,* and *Canção Arabe* have been published.

Brasilio ITIBERÉ (1896———) was born in Paraná and studied composition in his native town. From the very first he dedicated himself to Brazilian folklore. He has written effective piano pieces and songs in the Afro-Brazilian manner, depicting the ritualistic dances of Brazilian Negroes. He has also written music in classical forms: two string quartets, a piano Trio, and pieces for the harpsichord, in which he adapts Bach's contrapuntal technique to Brazilian rhythms. His song *Cordão de Prata* was published as a supplement to *Musica Viva* in 1940.

João Batista JULIÃO (1886———) is a composer of choral music and educational pieces for schools, who is active as a pedagogue in São Paulo. His short piano pieces and choruses are published.

Hans-Joachim KOELLREUTTER (1915———) is a young German composer, resident in Brazil. He studied flute and composition, and gave concerts as a flutist all over Europe. In 1937 he settled in Brazil, where he is active as teacher, composer, and flutist. He has written a Piano Sonata; two violin sonatas; a Sonata for Flute and Piano; *Inventions,* for oboe, clarinet, and bassoon; Variations for String Quartet; and a set of *Brazilian Poems,* scored for voice, English horn, viola, bass clarinet, and military drum. He has also written *Variations 1940* and *Musica 1941* for full orchestra. In 1940 he launched, in São Paulo, the publication of a modern periodical, *Musica Viva.* Since 1943 Koellreutter has been flutist in the *Orquestra Brasileira* in Rio de Janeiro. Koellreutter writes exclusively in an atonal idiom. Since 1940 he has adopted the twelve-tone technique according to Schoenberg. The piano version of his *Musica 1941* has been published by the *Editorial Cooperativa Interamericana de Compositores* in Montevideo, and his *Inventions* and *Bagatelas* for piano were issued as a supplement to *Musica Viva.*

Souza LIMA (1898———), the pianist and composer, was born in São Paulo, and studied piano and composition in his native town. In 1919 he was given a government stipend for a trip to Paris, where he studied at the Conservatory in the class of piano and composition. Upon graduation in 1922, he traveled widely in Europe as a pianist. Souza Lima has written a number of piano pieces and songs, as well as an orchestral poem, *O Rei Mameluco* (The Mameluke King). Since 1936, Lima has conducted orchestral concerts in Brazil. Some of his piano music has been published by Ricordi.

Francisco MIGNONE, one of the foremost Brazilian composers, was born in São Paulo in 1897. He studied flute with his father, and later piano and composition at the Conservatory of São Paulo. In 1920 he went to Milan, where he studied with Ferroni. Mignone began to compose at an early age, and from the very first turned to Brazilian folklore for inspiration. Apart from his serious music, he has also written numerous popular dances and songs under the nom de plume Chico-Bororó (after the tribe of Bororó Indians). His first appearance as a composer took place in São Paulo on September 9, 1918, when he played his piano pieces. On December 16, 1918, his father and teacher conducted his first orchestral compositions, *Caramurú* and *Suite Campestre*. During his stay in Italy (1920–1924), he wrote his first opera, *Contractador dos Diamantes*. The action of the opera unfolds in eighteenth-century Brazil, and the central figure is a merchant of diamonds. The *Congada* from the second act of this opera has become Mignone's most successful orchestral piece. It was first performed with the title *Dansa* in São Paulo on September 10, 1922, under the direction of the composer. The opera was performed in its entirety at the *Teatro Municipal* in Rio de Janeiro on September 20, 1924. Mignone's second opera, *L'Innocente*, was produced in Rio de Janeiro on September 5, 1928. The subject of this opera is taken from Spanish history. Both operas are written to Italian libretti.

Of Mignone's numerous symphonic works, the early scores, *Farandola das Horas, Romanza, Dansa das Bruxas* (Witches' Dance), *La Signora del Fuoco, Marcha Triumphal*, and *Notturno Improvisto*, remain unperformed. *No Sertão* (In the Country), a symphonic dance of the *Congada* type, was performed in São Paulo on October 17, 1921. *Interludo* was performed in Rome, Italy, on January 12, 1923. The *Notturno-Barcarolla*, in two sections connected by a flute cadenza, was performed in São Paulo on August 15, 1923. On the same program was performed Mignone's symphonic dance *Scenas da Roca*. The following symphonic compositions by Mignone's have also been performed: the symphonic poem *Festa Dionisiaca*, in Rome on October 24, 1923;

Velha Lenda Sertaneja (Old Country Legend), in São Paulo on March 15, 1924; *Pelos Estrados Silenciosos* (Along the Silent Paths), in São Paulo on October 19, 1924; *Intermezzo Lirico* for orchestra, in São Paulo on May 13, 1925; a *Berceuse* for strings, harp, celesta, flutes, and oboes, *Ao Anoitecer* (Towards Night), on August 16, 1925; an orchestral song, *Cantiga de Ninar*, in São Paulo on November 6, 1926; and *Dansa Asturiana*, in São Paulo on May 18, 1930.

Mignone has written four characteristic Brazilian pieces for piano and orchestra entitled *Fantasia Brasileira*. The first was performed in São Paulo on March 20, 1931, Mignone conducting; the second in Rio de Janeiro on June 20, 1934, Villa-Lobos conducting; and the third and fourth in São Paulo on May 10, 1934, and October 30, 1937, respectively, with the composer conducting. To the same period belong a humorous symphonic poem, *Momus* (the nickname of a popular carnival character, usually called *Momo*), composed in 1929, and performed by Villa-Lobos in Rio de Janeiro on April 24, 1933; and *Seguida-Mirim* (meaning a "little suite" in the Guarany language), composed in 1931. To these works, all of which are based on native Brazilian rhythms and melodies, should be added *Maxixe* (1925). There followed the ballet *Maracatú de Chico-Rei* (the *Maracatú* of the Little King), produced under Mignone's direction in Rio de Janeiro on October 29, 1934. *Suite Brasileira*, in three descriptive movements, *Cucumbyzinho* (a little *cucumbi*), *Lenda Sertaneja* (Country Legend), and *Cateretê* (popular Brazilian dance) were performed in Rio de Janeiro by Burle Marx on December 9, 1933. *Butucajé*, performed in São Paulo on March 28, 1936, is an orchestral dance scored for modern orchestra with the inclusion of the native instruments *reco-reco*, *chocalho*, and *cuica*. *Babaloxá* (the name of an Afro-Brazilian chief) was performed in São Paulo on November 6, 1937, under Mignone's direction. On June 28, 1941, Mignone conducted in São Paulo his Variations on a Brazilian Theme. *Sonho de um Menino Travesso* (Dream of a Spoiled Child) is an orchestral stylization of an animated cartoon, in four movements. Mignone conducted this score in São Paulo on October 30, 1937. His humorous ballet, *O Espantalho* (Scarecrow), composed in 1941, is scored for an orchestra including a steam siren, police sirens, and a train whistle. His *Ouverture das Tres Mascaras Perdidas* (Overture to Three Lost Masks) was performed in Rio de Janeiro on November 28, 1936.

Parallel to the composition of symphonic works in a Brazilian vein, Mignone has, since 1939, turned his attention to music of social and religious content, as typified by his *Sinfonia de Trabalho* (Symphony of Labor), in four movements subtitled Song of the Machine, Song of the Family, Song of the Strong Man, and Song of Fruitful Work; and by *Festa das Igrejas* (Festival of Churches). *Festa das Igrejas*, depicting four well-known cathedrals of Brazil, was conducted by Mignone with the NBC orchestra of New York City on April 22, 1942, during his visit in the United States. Other symphonic works to be noted are *Seresta* (Country Serenade) for cello and orchestra, performed in Rio de Janeiro on March 31, 1939; *Leilao*, a ballet in six movements; and a symphonic dance, *Miudinho*, conducted by Mignone in São Paulo on June 28, 1941.

Among Mignone's compositions for chamber music, the most important is his Sextet for piano, flute, oboe, clarinet, bassoon, and horn. He has written a Violin Sonata, a String Quartet, eight pieces for violin and piano, and three for violoncello and piano. For piano solo he has written a Sonata, six Preludes, six Transcendental Etudes, and a great number of concert pieces, among them eleven Brazilian pieces entitled *Lenda Sertaneja*. There are also piano versions of Mignone's orchestral pieces, *Danza das Bruxas, Maxixe, Congada, Cucumbyzinho, Catereté*. Most of Mignone's piano pieces and songs are published by Ricordi, Carlos Wehrs, and the Casa Mozart. His Sextet has been printed by the University of Rio de Janeiro, 1937. Edward B. Marks in New York has reissued several of Mignone's *Lendas Brasileiras, Miudinho, Tango Brasileiro*, and other piano pieces. The following scores by Mignone are in the Fleisher Collection in Philadelphia: *Fantasias Brasileiras* No. 2 and No. 3, *Batucajé, No Sertão, Sonho de um Menino Travesso, Ao Anoitecer, Notturno-Barcarolla, Festa das Igrejas, Plenilunio, Suite Brasileira*, and *Congada*. Mignone's *Canção Brasileira* for voice and piano is included in the musical supplement to Volume I of the *Boletín Latino-Americano de Música*. It is recorded in the album *South American Chamber Music* issued by Columbia.

Mignone's melodic style is characterized by great emotional expressiveness. His harmonies tend towards the usage of the modern Italian school of composition. The rhythm of Mignone's music is characteristic of native dances, particularly the Negro dances of Brazil.

Leopoldo MIGUEZ (1850–1902) studied the violin, and began to compose rather late, in 1876, when he wrote a *Nuptial March*. He composed mostly for the orchestra and the theater. Of his symphonic works, the following are the more important: *Symphony, Parisina, Prometheus, Suite à l'Antique*, and *Scherzetto Fantastico*. His *Hymn of the Republic* was awarded first prize at the competition in 1889, upon the fall of the Empire. In 1890 he was appointed director of the *Instituto Nacional de Musica* in Rio de Janeiro, a post which he held until his death. Miguez wrote two operas: *Pelo Amor* (For the Sake of Love, to an episode from Scottish history) and *Os Saldunes* (The Comrades, from the era of Caesar's Gallic Wars). The first was produced in Rio de Janeiro on August 24, 1897, and the second on September 20, 1901. Both operas are imitative of early Wagner, while Miguez's symphonic music is redolent of German romanticism. The vocal scores of the operas were published in Germany. The scores of *Parisina* and *Scherzetto Fantastico* are included in the Fleisher Collection in Philadelphia. See *Leopoldo Miguez e o Instituto Nacional de Musica* in *Revista Brazileira de Musica*, 1940.

Radames MOSCA (1908——) studied piano at the Conservatory of São Paulo, and upon graduation traveled in Brazil as a pianist. He has written a number of piano pieces, particularly for children.

Arthur NAPOLEÃO, the pianist and music publisher, was born in Oporto, Portugal, in 1843, and died in Rio de Janeiro in 1925. He went to Brazil in 1865, and established in 1868 the music publishing firm which bears his name. He has also written some piano pieces and songs.

Ernesto NAZARETH (1863–1937) was a composer of popular music. Largely self-taught, Nazareth had an instinctive flair for native music and wrote a number of piano pieces in the Brazilian vein. His technique of writing for the piano was influenced by Chopin. Villa-Lobos said of Nazareth that he is "a true incarnation of the soul of musical Brazil."

Alberto NEPOMUCENO (1864–1920), the pioneer of Brazilian national music, studied piano with his father in his native town of Fortaleza, and in Recife. In 1880 he went to Europe, where he studied organ and composition at the Santa Cecilia Academy in Rome, and later in Berlin and in Paris. He returned to Brazil in 1895, and on August 4, 1895, gave a concert in Rio de Janeiro, appearing as organist, pianist, and composer of songs to German, French, and Italian texts. In Brazil he wrote a Symphony, *Suite Antique* for strings, and a lyric drama, *Artemis*, which was performed on June 14, 1898. To the same period belongs his first work in the Brazilian manner, *Suite Brasileira* for orchestra. In it Nepomuceno used folk themes of the Brazilian Negroes. The last movement is a *Batuque*. Another work of native inspiration was an introduction to the unfinished lyric drama *O Garatuja*, performed in Rio de Janeiro on October 26, 1904. In 1902 Nepomuceno was appointed director of the *Instituto Nacional de Musica,* a post which he held, off and on, until 1916. In 1910 he was delegated to the Brussels Exposition to conduct concerts of Brazilian music. He repeated these concerts in Geneva and Paris. His opera *Abul,* on a Biblical subject, was presented in Buenos Aires on June 13, 1913. Nepomuceno's music has been published by Arthur Napoleão: twelve piano pieces, a piano transcription of *Suite Brasileira,* songs and excerpts from operas, and songs to French and Italian texts. The score and parts of Nepomuceno's Symphony were published posthumously in 1937, under the auspices of the University of Rio de Janeiro. The full score of *Suite Brasileira* is in the Fleisher Collection. The historic role of Nepomuceno is that he was the first who determinedly introduced Brazilian folk music into orchestral literature.

Barrozo NETTO (1881–1941) studied at the *Instituto Nacional de Musica,* and after graduating embarked on a double career as pianist and composer. In 1906, he was named professor at the *Instituto.* As a composer, Netto excels in shorter forms. Without resorting to actual quotations from folk songs, he re-creates the spirit of Brazilian folklore in adeptly contrived rhythms. His best-known piano composition is *Minha Terra* (My Land), written in the style of a nineteenth-century salon piece. At least 120 of Netto's piano pieces and songs have been published in Brazil. Barrozo Netto also edited a number of piano pieces from the classical repertoire. An arrangement of *Minha Terra* for string orchestra and similar arrangements of Netto's short compositions—*Dansa Caracteristica, Ideal, Berceuse, Moto Perpetuo, Intermedio,* and *Paz*—are in the Fleisher Collection in Philadelphia.

João OCTAVIANO (1896——) studied piano and composition at the *Instituto Nacional de Musica* in Rio de Janeiro. On May 15, 1915, he presented the first concert of his own works. On June 30, 1919, he conducted in Rio de Janeiro the first performance of his symphonic poem *Victoria,* and on August 30, 1920, he presented his First Symphony. On November 2, 1923, Octaviano conducted his cantata, *Poema de Vida* (Poem of Life). On April 6, 1937, the opera of Rio de Janeiro performed Octaviano's one-act opera *Iracema,* to the legend of romantic passion induced by drinking a love potion. Another opera, *Sonho de Uma Noite de Luar* (The Dream on a Moonlit Night), has not yet been performed. On June 24, 1937, Octaviano conducted at the *Teatro Municipal* in Rio de Janeiro his ballet *Ondinas.* He has also composed *Batuque-Fantasia* for orchestra, based on the rhythms of the Afro-Brazilian jungle, several pieces in classical forms for string orchestra, and pieces for violin and violoncello. Over a hundred of his piano pieces and songs have been published by Arthur Napoleão. His style of writing is technically brilliant, while his harmonic idiom is academic. Of his many transcriptions of Brazilian popular songs for piano, the best known is *A Casinha Pequenina*. Octaviano is also active as a musical pedagogue, and is on the faculty of the *Escola Nacional de Musica* in Rio de Janeiro. He is the author of several manuals of theory and harmony.

Henrique Oswald (1852–1931) was the son of a Swiss named Oschwald, who abbreviated his name to Oswald. Henrique Oswald occasionally used the Brazilianized form Oswaldo. He studied music in Florence, Italy, and for some years served in Europe as a consular representative of Brazil. He was director of the *Instituto Nacional de Musica* in the years 1903–1906. He composed two grand operas, *La Croce d'Oro* and *Le Fate*, and a comic opera *Il Néo*. They were never performed. Oswald's Symphony in C major was presented at the Ibero-American Music Festival in Barcelona, on October 2, 1929. His Piano Quintet was published posthumously in 1937. Three of Oswald's works, the Symphony, *Paysage d'Automne*, and *Andante con Variazioni* for piano and orchestra, are in the Fleisher Collection in Philadelphia. Ricordi has published Oswald's *Serrana*, a short piece for piano, violin, and violoncello based on Brazilian rhythms, as well as six pieces for piano, and songs. Oswald's best-known piano composition is *Il neige*, which won the *Figaro* prize in Paris in 1902.

Jaime Ovalle (1894——) began to study music rather late, and played the violin and guitar in street bands of Rio de Janeiro and other Brazilian cities. At the same time he studied finance, and in 1933 was appointed financial attaché at the Brazilian embassy in London. He held this post until 1937, when he returned to Brazil and took the job of a customs inspector. As a composer, Ovalle has written primarily piano pieces and songs, based on Afro-Brazilian folklore. Of his piano works the most interesting are the three *Legendas*, which exploit native melodies in a quasi-Lisztian virtuoso manner. In the same vein is the suite *Descobrimento do Brasil*, originally intended as a symphonic composition in four movements. But it is in his songs that Ovalle succeeds most in bringing the spirit of Brazilian folklore to life. *Berimbau*, a jungle incantation, is particularly effective. The three *Legendas*, the *Descobrimento do Brasil*, several short piano pieces, and a number of Afro-Brazilian songs by Ovalle have been published by Arthur Napoleão.

Newton PADUA (1894———), violoncellist and composer, studied composition with Francisco Braga and later went to Rome, where he studied violoncello and church music. He has written several orchestral suites in the traditional European style, occasionally using Brazilian themes.

Arthur PEREIRA (1894———) went to Europe in 1915, where he studied at the Conservatory of Naples. Upon his return to Brazil, he was appointed instructor of composition at the São Paulo Conservatory. He has composed very little. His *Seis Peças Simples Monotonais Sobre Temas do Folklore Brasileiro* for piano has been published in São Paulo.

Assis REPUBLICANO (1897———), the Negro composer, studied with Francisco Braga and began to compose at an early age. His predilection is for vocal music, but he has also written several symphonic poems, mostly to native subjects, although without emphasis on specific Afro-Brazilian folklore. He has written four operas. The first, *O Bandeirante* (The Pioneer), was produced at the *Teatro Municipal* in Rio de Janeiro on October 3, 1925, and the second, *A Natividade de Jesus*, on March 25, 1937. The third, *Amazonas*, and the fourth, *O Ermitão da Gloria* (The Hermit of Glory), are as yet unperformed. Among Republicano's other works in large forms are a *Symphony of Multitudes*, for orchestra, chorus, and military band, and *Improviso*, for violoncello and orchestra. In his operatic style, Republicano follows the Italian tradition, and his harmonic idiom is conventional. His song *Magdala* has been published. The score of Republicano's *Improviso* is in the Fleisher Collection in Philadelphia.

Claudio SANTORO (1919———), the young violinist and composer, studied composition with Hans-Joachim Koellreutter, who initiated him into modern music. Santoro has adopted the twelve-tone technique, and writes exclusively in absolute forms, without reference to Brazilian folklore. He has written a Symphony for Two String Orchestras, a Symphony for Two Pianos and Chamber Orchestra, two violin sonatas, a Sonata for Violin Solo, a piano Trio, and *Divertimento* for seven instruments. His Sonata for Violin Solo, in the strict twelve-tone technique, has been published by the *Editorial Cooperativa Interamericana de Compositores* in Montevideo.

José SIQUEIRA (1907———) was born in Conceição, where he learned the rudiments of music from his father, the leader of the local military band. Later he played the trumpet. In 1927 he went to Rio de Janeiro, where he studied composition with Francisco Braga and conducting with Burle Marx. In 1940 he was appointed administrative director of the newly organized *Orquestra Brasileira,* and conductor of radio concerts with that orchestra. In 1944 he visited the United States. Siqueira has written prolifically, for the orchestra, for chamber combinations, for piano, and for voice. For the orchestra he has composed two overtures: *A Musa em Festa* (The Muse on a Holiday), *Visão* (Vision); three symphonic poems: *Os Pescadores* (The Fishermen), *Alvorada Brasileira* (Brazilian Aubade), *O Despertar de Ariel* (The Awakening of Ariel); Symphony in D minor; three symphonic Preludes; a symphonic suite *Cenas do Nordeste Brasileiro* (Scenes of Northeastern Brazil); five pieces for string orchestra; four *Dansas Brasileiras; Frevo* for brass ensemble; *Elegia* for violoncello and orchestra; and three works for voice and orchestra. For chamber music, Siqueira has written a piano Trio, a Violin Sonata, and a String Quartet. He has furthermore composed nine short violin pieces, seven compositions for violoncello, and sixteen pieces for piano, as well as choruses and songs. Siqueira is particularly successful in his Brazilian compositions, based on native folklore. His style of writing is rich in harmony, and his orchestration is brilliant. For atmospheric effects, Siqueira frequently resorts to parallel chord formations, progressions in whole-tone scales, and instrumental cadenzas. None of his compositions have been published. The following orchestral scores by Siqueira are in the Fleisher Collection in Philadelphia: *Dansas Brasileiras* No. 2 and No. 4; *Cenas do Nordeste Brasileiro, Mebo, Os Pescadores, O Despertar de Ariel,* and *Alvorada Brasileira.* The orchestral scores and parts of Siqueira's *Cenas do Nordeste Brasileiro, 5 Dansas Brasileiras, Senzala, Toada,* and *Uma Festa Na Roça,* are available at the Associated Music Publishers in New York.

Hekel TAVARES (1896——) was born in Satuba, the son of a wealthy plantation owner. He developed a predilection for folk music, and improvised airs in the native manner. Without the benefit of formal education, Tavares writes prolifically, in all forms, including symphonic composition. His Concerto for Piano and Orchestra bears the opus number 105. It is in three movements, entitled *Modinha, Ponteio,* and *Maracatú,* which represent three types of Brazilian folk song, urban, rural, and Negro. Tavares has also written a symphonic suite, *André de Leão e o Demonio de Cabelo Encarnado* (André de Leão and the Red-Haired Demon), based on Brazilian themes. While Tavares's style of writing is ingenuous, he compensates for his lack of technique with an innate feeling for Brazilian folklore. Several of his songs have been published.

Fructuoso VIANNA (1896——) studied piano and composition with Henrique Oswald in Rio de Janeiro, and in 1923 went to Paris for further study. Upon his return to Brazil, he was appointed instructor at the Conservatory of São Paulo. Vianna has written almost exclusively in small forms, for piano and for voice. His musical resources are rooted in Brazilian folklore, for which he has an intimate understanding. His style of writing tends toward impressionism, somewhat in Ravel's manner. His 7 *Miniaturas Sobre Temas Brasileiros, Dansa de Negros*, a children's suite for piano, and several songs have been published. His brilliant Brazilian dance *Corta-Jaca* is included in the album *Musique Brésilienne Moderne* (Rio de Janeiro, 1937).

Heitor VILLA-LOBOS, the foremost Brazilian composer, was born in Rio de Janeiro on March 5, 1887. This date has been incontrovertibly established by documentary evidence. His father, who was a writer and amateur musician, gave him his first instruction in the elements of music at the age of six. Soon afterwards, Villa-Lobos began to play on the viola, holding it like a small violoncello, in vertical position. At the age of nine he improvised variations on popular Brazilian tunes. His first organized composition was a piece for guitar which he called *Panquéca*, a made-up word for pancake. Very early in life, Villa-Lobos played the violoncello in the theaters and cinemas of Rio de Janeiro, and at the same time composed pieces for the guitar, piano, voice, and even for the orchestra. His first published composition was a salon waltz, but, after the first groping efforts, Villa-Lobos definitely engaged himself in the stylization of Brazilian folklore, with the purpose of shaping it into an art form. This has remained his principal ambition throughout his career as composer.

As a young man, Villa-Lobos traveled widely in the North and South of Brazil, and engaged in varied pursuits, including working in a match factory. He gave concerts in the interior of Brazil, and eagerly collected folk songs, seeking to establish the nature of national musical resources. His first composition in the Brazilian manner was a suite for small orchestra entitled *Canticos Sertanejos* (Country Airs), which he wrote in 1909. Returning to Rio de Janeiro, he took lessons in composition with Francisco Braga. He also read Vincent d'Indy's *Traité de Composition*. In 1918 he met in Rio de Janiero the pianist Artur Rubinstein and the

French composer Darius Milhaud, and heard for the first time the piano music of Debussy, which produced a profound impression upon him. In 1923 he went to Paris and became acquainted with the modern school of composition. By that time he was already the author of a great many works in all genres. He returned to Brazil in 1927. In 1932 Villa-Lobos was appointed Director of Music Education in the district of Rio de Janeiro by President Vargas. This appointment gave Villa-Lobos the occasion to test his revolutionary theories of musical instruction. Each year, on Brazil's Independence Day, September 7, he conducts an "orpheonic concentration" of several thousand school children, in a repertoire ranging from Handel to popular songs and patriotic hymns. The vocalization comprises not only recognizable words, but the so-called "orpheonic effects," percussive and explosive sounds, sibilation, and clapping hands. He has composed special rhythmic scores for chorus with orpheonic effects, of which the *Invocation to Metallurgy* is typical. Villa-Lobos has also developed a chironomic system of solfeggio, in which the position of the fingers indicates degrees of the scale. Coordinated with this educational program is the publication of Villa-Lobos' choral arrangements of Brazilian popular songs, in a volume *Guia Pratico* (Practical Guide), constantly supplemented by new editions. In recognition of the President's role in the educational program for Brazilian music, Villa-Lobos published a laudatory pamphlet, *A Musica Nacionalista no Governo Getulio Vargas.*

The creative productivity of Villa-Lobos is very large. He has written operas, oratorios, symphonies, symphonic poems, concertos, quartets, trios, sonatas, and a great number of piano pieces and songs. Much of Villa-Lobos' music for piano and for voice has been published, but many large works still remain in manuscript. It is difficult to compile a comprehensive catalogue of Villa-Lobos' unpublished works, in view of frequent duplication of material in compositions bearing different titles. For this side of Villa-Lobos, see *Some Aspects of Villa-Lobos' Principles of Composition*, by Lisa Peppercorn, in the February, 1943, issue of *The Music Review* of London.

Villa-Lobos has written five operas, *Aglaia, Izaht, Jesus, Zoë,* and *Malazarte,* but only one, *Izaht,* has been completed and fully orchestrated. The opera, written in 1913, shows the influence of the Italian *verismo,* somewhat in the Puccini tradition. The subject of *Izaht* is concerned with a Gypsy girl by that name, who is a member of the Apache gang in Paris. She falls in love with a viscount, not realizing that she is his illegitimate daughter, and is saved from incest when she dies protecting him from the gang. *Izaht* was produced in Rio de Janeiro in oratorio form, without stage action, on April 6, 1940.

Villa-Lobos' oratorio *Vidapura* (*Vida Pura*, Pure Life) was produced in Rio de Janeiro on November 28, 1934. It is defined by Villa-Lobos as "an oratorio written in the spirit of liturgic music, with all the rules and restrictions that this type of music requires." Villa-Lobos has written seven symphonies and a symphonietta. The First Symphony subtitled *O Imprevisto* was performed in Rio de Janeiro on August 30, 1920; the Second is subtitled *Ascension*. The Third Symphony is named *Guerra*. It is scored for a very large orchestra, with thirty-seven extra brass instruments. It was performed in Rio de Janeiro on July 30, 1919. The Fourth Symphony bears the subtitle *Victory*, and the Fifth, scored for orchestra and chorus, is named *Peace*. In 1944–45 Villa-Lobos wrote two more symphonies. The symphonietta is based on two themes of Mozart.

As a result of his travels in the interior in 1914, Villa-Lobos wrote an orchestral suite entitled *Dansas Africanas*, with the subtitle *Dansas dos Indios Mestisos do Brasil* (Dances of Mestizo Indians of Brazil). The Suite in three movements, with the Afro-Brazilian subtitles *Farrapos*, *Kankikis*, and *Kankukus*, was first performed in Paris on April 5, 1928. Also of jungle inspiration is Villa-Lobos' symphonic poem *Uirapurú*, written in 1917, which depicts nocturnal gatherings of Indians in the forests. Uirapurú is the name of a legendary Indian chief, whose playing upon the flute was said to exercise irresistible attraction to young Indian girls. The symphonic poem *Amazonas*, composed in 1917, portrays the experiences of an Indian virgin alone in the tropical jungle, pursued by unseen monsters. The orchestration of *Amazonas* abounds in novel effects, such as playing on the string instruments below the bridge, and the use of harmonics *glissando*. *Amazonas* was performed in Paris on May 30, 1929, and produced something of a sensation. The score is also arranged for a ballet under the title *Miremis*. To the same category of symphonic compositions on Indian themes belongs the suite *Tres Poemas Indigenas* for voice and orchestra (1926). *Suite Indigena Brasileira* was composed in 1920. Numerous other symphonic scores, which Villa-Lobos wrote between 1916 and 1920, were left unfinished, and in more than one case the manuscripts were lost. Several orchestral works were later converted into ballets, which accounts for the duplication of some of the orchestral scores in the catalogue of Villa-Lobos' works.

Not only the folklore of the jungle, but also the popular songs of the carnival and the historic airs of colonial Brazil have attracted Villa-Lobos. Thus, in *Descobrimento do Brasil* (Discovery of Brazil, originally written for a film in 1936), Villa-Lobos depicts the voyage of discovery, the settlement, and the thanksgiving. For his themes, Villa-Lobos uses old Portuguese songs, Indian folk songs, and, in the concluding section, a double chorus *a cappella*, in which the male voices sing a Gregorian chant, while the female chorus intones Indian songs in the Guarany language. From *Descobrimento do Brasil* Villa-Lobos drew four concert suites, comprising the following movements: *Introduction, Alegria, Adagio Sentimental, Ualalocé* (Amerindian chant), *Cascavel* (Bagatelle), *Impressão Moura* (Moorish Impression), *Impressão Iberica* (Iberian Impression), *Festa nas Selvas* (Festival in the Forest), *Procissão da Cruz* (Procession of the Cross), and *Primeira Missa no Brasil* (First Mass in Brazil).

Momoprecoce, composed by Villa-Lobos in Paris in 1929, is a suite drawn from the piano composition *Carnaval das Crianças Brasileiras* (Carnival of Brazilian Children), and arranged for piano, orchestra, and Brazilian percussion instruments. The title is the telescoped form of *Momo Precoce,* precocious *Momo,* or Child Carnival King.

The most original contribution of Villa-Lobos to Brazilian music is a group of twelve works entitled *Chôros.* Properly, *Chôros* is a street band of players of popular songs, but Villa-Lobos extends the name to mean any composition "in which the various aspects of Brazilian music, Indian and popular, achieve their synthesis." The first *Chôros,* in the popular vein, is written for the Brazilian guitar (*violão*) solo. The second *Chôros* is a duet for flute and clarinet, extremely dissonant in treatment, and reflecting some characteristics of Brazilian popular song. *Chôros* No. 3 is scored for several wind instruments and a male chorus. *Chôros* No. 4 is a quartet for brass instruments. *Chôros* No. 5, subtitled *Alma Brasileira* (Brazilian Soul), for piano solo, is one of the most popular of Villa-Lobos' compositions. It is cast in simple ternary form, with an explosively rhythmic middle section containing a quotation from a popular Brazilian song. *Chôros* No. 6 is a lengthy work, scored for an unusual combination of instruments, including the bombardine, guitar, and native percussion. *Chôros* No. 7 is written for flute, oboe, clarinet, saxophone, bassoon, violin, and violoncello. *Chôros* No. 8, No. 9, No. 10, No. 11, and No. 12, are complex works, requiring a large orchestra and a battery of native percussion instruments. The score of *Chôros* No. 10 includes a mixed chorus, which intones with savage intensity a popular

Brazilian song, *Rasga o Coração*. In his program notes for *Chôros* No. 10, Villa-Lobos writes: "This work represents the reaction of a civilized man to stark nature; his contemplation of the valleys of the Amazon, and the land of Mato Grosso and Pará. The vastness and majesty of the landscape enrapture and captivate him. The sky, the waters, the woods, the birds fascinate him. But little by little his humanity asserts itself: there are living people in this land, even though they are savages. Their music is full of nostalgia and of love; their dances are full of rhythm. The Brazilian song *Rasga o Coração* is heard, and the Brazilian heart beats in unison with the Brazilian earth." *Chôros* No. 11 is longer and more complicated in rhythm and harmony than *Chôros* No. 10. It is scored for piano and large orchestra, and takes over an hour to perform. *Chôros* No. 12, somewhat eclectic in style, is also written for a large orchestra, with Brazilian percussion instruments. To this list should be added a supernumerary *Chôros bis*, for violin and violoncello, short but extremely difficult to play.

Few performances of these large-scale compositions have been given. *Chôros* No. 10 was performed in Rio de Janeiro on December 15, 1926; *Chôros* No. 8, in Paris on October 24, 1927; *Chôros* No. 9 was conducted by Villa-Lobos in Rio de Janeiro on July 15, 1942; and *Chôros* No. 6, together with *Chôros* No. 11, on July 18, 1942. *Chôros* No. 12 was first performed by Villa-Lobos on his concert tour in the United States, when he conducted the Boston Symphony Orchestra, on February 23, 1945.

Villa-Lobos is not averse to humorous subjects, in the Gallic manner. Characteristic of this manner is his suite for strings, in three movements, *Musica Timida, Musica Misteriosa*, and *Musica Inquieta*. In similar vein is the suite of eight pieces for voice and chamber orchestra, *Epigrammes Ironiques et Sentimentales*. In 1929, in Paris, Villa-Lobos composed *Suite Suggestive*, subtitled *Cinemas*, in which he caricatured typical cinema programs, with parodied versions of Rossini's *William Tell Overture* and Sousa's *Stars and Stripes*. One of the movements is scored for three metronomes and two voices, with the accompaniment of violins, scraping bows against the back of the instrument. His *Saudades da Juventude* (Nostalgic Memories of Youth), written in 1940, in ten short movements, depicting the sounds and sights of the city streets, is half-humorous, half-sentimental in character.

Villa-Lobos likes unusual titles. His tremendously difficult Concerto for Violin and Orchestra, in two movements, *Alma Convulsa* (Convulsed Soul) and *Contentamento*, composed in 1920, was performed in Rio de

Janeiro on December 15, 1922. In 1941, Villa-Lobos added another movement *Serenidade*, and labeled the whole work *Fantasia dos Movimentos Mixtos*, so as to indicate the diversity of styles inherent in the music. His Concerto for Violoncello and Orchestra (1916), however, is free of such connotation. The suite *Martirio dos Insectos* (Martyrdom of Insects), written in 1916 for violin and piano, is in three parts with fanciful titles: *A Cigarra no Inverno* (Cricket in the Winter), *O Vagalume na Claridade* (The Glow-worm in the Light), and *Mariposa na Luz* (Butterfly in the Light).

Villa-Lobos combines a keen sense of humor with ostentatious science. He has developed a method of composition which consists of transferring the outline of a geometrical curve, or a photograph, to music paper, using the resultant melodic line as a subject for musical composition. At the instigation of an American journalist, he projected a photograph of the city of New York on music paper, harmonized the melody, and orchestrated the result. The orchestral version of this composition, under the title *New York Skyline*, was broadcast from Rio de Janeiro on the occasion of the opening of the Brazilian Pavilion at the New York World's Fair, on April 7, 1940. Villa-Lobos has similarly harmonized the outline of the mountain landscape at Bello Horizonte in Brazil.

His preoccupation with science has led Villa-Lobos to an audacious, but remarkably successful experiment, of applying Bach's contrapuntal technique to Brazilian folklore. The product of this experiment is the series of seven suites named *Bachianas Brasileiras*. The separate movements bear double titles, one Bachian and one Brazilian, as, for instance, Introduction (*Embolada*), Prelude (*Modinha*), Chorale (*Canto de Sertão, i.e.* Country Song), and Dance (*Miudinho*). In the second suite, the fourth movement, a *Toccata*, bears the subtitle *O Trenzinho do Caipira* (Little Train of a Rustic), alluding to the noise of local trains in the small communities of Brazil's interior. In the fourth suite, the *Chorale* has a constantly repeated B flat in the treble, which according to Villa-Lobos represents the cry of the jungle bird, Araponga. *Bachianas Brasileiras* are written for various instrumental combinations, and also exist in piano form.

In contrast to his music governed by an intellectual idea, Villa-Lobos' numerous compositions for children, most of them for piano, use the immediate appeal. His *Caixinha de Boãs Festas* (Little Box of Holy Night) is a fairy tale in eight pictures. In its orchestral form, it was performed in Rio de Janeiro on December 8, 1932. In 1929, Villa-Lobos composed a piano suite of ten pieces, entitled *Francette et Pia*, which depicts the visit of a Brazilian Indian boy, Pia, to France, where he meets the French girl, Francette. *Carnaval das Crianças*, from which Villa-Lobos drew the orchestral work *Momoprecoce*, is a piano suite of eight pieces illustrative of carnival scenes. Villa-Lobos' two suites of piano pieces, *Prole do Bébé* (Baby's Family), are a musical gallery of baby's toys and dolls. They are somewhat in the manner of Debussy's *Children's Corner*, but much more complex in pianistic and harmonic idiom. *Polichinelle* from *Prole do Bébé* No. 1 is very popular. Among his earlier children's piano pieces, written between 1914 and 1920, are two series entitled *Suite Infantil*; a group of twelve pieces, *Cirandinhas* (little rounds); and a group of sixteen pieces, *Cirandas* (rounds). The most popular piece from *Cirandas* is *Xô, Xô, Passarinho* (Hey, Hey, Little Bird).

Villa-Lobos' most formidable composition for piano is *Rudepoema* (Rude Poem), a lengthy work written in 1926 for Artur Rubinstein, and presenting great technical difficulties. *Rudepoema* has been orchestrated by Villa-Lobos, and the orchestral version was performed under his direction in Rio de Janeiro on July 15, 1942. Among piano compositions in folkloric vein, the *Saudades das Selvas Brasileiras* (Nostalgia of Brazilian Forests) and *Ciclo Brasileiro* are the most expressive. The *Ciclo Brasileiro* (1936) is in four movements, named *Plantio do Caboclo* (Lament of the Peasant), *Impressões Seresteiras* (Country Impressions), *Festa No Sertão* (Country Fiesta), and *Dansa do Indio Branco* (Dance of a White Indian). The piano writing here is effective without being too difficult. In similar vein is the poetic *Lenda do Caboclo* (Tale of a Peasant).

Villa-Lobos has written a considerable amount of chamber music: *Nonet* for flute, oboe, clarinet, saxophone, bassoon, harp, celesta, percussion, and mixed choir; a Quartet for flute, saxophone, harp, celesta, with the addition of female chorus; five string quartets; Trio for oboe, clarinet, and bassoon; three piano trios; two violoncello sonatas; and *Sonata-Fantasia*, subtitled *Désesperance*, for piano and violin. In 1923 Villa-Lobos wrote a Suite for voice and violin, in three movements, characteristic of Brazilian folklore. The violin is here made to imitate the guitar, while the vocal part presents a percussive recitative. To the category of chamber music also belong *Chôros* No. 2, No. 4, No. 6, No. 7, and *Chôros bis*. For voice and instruments Villa-Lobos has written an expressionist creation, *Poema da Criança e Sua Mama* (Poem of a Child and its Mother).

Among vocal works of Villa-Lobos, his twelve *Serestas* are outstanding. Varied in form and mood, these *Serestas* follow the idea of folkloric synthesis typified by the *Chôros*. Like the *Chôros*, the *Serestas* approach the *Serenade* in conception. *Historiettes* (1920) are impressionistic in character. Villa-Lobos has also made numerous arrangements of popular Brazilian songs, of which *Chansons Typiques Brésiliennes* are the most important.

The technique of composition applied by Villa-Lobos varies from the simplest kind of harmony (as in his music for children) to the ultimate in complexity (as in *Rudepoema* or *Chôros* No. 11). Of the same generation as Stravinsky, Villa-Lobos was not acquainted with Stravinsky's music until 1923, when he was forty-two years old, and certain parallels of technical procedures in his and Stravinsky's music should be regarded as coincidental. During his Paris period (1923–1926), Villa-Lobos was influenced by the impressionist style of composition. But owing to his lack of formal musical education, Villa-Lobos was compelled to rely on his own resources in musical technique. By predilection, he uses sonorous harmonies, often supported by powerful pedal points. Polytonality (particularly as typified by the combination of C major with F sharp major) is a frequent device in Villa-Lobos' music. This polytonality is also implied in his piano writing (as in *Prole do Bébé*), when the right hand plays on the white keys, and the left on the black keys. For special effects, Villa-Lobos uses clusters of chromatic tones, particularly in the low register of the piano. There is little polyphony in Villa-Lobos' music, and the contrapuntal lines are usually subordinated to the harmonic idea, even in such contrapuntally designed works as *Bachianas Brasileiras*. The rhythmic element is naturally rich and varied. Villa-Lobos' orchestration abounds in color, and the spirit of free improvisation pervades the score. Brazilian native instruments are used as a background rather than a substitute for standard percussion.

Villa-Lobos' orchestral and chamber music has been published by Max Eschig in Paris, including *Amazonas; Dansas Africanas; Chôros* Nos. 2, 3, 4, 7, 8, 10, and *Chôros bis; Nonet;* Suite for voice and violin; *Poema da Criança e Sua Mama;* Quartet for flute, saxophone, harp, and celesta, with female chorus; piano score of the Concerto for Violoncello and Orchestra; Trio for oboe, clarinet, and bassoon; piano Trios No. 2 and No. 3; String Quartets No. 2 and No. 3; *Sonata-Fantasia* for violin and piano; *Chansons Typiques Brésiliennes* (harmonizations of Brazilian melodies); *Rudepoema* for piano; *Saudades das Selvas Brasileiras* for piano; and the second suite of *Prole do Bébé*.

The piano pieces and songs have been published by Arthur Napoleão in

Brazil: *Carnaval das Crianças; Chôros* No. 5; *Cirandas; Cirandinhas; Dansas Africanas; Lenda do Caboclo; Prole do Bébé* No. 1; *Suite Floral;* two collections entitled *Suite Infantil; Ciclo Brasileiro; Bachianas Brasileiras* No. 4; *Sul America* (South America, based on folk themes of several South American countries); song collections in Portuguese and French, among them *Epigrammes Ironiques et Sentimentales; Historiettes; Serestas; Mariposa na Luz* for violin and piano, and several arrangements for violin of original piano pieces; *Pequena Suite* (Little Suite) for violoncello and piano, and also versions for violoncello of violin pieces; *Chôros* No. 1 for guitar; choral compositions, educational pieces, etc. Two *Preludios* for guitar by Villa-Lobos have been published as a supplement to *Musica Viva* (São Paulo, January, 1941). The *New York Skyline* and the "millimetrization" of the mountain chain at Bello Horizonte were published in the Brazilian issue of *New Music* of October, 1942. *Dansa* from *Bachianas Brasileiras* No. 4 is included in the Schirmer collection *Latin-American Art Music for the Piano* (New York, 1942). Several popular piano pieces by Villa-Lobos have been reissued in the United States by the Associated Music Publishers, Marks, Axelrod, and others. The following orchestral scores are in the Fleisher Collection in Philadelphia: *Amazonas; Bachianas Brasileiras* Nos. 1, 2, and 4; *Caixinha de Boās Festas; Chôros* Nos. 7, 8, 10, and 11. Concerto for Violoncello and Orchestra; *Descobrimento do Brasil; Momoprecoce;* Suite for string orchestra; *Suite Suggestive;* Symphony No. 3; and *Fantasia dos Movimentos Mixtos.* Various pieces by Villa-Lobos have been recorded in the albums *South American Chamber Music* (Columbia) and *Festival of Brazilian Music* (Columbia). Recordings of Villa-Lobos' chamber music have also been made in Brazil.

Several monographs on Villa-Lobos have appeared in the music press. See particularly "Brazilian Portrait—Villa-Lobos," by Burle Marx, published in *Modern Music,* October, 1939, and also "A Visit with Villa-Lobos," by Nicolas Slonimsky, in *Musical America,* October 10, 1941. Villa-Lobos' own autobiographical calendar, arranged year by year (but giving his birthday as 1888), was published in *Musica Viva,* No. 8 (1941).

Chile

. . . *la Patria Chilena, de mitros*
y de lauros coronada . . .
[LEONARDO ELIZ]

Chile occupies a narrow strip of land along the Pacific coast of South America, below the Tropic of Capricorn. Chile's length is thirty times its average width. The population of Chile numbers about five million, of which one hundred thousand are Araucanian Indians.

Chilean folklore is primarily Hispanic. The Araucanian Indians still surviving in the country are too few in number and too remote from the centers of cultural activities to exercise a marked influence on the national arts. Araucanian music exists as a heritage from the past, isolated from the present trends of Chilean folklore. There is much in Araucanian music which distinguishes it from that of other Indian branches. The Araucanian scales are not exclusively pentatonic, but contain intervallic divisions smaller than a semitone. The Araucanian instruments differ in many respects from those of other Indians. The Araucanian reed pipe, the *Trutruca,* which reaches two meters in length, is capable of producing only one sound, somewhat lugubrious in character. A smaller reed pipe is called the *Pifulka.* A unique instrument is the double musical bow, called the *Künkülkawe,* which consists of two strips of wood, or two animal bones, bent with a bowstring and interlocked like a chain of two rings. The sound is produced by rubbing on the bowstrings. Other musical instruments used by the Araucanians are the *Wada,* or *Huada,* which is a fruit shell filled with dry seed; the *Küllküll,* which is an animal horn, the *Pinkülwe,* a vertical flute; and the *Kultrun,* a flat drum. An illustrated description of Araucanian instruments is given by Carlos Isamitt in his articles published in Volumes I, III, and IV of the *Boletín Latino-Americano de Música.*

The living music of Chile is essentially Spanish in its inspiration and historic origin. The most popular air of Chile is the *Zamacueca*. It appeared in Chile in 1824, possibly by way of Lima. Its early popularity is attested by the fact that a *Zamacueca* was sung in the singing lesson scene in the opera *Barber of Seville*, when it was first produced in Chile about 1830. Up to 1850, the *Zamacueca* was sometimes called *Sambacueca*. There is no connection between the *Zamacueca* and the Brazilian dance *Samba*, which is of Negro origin.

The derivation of the name *Zamacueca* is obscure. The common theory is that the word comes from the compound *Zamba*, a Moorish festival, and *Clueca*, the clucking of the hen. In Bolivia and Argentina, the *Zambacueca* is called *Cueca*, *Cueca Chilena*, or simply *Chilena*. In Chile itself, the shorter name *Cueca* is commonly used for *Zamacueca*. In Peru, the *Cueca Chilena* was very popular up to the time of the war between Peru and Chile in 1879, when the name of the dance was changed, for patriotic reasons, to the *Marinera*, in honor of the Peruvian Marine forces.

The *Zamacueca* is always in the major key. Some writers see in this a reflection of the sunny and optimistic character of the Chilean people. Diego Portales, a powerful Chilean politician of the early republic, is said to have declared publicly: "I would not exchange the *Zamacueca* for the presidency itself." Portales never became president.

The *Zamacueca* is usually written in six-eight time, with the accompaniment in three-four time. Humberto Allende gives the following description of the *Zamacueca:* "Neither the words nor the music obey any fixed rules; various motives are freely intermingled. The number of bars is from twenty-six to thirty, and there is usually an instrumental introduction eight to ten bars in length. The last note of the melody is either the third or the fifth of the scale, never the octave."

Like most Latin American airs, the *Zamacueca* is sung as well as danced. The singing version is analyzed by Pablo Garrido, in his monograph *Biografía de la Cueca* (Santiago, 1943), as consisting of a quatrain corresponding to the Spanish *Malagueña*, and a period of eight verses corresponding to the *Seguidilla*. There is also a coda which summarizes the salient points of the verse, or proffers a moral. Garrido states also that only the tonic and the dominant are employed, modulations, particularly into the minor, being extremely rare. A typical *Zamacueca*, entitled *Tus Amores*, is included in Garrido's monograph.

Among the popular songs of the Chilean countryside, the *Tonada Chilena* enjoys great popularity. It is a lyrical air, usually in two sections, a slow part in three-four time, and a lively movement in six-eight time.

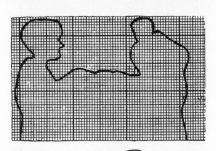

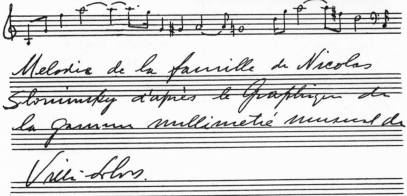

Heitor Villa-Lobos' "Melody of a Family"

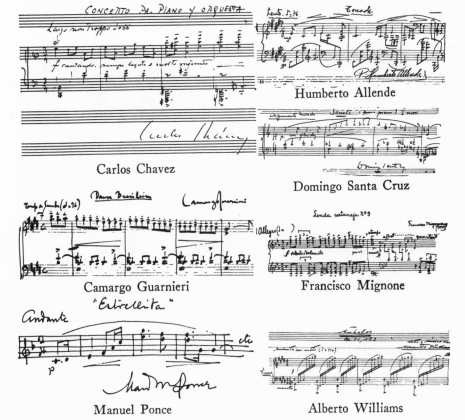

Humberto Allende

Carlos Chavez

Domingo Santa Cruz

Camargo Guarnieri

Francisco Mignone

Manuel Ponce

Alberto Williams

Some Musical Autographs

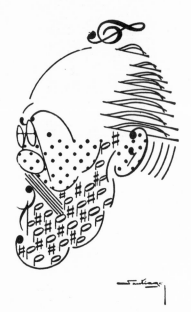

Carlos Pedrell, by Santiago

Julian Carrillo, by Enrico Caruso

Alejandro García Caturla,
by García Mora

Vicente Emilio Sojo, by
Alberto Egea López

"Tus Amores," a Chilean Cueca (*Garrido*)

Among urban songs, the *Esquinazo*, literally a street corner song, is a serenade, but is also sung as a Christmas carol.

The *Zapateo*, literally a shoe dance, which is common to all Latin America, has been popular in Chile for centuries. In his book, *Rélations du Voyage de la Mer du Sud*, the French traveler Frézier gives the musical notation of a *Zapateo* danced in Chile in 1713. The Spanish *Fandango*, which was popular in Chile in the eighteenth century, incurred the condemnation of the ecclesiastical authorities, as "an infamous dance, cultivated in the low classes, which leads to excesses of bestiality." A native air, called *Chocolate*, was also banned on account of its licentious and vulgar character.

The once popular air *El Parabién* shows the combined influence of Italian opera and Spanish operetta styles. It is characteristic of the salon music popular in Chile in the middle of the nineteenth century.

The first native-born Chilean composer was Manuel Robles (1780–1837), the author of the first Chilean National Anthem. The present Chilean Anthem was written by the Spanish musician Ramón Carnicer (1789–1855), who never visited Chile.

The first German musician to settle in Chile was Wilhelm Frick. In 1840, he published a piano piece entitled *Ein Deutscher Gruss aus Chile*. Another German, Aquinas Ried, wrote the first opera on a native subject,

Telésfora, which was produced in Valparaiso on September 18, 1846.

Chile possesses an excellent symphony orchestra, the *Orquesta Sinfónica de Chile,* established in Santiago in 1928, under the direction of its permanent conductor Armando Carvajal.

The first Conservatory of Music in Chile was established in Santiago by a government decree on October 26, 1849. Its history up to the year 1911 is presented in the now extremely rare edition *Reseña Histórica del Conservatorio Nacional de Música y Declamación 1849 a 1911,* which contains biographical sketches of 121 professors of the Conservatory, with 34 photographs.

A great impetus to the cultivation of native music in Chile was given by the formation of the *Instituto de Extensión Musical,* founded by the government decree of October 2, 1940, with the Chilean composer Domingo Santa Cruz as Director. Under the joint auspices of the University of Chile and the Institute, a national music festival was held in Santiago in November 1941, and numerous prizes were awarded for the best compositions by Chilean musicians. The University of Chile has also sponsored the publication of piano pieces and songs by Chilean composers, and books on native music. Of these, the scholarly volume by Eugenio Pereira Salas, *Los Origenes del Arte Musical en Chile,* published in 1941, and an annotated collection of native airs, under the title *Chile* (Santiago, 1943), are basic source books for the student of Chilean music. In May 1945 the *Instituto de Extensión Musical* began publishing a music periodical *Revista Musical Chilena.*

MUSICIANS OF CHILE

Adolfo ALLENDE (1890——), the music critic and composer, is the younger brother of Humberto Allende. He has written little. Among his published pieces of Chilean inspiration are *Nocturno Chileno* and six songs under the title *Talagante,* after a town of that name.

The pioneer of modern music in Chile is Humberto ALLENDE (1885——). He studied at the National Conservatory of Music in Santiago, where he was graduated in violin (1905) and composition (1908). He gave, at the Conservatory, the first performances of his Suite for String Orchestra on December 30, 1903, and an Overture in G major on September 15, 1904. In 1910, Allende received a prize for his Symphony in B flat in the competition on the occasion of the Centennial of the Independence of Chile. The prize money of 1500 Chilean pesos enabled him to make a trip to Europe. He visited Spain, Italy, Switzerland, and Germany. After a brief visit to Paris, he returned to Chile in May, 1911, and on May 10 he was named a member of the *Sociedad de Folklore de Chile*. In 1913, Allende wrote a symphonic suite in the native manner, entitled *Escenas Campesinas Chilenas*, in three movements: *Hacia la Era* (At the Threshing-Floor), *A la Sombra de la Ramada* (Under the Shade of the Foliage), and *La Trilla a Yeguas* (The Equestrian Tournament). This work, in which Allende uses some modernistic progressions, such as whole-tone scales, aroused the admiration of Felipe Pedrell, who called Allende *"El primer compositor futuro de su patria."* In 1915, Allende composed a Concerto for Violoncello and Orchestra, the score of which he sent to Debussy, and received a cordial reply in which Debussy commended the music for its rhythmic freshness. In 1920, Allende wrote his second symphonic poem in a Chilean style, *La Voz de las Calles*, performed in Santiago on May 20, 1921; it is based on the tunes of the street cries of Santiago vendors of eggs, lemons, or bottles. In the score of *La Voz de las Calles*, Allende makes use of the method of thematic integration, with the themes built up by the process of cumulation from melodic fragments in the exposition, a method suggested to Allende by a designer's drawings from a rendering, with the details filled in at the final stage. Between 1917 and 1922, Allende wrote twelve piano pieces, *Tonadas de Carácter Popular Chileno*, stylized native airs in harmonies touched with Gallic dissonance. Three of these *Tonadas*, arranged for orchestra and chorus *ad libitum*, were performed in Paris on January 30, 1930, with considerable success. Florent Schmitt found in the music "the folklore of the Andes, a synthesis of Inca airs and Arabic elements, imported in times immemorial by some Iberian Attila." Emile Vuillermoz praised the "ardent vitality" and "voluptuous rhythms" of the music, while Louis Aubert was impressed by the "strangely original inflections, which at once surprise and enchant." The orchestral version of three other *Tonadas* for large orchestra without chorus was performed by the *Orquesta Sinfónica de Chile* on April 27, 1936. *Tonada* No. 2 was played in Buenos Aires on November 23, 1941, in a transcription for twenty-two violoncellos and four double basses, made by A. Schiuma.

Among Allende's later works of large dimensions are *La Despedida* for two sopranos, contralto, and large orchestra (performed in Santiago on May 7, 1934), and two songs for soprano and orchestra (performed on July 4, 1938). His Concerto in D major for Violin and Orchestra, which received the second prize at the Quadricentennial Music Contest in Santiago in November, 1941, is more academic than his early works. It was first performed in Santiago on November 27, 1942.

Allende's international connections are wide. On March 24, 1924, he was elected a correspondent of the Folklore Society of Kharkov, Russia. When he made a trip to Europe in 1928, he was vice president of the Chilean delegation at the International Congress of Folk Arts in Prague, and on July 15, 1928, was elected director and European representative of the League to Combat Alcoholism. In 1929 he went to Europe once more, as the Chilean delegate at the Ibero-American Music Festival in Barcelona. Since 1928, Allende has taught composition at the National Conservatory in Santiago. Among his pupils were Amengual, Letelier, Nuñez Navarrete, and Urrutia Blondel. Allende is the author of *Metodo Original de Iniciación Musical* (1937) in which modern harmony is taught by progressively complex harmonizations of twenty Chilean songs.

The orchestral score of *La Voz de las Calles* was published in 1922 by the Chilean Ministry of Education. The miniature score of three *Tonadas* for orchestra and chorus was published by Sénart in Paris. Sénart has also published twelve *Tonadas* for piano; a *Preludio* for piano; four *Études* for piano; *El Encuentro* and *Debajo de un Limon Verde* for soprano and contralto with piano accompaniment; and *Ave Maria* for soprano and piano. The piano score of the second movement of the Cello Concerto is included in the collection *Músicos Chilenos* (Santiago, 1917). The University of Chile has published some of Allende's piano works: *Estudios* Nos. 5, 6, 7, 8, and 9; and six *Greek Miniatures*. Allende's songs *Mientras Baja la Nieve, El Surtidor, A las Nubes,* six *Cantos Infantiles,* and several school choruses have been published by the composer. Three songs and the *Prelude and Fugue* are included in the music supplements to Volume I and Volume IV of the *Boletín Latino-Americano de Música*. The English translation of Allende's paper on Chilean folk music is published in the Bulletin of the Pan American Union for 1931. *Tres Tonadas, La Voz de las Calles,* the Cello Concerto, and the Violin Concerto are available in the Fleisher Collection in Philadelphia.

A pupil of Allende, Pedro Nuñez Navarrete has prepared an extensive biography of Humberto Allende, which remains in manuscript. The September, 1945, issue of *Revista Musical Chilena* was dedicated to Allende when he received the National Music Prize of 100,000 Chilean pesos. Carlos Isamitt wrote a paper on Allende in Volume II of the *Boletín Latino-Americano de Música*. See also N. Slonimsky, "Humberto Allende—The First Modernist of Chile," in *Musical America*, August, 1942.

René AMENGUAL ASTABURUAGA (1911——) studied composition with Humberto Allende at the National Conservatory in Santiago. His early compositions, an orchestral piece, *Preludio* (1934), and a symphonic *Suite* (1937), are of little importance. Beginning with 1938, Amengual shows an awakening of talent. His Sonatina for Piano (1938), Ravelesque in spirit, is finely done, as is the brilliant *Introduction and Allegro* for two pianos (1939). His Concerto for Piano and Orchestra (1939–1941), written in a modern pianistic style, received first prize at the music contest in Santiago in November, 1941, and was performed on June 30, 1942. In 1943, Amengual made a trip to the United States. Amengual's *Album Infantil* for piano, and a song, *Caricia*, have been published by the University of Chile. *Transparencias* for piano is included in the music supplement to Volume IV of the *Boletín Latino-Americano de Música* (1938), and *Burlesca* in the album *Latin-American Art Music for the Piano*, published by Schirmer (1942). The score of Amengual's composition for voice and chamber orchestra, *El Vaso* (first performed in Santiago on August 25, 1944) is available through the Associated Music Publishers in New York.

Claudio ARRAU (1904——), the internationally known pianist, was born in Chillán, Chile. After a Conservatory course in Santiago, he went to study in Germany. His first appearance in the United States was with the Boston Symphony Orchestra on February 4, 1924. Since then he has toured widely in Europe and in South America. In 1927 he received the *Grand Prix International des Pianistes* at Geneva. His chief characteristics as a pianist are an unlimited technique and the extraordinary ability to digest all styles of classical and modern music.

Prospero BISQUERTT PRADO (1881——), composer, studied both music and military engineering. Between 1913 and 1923 he was employed in the Department of Domestic Revenue, and later was manager of several business concerns. Among his early compositions worthy of mention are *Preludio Lírico*, which received a prize on the occasion of the Centennial of the Independence of Chile; *Poema Pastoril* (1918); and a symphonic picture, *Primavera Helenica* (1919). His first musical work of native background is *Taberna al Amanecer* (Tavern at Dusk), in which he makes use of the rhythms of the Chilean national dance, *Cueca*. The work was first performed in Santiago on June 28, 1924, but the manuscript was subsequently lost when the trans-Andean train which carried a shipment of Chilean music to Buenos Aires burned on June 7, 1927. Bisquertt revised the score from memory in 1928. He went to Paris in 1930, and the first performance of the new version took place there on December 20, 1930. Bisquertt's symphonic poem *Procesión del Cristo de Mayo* was performed in Paris on January 15, 1931. His symphonic poem *Destino*, presented by the *Orquesta Sinfónica de Chile* on August 19, 1935, is characterized by parallel harmonic progressions, using the whole-tone scale profusely. His "symbolic drama" *Sayeda* was produced at the *Teatro Municipal* in Santiago on September 21, 1929. His suite for orchestra, *Nochebuena* (Christmas Eve) was performed by the *Orquesta Sinfónica de Chile* on July 27, 1936; a group of five orchestral sketches, entitled *Miscelaneas*, on June 7, 1937, and *Dos Emocionales* (*Elegía* and *Evocación*) on May 22, 1943.

Bisquertt's major work is a ballet in five movements, entitled *Metropolis*. The first movement, *Colonia*, is a minuet in the classical style. The second, *Pregón del Motero* (Vendor of Maize), evokes Chilean street folklore. The third, *Ciudad Moderna*, is a tribute to the machine age. The fourth movement, *El Botellero*, is the musical characterization of a bottle vendor. The fifth and last movement, *En una Fábrica* (In a Factory), employs special instrumental effects, such as soundless blowing in the trombones. Bisquertt has written a string quartet in three movements named *Aires Chilenos*. *Miscelaneas* (in the piano version) and *Tres Trozos* for piano have been published by the University of Chile. *Trois Esquisses pour Piano* (*Air Chilien, Marine, Paysage*) were issued in Paris in 1930. *Fiesta*, for piano, is included in the music supplement to Volume IV of the *Boletín Latino-Americano de Música*. The scores of *Taberna al Amanecer, Destino, Nochebuena*, and *Metropolis* are in the Fleisher Collection in Philadelphia.

Armando CARVAJAL (1893———) studied violin, piano, and composition at the National Conservatory in Santiago. From 1915 to 1927, he was the concert master in the opera at the Municipal Theater at Santiago, and, at the same time, taught violin at the Conservatory. In 1921, he was appointed conductor of the *Orquesta Sinfónica de Chile*. Virtually all first performances of Chilean works have been conducted by him. As a composer, he has written some children's pieces, which have been published by the University of Chile and by *New Music* (1939).

Juan CASANOVA VICUÑA (1895——), the conductor and composer, has since 1920 conducted concerts of symphonic music in Santiago and Viña del Mar. Casanova's suite of four pieces, *Cuatro bosquejos*, was performed by the *Orquesta Sinfónica de Chile* on May 30, 1931, and his symphonic poem, *El Huaso y El Indio*, on August 13, 1943.

Acario COTAPOS (1889——) studied piano and composition in Santiago, and in 1916 went to New York, where he took additional lessons with ten different teachers, including Ernest Bloch. In New York Cotapos became associated with the International Composers' Guild, under whose auspices his *Three Preludes for Orchestra* were performed on February 8, 1925. From New York, Cotapos went to Paris, where his *Four Preludes for Orchestra* were given on May 10, 1930, and *Voces de Gesta* on June 21, 1933. Cotapos has also written *L'Appel de la Terre* (1926) and *Le Détachement Vivant* (1928), for voice and chamber orchestra. Cotapos has developed a technique of thematic mottoes. For instance, his Prelude No. 4 for orchestra is based on a single combination, D-F-G♯-B-C♯-E-F♯-G, used both harmonically and melodically. The only published music by Cotapos is an excerpt from *Voces de Gesta*, in a reduction for voice and piano, and a piano Prelude printed by the University of Chile in 1938.

Pablo GARRIDO (1905——), the conductor and composer, was born in Valparaiso. At the age of eight, he lost his right leg in a trolley car accident, a handicap which, however, did not deter him from a musical career. In 1923, he formed the first Chilean jazz band. On January 21, 1925, he presented in Valparaiso a program announced as a concert of futurist music, which featured works of European modernists. He has traveled widely in the Americas and in Europe, associating himself with the intellectual and musical vanguard. As a result of his cosmopolitan connections, he was arrested at Antofagasta in 1932 on a charge of being a Soviet agent. This episode forced him to abandon Valparaiso and to settle in Santiago, where he is now president of the Orchestral Syndicate. Garrido has written two orchestral works, *Fantasía Submarina* for strings and piano and *Rapsodia Chilena* for piano and orchestra, the latter presenting a species of Chilean jazz. He conducted these scores for the first time at a concert of his compositions given in Santiago on August 3, 1938. His other works on the same program were *Ventana de Jazz*, *Interludio Dramatico*, *Pieza a Cuatro*, *Apunte Afro-Cubano* (all for various instrumental combinations), and five songs. None of his compositions are published. *Fantasía Submarina* and *Rapsodia Chilena* are in the Fleisher

Collection. Garrido has published a pamphlet, *Tragedia del Músico Chileno*, in which he deplores the lack of musical opportunities in Chile, and an important monograph, *Biografía de la Cueca* (1942). In March, 1945, he launched the publication of a music periodical, *Vida Musical*.

Carlos Isamitt (1885——) both as painter and musician, leans towards nativism. He has made a study of the music of the Araucanian Indians, and has arranged the native airs in his *Friso Araucano*, a collection of ten songs of different moods: songs for a child, women's chants, songs of the laborer in the field, music for games, rituals, and burials. Araucanian folklore is also reflected in his piano sonata, titled *Evocación Araucana*. *Pastorales* for violin and piano present Araucanian melodies in an atonal setting. Isamitt's major work is a *Suite Sinfónica* (first performed in Santiago on May 18, 1936), in three movements subtitled respectively: *Pregón Santiaguino* (Santiago Street Vendor), *Se Atraviese un Bosque* (Going through the Woods), and *Wirafun Kawellu* (Horses Galloping), the latter being an Araucanian dance, arranged in dissonant harmonies. The spirit of Araucanian music pervades Isamitt's ballet *El Pozo de Oro*, which received the second prize for a theatrical work at the national contest in November, 1941. Isamitt's piano pieces, *Pichi Purun* and *Estudio*, and a song, *Quietud*, have been published by the University of Chile. The piano version of *Wirafun Kawellu* is printed in the music supplement to Volume I of the *Boletín Latino-Americano de Música*, and *Estudio* No. 3 is included in the supplement to Volume IV of that publication. Isamitt has contributed several papers on Araucanian instruments to the *Boletín* and other publications.

Carlos Lavín (1883——) is a musician whose major interest is folklore. He spent a number of years in Europe, working in the libraries of the entire continent. He settled in Barcelona, and contributed a number of articles to Spanish musical publications. In 1943, Lavín returned to Chile, where he resumed his research work in native folklore.

Alfonso Leng, the composer and dentist, was born in Santiago in 1884. His father was German and his mother British. As a dentist, he has achieved a prominent position in his country, and has published a treatise on parodontia. Leng studied music with Enrique Soro at the National Conservatory of Santiago. His early works are songs generally in the Schumann tradition, to German and French texts. Leng's first symphonic work of importance is *La Muerte de Alsino* (Alsino is a Latin American Icarus), which was performed in Santiago on May 30, 1931. *Canto de*

Invierno, for orchestra, is a short work of romantic inspiration. It was first performed in Santiago on May 19, 1933. Leng's most effective work is a *Fantasía* for piano and orchestra, which employs modern harmony, and which concludes on an unresolved chord of the tonic seventh. *Fantasía* was first performed in Santiago on August 28, 1936, and was also played in London by the BBC Orchestra on April 10, 1941. The University of Chile has published several of Leng's pieces: *Doloras, Four Preludes, Poema, Preludio* No. 6, *Otoñales* for piano, and *Cima* for voice and piano. *Preludio* No. 7 for piano was published in the music supplement to Volume IV of the *Boletín Latino-Americano de Música.* The Fleisher Collection in Philadelphia has the scores of *La Muerte de Alsino* and *Fantasía.*

Alfonso LETELIER LLONA (1912——) studied music with Humberto Allende at the National Conservatory, and at the same time enrolled at the Agricultural College, graduating in both music and agronomy in 1935. Letelier began to compose at an early date, and at the age of fourteen presented his Suite for string orchestra in public performance. He then undertook the composition of a sacred opera, *Maria Magdalena,* but it was left unfinished. His *Dos Canciones* for voice and orchestra were performed in Santiago on June 15, 1936. His most mature orchestral work is *La Vida del Campo,* for piano and orchestra, which received the third prize at the Quadricentennial Music Contest in Santiago in 1941. Letelier writes in a romantic vein, and his music is characterized by chromatic harmony and flowing melody. His eight *Canciones* for mixed choir are published by the *Editorial Cooperativa Interamericana* in Montevideo. The University of Chile Press has printed Letelier's *Suite Grotesca* for piano, and a song, *Otoño.* The Fleisher Collection in Philadelphia has the score of *Vida del Campo.*

Carmela MACKENNA (1879——), great-granddaughter of General Mackenna, the hero of Chilean independence, and the maternal aunt of the Chilean composer Alfonso Leng, did not begin to study music until the age of fifty, when she took lessons with Hans Mersmann in Berlin. Since 1931, she has written a number of compositions distinguished by a compact polyphonic style: four Preludes for piano (1931), a Sonata for Violin and Piano (1931), a Trio for flute, violin, and viola (1932), a Concerto for Piano and Chamber Orchestra (1933), two *Orchesterstuecke* (1935), a Mass (1936), and a Trio for violin, viola, and cello (1936). Her Concerto for Piano and Chamber Orchestra was performed by the

Radio Orchestra in Berlin, on May 21, 1934. Its score, privately published in Germany, is in the Fleisher Collection in Philadelphia.

Hector MELO GORICOYTÍA (1899——) has studied mining engineering as well as music. His short orchestral piece, *Lobo* (1923), is crude, but some of his other music, as, for instance, *La Trilla* for piano, is of interest. His piano pieces, *Manchas de Color*, were published in 1930.

Samuel NEGRETE WOOLCOCK, the composer, was born in Santiago in 1893. (The name Woolcock is that of his maternal grandfather, who was British.) He studied music and architecture, and became a professor of music theory in 1920. At one time, Negrete taught mathematics. His major work is *Escenas Sinfónicas*, first performed by the *Orquesta Sinfónica de Chile* on July 2, 1934, and based on Chilean rhythms. His harmonic technique is that of early Debussy; whole-tone scales are employed for atmospheric effects. Negrete has written two string quartets and several piano pieces, of which *Sendero* has been published by the University of Chile. Negrete's *Danza* is published in the music supplement to Volume IV of the *Boletín Latino-Americano de Música*. The score of *Escenas Sinfónicas* is included in the Fleisher Collection in Philadelphia.

Pedro NUÑEZ NAVARRETE (1906——) studied in Santiago with Humberto Allende. He has written songs, violin pieces, and piano compositions, of which *Evocación* for piano is published. In 1939 he wrote a String Quartet, and in 1941 completed his magnum opus, *Sinfonía de los Andes*, a lengthy orchestral score in four movements portraying morning, afternoon, evening, and night in the Andes. The static harmonies of the music are explained by the composer as reflecting the "immanent statism" of the Andean landscape. The score of the *Sinfonía de los Andes* is included in the Fleisher Collection in Philadelphia.

Domingo SANTA CRUZ WILSON (1899——) is well-known as both composer and educator. The name Wilson is that of his maternal ancestors. He studied law, and after completing his studies in jurisprudence he became second Secretary of the Chilean Legation in Spain (1921–1924). He studied music with Enrique Soro (1917–1920), and later with Conrado del Campo in Madrid. In 1928, he was appointed professor of Music History and Analysis at the National Conservatory in Santiago. In 1933, he became Dean of the Faculty of Fine Arts of the University of Chile. On October 2, 1940, Domingo Santa Cruz was appointed President of the

Council of the newly created *Instituto de Extensión Musical*, and charged with organization of musical activities in Chile, the funds to be derived from a special tax. Under his direction, the Faculty of Fine Arts of the University of Chile has inaugurated the policy of furthering the cause of national music. He has arranged the publication of piano pieces and songs by Chilean composers, and supervised recordings of Chilean compositions by the Santiago branch of the Victor Company. Urrutia Blondel has described Domingo Santa Cruz as "a Hercules of a hundred deeds and a thousand worries."

As a composer, Santa Cruz cultivates a neoclassical type of composition, contrapuntally conceived, but not without romantic connotations. As a craftsman, he has been called the Chilean Hindemith. Domingo Santa Cruz has written in all genres. His *Viñetas* for piano (1927), in four brief movements entitled *Galante, Desolada, Clasica*, and *Grotesca*, follows the plan of a classical suite. *2 Canciones* for four voices (1926) are modern counterparts of Bach's chorales. *5 Poemas Tragicas* for piano come close to atonality. The last of these "tragic poems" is built around a persistent B flat, which is repeated 689 times. *4 Poemas de Gabriela Mistral* (1928) are in a neoromantic vein. *Imagenes Infantiles* (1933), in two series of four pieces each, are polytonal pieces for children. The String Quartet (1932) is neoclassical in texture. *3 Piezas* for violin and piano, *Canción, Recitativo*, and *Arabesco* (1938) are effective concert pieces. *Cantos de Soledad* (1936)—a group of three songs, *Dolor, Madre Mia*, and *Canción de Cuna*—are notable for their romantic coloring. The most characteristic work of Santa Cruz's neoclassical period is a suite for string orchestra, *5 Piezas Breves*. Composed in a week's time, it was first performed by the *Orquesta Sinfónica de Chile* on May 31, 1937. In a similar manner are the Variations in three movements for piano and orchestra, first performed in Santiago on June 25, 1943. The most significant work of Domingo Santa Cruz is the *Cantata de los Rios de Chile*, for chorus and orchestra, in three parts subtitled Madrigals, each representing a familiar landmark of the Chilean landscape. The first Madrigal depicts the mighty mountain stream, Maipo; the second, the great mountain Acancagua; and the third, the lake country, Valdivia. Despite the programmatic intent, there are no quotations from Chilean folklore, the sole exception being the oboe theme in the second movement, which is a reminiscence of the police whistle heard by Santa Cruz in his childhood. The choral writing of the *Cantata de los Rios de Chile* is free and unimpeded by the orchestra. The tonality is enhanced by the addition of diatonic tones to the fundamental chords. Thus, the first Madrigal ends on an unresolved chord of the tonic seventh.

The *Cantata* was awarded the first prize of 25,000 Chilean pesos at the Santiago Music Contest in November, 1941, but the award was declared void by the Government Committee under the specious pretext that Domingo Santa Cruz, in his capacity of Dean of the Faculty of Fine Arts, had no moral right to submit a work of his own, a decision which aroused violent protests on the part of the Society of Chilean Composers. On November 27, 1942, the first and second movements of the *Cantata* were performed in Santiago with great success.

Alfonso Leng gives the following appreciation of Santa Cruz as a musician: "In Santa Cruz's technique, we admire the extraordinary ability in moving four, five, or more voices with complete freedom of expression. This Santa Cruz owes to his patient and constant study of the polyphonic works of Bach. We admire, too, the vigor of his propulsive rhythms, the wealth and sobriety of his harmony, and the force of his palpitating counterpoint, which intensifies the inner drama of his music. The art of Santa Cruz is truly modern, not only in its material, but also in its spirit."

The following compositions by Santa Cruz have been published in Santiago: *Viñetas, 2 Canciones,* the second of the *4 Poemas de Gabriela Mistral, 5 Poemas Tragicas, Cantos de Soledad,* and *Imagenes Infantiles. Serenidad* for piano is included in the music supplement to Volume IV of the *Boletín Latino-Americano de Música. 3 Piezas* for violin and piano are published by *New Music.* The pieces appeared in the April, 1939, issue of *New Music,* but, because of numerous misprints, the edition was withdrawn, and reissued in 1941, with the errors corrected. These violin pieces have been recorded in the album *South American Chamber Music,* issued by Columbia in 1941.

Enrique SORO (1884————), having shown musical aptitude at an early age, was sent by the Chilean government to Italy for study. On June 18, 1903, his first composition, a String Quartet, was played at the Milan Conservatory. He graduated from that Conservatory in 1904, and subsequently gave concerts of his compositions in Italy and France. Upon his return to Chile in 1905, he was named professor of harmony and counterpoint at the National Conservatory at Santiago.

Soro has traveled widely as a pianist, in South America, North America, and Europe, and up to 1938 he had given 163 concerts in Chile and 112 abroad. From 1919 to 1928, Soro was director of the National Conservatory of Santiago. In a eulogistic brochure by Alvaro de Triana, entitled

Una Gloria del Arte Nacional, Soro is described as "the pride of Chile, of America, and of the Latin race."

The catalogue of Soro's works issued in Santiago in 1928 gives a lengthy list of his music published by Schirmer and Ricordi, including fifty pieces for piano, three sonatas, eighteen songs, a Violin Sonata, three pieces for violin with piano accompaniment, a Trio, a Quintet, six pieces for theater orchestra, a symphonic Suite, and a Piano Concerto. Among Soro's unpublished works are an early String Quartet, a Violin Sonata, and a Piano Sonata. Of his orchestral works, *Sinfonía Romantica,* in four movements, and *Suite Sinfónica No. 1,* in five movements, remain in manuscript. *Suite Sinfónica No. 2* is published by Ricordi. It is in five movements with romantic titles: *Nocturno, Recuerdo Lejano, Inquietud, Meditación,* and *Hora Mística.* The suite was first performed by the Santiago Symphony Orchestra, with Soro conducting, on May 9, 1919. Soro's music is agreeable to the ear, and effectively written for the instruments. His harmony and form are, however, entirely within academic precepts.

Jorge URRUTIA BLONDEL (1905——) studied with Humberto Allende and Domingo Santa Cruz. On April 12, 1928, Urrutia became the Secretary of the National Conservatory of Santiago, and in July, 1928, he received a scholarship for a trip to Europe. He studied with Paul Dukas, Nadia Boulanger, and Charles Koechlin in Paris, and with Hindemith in Berlin. Upon his return to Chile, in 1931, Urrutia began to compose in the native vein, drawing inspiration from Chilean folklore. His *3 Coros Infantiles de Carácter Chileno* (1938), written for two and three voices, *a cappella,* are, in the words of Carlos Isamitt, "designed to familiarize the children with the musical expression of the people of Chile, in the musical language of today." In 1941 Urrutia wrote a suite scored for a small orchestra of strings, harp, and celesta, entitled *Estampas de Chile,* which received a prize at the Music Contest in Santiago in November, 1941. The score of the *Estampas de Chile* is included in the Fleisher Collection of Philadelphia. Urrutia is also the author of a ballet, *La Guitarra del Diablo* (1941), partially performed in Santiago on November 27, 1942.

Colombia

. . . *el bello nombre de Colombia* . . .
[JOSÉ JOAQUÍN OLMEDO]

Colombia is the fourth largest South American republic, and has a population of nine million, of which nearly one-third are of Spanish extraction, one-half Mestizos, and the rest Negroes and Indians. Colombia's capital, Bogotá, is often called the Athens of Latin America, for its cultivation of literature and science.

The musical folklore of Colombia is derived from Spanish, Negro, and Indian sources. The Spanish influence is strongest in the melodic inflection of country dances. The Negro element enters strongly in the percussive rhythms of Colombian popular music. The monotonous chants of the Indians survive in their primeval solemnity in the interior.

In his book *Folklore Colombiano* (Barranquilla, 1942), Emirto de Lima characterizes Colombian folk music in these words:

In Colombian music we find elements of the culture of three races that have passed through Latin America. Listening to the beat of a drum, one conjures up a picture of African slaves driven down the coast during an era now happily past. In the dolorous chants of the Indians of the Amazon region, there is the wistfulness of the aborigines, who express their yearnings in the melancholy sounds of the flutes. And when a dapper boy, or a young lady of Santander or Cundinamarca, picks up a guitar and recites a sentimental ballad, one is transported as if by magic into ancient Spain. What a delight it is to recapture in these rhythms, chords, dissonances, accents, and gambols, the aura of the old romance, the passions and ardors of bygone days.

The most characteristic of Colombia's airs and dances is the *Bambuco*. Its name points to African origin, for there is a town in Western Africa named Bambuk, whence slaves were first imported into Colombia. In its present form, the *Bambuco* is a dance-song in the characteristic combined meter of three-four and six-eight, with an opening upbeat of three eighth-notes. In choreography it is a "pursuit dance," in which the male partner pursues the female, until they unite and continue the dance together. The

Bambuco is usually sung to the accompaniment of a *tiple* (a three-string guitar) and *bandolas* (Latin American lutes).

A Colombian poet finds in the *Bambuco* the combined strains of Indian melancholy, African ardor, and Andalusian valor:

> . . . *ha fundado aquel aire*
> *la indiana melancolia,*
> *con la africana ardentia,*
> *y el guapo andaluz donaire.*

The Colombian *Pasillo* is closer to Spain than the *Bambuco*. Like the *Bambuco*, it is cast in the dual meter of three-four and six-eight, but it is more flowing, less sharply accented. Emirto de Lima writes on the *Pasillo:* "Its rhythm stresses the first beat in the classical manner, then abandons itself to the blandishments of a tender second beat, and joyfully explodes on the third and last beat. The *Pasillo* possesses the aristocracy and the distinction of the *Waltz*, the light cadence of the *Contradanza*, the winged subtlety of the *Gavotte*, and the serene grace of the *Minuet*."

If the *Bambuco* is African, and the *Pasillo* is Spanish, the *Torbellino* is Indian. Its rhythm is more persistent, with the emphasis laid on the strong beat. The meter remains three-four. A rustic dance, the *Porro*, popular in the province of Santa Marta, has lately acquired the rhythm of a Foxtrot, and has now spread in this form in dance bands.

The *Guabina*, a quick dance in two-four, is popular in the provincial towns of Colombia. It is danced by couples holding hands. The *Galerón*, which is a ballad of the plains of the interior, should be mentioned. Here the melody and the rhythm are subordinated to the text, and follow the prosody of the lines of the narrative. *La Chispa*, an old air, sung to the accompaniment of the *Gaita*, *Tambor*, and *Guacharaca*, is still heard in the northern provinces.

The natives of Colombia still use musical instruments of the pre-Columbian era. There is a jungle drum *Manguaré*, which is a hollowed-out trunk of a tree. Another jungle drum, the *Cununú*, is covered on one side with an animal hide, and is stood up vertically. The *Bombo* has membrane covers on both ends, and is played with fingers or hands.

A curious native instrument is a musical bow, the *Timbirimba*, on which the sound is produced by rubbing the string with a wooden stick. The pitch depends on the tautness of the string, which may be altered at will.

The Cuban *Maracas*, or shakers, are also widely used in Colombia and are known under a variety of names, *Chucho*, *Alfandoque*, *Guaché*,

Colombian Chispa (*Emirto de Lima*)

Guazá, Carangano, or *Sonaja.* The indigenous notched gourds, similar to the Cuban *Güiro,* are called *Carraca* or *Guacharaca.*

Colombia's recorded music history dates back to a Jesuit priest José Dadey (1574–1660) who established a system of teaching church music. Towards the end of the eighteenth century attempts were made to introduce music on state occasions. An instrumental ensemble called *La Banda de la Corona* was formed in Bogotá in 1784. The first original compositions written in Colombia were two patriotic songs, *La Vencedora* and *La Liberadora,* the latter dedicated to Bolivar. Early in the nineteenth century, European musicians began to settle in Colombia. Among them was an Englishman, Henry Price (1819–1863), a prolific composer of popular songs and marches, who organized the first professional music school in Bogotá in 1847. His son, George W. Price, took over the direction of the school after his father's death. In 1910, the Colombian composer, Guillermo Uribe-Holguin, assumed the leadership of the institution, which was then officially renamed *Conservatorio Nacional de Música.*

European operatic music was popularized in Colombia by Italian opera companies. An Italian tenor, Oreste Sindici, was the author of the Colombian National Anthem.

The first opera written by a native composer was *Esther* by José María Ponce de León (1846–1882), which was produced in Bogotá on July 2, 1874. Other Colombian musicians of the nineteenth century whose names are preserved in the musical annals are Nicolas Quevedo Rachedell (1803–1874), Juan Crisóstomo Osorio y Ricaurte (1836–1887), José Joaquín Guarin (1825–1854), and Julio Quevedo Arvelo (1829–1897). Diego Fallon (1834–1905) has left a mark upon Colombian musical science as the inventor of a syllabic musical notation in which vowels represent note values, and consonants the degrees of the scale.

Of the later generation of Colombian composers, the names of Carlos Umana Santamaría (1862–1917), Andres Martinez Montoya (1869–1933), Santo Cifuentes (1870–1932), and Alejandro Villalobos (1875–1938) are to be mentioned.

A detailed history of music in Colombia, from aboriginal times to the twentieth century is given in the special articles in Volume IV of the *Boletín Latino-Americano de Música*, published in Bogotá in 1938, under the auspices of the Ministry of Education of Colombia, and under the editorship of Francisco Curt Lange.

The first concert of orchestral music in Colombia was presented on December 6, 1905, by a student orchestra of the Conservatory of Bogotá, under the direction of Guillermo Uribe-Holguin. This ensemble provided a nucleus for a national symphony orchestra, *Orquesta Sinfónica Nacional*, which was officially inaugurated on May 27, 1936, under the leadership of a native musician, Guillermo Espinosa. In August 1938, on the occasion of the four-hundredth anniversary of the foundation of Bogotá, the government of Colombia organized a Festival of Ibero-American music, and engaged several conductors from other American republics to take part in concerts of the *Orquesta Sinfónica Nacional*.

Formal music education is dispensed in Colombia through music schools and Conservatories. The Conservatory of Cali, which occupies a specially designed modern building, is by far the most sumptuous musical institution in Colombia, and indeed in all South America. But because Cali is not the music center of the Republic, the Conservatory cannot make full use of its facilities.

An important adjunct to the cause of music education in Colombia is the extraordinary development of radio broadcasting. There are now in existence one hundred and eleven radio stations scattered all over the country, and reaching to the heart of the jungle itself.

MUSICIANS OF COLOMBIA

Jesús BERMUDEZ SILVA (1884——) studied with Uribe-Holguin, and from 1910 to 1919 was instructor at the *Conservatorio Nacional* in Bogotá. In 1931 he went to Madrid, where, on March 24, 1933, he conducted his symphonic piece *Torbellino*, named after a traditional Colombian dance. Bermudez Silva has also written a Symphony in C, several orchestral dances in the native manner, and numerous choral works, all in an effective but conventional style. In 1942 he was named director of the Conservatory in Tolima. The orchestral score of *Torbellino* is in the Fleisher Collection in Philadelphia.

Gabriel Escobar Casas (1900——) was born in Barranquilla and studied in his native town. He has composed numerous piano pieces and songs, and a ballet, *Descubrimiento de America.*

Guillermo Espinosa (1905——), after a brief period of study in Bogotá, went to Europe, where he took lessons with Weingartner. Later, Espinosa gave orchestral concerts in Germany, Italy, and Denmark. In 1936, he was appointed conductor of the newly created *Orquesta Sinfónica Nacional* in Bogotá. Francisco Curt Lange published an extensive study on Espinosa and the orchestra in Volume IV of the *Boletín Latino-Americano de Música.*

Emirto de Lima (1892——) studied music in Europe, and took a course at the *Schola Cantorum* in Paris under Vincent d'Indy. He has written a number of dances and airs in the manner of Colombian folklore. He is also the author of a Concerto for Piano and Orchestra, a String Quartet, and two operettas. His treatise, *Folklore Colombiano* (1942), is an important source book.

Adolfo Mejia (1909——) was born in Cartagena de Indias. He did his early studies in his native town and in Bogotá. In 1938 he went to Paris, where he took a course in composition at the *École Normale de Musique.* He returned to Colombia in 1940. He has written in various genres, in a competent manner. His *Danza Ritual Africana* for orchestra was performed in Bogotá on November 15, 1940.

Emilio Murillo (1880–1942) was a composer of popular music. His genuine feeling for native folklore compensates for his weakness of technique. He wrote a number of *Pasillos*, some of which were lithographed. Several appreciative pages are devoted to Murillo's role in Colombian music in Cortijo's compendium, *La Música Popular y los Músicos Celebres de la America Latina* (Barcelona, 1919).

Carlos Posada-Amador (1908——) studied in Paris with Nadia Boulanger and Paul Dukas. From 1935 to 1937, he was director of the Conservatory in Medellín. His symphonic poem, *La Coronación del Zipa en Guatavita,* first performed at the Ibero-American Festival in Bogotá on August 27, 1938, portrays the election of a new chief of the Chibcha Indians, and is based on the pentatonic scale, while the harmony is Wag-

nerian. His stylizations of troubadour songs, *Cinco Canciones Medioe-
vales,* for mixed chorus *a cappella,* are published by the *Editorial Cooperativa Interamericana de Compositores* in Montevideo.

José Rozo CONTRERAS (1894——), the band leader and composer,
studied in Vienna, where his first orchestral work, *Tierra Colombiana,*
based on native themes, was performed on December 14, 1930. Upon
his return to Bogotá in 1933, Rozo Contreras was named director of the
Banda Nacional of Bogotá.

Guillermo URIBE-HOLGUIN (1880——) is the leading composer of
Colombia. As a boy, he studied the violin with Narciso Garay. In 1905,
he became instructor of violin and harmony at the *Academia Nacional
de Música* in Bogotá. He organized a student orchestra, and conducted
its first concert on December 6, 1905. In 1907, Uribe-Holguin went to
Paris, where he studied with Vincent d'Indy at the *Schola Cantorum.*
Among his classmates were Joaquín Turina and Erik Satie. He later
went to Brussels where he studied violin with César Thomson. Returning to Colombia in 1910, he was appointed director of the *Academia Nacional,* whose name was now changed to *Conservatorio Nacional.* He resumed the concerts of the student orchestra, with which he performed
altogether 252 compositions, including a number of his own symphonic
works. In September, 1935, Uribe-Holguin resigned his post and retired
to private teaching, and to the administration of the coffee plantation
which he owns. In 1941, he published his autobiography, *Vida de un
Músico Colombiano.*

Uribe-Holguin is a prolific composer. His first important work was a
Violin Sonata, which was performed in Paris on June 15, 1909. His first
symphonic composition, *Del Terruño,* a suite of character pieces based on
native Colombian rhythms, was performed in Bogotá, under his direction on October 20, 1924. He conducted his *Tres Danzas* in Bogotá on
May 27, 1927. This suite was subsequently reorchestrated, and performed in a new version on April 12, 1940. Other orchestral works,
performed under the composer's direction, are *Marcha Festiva* (August 20, 1928), *Serenata* (October 29, 1928), *Carnavalesca* (July 8,
1929), *Cantares* (September 2, 1929), *Villanesca* (September 1, 1930),
Bajo Su Ventana (October 20, 1930), *Suite Típica* (November 21, 1932),
and a symphonic poem *Bochica* (April 12, 1940). He has also written
a Concerto for Piano and Orchestra in the classical manner, performed in
Bogotá on October 15, 1939, and a Concerto for Violin and Orchestra.

In the field of chamber music, Uribe-Holguin has five violin sonatas and two suites for violin and piano, two violoncello sonatas, three string quartets, a piano quartet, and two piano quintets. He has also composed over three hundred piano pieces under the general title *Trozos en el Sentimiento Popular,* which are couched in the native style and are brilliantly written for the instrument. Of the entire bulk of Uribe-Holguin's output, three piano preludes have been published in *New Music,* April, 1939. His early Violin Sonata, published in Paris, is now out of print.

The style and technique of Uribe-Holguin's music are impressionist, in the French manner, and his harmonic texture often approaches polytonality, while the basic rhythms and melodic inflections are native in derivation.

A detailed biography of Uribe-Holguin by Francisco Curt Lange was published in Volume IV of the *Boletín Latino-Americano de Música.* The following scores of Uribe-Holguin are included in the Fleisher Collection in Philadelphia: *Carnavalesca, Tres Danzas, Marcha Festiva, Serenata, Cantares, Bajo Su Ventana, Bochica.* One of the *Trozos en el Sentimiento Popular* and a movement from a violin Suite are recorded in the album of *South American Chamber Music* issued by Columbia.

Antonio María VALENCIA (1903——) studied the rudiments of music with his father and later went to Paris where he attended the class of Vincent d'Indy at the *Schola Cantorum.* In Paris, Valencia presented piano recitals and wrote chamber music and piano pieces, notable for their coloristic quality. Upon his return to Colombia, in 1930, he became instructor at the Conservatory in Bogotá. In 1937 he founded the Conservatory of Cali, housed in a specially erected modern building.

Costa Rica

¡Costa Rica es mi patria querida!
[PATRIOTICA COSTARRICENSE,
1856]

Costa Rica is situated between Nicaragua and Panama, and is the second smallest Central American Republic, after El Salvador. There are about 650,000 inhabitants in Costa Rica, mostly of Spanish stock. Some Indians survive in the coastal regions.

Costa Rican music is a white man's music, and of all Latin American countries is the least influenced by either the Indian or the Negro culture. Costa Rican dances and songs are Spanish in character, and European in melodic structure. It is only recently that native Indian music began to attract the attention of Costa Rican musicians. In 1907, the chief of the Talamanca Indians visited San José, the capital, and sang Indian songs, which still preserve the pentatonic scale of pre-Columbian America.

In the January 1942 issue of *Educación,* organ of Costa Rican School Inspectors, we find the following review of native music: "Our country is not as rich in folklore as Mexico or Colombia, but it possesses its own musical form of expression. The guitar, the accordion, the mandolin, the marimba, are the favorite instruments of our people, and are found even in the remotest villages. One hears in the afternoon the strumming of the guitar and the plaintive voice of the villagers who seek to brighten their leisure with songs. Our marriage ceremonies and field festivals are conducted to the accompaniment of this music. The province of Guanacaste has given us that inimitable dance, *Punto Guanacasteco,* and there are other characteristic country airs."

A number of Costa Rican songs and dances have been published by the Department of Education, under the titles *Colección de Bailes Típicos de la Provincia de Guanacaste* (1929) and *Colección de Canciones y Danzas Típicas* (two volumes, 1934, and 1935). The first of these col-

lections contains an illuminating essay on Costa Rican music, written by
Luis Dobles Segreda:

Four types of popular music are represented in Costa Rica: *Callejeras,*
Patrioticas, Pasillos, and *Danzas.* The music of *Callejeras* (literally, street
songs) is voluble. Like a fickle woman, who flirts with anyone, the Callejera
assumes a hundred different forms, at times drunk with joy, at others as sweet
as caramel candy, dissolving in the mouth and poisoning the heart. This street
music is scarcely more than an improvisation, but it has in it a fragment of the
village's soul; it sings, as if bewitched by the warm, silent, moonlit night.

Then come the patriotic songs, in a more subdued and more solemn manner,
marking rhythms, exuding tobacco smoke and sweat, gun powder and
blood . . . There is the *Pasillo Guanacasteco,* a dance quite different from the
Colombian *Pasillo.* Musically, it is the most original of all, for in it the melody
proceeds in compound binary time, while the accompaniment goes on in simple
triple time. Finally comes the *Danza;* it is the old *Danza,* differing from the
Habanera by its vivacious pace and salty flavor. Technically the difference lies
in the characteristic form of the accompaniment. Sometimes, two-four time
alternates with three-four time. *Danza Guanacasteca* is a kind of music that
inflames, a music that dreams, laughs, and amuses; but it also breathes passion,
zest, and valor.

Segreda warns against an over-critical attitude towards the homely
native product:

Do not let harmony professors examine the water in our musical vessel
through a microscope, lest they discover ingredients that are Spanish, or Indian,
and decide that our music lacks originality . . . For, if the elements appear
mixed, they are filtered through the sands of our own soil.

Callejera, from Guanacaste, Costa Rica

Music history in Costa Rica begins with the creation of the National
Anthem. Its author was one Manuel Gutiérrez (1829–1887). The story
goes that he was ordered by the President of Costa Rica to write a patriotic

song, and when he pleaded that his learning was inadequate for such a task, he was thrown into jail, where he remained until the Anthem was ready. The first public performance of the Anthem was given in the Hall of the National Assembly in San José, on June 11, 1853.

In the January 1942 issue of *Educación* we find a long list of names of Costa Rican musicians of the last century. Among these, the following are prominent: Rafael Chavez Torres (1839–1907), who was a military band leader, and composed waltzes and funeral marches; Pedro Calderón Navarro (1864–1909), a religious composer; José Campabadal (1849–1905); and his son Roberto Campabadal (1881–1931), who wrote sacred music and patriotic songs; Rafael Angel Troyo Pacheco (1875–1910), who perished in the earthquake of 1910; Pilar Jiménez Solis (1883–1922); Gordiano Morales (1839–1917); and Fernando Murillo Rodriguez (1867–1928).

The dean of contemporary Costa Rican musicians is Alejandro Monestel, who is the first Costa Rican composer who has used native folk songs as themes for his works in established art forms. Of Costa Rican musicians of a later generation, Julio Fonseca is the romanticist and Julio Mata the modernist. The names of Cesar A. Nieto, a composer of ballet music, and that of Ismael Cárdona should also be mentioned.

There is a national theater in San José, inaugurated on October 21, 1897, which is used for performances by visiting opera companies. San José has an excellent military band, led by Roberto Cantillano, which gives frequent concerts, featuring compositions by native musicians. A National Conservatory of Music was established in San José in 1942.

The National Museum of Costa Rica possesses numerous specimens of old musical instruments dating back to the pre-Colombian era. Particularly remarkable is an Ocarina with six holes, which is capable, by combining the stops, of producing eighteen successive chromatic tones.

Writing in the October 1940 issue of *Revista Musical*, a music periodical published under the auspices of the *Asociación de Cultura Musical* of San José, Julio Fonseca laments the lack of appreciation of native culture. "Some resident foreigners," he writes, "regard the people of Costa Rica as apathetic, devoid of all interest in the arts, and capable of getting excited about anything only under the influence of liquor. It is a lamentable misconception. The Costa Ricans like entertainment and appreciate music. This fact was convincingly demonstrated when the Association of the National Manufacturers of Alcoholic Beverages arranged a music contest, which aroused so much interest that over two hundred songs were sent in from all corners of the Republic."

MUSICIANS OF COSTA RICA

Roberto CANTILLANO (1887——), the Costa Rican band conductor, arranger, and composer, was born in Santo Domingo de Heredia. He studied music in his native town, and in 1903 was named conductor of a provincial military band. He subsequently played the second flute in the band of San José, and in 1919 became the conductor of this band, a post which he occupies at present. Cantillano has composed a number of pieces in the popular genre. On March 25, 1936, he presented, with the band of San José, his symphonic poem *Amanecer Guanacasteco*.

Ismael CÁRDONA (1877——) is both a violinist and composer. Most of his music consists of salon pieces. His *Suite Miniature* in three movements (*Gavot, Idyll, Canzonette*) was performed by the Symphonic Ensemble of San José on March 26, 1935. It is included in the Fleisher Collection in Philadelphia.

Julio FONSECA (1885——) was, in 1902, sent by the Costa Rican government to Europe for musical study; he took courses at the Milan Conservatory. Upon his return to Costa Rica, Fonseca was appointed professor of music at the Young Ladies' College of San José, and organist at the Church of Our Lady of Mercy. The bulk of Fonseca's musical production consists of salon dances, but he has also written for orchestra and military band. Fonseca adopts in his music certain elements of modern harmony. In his *Cantata a la Música* (presented at the "Fiesta de la Raza" in San José on October 11, 1935), the principal theme is built on the whole-tone scale. At the concert of Fonseca's works given in San José on December 4, 1934, he conducted his *Suite Tropical* for orchestra, based on Costa Rican folklore. The score is included in the Fleisher Collection in Philadelphia. Some of Fonseca's salon music has been published. Fonseca's son, Jimmy Fonseca, has a promising musical gift. His *Gran Marcha de la Exposición* was presented by the Military Band of San José on July 20, 1938.

Julio MATA (1899——) studied music in San José, and later went to the United States, where he took courses at the Brooklyn Academy of Music. Mata has written music for military band, for orchestra, and for the theater. His light opera, entitled *Toyupán*, is based on native folklore. His operetta, *Rosas de Norgaria*, was presented in excerpts by the military band of San José on October 14, 1936. The same band performed his march *Patria y Afectos* on August 17, 1932. Mata's orchestral *Suite Abstracta*, performed in San José at a concert of Mata's compositions on May 23, 1941, follows a "disoriented tonality," according to the composer's definition. However, the names of the separate movements, Anger, Love, Melancholy, and Joy, imply a programmatic plan. The *Suite Abstracta* is included in the Fleisher Collection in Philadelphia.

Alejandro MONESTEL (1865———), the composer, studied the organ and in 1884 became organist and choirmaster at the Cathedral of San José. In 1902 he went to the United States, as church organist in Roslyn, Long Island; Brooklyn, New York; and Ridgewood, New Jersey. In 1937 he returned to Costa Rica, where, on July 25, 1937, a gala concert of his works was presented by the military band of San José. Monestel is a prolific writer of religious music, having composed fourteen Masses, four Requiems, two *Ave Marias*, two *Salve Reginas*, two *Tantum Ergos*, as well as a communion service for the Protestant Church. He is the author of five cantatas on the life of Jesus Christ from birth to resurrection. Some of his religious music has been published by Schirmer. His music for military bands is important as a means of popularizing Costa Rican folk melodies. Of these band compositions, the *Rapsodia Costarricense*, first performed in San José on August 28, 1935, and two *Rapsodias Guanacastecas*, performed respectively on July 25, 1937, and October 20, 1937, are particularly rich in indigenous folklore. Among Monestel's light pieces for the orchestra are *El Amante y la Coqueta*, *As Orillas de un Arroyo*, and *6 Canciones*. These pieces, as well as the three rhapsodies on Costa Rican themes, are included in the Fleisher Collection in Philadelphia.

Cesar NIETO (1892———), the composer, was born in Barcelona, Spain, went to Costa Rica in 1899, and became a Costa Rican citizen in 1936. Nieto is now conductor of a choral society in San José. As a composer, he has written a ballet, *La Piedra del Toxil*, based on pentatonic Inca themes, and harmonized in the traditional nineteenth-century style. He has also composed salon music, waltzes, marches, etc. The score of *La Piedra del Toxil* is included in the Fleisher Collection in Philadelphia.

The military band leader and composer José QUESADA (1894———) was born in San Rafael, Costa Rica. He studied music in San José, and later became the leader of a military band there. He conducted in San José the first performance of his orchestral piece, *El Son de la Luna*, on

December 20, 1930. The score of this composition is in the Fleisher Collection in Philadelphia. The band arrangements of Quesada's two *Costa Rican Dances* are published by Axelrod.

Cuba

¡Oh tierra de mi amor! . . *¡Oh cara Cuba!*
[JOSÉ FORNARIS]

¡Perla del Mar! ¡Cuba hermosa!
[GERTRUDIS GOMEZ DE AVELLANDEA Y ARTEAGA]

¡Oh Cuba, nombre dulce indefinible!
[JOAQUÍN LORENZO LUACES]

¡Cuba, Cuba, que vida me diste,
Dulce tierra de luz y hermozura!
[JOSÉ MARÍA HEREDIA]

Cuba, the largest of the West Indies islands, has been called the Pearl of the Antilles, the Castle of Indolence, the Land of Sugar and Spendthrifts, Spain's Lost Jewel, and the Garden of Delight. Cuba numbers 4,300,000 inhabitants, of whom over half a million live in Havana. Twenty per cent of the population are Negroes. The Indians are virtually extinct.

Among Latin American airs and dances, the music of Cuba was the first to spread in Europe and North America. The *Habanera* (that is, a Havana air) became known a century ago. More recently the *Rumba* has swept the world. But it must be pointed out that Cuban popular music as performed in Europe and America sounds false and perverted to native ears. The late Cuban musicologist, Emilio Grenet, writes in a preface to his valuable collection, *Música Popular Cubana:* "Our music has invaded all lands and all climes. But while this conquest is an undisputed reality, it is no less true that most musicians cultivating Cuban music abroad fail to understand the nature of the new rhythms which have infiltrated into their countries. And that is the reason why our sister nations, the United States, which is our geographical neighbor, and Spain, which is our racial relative, distort the character of our music and invest it with an alien spirit . . . To our neighbors to the north, all Cuban music is reduced to the *Rumba.* But even the *Rumba,* that creature of our robust virility, is diluted and emasculated . . . The Spanish are a step ahead in their comprehension of our music. They interpret it as a tropical siesta, in a slow cadence of the *Habanera* and the *Danzón,* no doubt because these dances are so ostentatiously Hispanic . . ."

Two racial strains combine to produce Cuban popular music: the Spanish and the African. Little is left of the pentatonic melos of the aboriginal Indians. The Spanish element is strong in the rustic airs of the interior, while the Negro influence is felt in the city songs. The Spanish rhythms are characterized by the combined six-eight and three-four time, while the Afro-Cuban type is marked by syncopation in two-four time. The typical rhythm of Cuban popular music is represented

by a two-bar pattern, $\frac{2}{4}$ 𝅘𝅥𝅭 𝅘𝅥𝅮 | 𝄿 𝅘𝅥𝅮 𝄿 | In performance

this formula is often transformed into a group of five notes, 𝅘𝅥 𝅘𝅥𝅮𝅘𝅥𝅮 𝅘𝅥𝅮𝅘𝅥𝅮

which is known as the Cuban *Cinquillo.* This *cinquillo,* in its turn, may

become shortened into a group of three notes, 𝅘𝅥𝅭 𝅘𝅥𝅭 𝅘𝅥

There is a wide divergence in rhythmic interpretation of a popular song as sung by the peasants of the interior, and the slick, jazz-like version of the professional musicians in a Havana café. Emilio Grenet transcribes two versions of a popular song, *Mama Iñes,* as performed in the country and in Havana. The first version is "straight," whereas the second is convulsed with syncopation:

"Mama Iñez," Straight and Syncopated (*Grenet*)

The distinctive Cuban rhythms are punctuated by a variety of native percussion instruments. The basic rhythm is usually given by the *Claves,* a pair of cylindrical wooden blocks struck one against the other, with the cupped palm of the hand serving as the resonator. Fernando Ortiz, in his essay *La Clave Xilofónica de la Música Cubana,* describes the sound of the *Claves* as "the most profound emotional expression of Cuba's soul."

The Cuban *Maracas,* which is a pair of gourds filled with dry seeds, and the *Güiro,* a serrated calabash, rubbed with a stick, are the customary ingredients of every native band, not only in Cuba, but all over Latin America. Then there is in Cuba a variety of primitive drums. Of these, the *Conga* is the largest. It is made of a tree trunk, burned out inside, and covered with a parchment. So strong is its sound, that the *Conga* can be heard for miles in the jungle. Because the *Conga* serves as a means of jungle telegraphy among the natives, the Cuban government felt obliged to forbid its manufacture and use, to forestall an outbreak of native unrest.

A smaller drum of the *Conga* type is called *Enkomo.* The Cuban twin drums, the *Bongos,* which have gained great popularity, are placed on the knees, and tapped with the fingers. The *Cencerro,* which is a piece of metal, is used in native bands as a bell. The most unusual instrument in the primitive Cuban orchestras is the *Quijada del Burro,* the jawbone of an ass, which is furnished with small bells and used as a tambourine. A detailed description of Cuban percussion instruments is given by Harold Courlander in his monograph on the subject, published in the April 1942 issue of *The Musical Quarterly.*

Among the native dances of Cuba, the Spanish element is strongest in the *Habanera, Guajira, Punto,* and the *Guaracha.* The Afro-Cuban dances are the *Rumba,* the *Conga,* and the *Son Afro-Cubano.* The hybrid Spanish-African style is represented by the *Bolero-Son,* which is in two-four time, and in syncopated rhythm, whereas the original Spanish *Bolero* is in three-four time.

The *Habanera* is characterized by the unmistakable swaying rhythm

$\frac{2}{4}$ ♩. ♪♫ which is also the formula of the Argentine *Tango.* The earliest known *Habanera* is *El Areglito* by the Spanish composer Yradier, published in the 1840's with the subtitle *Chanson havanaise.* This is the *Habanera* that Bizet picked up in Spain and used in *Carmen.* Among modern composers, Ravel and Stravinsky wrote *Habaneras* in stylized adaptations.

The Argentine music scholar, Carlos Vega, traces the origin of the *Habanera* to the English Country Dance. This unexpected genealogy is made extremely plausible by Vega. According to his theory, the Country Dance, which became *Contredanse* in France, and *Contradanza* in Spain, was imported into Cuba, where it was known as the *Danza*, and later as the *Danza Habanera*. Then the word *Danza* was dropped, leaving the name simply *Habanera*.

The *Guajira* takes its name from the *guajiros*, the peasants of the interior, and is written in the characteristic Hispanic meter of six-eight, superimposed on three-four. It is sung to the accompaniment of the guitar, with a melody not exceeding the range of a minor seventh. Close to the *Guajira* in rhythm, melody and harmony, is the Cuban *Punto*, which is also related to the *Punto* of Panama.

The *Guaracha* is an old Spanish-Cuban dance in the characteristic six- eight time, alternating with three-four time. In Cuba, it is rarely heard among the people, but is popular in dance bands. There is a *Guaracha* in Auber's opera *La Muette de Portici*, written in 1828.

The choreography of the Cuban dances of Spanish origin is interesting in that the partners are separated, and wave handkerchiefs at each other, without coming into physical contact. A special phase of these dances is *El Zapateo*, from *Zapato*, shoe. It is a tap dance, in which the dancers stamp on the ground in rapid tempo.

The *Danzón* was introduced into Cuba in 1879 by a Negro composer, Miguel Failde. It is related to the old Spanish *Contradanza*, but is greatly influenced by African elements. It is danced by couples holding hands. The *Danzón* was very popular for a time, but was displaced by the *Son*, a dance-song which appeared in 1916 in the eastern provinces of Cuba. The *Son* is more highly syncopated than the *Danzón* and usually has an introduction for a solo singer. Its rhythmic structure is usually a *cinquillo*, in which the last eighth-note is split into two sixteenth-notes. The *Son Afro-Cubano* is the extension of the *Son*, with Negro melodies and ritualistic African words.

The *Rumba* and the *Conga* are the characteristic creations of the Cuban Negroes. In the slums of Havana, the *Rumba* is often accompanied by an ensemble made up of domestic utensils such as bottles, pans and spoons.

The rhythm of the *Rumba* is varied, often with a different pattern in every bar, as for example,

The *Conga* is a Carnival dance, performed during the so-called *Comparsas* or parades, and its rhythm is essentially that of a march, the only peculiarity being that in every other bar the second beat is anticipated by a sixteenth-note. The American *boogie-woogie* players often use the *Conga* rhythm as the basic accompaniment pattern.

The *Rumba* and the *Conga* are often used as political campaign songs. In the presidential campaign of 1924, a *Conga* was used as a "smear" song against Menocal. Here is the first stanza: "The King of Spain sent a word to Menocal, saying, return to me the steed you have no skill to mount." Menocal lost the election.

The history of music in Cuba can be but sketchily traced. The nineteenth century in Cuba was the century of Italian music. Italian operatic music dominated the salons of Havana, and the Cuban salon dances of the time reflect this influence. The first Italian opera company visited Cuba in 1839. There is also a record of the arrival of several musicians from Bohemia in the year 1853, who presented a symphonic concert of classical music on March 10 of that year. The first Cuban composer who cultivated native themes was Ignacio Cervantes (1847–1905), who has been called "the Glinka of Cuban music."

Military bands were formed in Cuban towns for the purpose of supplying the population with cultured recreation. Of these bands, the most important is the *Banda de la Policía,* established on August 15, 1899.

In July 1922, an orchestral organization, *Orquesta Sinfónica de la Habana,* was founded under the directorship of the Cuban conductor and composer Gonzalo Roig. Two years later a rival organization, the *Orquesta Filarmónica de la Habana,* was founded. Its first concert was given on June 8, 1924, under the direction of the Spanish musician Pedro Sanjuán. After Sanjuán's departure, Amadeo Roldán became the conductor, retaining the post until his death in 1939. Massimo Freccia, an Italian musician, became Roldán's successor until 1944, when Erich Kleiber was invited to serve as principal conductor.

There is a municipal conservatory in Havana which provides adequate musical courses. The *Conservatorio Bach,* under the direction of Antonio and María de Quevedo, performs an important cultural role by presenting concerts of classical and modern works. The Quevedos are also the publishers of the progressive music periodical *Musicalia*, which has appeared, albeit with interruptions, since 1927.

The recently deceased Cuban composer Eduardo Sanchez de Fuentes is the author of operas and ballets, as well as of popular music, of which the Habanera *Tu* (1890) has become a classic in its genre. The Cuban-born composer Joaquín Nin y Castellanos spent virtually all his life in Paris, returning to Havana in 1939. His son, Joaquín Nin-Culmell, also a composer, was born in Berlin, lived in France, and eventually settled in the United States.

Two Cuban composers, both of whom died a tragic death in their early thirties, Amadeo Roldán and Alejandro García Caturla, share the honor of being the founders of the modern school of native composition. Both were inspired in their music by Afro-Cuban folklore. Roldán was a mulatto, and Caturla, although of white stock, married into a Negro family.

The present tendency of Cuban music is directed towards neoclassicism rather than folkloric nationalism. This new trend is cultivated by José Ardévol, a Spanish musician who settled in Havana in 1934, and a group of young men and women who have banded together in a modern music society, *Grupo de Renovación Musical*. This group presented its inaugural concert in Havana on January 19, 1943, in a program of works by Harold Gramatges, Juan Antonio Cámara, Julián Orbón, Hilario González Iñiguez, Esther Rodriguez, Virginia Fleites, Gisela Hernández Gonzalo, and Edgardo Martín.

MUSICIANS OF CUBA

José Ardévol (1911———) was born in Barcelona, Spain. He studied with his father, a well-known musician, and appeared as pianist in concerts at an early age. In 1930, he settled in Havana, where he founded a Society of Chamber Music Concerts. The programs of these concerts are reproduced in Volume III of the *Boletín Latino-Americano de Música*. Ardévol's *Scherzo* for orchestra, composed at the age of eighteen, was first performed by the *Orquesta Filarmónica* in Havana on October 23, 1932. In 1937, Ardévol wrote two Concertos Grossos, and in 1938, a Concerto for Three Pianos and Orchestra. The titles of his works indicate the neoclassical trend of Ardévol's style. He has also composed *Tres Ricercari* (1936); *Chamber Music for Six Instruments* (1936); a Sonata for Oboe, Clarinet, and Cello (1937); a Sonata for Two Flutes and Viola (1938); and a Sonata for Two Trumpets and Trombone. The nine *Pequeñas Piezas* (1933) are humorous in their intent; one of the pieces bears the title, *Hymn of 2 Plus 2 Equals 4*. He has also exploited the resources of the percussion orchestra, and wrote in 1934 a Suite for thirty percussion instruments. The score of this Suite and that of Ardévol's *Six Synthetic Poems* are included in the Fleisher Collection in Philadelphia. His Sonatina for Piano was published in *New Music* in July, 1934.

Juan Antonio CÁMARA (1917———) was born in Havana. He studied music with Amadeo Roldán and José Ardévol, and in 1943 joined the *Grupo de Renovación Musical*, founded by a group of young Cuban composers. He writes in a neoclassical style, emphasizing the contrapuntal aspect of the music. His Suite for flute, clarinet, and bassoon was performed in Havana on August 2, 1944.

Alejandro García CATURLA, one of the most significant composers of Cuba, was born in Remedios in 1906, and tragically assassinated there on November 12, 1940. He studied in Havana with Pedro Sanjuán, and in Paris in 1928 with Nadia Boulanger. His compositions are distinguished by native color and ultra-modern harmony. Although of pure Spanish blood, he married a Negro woman, and in his creative work was inspired by Afro-Cuban folklore. His orchestral suite *3 Danzas Cubanas*, first performed by the *Orquesta Filarmónica* in Havana on December 9, 1928, shows his instinctive feeling for native rhythms. In *Bembé*, an Afro-Cuban suite for fourteen instruments, performed in Paris on December 21, 1929, he reveals a great talent for composition in·an advanced harmonic idiom. *Yamba-O*, a ritualistic symphonic poem for large orchestra, based on a Negro liturgy, is his most complicated and most significant work. It was given by the Philharmonic Orchestra of Havana on October 25, 1931. *La Rumba*, performed in Havana on December 31, 1933, is based on popular Cuban rhythms. A similar stylization of Cuban rhythms and melodies is present in Caturla's *Primera Suite Cubana* for piano and six wind instruments. Adolfo Salazar, in his monograph on Caturla in *La Revista Cubana* of January–March, 1938, states that Caturla's general esthetic code is that of the Cuban *Son*, characterized by a "generally pentatonic melody, presented by an instrument of a distinct timbre, in a tonally indefinable sonorous atmosphere, sustained by the multiplicity of simultaneous rhythms played by native instruments."

Alberto Williams   Alberto E. Ginastera

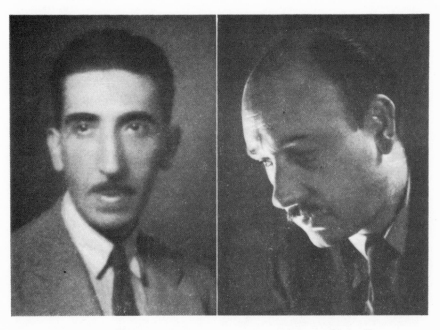

Luis Gianneo   Honorio Siccardi

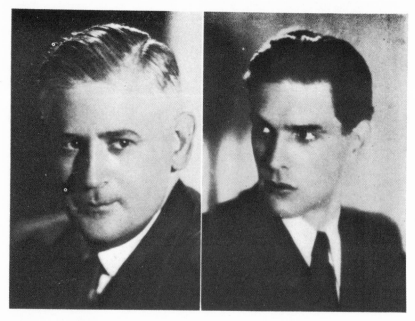

Jacobo Ficher   José María Castro

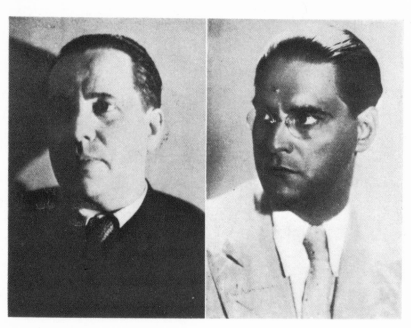

Juan Carlos Paz   Juan José Castro

Caturla's songs *Mari-Sabel, Yuego Santo, Bito-Manué, Mulata,* and *Yambambo,* piano arrangements of the *Danza del Tambor* and *Danza Lucumi* from *3 Danzas Cubanas,* and *Bembé* were published in Paris. The Sonata and Prelude for Piano, the piano version of *Comparsa,* and the score of *Primera Suite Cubana* are published by *New Music.* Caturla's piano piece *Son* was issued as a supplement to the periodical *Musicalia* in Havana. The orchestral scores of Caturla's *Danzas Cubanas, Bembé, Primera Suite Cubana, Yamba-O,* and a chamber orchestra version of *3 Danzas Cubanas* are included in the Fleisher Collection in Philadelphia. See Nicolas Slonimsky, "Caturla of Cuba," in *Modern Music* (January, 1940).

Virginia FLEITES (1916———) studied with Roldán and Ardévol; she has written chamber music, piano pieces, and songs. She is a member of the *Grupo de Renovación Musical* in Havana.

Hilario GONZÁLEZ IÑIGUEZ (1920———), of the modern generation, studied with José Ardévol, and in 1943 joined the *Grupo de Renovación Musical,* formed by a group of young Cuban composers. González Iñiguez cultivates native folklore in his piano pieces and songs.

Harold GRAMATGES (1918———), also one of the youthful school of Cuban composers, studied with Amadeo Roldán and José Ardévol in Havana, and in the summer of 1942 at the Berkshire Academy in the United States, with Aaron Copland. He has written music in various genres, for orchestra, for piano, and for voice. He adheres to the precepts of neoclassicism, without injecting elements of folklore. In association with a group of young Cuban composers (Julián Orbón, Hilario González, Edgardo Martín, Virginia Fleites, Esther Rodriguez, and others), Gramatges founded the *Grupo de Renovación Musical,* which presented its inaugural concert of chamber music by its members, in Havana, on January 19, 1943.

Gisela HERNÁNDEZ (1910———) has studied with José Ardévol, and in 1943 she joined the *Grupo de Renovación Musical* in Havana. She writes in a neoclassical manner.

Ernesto LECUONA (1896———) began composing at the age of eleven, and at sixteen was a teacher at a Havana music school. Graduating from the National Conservatory in 1913, he traveled in the United States, Spain, and France, where he gave piano recitals. Although Lecuona has written works for the symphony orchestra, it is in the field of popular music that he has become famous. His rumba band, Lecuona's Cuban Boys, has established itself all over Latin America, and it is featured in night clubs and other places of entertainment as a type of popular music, even when Lecuona does not conduct it personally. Of his songs, *Siboney, Canto Karabali, Say Si Si,* and *Malagueña* have had an extraordinary popular success, and have sold in thousands of copies and recordings. His piano pieces in Cuban manner enjoy similar popularity. On October 10, 1943, he presented at Carnegie Hall, New York, a concert of Cuban music, at which he gave the first performance of his *Rapsodia Negra* for piano and orchestra.

Edgardo MARTÍN (1915——) studied with José Ardévol, and in 1943 joined the *Grupo de Renovación Musical* in Havana.

Joaquín NIN Y CASTELLANOS (1879——) was born in Havana, went to Barcelona at an early age, and later moved to Paris, where he studied composition at the *Schola Cantorum,* and piano with Moszkowski. He is particularly interested in old Spanish music, and has edited several collections of works by Spanish composers. As a composer, Nin writes in a Hispanized French style. His piano pieces and songs have been published in Paris. In 1939, Nin returned to Havana. His son, Joaquín Nin-Culmell, who was born in Berlin on September 5, 1908, is a composer of great attainments. He lived in France and in the United States, and served in the Cuban Army. In 1944 he joined the faculty of Williams College.

Julián ORBÓN is the youngest of Cuban composers. Born in Spain on August 7, 1925, he was taken to Havana as a child. He studied with José Ardévol, and joined the *Grupo de Renovación Musical.* His music is in a neoclassical style. His *Capriccio Concertante* for chamber orchestra was performed for the first time in Havana on June 21, 1944. Orbón has also composed incidental music for *La Gitanilla* of Cervantes and a Toccata for piano.

Esther RODRIGUEZ (1920——) studied with Roldán and Ardévol, and has written chamber music, choruses, songs, and piano pieces. Her String Quartet was performed at the inaugural concert of the *Grupo de Renovación Musical* in Havana, of which she is a member, on January 19, 1943.

Gonzalo ROIG (1890——) is the founder and permanent conductor of the *Orquesta Sinfónica* of Havana. He has written a lyric comedy, *Cecilia Valdes,* and numerous songs.

Amadeo ROLDÁN (1900–1939), the Cuban mulatto composer, was born in Paris. He studied violin in Madrid, and composition in Havana with Pedro Sanjuán. In 1924, Roldán was concertmaster of the *Orquesta Filarmónica* in Havana, and in 1932 succeeded Sanjuán as conductor, a position he held up to the year of his death. All of Roldán's music is inspired by Afro-Cuban folklore. His first important work was *Obertura Sobre Temas Cubanos*, performed by the *Orquesta Filármonica* of Havana on November 29, 1925. There followed *Tres Pequeños Poemas*, first performed in Havana on January 9, 1927. The first of these poems, *Oriental*, introduces the atmosphere of eastern Cuba; the second poem, *Pregón*, is derived from a street vendor's cry; and the third movement, *Fiesta Negra*, is based on Afro-Cuban motives. The spirit of Negro ritual music finds its most powerful expression in Roldán's ballet *La Rebambaramba*, in which he employs Cuban percussion instruments in six separate groups. An orchestral Suite of five numbers arranged from this ballet was performed by the *Orquesta Filarmónica* in Havana on August 12, 1928. Roldán's ballet *El Milagro de Anaquillé* was produced in Havana on September 22, 1929. Other works of Roldán inspired by Afro-Cuban rhythms are *Danza Negra*, for high voice and seven instruments (first performed in Paris on April 23, 1929), *Chango*, and *Poema Negra* for string quartet (1930). Further, there are *Motivos de Son* (1930), for high voice and nine instruments, and *3 Toques* (subtitled respectively *De Marcha*, *De Rito*, and *De Baile*) for chamber orchestra (1931). Of interest from the instrumental standpoint are Roldán's *Rítmicas*. The first four, written for flute, oboe, clarinet, bassoon, horn, and piano, were presented in Havana on August 3, 1930. *Rítmicas* Nos. 5 and 6 are scored for Cuban percussion instruments only, including the *Quijada del Burro* (Jawbone of an Ass). *New Music* has published the orchestral score of *Motivos de Son*, and the vocal score of three numbers from the same suite. The scores of the *Obertura Sobre Temas Cubanas* and *La Rebambaramba* are included in the Fleisher Collection in Philadelphia.

Eduardo SANCHEZ DE FUENTES (1874–1944) was born and died in Havana. He studied piano and musical theory. At the age of eighteen Sanchez de Fuentes wrote his first piece, a Habanera entitled *Tú*, which was published in 1894, and soon acquired universal popularity. Subsequently he devoted his energies to the cultivation of Cuban national music. In 1911 he was appointed secretary of the Music Department at the Academy of Arts and Letters in Havana. Sanchez de Fuentes wrote six operas: *Yumurí* (produced in Havana on October 26, 1898), *El Náufrago* (after Tennyson's *Enoch Arden,* produced on January 31, 1901), *La Dolorosa* (performed on April 23, 1910), *Doreya* (produced on February 7, 1918), *El Caminante* (produced on July 7, 1921), and *Kabelia* (produced on June 22, 1942). His oratorio, *Navidad,* was performed in Havana on December 29, 1924, and his aboriginal Symphonic Poem *Anacaona* (named after the sixteenth-century Indian Queen of the island of Hispaniola) was performed in Havana on December 2, 1928. His ballet, *Dioné,* was produced in Havana on March 4, 1940. Among his works for orchestra based on native folklore are *Triptico Cubano, Bocetos Cubanos,* and *Rapsodia Cubana.* He was also the author of several operettas and numerous songs in the native manner. In recognition of his service to Cuban culture, the government designated April 3, the birthday of Sanchez de Fuentes, as *El Día de la Canción Cubana,* to be celebrated annually by performances of Cuban songs.

Dominican Republic

> Brillantes, oro y rubies,
> ¡República Dominicana!
> [RUBÉN DARÍO]

The Dominican Republic occupies the eastern two-thirds of the island of Santo Domingo. The aboriginal name of the island was Quisqueya, which means "mother of the earth." Columbus called the island Hispaniola. The population of the Dominican Republic numbers about 1,800,000, of which 35 per cent are whites, 50 per cent mestizos, and 15 per cent Negroes. There are virtually no Indians of pure stock left in the Dominican Republic. The capital of the Dominican Republic, Santo Domingo, the oldest permanent European settlement in the Western Hemisphere, was renamed Ciudad Trujillo in 1930, after the president of the republic, Generalissimo Rafael L. Trujillo Molina.

Santo Domingo is the cradle of New World music. Here it was that a tribal Queen, Anacaona, gave the earliest demonstration of native dances. Columbus' historiographer, Gonzalo Fernandez de Oviedo, in his *Historia General y Natural de las Indias*, gave a vivid description of the event:

The inhabitants of this island have a fine custom of commemorating ancient events in their songs and dances, which they call *Areitos*, and which we would call singing dances . . . At times, they combine the singing with the playing of drums made of round pieces of wood, hollow inside, and as thick as a man's body . . . And so, with drums or without, they recite in a singing tone their memories and past histories, and relate in these recitations the deeds of the great chieftains . . . Sometimes, they change the melody and step of the dance, and tell a new story, or the same story to a new tune. In 1520, Queen Anacaona, wife of a native chief named Caonabo, danced an *Areito;* and in this dance more than three hundred damsels took part. While they danced and sang, other Indian maidens passed drinks around to the dancers. When a dancer becomes intoxicated, he falls out, while others keep dancing, so that drunkenness sets the end of the *Areito*. This happens at *Areitos* celebrating marriages, deaths and battles; on other occasions, *Areitos* are danced without getting drunk.

Further testimony as to the native love for dance and song is found in *Historia de las Indias* by Bartolomé de las Casas, the sixteenth century Spanish bishop known as "the Apostle of the Indians": "The Indians of the island of Santo Domingo are very fond of dancing, and in order to keep time and to mark step, they flourish cleverly made rattles with pebbles inside, which produce a rather raucous sound."

Bartolomé de las Casas was also the first to give a performance of a religious musical work in the New World. In 1510, he celebrated Mass, with the participation of a chorus, in the church of the town of La Vega.

The first musician born in the western hemisphere was also a native of Santo Domingo, Cristóbal de Llerena, the organist at the Cathedral of Santo Domingo in the latter part of the sixteenth century. He was an educated musician, described, in a letter written to Philip II of Spain, as "a man of rare ability, who knows enough Latin to qualify for the position of Professor at the University of Salamanca, and enough music to be a choirmaster at the Chapel of Toledo."

Spanish music was for centuries a dominating influence in Santo Domingo, first through the Church, and then through the importation of Spanish popular dances and the spread of the Spanish guitar. So strong was the spirit of music-making in colonial Santo Domingo that in times of stress music had to be banned in the streets. In 1813, the Spanish Governor of Santo Domingo issued an order forbidding "the performance of serenades and songs to the sound of the guitar after ten o'clock at night."

With the importation of African slaves into the West Indies, the songs and dances of the islands began to acquire a rhythmic accent characteristic of Negro music. The extent of this influence is disputed by Dominican musicologists. Flerida de Nolasco, in her valuable essay, *Música en Santo Domingo* (Ciudad Trujillo, 1939), writes: "Our songs stem from Spanish rhythms . . . Even should we admit that our musical folklore is the product of a double culture, the Spanish and the African, the art invariably follows a nobler and purer strain. Dominican folk music is Spanish music adjusted to native tastes, and it is only by accident that it is affected by the savage African rhythms."

On the other hand, the late Afro-Dominican musician Esteban Peña Morell sees in the Negro contribution a legitimate part of the national art. Another Dominican musician, Julio Arzeno, in his posthumous book *Del Folklore Musical Dominicano* (1927), writes: "We must relinquish alien rhythms. We must become Dominican musicians, not German or Puerto Rican. We must create an art based on the natural and spontaneous resources of our vigorous native music." Enrique de Marchena, the foremost Dominican music scholar and composer, in his book *Del Areito de Anacaona al Poema Folklórico* (1942), asserts that "every Dominican musician instinctively writes music that is Dominican."

The national "singing dance" of the Dominican Republic is the *Merengue*. It is a gay air, symmetrically constructed of two periods of sixteen bars each, in two-four time. The first section is usually in a major key, and the second in the major dominant, or in the relative minor key, with the return to the original key indicated in the cadence. The rhythm is characterized by moderate syncopation.

The typical *Merengue* contains a short introduction, called *Paseo*, or promenade, and interludes, called *Jaleo*. A detailed description of the *Merengue* is found in a paper by Dr. Pedro Henriquez Ureña, *Música Popular de America*, published by the *Biblioteca del Colegio Nacional de la Universidad de la Plata*, Volume I, 1930.

The origin of the *Merengue* is uncertain. Some believe it was imported from Cuba by the Negro slaves, others that it originated in Puerto Rico or in Haiti. Peña Morell asserts that there is a verb *Merenguearse*, to dance with great abandon, and that the word *Merengue* is a noun derived from that verb.

Among other Dominican airs, the *Punto Cibaeño* (a *Punto* from the province of Cibao) is similar to the *Merengue*, but is cast in a ternary form, so that the first section is repeated. The *Barcarola Criolla* (a native Barcarolla) follows the European model with some slight syncopation. The Dominican *Bolero* is identical with the Cuban *Bolero*, and is in two-four time, whereas the classical Spanish *Bolero* is always in three-four time.

Among the native dances now obsolete is the *Mangulina*, which, when played rapidly, resembles a *Tarantella*. Then there is a *Tonada Maguanera*, from the province of Maguana; the *Zapateado Montuno*, a "shoe-dance," also known as the *Sarambo*; and the *Media-Tuna*, a lively air, often sung by laborers going to work.

The topical ballads of the Dominican Republic, similar to the Mexican *Corridos*, are interesting in that they often reflect the popular reaction to historical events. The American intervention of 1916, for instance, is remembered in the following quatrain:

> *Vinieron los Americanos*
> *A cojer la fortaleza,*
> *Y mataron al capitan*
> *De un balazo a la cabeza.*

The "father of Dominican music" was Juan Bautista Alfonseca (1810–1875). He was the first to make use of national folklore in his music. He was also the author of the first National Anthem, *Himno de la Independencia*. His pupil, José Reyes (1835–1905), continued the national tradition established by Alfonseca. Among other nineteenth-century Dominican composers are Alfredo Maximo Soler, who wrote music in a light vein; Pablo Claudio, the author of two operas and over seven hundred other works; and José María Arredondo, the composer of a number of popular dances.

The names of two Dominican-born sisters have been retained in the annals of native music. One, Julieta Licairac Abreu (1890–1925), wrote piano music, somewhat Chopinesque in character. Her sister, Lucila, a child prodigy, was born on February 21, 1895, and died on November 21, 1901, at the age of six years and nine months. Her naive improvisations were collected and published by the family.

The state of music in the Dominican Republic has now advanced to an astonishing degree. Ciudad Trujillo, the capital, possesses its own Symphony Orchestra, which was inaugurated on October 23, 1941, under the direction of the Spanish musician Enrique Casal Chapí, in a program of works by native musicians. In order to encourage creative composition, the government of the Republic announced a music contest for the best works in all genres by native musicians, held on the occasion of the centennial of Dominican Independence, in February 1944. The largest prize, for an orchestral work, was one thousand American dollars.

The cause of musical education in Santo Domingo received further encouragement with the establishment, in 1941, of the National Conservatory of Music. Ciudad Trujillo also possesses a powerful radio station HIN y HI1N, with Enrique de Marchena in charge of the musical programs.

Two albums of Dominican popular songs and dances have been published in New York by the Famous Music Corporation and the Alpha Music Company. An excellent collection of sixty-four Dominican airs, *La Patria en la Canción,* compiled by Emilio Jiménez, was published in Barcelona in 1933, but it is now out of print. Similarly unavailable is Julio Arzeno's treatise *Del Folklore Musical Dominicano.* An authoritative report on the state of music in the Dominican Republic by J. M. Coopersmith is published in the January and April, 1945, issues of *The Musical Quarterly.*

MUSICIANS OF THE DOMINICAN REPUBLIC

One of the most prolific of Dominican musicians was Clodomiro ARREDONDO-MIURA (1864–1935). He wrote religious music as well as marches, waltzes, and indigenous barcarollas. His son, Horacio Arredondo-Sosa (born in 1912), is also a musician, and has compiled, in association with José G. Ramirez-Peralta, a collection of popular Dominican airs published by the Alpha Music Corporation in New York.

The youthful Bienvenido BUSTAMENTE (1924——) studied music with his father, José María Bustamente (1867–1940). His orchestral *Fantasia* was performed in his native city, San Pedro de Macoris, on August 16, 1942, when the composer was eighteen years old.

José Dolores CERÓN (1897——), a Negro musician, studied with José de Jesús Ravelo and Peña Morell. Cerón has written popular music, as well as symphonic compositions. His symphonic poem *Enriquillo* (named after a sixteenth-century Indian chief) was performed at the inaugural concert of the *Orquesta Sinfónica Nacional* in Ciudad Trujillo, on October 23, 1941.

Enrique Casal CHAPÍ (1909——), naturalized in Santo Domingo, came originally from Madrid in Spain. His grandfather was Ruperto Casal Chapí, the well-known composer of *Zarzuelas*. Casal Chapí studied at the Madrid Conservatory, and graduated in 1936, when he was twenty-seven, in the class of composition of Conrado del Campo. He was active in the cultural life of the Spanish Republic, and upon the defeat of the Loyalists made his way on foot to the French frontier. He finally found refuge in the Dominican Republic, where he arrived on April 21, 1940. On August 5, 1941, he was appointed conductor of the newly founded *Orquesta Sinfónica Nacional* in Ciudad Trujillo. He has established a policy of encouraging native composers, several of whom have studied with him. Of his own orchestral works, Casal Chapí has conducted an Overture (November 30, 1942). He writes in an advanced modern style, marked by technical mastery.

Gabriel DEL ORBE (1888——), who has written over one hundred violin pieces, is a native of Moca, Santo Domingo. He studied in Germany, where he gave violin recitals. Upon return to his native land, he was appointed instructor in violin at the Conservatory in Ciudad Trujillo.

The composer of popular music, Juan Bautista ESPINOLA Y REYES (1894–1923) was a native of La Vega. He played the clarinet in military bands, and composed more than five hundred pieces in the popular vein— merengues, waltzes, and barcarollas.

Juan Francisco GARCÍA (1892——) was born in Santiago de los Caballeros. He was largely self-taught, but acquired a solid technique of composition which enable him to write in symphonic forms. His *First Symphony*, subtitled *Sinfonía Quisqueya* (*Quisqueya* is the ancient name of the island of Santo Domingo) was performed in Ciudad Trujillo on March 28, 1941, and his *Scherzo Clasico* on October 23, 1941. García's *Second Symphony* received the first prize at the Dominican national contest for the best symphonic composition in 1944. In April, 1944, García was appointed director of the Conservatory of Ciudad Trujillo. Apart from his symphonic works, García has written a number of dances in the popular style, and has introduced new forms of native compositions, *Sambumbia*, or a Dominican Rhapsody, and *Melodanza*, a melodic dance in the native vein. A collection of his piano pieces, *Ritmos Quisqueyanos*, was published in New York in 1927.

Julio Alberto HERNÁNDEZ (1900——), saxophonist and composer of popular music, is a native of Santiago de los Caballeros. He studied the saxophone, and acquired practical knowledge of the orchestra as a band conductor. He has compiled a valuable collection, *Album de Música Nacional* (1927).

Rafael IGNACIO (1897——) played the trumpet, flute, and double-bass in military bands, and later conducted a dance orchestra called *Amores y Amorios*. After a period of musical activities in Ciudad Trujillo, the capital, Rafael Ignacio was appointed in 1941 assistant conductor of the military band in Santiago de los Caballeros. Ignacio is the author of a Symphony in C minor, and *Suite Folklórica*, based on native themes. He has also written numerous popular dances and songs.

Manuel de Jesús LOVELACE (1871——) learned the rudiments of music by playing the piccolo in military bands. He is the author of numerous popular dances. Of his larger works, *Escenas Dominicanas*, for orchestra in three movements, reflects the folkways of Santo Domingo.

Enrique de MARCHENA (1908——) studied composition with Esteban Peña Morell in Santo Domingo. Marchena's style of writing is romantic, with touches of impressionistic color. He has written over one hundred piano pieces, a symphonic poem *Arco Iris*, and a Concerto for Violin and Orchestra. His *Suite de Imagenes*, in three movements, inspired by native folklore, was performed for the first time by the *Orquesta Nacional* in Ciudad Trujillo on April 29, 1942. Since 1930, Marchena has been the music critic of *Listín Diario*. He is also in charge of the musical programs of the Dominican radio station HIN y HI1N in Ciudad Trujillo. In 1943 he made a lecture tour in the United States. In his book, *Del Areito de Anacaona al Poema Folklórico* (1942), Marchena traces the history of folk music in Santo Domingo from the days of the legendary Queen Anacaona to the present time. The orchestral score of Marchena's *Suite de Imagenes* is included in the Fleisher Collection in Philadelphia.

Enrique MEJIA-ARREDONDO (1901——) studied with his grandfather, José María Arredondo. His Symphony in A major, performed on October 23, 1941, at the inaugural concert of the *Orquesta Sinfónica Nacional* in Ciudad Trujillo, has a program relating to the civil war in Santo Domingo in 1863. His Second Symphony, *Sinfonía de Luz*, is romantic in essence. The symphonic poem *Renacimiento* pictures the work of recovery after the hurricane that struck the island on September 3, 1930. *Evocaciones*, a suite of three orchestral pieces, was performed in Ciudad Trujillo on

February 23, 1942. While Mejia-Arredondo's harmonic style is not advanced, and the instrumentation is conventional, his music presents interest from a folkloric standpoint. Two of his *Danzas Quisqueyanas* and *En el Templo de Yocari* for piano have been published by the Alpha Corporation in New York.

Luis E. MENA (1895———) studied with José de Jesús Ravelo, and has acquired an adequate technique of composition. Mena has written religious, symphonic, and popular music. For the orchestra, he has composed a *Sinfonia de Juguetes,* based on the themes of children's games, an Overture (performed by the *Orquesta Sinfónica Nacional* in Ciudad Trujillo on October 23, 1941), two symphonic dances, a *Sinfonia Giocosa,* a Suite for flute and string orchestra, and *Homage to the Dominican National Anthems,* in which he incorporated two old anthems, and the present official anthem of the Republic. Mena's capriccio for piano, *Elila,* is published by the Alpha Music Corporation in New York.

Ramón Emilio PERALTA (1868–1941) was a composer of popular music. His list of compositions includes twenty-five *Danzas,* seven waltzes, five mazurkas, three operettas, and also polkas, marches, and *habaneras.*

Rafael PETITÓN GUZMÁN is a Dominican who, since 1939, has been living in New York. Guzmán is a native of Salcedo, where he was born on December 18, 1894. He has composed numerous popular dances and a *Suite Antillana,* in three movements, reflecting the folklore of Puerto Rico, Cuba, and Santo Domingo.

José de Jesús RAVELO (1876———) has written over two hundred compositions of various types, all in a traditional European style. His oratorio, *La Muerte de Cristo,* published by Schirmer, bears the opus number 144. It was performed on April 7, 1939, at the Basilica of the Santa María Cathedral in Ciudad Trujillo.

Luis RIVERA (1902———) studied violin and piano. As a composer, he cultivates the native folklore. His *Poema Indio* for orchestra, baritone, and narrator was performed by the *Orquesta Sinfónica Nacional* in Ciudad Trujillo on July 29, 1942. He has also written two Dominican Rhapsodies for piano and orchestra, the first of which was performed in Ciudad Trujillo on September 23, 1941.

Fernando A. RUEDA (1859–1939), the composer of salon music, was a native of Santo Domingo. He wrote a number of popular dances for the military band, of which *Bodas de Oro,* first performed in Santo Domingo on August 16, 1913, is still widely popular in the Dominican Republic.

Manuel Simó (1916——) played in a military band, and later in the *Orquesta Sinfónica Nacional* in Ciudad Trujillo. He studied with Casal Chapí, and has shown interest in contrapuntal constructions. He has written short pieces for piano, and a symphonic composition, *Pastoral.*

Esteban Peña Morell (1894–1939), a Negro musician, was born in Santo Domingo; died in Barcelona, Spain. He fought in the Revolution of 1913, and was wounded seven times. At one time he played the bassoon in the Havana Philharmonic Orchestra. He has written a symphonic poem, *Anacaona,* and a *Sinfonía Barbara* for military band, in which he makes use of special percussion effects. His compilation of native folk songs, *La Folklo-Música Dominicana,* was to have been published in 1930, but the catastrophic cyclone that struck the island on September third of that year frustrated the plans.

Augusto Vega (1885——) has written an orchestral suite based on native themes, entitled *Folklore Sinfónico;* an overture, *Duarte,* portraying the patriotic deeds of a hero of the Dominican wars for independence; an opera, *Indigena;* and songs.

Ecuador

> . . . *Concedió bellos presentes*
> *Providencia a las gentes*
> *Del Ecuador feliz* . . .
> [ANDRÉS BELLO]

Ecuador takes its name from its geographical position astride the Equator. The country presents a great variety of climatic and topographical conditions, from the jungle lowlands to the forbidding mountain landscapes. Ecuador's population is about three million, the Indians being in considerable majority. The capital, Quito, is one of the highest cities in the world, nearly two miles up in the air.

The folklore of Ecuador is part of the ancient culture of the Andean plateau, which includes contemporary Peru and Bolivia. Here, the Indians still live in primeval isolation in their mountain retreats. This isolation has largely contributed to the preservation of ancient melodies, untrammeled by post-Columbian influences. Padre Raimundo M. Monteros has published a number of Indian melodies from the eastern part of Ecuador in a brochure entitled *Música Autóctona del Oriente Ecuatoriano* (Quito, 1942). The intervallic structure of most of these melodies is rudimentary, and the pentatonic scale is never complete.

Indian Melodies from Ecuador (*Padre Monteros*)

At a more advanced stage of melodic development, the native chants of Ecuador adhere to the pentatonic scale. Many such melodies are found in the essay on Ecuadorian music by Segundo Luis Moreno, published in the second volume of *El Ecuador en Cien Años de Independencia* (Quito, 1930), and in *La Musique des Incas et ses Survivances* (Paris, 1925), by d'Harcourt.

With the advent of the Conquistadores, the aboriginal pentatonic scale was extended to the seven-tone scale. Minor keys are more commonly employed in Ecuador's folk music than the major, a circumstance that some consider a sign of decadence. The historical explanation of the prevalence of minor modes in Ecuador's music is that ancient chants of the Indians often begin with the interval of a minor third, which influenced the formation of later folk songs in the direction of minor tonality.

The rhythm of Ecuador's folk music is Hispanic in character. The meter is characteristic: it is dual three-four and six-eight time, which is assimilated into two-four time by the conversion of six-eight into two groups of duplets. The Negro element, so strong in the music of the West Indies and Brazil, is here negligible.

The national air of Ecuador is the *Sanjuanito*, named after Ecuador's patron saint, St. John. The music of the *Sanjuanito* is invariably cast in a minor key, in two-four time. Its rhythm is characterized by mild syncopation, and the conversion of a syncopated group of a sixteenth-note, an eighth-note, and a sixteenth-note into a triplet figure is common.

The *Pasillo*, which is indigenous to the entire North of the South American continent, assumes in Ecuador a minor tonality, whereas the Colombian *Pasillos* are mostly in the major. The *Yarawi*, a melancholy Indian song, is also heard in Ecuador's highlands.

Other airs peculiar to Ecuador are the *Pasacalle* (not to be confused with the classical *Passacaglia*) of Bolivian origin, the *Danzante* and the *Guaranda*, which are festival dances, and an Indian air, the *Cachullapi*. These airs are in six-eight or two-four time. Popular among Ecuador's Negroes is a sentimental ballad *Amor Fino*, which is embellished with considerable syncopation.

Several hybrid musical forms in Ecuador's folklore are a product of assimilation of native rhythms and European dances. Such is, for instance, the *Pasillo-Mazurka*, which preserves the character of the South American *Pasillo*, while retaining the rhythmic cadence of the *Mazurka*, with its typical accent on the second beat. The Americanization of the native *Sanjuanito* results in a ludicrous creation named *Foxtrot Incaico*.

These airs are sung and danced to the accompaniment of the guitar or harp. The typical instrument of native origin is the *Rondador*, a panpipe made of a series of bamboo reeds or condor feathers. Also popular among the natives are vertical flutes, known under the generic name of *Pingullo*. The Cuban *Maracas* is called *Chil-Chil* in Ecuador.

The cultivation of serious music in Ecuador lags behind the rich development of folk music. An interesting account of the status of music in Ecuador a hundred years ago is found in *Four Years Among Spanish Americans* (New York, 1868), by F. Hassaurek, who served as United States Minister to Ecuador. He writes:

There are about one hundred and twenty pianos in Quito, very indifferently tuned; but there are very few ladies who play well. The guitar and the harp are great favorites, especially with the middle and lower classes; but a woman who plays either of these instruments scarcely ever knows a note. Her stock of music is therefore easily exhausted, whenever she is called upon for songs.

Moreover, they sing chiefly through the nose, especially when they sing one of their national tunes.

Some information of the history of music in Ecuador is found in the essay by Segundo Moreno in the centennial edition *El Ecuador en Cien Años de Independencia*. Here are a few salient points. The first church organ in Ecuador was installed in the Cathedral of Cuenca in 1730, and is still in practical use. The first national conservatory was founded in Quito by the government decree of February 28, 1870. Its first director was Antonio Neumane, a native-born musician of German extraction, and the author of Ecuador's National Anthem. The Italian musician Domenico Brescia, who was director of the Conservatory between 1903 and 1911 and who wrote an *Ecuadorian Symphony*, was the first to cultivate native folklore in serious composition. Among Brescia's disciples, Segundo Luis Moreno and Luis H. Salgado have distinguished themselves in the field of native-inspired composition. The name of Pedro Traversari, pedagogue and composer, should also be mentioned.

MUSICIANS OF ECUADOR

Segundo Luis MORENO (1882——) in 1906 entered the Conservatory of Quito, where he studied composition with Domenico Brescia. Having completed his studies, he joined the faculty of the Conservatory and was also appointed leader of the military band in Quito. He has composed numerous piano pieces and songs, as well as popular dances. For the orchestra, he has written a *Preludio*, first performed in Quito on July 20, 1910; an overture *10 de Agosto*, performed in Quito on July 4, 1911; an Overture *9 de Julio*, dedicated to the leader of the revolution of July 9, 1925; and—his most important work—*Suite Ecuatoriana*, composed in 1922, and performed in Cuenca on July 24, 1940. These scores, as well as a symphonic march, *La Coronación*, are included in the Fleisher Collection of Philadelphia. Segundo Moreno is the author of an exhaustive treatise on Ecuadorean folklore and music history, in three large sections, of which the first is published in the now rare edition, *El Ecuador en Cien Años de Independencia* (1930).

Luis H. SALGADO (1903——) received private instruction in pianoforte and composition from his father. In 1928 he was graduated from the Conservatory of Quito as a pianist, and later became instructor of harmony and musical dictation at the Conservatory. Salgado has written prolifically in all forms. His symphonic suite, *Atahualpa, or the Sunset of an Empire,* was first performed in Quito under his direction on August 29, 1933. Salgado's style of composition, while not advanced, possesses a certain element of sophistication. His orchestral dance, *Pasillo-Intermezzo,* is included in the Fleisher Collection of Philadelphia.

Pedro TRAVERSARI (1874——) studied in Ecuador and in Italy. In 1898, he was engaged by the Chilean government as instructor at the National Conservatory in Santiago. From 1915 to 1923 he was director of the Quito Conservatory. Traversari has written a symphonic suite, *Glorias Andinas,* which he conducted in Quito on August 14, 1930, on the occasion of the Centenary of Ecuador's Independence. He has further written several "indigenous melodramas," whose titles reflect the native folklore: *Cumanda, or the Virgin of the Jungle; The Prophecy of Huira-cochas* and *Kizkiz, or the Last Exponent of the Inca Spirit.* The style of his music is entirely within the academic tradition. The orchestral scores of Traversari's *Tríptico Indoandino* and *Himno Pentafónico* are included in the Fleisher Collection of Philadelphia. Traversari is the owner of a valuable collection of pre-Columbian native instruments.

Guatemala

¡Guatemala feliz!
[FROM GUATEMALA'S NATIONAL ANTHEM]

The aboriginal name of Guatemala is Quauhitemallan, which means "full of trees." Guatemala lies between Honduras and Mexico. Its population numbers 3,300,000 inhabitants, of which 60 per cent are Indians.

To the musical world, Guatemala is known as the land of the *Marimba,* a picturesque native instrument which consists of a series of bars and keys, made of sonorous wood, with gourds of different sizes suspended underneath for resonance. Jesús Castillo, the foremost musicologist of Guatemala, submits as proof of the native origin of the *Marimba* the fact that there is in Guatemala a mountain named Chinal Jul, which means, in the native dialect, "the *Marimba* of the Ravines."

Other native instruments of Guatemala are common to all Central America. They are the *Zu or Xul*, which is a vertical flute; a small wind instrument named *Tzijolaj*; the *Chirimía*, which is the general name for clarinet-like wind instruments; the *Tun* or *Teponaxtle*, which is a drum made of a hollowed-out tree trunk; and the *Tot*, which is an incrustated shell.

Jesús Castillo has classified the aboriginal melodies of the Quiché Indians of Guatemala into six categories. The first is characterized by a progression of five notes, in whole tones. The second and the third are identical with four notes (the dominant, tonic, supertonic, and mediant) of the major scale; the fourth is a minor hexachord; the fifth is composed of elements of major and minor scales; and the sixth represents the descending scale in the Mixolydian mode, with a semitone below the final note.

Six Basic Types of Quiché Melodies of Guatemala and Their Scale
Patterns (*Castillo*)

Six Basic Types of Quiché Melodies of Guatemala and Their Scale
Patterns—*Concluded* (*Castillo*)

Castillo propounds an interesting hypothesis regarding the origin of
some of these primitive scales, namely that they imitate the song of the
Guatemalan Cenzontle, a bird of the thrush family. The remarkable
circumstance is that these birds sing along the tones of a major scale. To
quote Castillo: "Through these native birds, nature has placed the Indian
in contact with constructive musical elements. The song of these birds
lies within a perfect major scale, from the Dominant to the Dominant,
and contains intervals of the second, third, fourth, fifth, and the sixth. In

the song of these birds one finds syncopation, rests, holds, rudimentary transitions from the Dominant to the Tonic, and even modulations."

The present-day popular dances in Guatemala are mainly native versions of European ballroom dances. The only native air is the *Son Chapín*, or *Son Guatemalteco*, as it is also called. It is in waltz time, with cross-accentuation resulting through the superposition of six-eight time on the basic three-four time signature.

Music history in Guatemala is not rich in events or personalities, but some names have been retained in its annals. Guatemala's first native-born musician of merit was Don José Escolástico Andrino, who was active in El Salvador, whither he went about 1845. Rafael González Sol, in his *Historia del Arte de la Música en El Salvador*, quotes the opinion of a Guatemalan musician about Andrino, couched in terms of extravagant praise: "Don José Escolástico Andrino was a colossus. He played the violin in Havana, and he was also a great composer. Among his creations were two symphonies, three Masses, and an opera, *The Generous Mooress*."

A nineteenth-century harbinger of musical culture in Central America, and in Guatemala in particular, was the Italian musician Juan Aberle. He taught a generation of native musicians. The grateful Government bestowed upon him a gold medal inscribed "To the Prince of Central American Music."

The first native musician to write music inspired by Guatemalan folk-lore was Luis Felipe Arias, who possessed a European education. When he was assassinated in Guatemala City in 1904, apparently by mistake, the cause of native music suffered a setback which was not soon remedied.

The Indian folklore of Guatemala is cultivated chiefly by Jesús Castillo, who has, apart from his musicological labors, written the first Guatemalan opera on an Indian subject, *Quiché Vinak*. Its performance in 1924 was a landmark in Guatemala's native musical culture. Jesús Castillo has also published an analytic survey of Central American music under the title, *La Música Maya-Quiché* (1941). His half-brother, Ricardo Castillo, had the benefit of musical study in Paris. He has written a suite of pieces, *Guatemala*, in which native rhythms and melodic inflections form the thematic foundation.

Technically, the best-equipped native composer of Guatemala is Raúl Paniagua, whose symphonic poem, *The Mayan Legend*, is a well-integrated work based on the melo-rhythmic elements of ancient Indian music of Central America. Franz Ippisch, an Austrian musician who settled in Guatemala, has contributed to native composition by selecting Guatemalan Indian themes as a basis of his *Sinfonía Guatemalteca*.

Alberto Mendoza has written some music in small forms, but he is chiefly active as a pedagogue in Guatemala City. Of the younger generation, Salvador Ley merits mention. His compositions, however, are in the European manner, without reference to native folklore.

José Molina Pinillo and Felipe Siliézar have written some instrumental music in the native manner. Mariano Valverde, principally known as a Marimba player, is the composer of popular waltzes. Julian Paniagua, an uncle of Raúl Paniagua, has written songs that have attained considerable popularity in Central America.

In a class by himself is José Castañeda, an experimenter in ultra-modern music. In 1934 he founded in Guatemala City an orchestral group significantly named *Ars Nova*, which was later developed into a symphony orchestra called *Orquesta Progresista*, which presented its first concert on January 7, 1936. In 1944 the *Orquesta Progresista* was discontinued, and a new organization was formed in its place, the *Orquesta Filarmónica de Guatemala*, which gave its first concert on September 8, 1944.

An important medium of musical culture and education is the radio station *La Voz de Guatemala*, which possesses modern equipment. It maintains a regular schedule of orchestral and instrumental music, and is powerful enough to be heard throughout Central America.

MUSICIANS OF GUATEMALA

One of the first cultured musicians of Guatemala was Luis Felipe ARIAS (1870–1908) who was assassinated in the streets of Guatemala City on March 24, 1908, possibly by mistake. His killers were apprehended and sentenced to six months in jail. Arias, whose death occurred when he was thirty-eight years old, was educated in Europe. He was active as a teacher, and left several compositions, mostly short pieces. The orchestral score of his *Moorish Dance* is included in the Fleisher Collection of Philadelphia.

José CASTAÑEDA (1898——) is a versatile musician and a writer in the field of music. When Castañeda returned to his native land, after spending some time in Paris, he directed for a brief period an orchestral ensemble *Ars Nova* in Guatemala City, and conducted concerts of Latin American music in New York at the World's Fair in 1939. In his theoretical investigations, Castañeda has developed a new notation of twelve chromatic tones, dispensing with sharps and flats.

Jesús CASTILLO (1877–1946), composer and music scholar, studied in his native city, Quezaltenango, and has always been devoted to the cultivation of native music. In 1896, he wrote his first symphonic work based on these native melodies, *Obertura Indigena*. Castillo's indigenous opera *Quiché Vinák* was performed in Guatemala City on July 24, 1924, in the orchestration of Fabian Rodriguez. The subject of the opera is based on the ancient prophecy of an Indian sorcerer who predicted the ruin of the Quiché empire. Later Castillo undertook the composition of another native opera, *Nicté*, and a ballet, *Guatema*. While his early works were quite conventional in harmony and technically inadequate, he later enlarged his harmonic vocabulary. As a scholar, Castillo has summarized the results of his research in a brochure, *La Música Maya-Quiché* (1941). Castillo's piano pieces from the suite *Popol Buj* (Guatemalan Indian sacred book) have been published in Paris. The following orchestral works by Castillo are included in the Fleisher Collection in Philadelphia: *Tecum Overture*, Minuet from the *Suite Indigena*, Prelude, and *Hymn to the Sun*.

Ricardo CASTILLO (1891———) is a half-brother of Jesús Castillo. In 1911, after making preliminary studies of music in his native town, Ricardo Castillo went to Paris, where he studied with Paul Vidal. During World War I, he enlisted in the French army, and in 1922 returned to Guatemala. His compositions, for piano, voice, and later for orchestra, are generally short pieces, notable for color and feeling for native melos. His suite for piano, entitled *Guatemala*, was published in Paris, and in its orchestral form it was first performed on November 8, 1934, in Guatemala City. The first movement of Castillo's Symphony, and his "symphonic evocation," *Xibalba*, on ancient Mayan themes, were performed at the concert of the *Orquesta Filarmónica de Guatemala* in Guatemala City on September 8, 1944. The following orchestral scores by Ricardo Castillo are in the Fleisher Collection of Philadelphia: *La Doncella Ixquic*, *Guatemala*, *La Procesión*, and the *Fairy of the Blue Mountain*.

Franz IPPISCH (1883———), an Austrian by birth, settled in Guatemala in 1938; his flight from Austria was made imperative because of his wife's non-Aryan background. On September 22, 1939, he was named Director General de Músicas Marciales in Guatemala City. He also conducts the ensemble class at the National Conservatory at Guatemala City. Ippisch is the composer of numerous symphonic works, distinguished by a solid mastery of the medium, albeit in an academic tradition. As a tribute to his adopted country, he composed a *Sinfonía Guatemalteca,* which he conducted on September 13, 1941, with the *Orquesta Progresista* of Guatemala City. Two previous symphonies, a Violin Concerto, an Overture, much chamber music, and instrumental pieces belong to the European period of his career. The Fleisher Collection of Philadelphia has the following scores by Ippisch: Concerto for Violin and Orchestra, *Eine Lustige Ouverture,* three symphonies, *Pastorale* for cello and chamber orchestra, *Pierrots Liebeswerben,* and *Suite for String Orchestra.*

Salvador LEY (1907———) went at the age of fifteen to Berlin to study piano and composition. He returned to Guatemala in 1934, and was appointed director of the National Conservatory of Music, a post which he held until 1937, and again since 1944. In 1939 he visited the United States, where he gave concerts of Latin American music. As a composer, he affects a modern percussive style. He has written a Concertino for Piano and Chamber Orchestra (1942).

Alberto MENDOZA (1889———), educator and composer, studied with Luis F. Arias. In 1925 Mendoza was appointed director of the National Conservatory of Guatemala, a post which he held until 1931. For some time, Mendoza was director of the oldest music organization in Guatemala, the *Sociedad Filarmónico-Religiosa,* founded in 1813. Mendoza has written several piano pieces and songs. Of his compositions for the military band, a triumphal march, *Glory to the General García Granados,* has received a prize.

José MOLINA PINILLO (1889———), of Guatemala City, studied with Julian Carrillo in Mexico and with Scharwenka in Berlin. His *Guatemalan Rhapsodies, Miniatura,* and *Cromos Nacionales,* written in an effective if conventional manner, are included in the Fleisher Collection in Philadelphia.

Raúl PANIAGUA (1898———) is a nephew of Julian Paniagua Martinez, the composer of popular music. He studied piano in Guatemala and composition in New York. Raúl Paniagua possesses a solid technique of composition in all forms, and his feeling for folklore enables him to write effective music in a native manner. His most representative work is *The Mayan Legend* for orchestra, first performed by the National Orchestral Association of New York on February 17, 1931. Paniagua has also written songs and piano pieces, in an impressionist style. The score of *The Mayan Legend* is in the Fleisher Collection in Philadelphia.

Julian PANIAGUA MARTINEZ (1856——), the composer of popular music, studied violin with his father, Francisco Paniagua. When he was thirteen years old, in 1869, he wrote a waltz entitled *La Tos Ferina*, which was the popular name of the epidemic that devastated the country at the time. As a youth, Paniagua Martinez enlisted in the army during the war with El Salvador, and, after the war, conducted the *Banda de Guerra* in Quezaltenango. Paniagua Martinez is the owner of a music store in Guatemala City, in which he has printed a dozen of his popular dances. The orchestral arrangement of his waltz *Martha* is included in the Fleisher Collection in the Free·Library of Philadelphia.

Felipe SILIÉZAR (1903——) received his preliminary musical education in Guatemala; then spent five years in New York. Returning to Guatemala, he conducted military bands in provincial towns. Later he abandoned music in favor of commerce, and is now the owner of a general store "La Economica" in Antigua, which sells featherweight tropical shoes, gasoline lamps, spectacles, and lottery tickets. The orchestral score of Siliézar's suite, *Bewitching Maya*, is included in the Fleisher Collection in Philadelphia.

Mariano VALVERDE (1884——), amateur composer and marimba player, is a native of Quezaltenango. He has written fifty-three popular compositions with picturesque titles, such as *Noche de Luna en las Ruinas*.

Haiti

Bing, Dahomé, bing, bing, bing, Dahomé!
Bing, Dahomé, bing, bing, bing, Dahomé!
[FROM A VOODOO SONG OF HAITI]

The Negro Republic of Haiti occupies the western third of the island of Santo Domingo. The population, which numbers about three million, consists of descendants of African slaves. Haiti is the only Latin American nation with French as its official language.

The music of Haiti is a music of drums. The rhythms are African rather than Latin. The Latin strain is revealed only in "civilized" songs of later date. There is nothing of the Indian left in the folklore of Haiti. Arthur C. Holly, the Haitian writer, says in his book *Les Daimons du Culte Vodu:* "We are Latin Africans. Our Latin culture is on the surface, while the primeval African strain dominates our souls . . . Our senses respond naturally to the syncopated rhythms of the sacred dances of the Voodoo ritual, which inspire us with passion."

The sound of the drums is full of meaning to the natives. The drums serve as the telegraph of the jungle, carrying messages of war and peace; they accompany all great events of family and community life; they are religious and medicinal symbols in the Voodoo rites. In Eugene O'Neill's drama *Emperor Jones,* the monotonous sound of the jungle drums spells the doom of the former Pullman porter who has become a Voodoo ruler.

W. B. Seabrook heard classical counterpoint in the beating of Haitian drums. He writes in his book *The Magic Island:* * "It was not syncopation. It was not remotely jazz. It was pure counterpoint, like a Bach fugue, except that the core of it was slow, unhurried, relentless. There was something cosmic in it, like the rolling of mighty waters."

The playing of drums together by native drummers is polyrhythmic. The smaller drums beat in fast time, while the big drums accentuate the main beat.

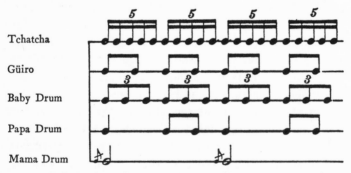

Polyrhythmic Design of Haitian Drum Ensemble (*Lamothe*)

Haitian drums bear picturesque names. Thus the drums of the Voodoo ritual are called Mama Drum, Papa Drum, and Baby Drum. The Mama Drum is the largest. Its sound is reputed to be capable of warding off the

* Harcourt, Brace & Co., 1929.

Zombies, the walking dead of the popular superstition. Among other Haitian drums, there is the *Assotor*, which is said to be so sensitive that it vibrates like the Aeolian harp in the breeze. There is a family of drums bearing the generic name *Petro*, and there is the work drum *Tambour-Travaille*, and a unique *Tambour Meringouin*, which is not a drum at all despite its name; it is a musical bow, consisting of a string attached on one end to a branch of a tree, and on the other, to a drumhead of cow hide, which covers a hole in the ground. When the branch is agitated the string vibrates. The hole in the ground serves as a resonator.

Like all islanders of the West Indies, the Haitians use gourds filled with dried seed, which are shaken in the air to make noise. These were the first native instruments of the islands found by Columbus. The Cubans call these shakers *Maracas*, but in Haiti the instrument is known under the onomatopoeic name *Tchatcha*. The only wind instrument of Haiti is a primitive trumpet called *Vaccine*. Finally, there are nondescript unclassified noise-makers used by the natives on various occasions, makeshift devices manufactured of wood, scrap metal, or anything that comes to hand.

A complete description of Haitian instruments, with photographs, is given in the authoritative article by Harold Courlander in the July, 1941, issue of *The Musical Quarterly*.

The native melodies of the Haitian Negroes are rarely more than instinctive incantations, alternating between shouts and mumblings, wherein certain vocables seem to be infused with a ritualistic significance. Melville Herskovits, in his book *Life in a Haitian Valley*,* gives the following account of native music: "The musical forms are almost entirely African in rhythmic structure, but European influence is traceable in their melodic line, which varies from unchanged European folk melodies to purely African songs. In the use of the falsetto, however, in the statement of a theme by the leader and its repetition by the chorus, and in the countless modulations introduced into the song, the singing is African."

European influence is strongly reflected in the songs popular among the population of towns and larger villages, where contact with the outside world is maintained in the cosmopolitan cafés and taverns. Later the gramophone and the radio brought to Haiti the folklore of other lands, and American jazz.

The authentic songs and dances of Haiti relate, to a greater or lesser extent, to the social and religious code of the Voodoo, or *Vodoun*, which

* Alfred A. Knopf, 1937.

is the way the natives pronounce the word. The names of these chants and dances indicate a mixture of African and French elements. Here are a few: *Baboule, Ka, Rada, Rara, Quitta, Bamboche, Juba, Bumba, Loangue, Salongo, Mousondi, Moutchétché*. Harold Courlander gives a comprehensive account of these dances in his book *Haiti Singing* (1939).

The most popular song-dance of modern Haiti is the *Meringue*, which is the French spelling of the *Merengue*, the national dance of the Dominican Republic, Haiti's neighbor. The Haitian *Meringue* is often in the minor key, while the Dominican *Merengue* is usually in the major. Then there is the difference in the language of the text, which in the Haitian song is French, in the Dominican, Spanish. Otherwise, the two types are identical in rhythm and in musical structure.

The Haitian composer, Ludovic Lamothe, who has been called "The Black Chopin," has given the following description of the *Meringue:* "Our rhythms are Spanish and Negro, and our national dance, the *Meringue*, shows the influence of both elements. The origin of the name *Meringue* is uncertain. Some derive it from the name of the French pastry; others trace it to the *Meringha*, an African dance in duple time. The *Meringue* is danced in the salons in a more dignified manner than by the populace in the streets. There it is a veritable earthquake of hips and thighs, as in Africa . . . The composers of the new school often include the *Meringue* in their compositions. This usage imparts a certain consistence to the music, but also a certain monotony."

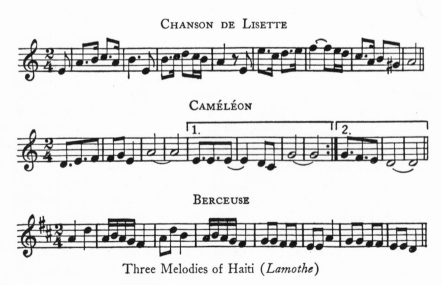

Three Melodies of Haiti (*Lamothe*)

The unique significance of Haitian music is that it is the instinctive expression of primitive emotions, virtually free from all considerations of measure and rhythm inherent in organized musical forms. As such, this Latin African art is a potential reservoir of new musical developments, awaiting the appearance of a native composer who will be able to concentrate this inchoate force in a recognizable musical form, as Caturla did in Afro-Cuban music and Villa-Lobos in his Afro-Brazilian inspirations. So far, Haiti has not produced such a composer. The first educated musician of Haitian birth was Justin Elie, who spent most of his life in New York. Another Haitian composer, Occide Jeanty, was a military band conductor. Ludovic Lamothe, dean of living Haitian musicians, is *Chef de Musique* at the Governor's Palace in Haiti's capital, Port au Prince.

MUSICIANS OF HAITI

Justin ELIE (1883–1931) was born in Cap Haitien and died in New York City. He studied the rudiments of music in Haiti and then went to Paris, where he entered the Conservatory. On his return to Haiti, he became interested in the ceremonial music of the Voodoo ritual, and wrote some pieces in a native manner. In 1922, he went to New York, and remained there until his death. His pieces for piano, violin, and voice have been published in the United States. Also published is the theater orchestra arrangement of his *Aboriginal Suite*. His music affects an orientalistic style, and its harmonic style is conventional.

A composer whose entire life of seventy-six years (1860–1936) was spent in Port-au-Prince is Occide JEANTY. He showed musical ability at an early age, and was sent to Paris by the government to continue his studies. Returning to Haiti in 1886, he was appointed musical director of the Republic. He was also active as a conductor of military bands. He has written a number of marches in the Sousa manner.

Ludovic LAMOTHE (1882——), the Negro composer, is also a native of Port-au-Prince. Lamothe showed musical aptitude at an early age, and, after a course of study in piano and elementary harmony, he went to Paris in 1910, where he took lessons at the Conservatory. Returning to Haiti, Lamothe devoted himself to the study of folklore. The simple charm of his music led some admirers to call him a "Black Chopin." He has recorded ten of his piano pieces for Victor, in an album entitled *Fleurs d'Haiti*. Two piano pieces, *Nibo* (*Meringue de Carnaval*) and

La Dangereuse (*Meringue Haitienne*), and a song, *Billet,* have been printed for the author in New York, Hamburg, and Paris, respectively. Ludovic Lamothe is now Chief of Music of the Republic of Haiti.

Honduras

¡Qué dicha tan grande nacer en Honduras!
[RAFAEL COELLO RAMOS]

The word Honduras means "the depths," the name having been applied by Columbus on his last voyage, when he found a great depth of water off the North coast of Honduras. Honduras borders on Nicaragua, El Salvador, and Guatemala. Its population numbers about 1,100,000, of which 70 per cent are Mestizos and 20 per cent Indians.

Music in Honduras is in a rudimentary state. In reply to a query, M. de Adalid y Gamera, a Honduran-born musician, and now a citizen of the United States, writes to the author: "There have never been in my country any Conservatories of Music. Musicians here are simple amateurs, without real musical training; yet they do not lack talent. There are at least fifty such amateurs who 'compose' music, among them Rafael Coello Ramos, who has been teaching solfeggio, Ignacio Galeano, Francisco Diaz Zelaya, and Camilo Rivera."

In their autobiographical notes, the "composers" themselves willingly admit the inadequacy of their training. Ramon Ruiz writes: "I use only chords I can find on my guitar." Ignacio Galeano complains that his addiction to alcohol has "rapidly led to bodily destruction and moral disintegration" and has prevented the development of his musical talent.

Recently the Inspector General of Music of the Republic, Rafael Coello Ramos, introduced a system of music instruction in public schools, which he called "Desanalfabetización Musical Hondureño" (Musical Dis-illiteratization of Honduras), but as he bitterly complains in his paper *La Cultura Musical del Pueblo Hondureño,* published in Volume IV of the *Boletín Latino-Americano de Música*, "it has not been possible for me to extend the radius of my activities to all schools of the country, because I cannot afford traveling expenses by plane, which is the only possible means of communication." "The avalanche of mechanical music," Coello Ramos continues, "has been disastrous for Honduras. While gramophones and radios are found in the majority of homes, pianos and other musical instruments are neglected and unappreciated. As a consequence, musical culture has dropped almost to the zero point. What is needed, besides the energetic intervention of the public authorities, is the aid of those who understand that art is the fountainhead of civilization."

Attempts have been made in the past to cultivate music in Honduras. José Trinidad Reyes (1797–1855), the Bishop of Honduras, who was a poet, an architect, a painter, and an astronomer, included music in the educational program of the government. In recent times, a musician named Leonidas Rodriguez established an Academy of Music in Tegucigalpa, the capital of Honduras. But he was killed in an automobile accident, and with his death the project was abandoned.

Concert music in Honduras, apart from rare visits by foreign musicians, is supplied mainly by military bands, which exist in every sizable town of the country. The best military band is the one in Tegucigalpa, bearing the proud appellation of the *Banda de los Supremos Poderes* (Band of the Supreme Powers).

MUSICIANS OF HONDURAS

Francisco Díaz Zelaya (1898———), now conductor of the *Banda de los Supremos Poderes* in Tegucigalpa, is a native of Ojojana.

The musician Camilo Rivera (1878———) is known chiefly as a conductor of military bands and as the composer of numerous popular dances.

Ramon Ruiz (1894———), the amateur musician resident in Honduras, is a Nicaraguan by birth. He admits that his musical equipment is limited to the chords he can find on his guitar.

Because of extreme poverty in his youth, Ignacio Villanueva Galeano (1885———) was unable to devote himself to serious study, and instead practiced music on a homemade flute. Later he became a band conductor. An unfortunate addiction to alcohol forced him eventually to abandon music. In his lucid moments Villanueva Galeano wrote military marches. The score of his *Pan American Union March* is included in the Fleisher Collection in Philadelphia.

Mexico

A Mexico el Criador en sus bondades
Le ha dado un aire diafano y sereno.
[MANUEL CARPIO]

The name Mexico comes from that of the Aztec war god, Mexitli. The population of the present Republic of Mexico is about twenty million, of whom Indians and Mestizos constitute a majority. Mexico City numbers a million and a quarter inhabitants.

The territory of Mexico was the ground on which the Spanish Conquistadores and the greatest of American Indian civilizations met, fought, and fused into a new nation. Three successive cultures existed in Mexico before the conquest: the Mayas, the Toltecs, and the Aztecs. Of these great civilizations, many monuments have been preserved. We know a great deal about the religion, the science, and the arts of ancient Mexico. We know something about pre-conquest music, thanks to musical instruments that have been preserved. Melody, rhythm, and tone-color were the media of musical expression among ancient Mexicans. The melody was given out by the wind instruments made of clay; the rhythm was punctuated on the drums; and tone-color was diversified by the use of different material, different shapes and sizes of these instruments.

The structure of the wind instruments in use among ancient Mexicans points to the predominance of the pentatonic scale, without semitones, and usually with the minor third at the base, la, do, re, mi, sol. Melodies of great antiquity are still sung by old Indians, who learned them by tradition from their fathers and grandfathers. One of these melodies, a Mayan Warriors' song, Los Xtoles, has been notated by Mexican folklore collectors.*

Carlos Chavez has collected several dance airs of Mexican Indians. One of these airs he used in the last movement of his symphonic poem, Cuatro Soles.

* Courtesy of the Music Section of the Secretariat of Education of Mexico.

LOS XTOLES

Song of Mayan Warriors (*Baqueiro Foster*)

Ancient Mexican Dance (*Chavez*)

The instrumental resources of ancient Mexican music were of six principal types: (1) Flutes, *Chililihtli;* and ocarinas and panpipes, *Tlapitzalli;* (2) Marine snail shell, *Atecocoli;* (3) Vertical drum, *Huehuetl;* (4) Horizontal drum, *Teponaxtle;* (5) Calabash rasps, *Tzicahuaztli;* and bone rasps, *Omichitzicahuaztli;* (6) Gourd filled with pebbles, *Ayacaztli.*

The *Chililihtli* was a vertical flute made of baked clay. Several tubes joined together formed a panpipe called *Tlapitzalli.* The tones produced by the *Chililihtli* and by the *Tlapitzalli* never exceed five. Some native melodies of ancient type are built on three different tones only. The Indians do not find their chants monotonous, for they color each tone with greatly varied dynamics; the manner of singing and the duration of each tone provide additional means of expression.

The marine snail shell instrument, *Atecocoli,* is capable of producing a low rumbling tone, foreboding and lugubrious in quality. In his piece *Xochipili-Macuilxochitl,* named after the Aztec god of music, flowers and love, Chavez uses the trombone in order to reproduce the sound of the Indian snail shell.

The *Huehuetl* is a vertical drum, made of a hollowed section of a tree, and covered with a drumhead of animal hide. The Mayan name for the

Huehuetl is *Zacatán;* the sound of this word suggests the rhythm of the anapest, expressed in music by two short notes and a long note. This rhythmic figure, two sixteenth-notes and an eighth-note, appears in *Los Xtoles,* song of the Maya Warriors. There were three sizes of *Huehuetl* drums: *Huehuetl* proper, which was of relatively small size; *Panhuehuetl,* of medium size; and *Tlapanhuehuetl,* of large size. (*Huehuetl* means drum, *Pan* means upon, and *Tla,* instrument.)

The *Teponaxtle* is the most important instrument of the ancient Mexicans. It is made of a large section of a tree trunk, and sometimes of stone. There is an aperture in the wall of the trunk. The drum is placed horizontally; the sounds struck to the right and to the left of the aperture differ in tone, usually by a minor or a major third. The pitch is as definite as that in the modern kettle-drums. The *Teponaxtle* was regarded by the Indians as a sacred instrument, and was not played except on solemn occasions. *Teponaxtles* belonging to priests and Indian chiefs had elaborate incrustations. An early Spanish traveler tells of seeing a *Teponaxtle* made of pure gold.

The rasps, *Tzicahuaztli,* were made of baked clay, notched and rubbed with a stick, or with animal and human bones. There are in the National Museum of Mexico several specimens of human femurs, striated, and rubbed with a piece of bone. These human *Tzicahuaztli* were called *Omichitzicahuaztli,* which means bone noise. Human skulls were also used as resonance boxes, or as drums.

The *Ayacaztli,* now called *Sonajas* in Mexico, and *Maracas* in Brazil and Cuba, were made of gourds with pebbles inside.

Other noise-producing instruments used by Mexican Indians are *Cascabeles,* metal jingles with pellets inside; *Tenabaris,* dried butterfly cocoons worn on the ankles by dancers; and the *Jicara de Agua,* made of half a fruit shell, inverted and placed in a basin, half-filled with water. It is played with sticks.

The ancient instruments of Mexico have been the subject of detailed study. Daniel Castañeda and Vicente T. Mendoza published in 1933 the first volume of a monumental work, *Instrumental Precortesiano,* with numerous illustrations, diagrams, and measurements of pre-Cortez instruments in the National Museum of Mexico. Mexican composers often include the *Huehuetl* and *Teponaxtle* in their symphonic works for the sake of authentic color. Carlos Chavez uses the *Huehuetl,* the *Teponaxtle* in his *Cuatro Soles,* and the *Jicara de Agua* in the *Sinfonia India.* In 1933, a special orchestra, named *Orquesta Mexicana,* was formed in Mexico

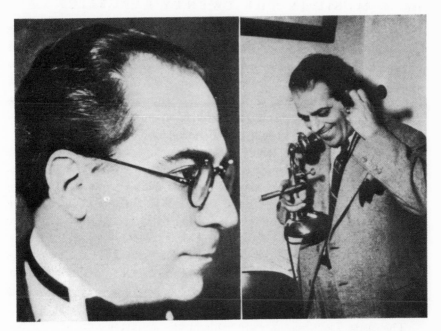

Oscar Lorenzo Fernandez   Heitor Villa-Lobos

Camargo Guarnieri   Francisco Mignone

Humberto Allende   René Amengual

Domingo Santa Cruz   Pablo Garrido

City, with the specific purpose of reviving the old instruments. This orchestra includes a variety of such instruments, the *Teponaxtle*, *Huehuetl*, *Jicara de Agua*, marine shells, *Sonajas*, *Tenabaris*, various rattles, such as *Grijutians*, *Jiruquias*, as well as modern instruments, a large harp, a large guitar, violins, guitars, flutes, trumpets, and the indigenous oboes, *Chirimías*. Carlos Chavez, Daniel Ayala, Luis Sandi, Blas Galindo, and other Mexican composers have written special compositions for this orchestra of native instruments.

In ancient Mexico music was part of religious and civic ceremonies. Instrumental music also accompanied native dances. Juan de Torquemada, a sixteenth-century Spanish missionary, left a description of a typical Indian dance in old Mexico:

When the dancers arrive at the place, they take their places to play the instruments. The two best singers then begin the song. A large drum, played with the hands, is called a *Huehuetl*. The other, played with sticks like the instruments of Spain, is called the *Teponaxtle*. . . . Wishing to begin the dance, three or four Indians raise very shrill whistles. The instruments sound in a low tone, and little by little increase in volume. When the dancers hear the instruments they begin to sing and dance. The first songs go slowly and in a deep tone. When one song is finished (and it seems long because it goes very slowly, though none lasts over an hour), the instrument changes tone, and the leaders begin another chant, a little higher and more lively. In this way, the songs keep rising, as though someone changed from a bass to a tenor voice.

In the early century of the Conquest, the Church militantly opposed ritual dances and songs. In his *Historia de la Música en Mexico*, Gabriel Saldivar quotes a report by a notary of the sacred office of the Inquisition in the province of Zapotitlán, dated November 8, 1623, in which he informs his superiors of the continued practice of "iniquitous and pagan" dances among the Yaqui Indians, and recommends the imposition of a fine of 500 ducats on the community and, in case of further disobedience, deportation of the Indians from their pueblos.

The dances and songs of contemporary Mexico are entirely Spanish in structure. But under the new skies these airs have acquired a tropical accent. The Mexican *Huapango* is ultimately traced to the Spanish *Son*, but its rhythm is definitely of the new world. The *Huapango* combines two-four time with three-four time and six-eight time, creating cross rhythms of great complexity. The word *Huapango* is derived either from a native vocable meaning "on a wooden stand" (the *Huapango* is danced on a platform), or it may be a contraction of *Huaxtecas de Pango*. *Huaxtecas* means a tropical valley, and *Pango* is the ancient name of the river Panuco. In colloquial usage the word *Huapango* assumes a generic significance, and is applied to any Mexican dance.

The *Jarabe* is a descendant of the Spanish *Zapateado*, and its rhythm resembles that of the *Mazurka*. It is in three-four time, with occasional interpolations of six-eight time. Despite its European derivation, the *Jarabe* is stamped with the Mexican spirit. The word *Jarabe* means syrup.

The *Jarana* (the word means merry clatter) is the characteristic dance of Yucatan, and is possibly closer to the melo-rhythmic foundation of ancient Mexican songs than any other native air. The verses of the *Jarana* are often in the Mayan language. The *Zandunga* is a Mexican air in Waltz time. The word means a graceful woman.

The most remarkable native variant of a Spanish musical form is the Mexican *Corrido*. It is a development of the Spanish *Romance*, in which historical or contemporary events, and often trivial gossip, are the subject. One of the Mexican *Corridos* comments on the expropriation of the foreign oil companies by the Mexican government. Vicente T. Mendoza made a thorough study in his valuable book, *Romance y Corrido*, 1939.

The distinctive quality of Mexican popular airs owes a great deal to the characteristic accompanying band. A typical Mexican ensemble is composed of violins, guitars, and the harp. No primitive Mexican instruments are used, yet this *"Orquesta Típica"* is regarded by the Mexicans themselves as their own. The orchestra may be enlarged to include flutes, clarinets and trumpets. The first concert of such a typical orchestra was given in Mexico City on September 30, 1884.

The *Orquesta Típica* is referred to in Mexico City and in the coastal regions as the *Mariachi* band. The origin of the word is obscure. Jacopo Dalevuelta, in his book *Estampas de Mexico*, suggests that it is a corruption of the French word *Mariage*, and that the name stems from the time of the French domination during the short reign of Emperor Maximilian. The *Mariachi* bands were supposed to have played at wedding ceremonies, hence the name. The first verified performance of a *Mariachi* orchestra took place as late as 1907, when an ensemble composed of eight musicians played at a reception for Elihu Root at Cocola. In its present form, *Mariachi* music serves to entertain the public in the Mexican cafés or accompany dancers and singers in village fiestas. The players are garbed in Indian *ponchos* and wear large-brimmed hats. In these urban bands the harp is excluded and a trumpet added. The typical *Mariachi* band consists of two violins, a large five-stringed guitar (*Guitarrón*) and a trumpet. The repertoire of the *Mariachi* band includes Mexican popular songs, *Corridos* and *Huapangos*. These airs are called generically *Sones Mariachi*, that is, *Mariachi* songs. The Mexican composer, Blas Galindo, has written a symphonic score entitled *Mariachi*. Aaron Copland uses the *Mariachi* type of harmony and tone color in his *El Salón Mexico*, named after a once popular night club in Mexico City.

In a *Mariachi* band, the guitar player takes up the singing part, after an instrumental introduction. The melody is apt to be a short musical phrase repeated many times with slight variations. The singing line runs in parallel thirds. This type of harmonization is particularly characteristic of the *Corrido*.

Mexican Corrido (*Mendoza*)

In the music history of the western hemisphere, Mexico holds the chronological honor of being the country where the first book containing musical notation was published. It was an Ordinary of the Mass, printed in Mexico City in 1556. In 1604, a volume of Gregorian melodies was printed in Mexico containing plainsong settings for the Office of Holy Week. The compiler of the volume, Juan Navarro, has been erroneously identified with the famous Spanish musician of the same name. However, documentary evidence has been uncovered showing that the Spanish Juan Navarro died in Palencia, Spain, on September 25, 1580, whereas the licence for the publication of the Mexican volume was issued in 1601, which proves the nonidentity of the two Navarros.

The first music school in Mexico was established by Pedro de Gante (1480–1572), a Flemish musician and a cousin of Emperor Charles V. He founded a chapel in the town of Texcoco in 1523 and taught ecclesiastical singing and musical notation. In 1527 he transferred his school to Mexico City and gave instruction to the natives and to the sons of Spanish officials in the art of instrumental and vocal music. The natives proved to be apt students. One Mexican named Sahagun composed 365 chants in the Aztec language, one for every day of the year.

European dance music made its incursion into Mexico in 1526, when Juan Ortiz petitioned the authorities to grant him permission to open a dancing school "for the embellishment of the city."

The name of Hernando Franco, a sixteenth-century Spanish musician, has been preserved in the annals of Mexican music as the author of the first vocal composition to a text in the Aztec language, a Hymn to the Virgin.

The eighteenth century was marked in Mexican music by the appearance of the first opera written by a native. It was *Parténope*, by Manuel Zumaya, produced in 1711 at the Viceregal Palace in Mexico City. The performance was in Italian, a significant circumstance, for it presaged two centuries of Italian domination in Mexican music.

Towards the end of the eighteenth century there were in Mexico composers of secular music who wrote in imitation of Handel. José Aldana was one of these. He was the author of numerous religious works; a Mass of his composition was recently uncovered in the archives and performed by Carlos Chavez at the Festival of Mexican Music at the Museum of Modern Art in New York City, in May 1940.

Pianofortes were imported into Mexico during the last decade of the eighteenth century. In 1796 a piano manufacturing shop was established in Mexico City. Soon it became fashionable for the upper classes to play the piano at home. The era of musical amateurs had dawned in Mexico as it did in Europe.

In the meantime, the popularity of European salon dances grew steadily in Mexico. The authorities took notice of the danger to public morals in dances in which both sexes participated. In 1779 such dancing was forbidden, and musicians who played for mixed dancing were punished by six months' imprisonment. This measure, however, could not stop the prevalence of dancing.

In 1815, an ecclesiastical official reported that the Waltz was becoming widespread. He denounced the Waltz (which he called *La Balsa*, a floating raft, a rudderless and perilous motion) as a "corrupt importation from degenerate France . . . All of man's depravity could not invent anything more pernicious, nay, not even Hell itself could spawn a monster more obscene. Only those who have seen the *Vals* danced with complete license are in a position to warn of its perils."

The Waltz continued to enjoy wide popularity during the entire nineteenth century, and beyond. It was a Mexican, Juventino Rosas (1868–1894), who gave the world one of the most celebrated Waltzes, *Sobre las Olas* (Over the Waves).

The staple of Mexican musical production in the nineteenth century was piano music of the salon type, enhanced by a more or less adroit imitation of Chopin and of Schumann. Among Mexican composers who excelled in this type of composition three names stand out, Felipe Villanueva, Aniceto Ortega and Melesio Morales. Villanueva cultivated Mexican themes in his numerous salon pieces, and therein lies his importance in the development of a national style of Mexican music. Aniceto Ortega (1823–1875), apart from his semi-popular marches and waltzes, was also the author of the first Mexican opera on a native subject, a one-act "musical episode" entitled *Guatimotzin*. The opera dealt with the last days of the Aztec Empire. Guatemoc (or Cuauhtemoc), the last Emperor of the Aztecs, was the tenor, and Cortez was the bass. The opera, which remains unpublished, is analyzed in great detail in *Panorama de la Música Mexicana* by Otto Mayer-Serra.

Melesio Morales (1838–1908) was the composer of several operas. He also composed a curious piece named *La Locomotiva*, written on the occasion of the opening of a new railroad and performed in Mexico City on November 16, 1869. A contemporary newspaper described the piece as "a musical imitation introducing new instruments in order to reproduce faithfully the roar of the steam engine, the whistle of the locomotive, and even the sound of the wheels turning on the rails, all this mixed with harmonies so strange that they seemed a hymn intoned by modern giants in praise of nineteenth-century civilization."

Numerous Italian and German musicians settled in Mexico in the nineteenth century in the capacity of teachers. One such musician, Hermann Roessler, came to Mexico in the retinue of Emperor Maximilian. He published several character pieces for piano, and also wrote vocal music to texts in the Aztec language.

The growing nationalism in Mexico demanded a national anthem. A special competition was held in 1854 for the best setting of the hymn. The winning composer was Jaime Nunó, a Spaniard by birth, who settled in Mexico and eventually went to the United States, where he died. It is interesting to note that the prize of 2000 pesos for the music was not paid to Nunó by the Mexican administration of Santa Ana. He collected the award only in 1901.

Music was always a favorite art in Mexico, even during the dictatorship of Porfirio Diaz (1877–1910). With the Revolution, new musical forces were released among the Mexican people. Popular waltzes, such as *La Adelita,* became revolutionary airs through adaptation of special sets of words. One of the most striking songs of the period was the anonymous air *La Cucaracha,* which became the fighting song of Pancho Villa during his revolutionary raids. The original text is a nonsense poem about a girl called *La Cucaracha* (Cockroach), who could no longer walk because she had no marijuana to smoke.

LA CUCARACHA

La Cu - ca - ra - cha, La Cu - ca - ra - cha,

Ya no pue - de ca - mi - nar, Por - que no

tie - ne, Por - que le fal - ta ma - ri - jua - na que fu - mar.

The father of music education in Mexico was José Mariano Elízaga (1786–1842). He wrote the first Mexican treatise on music theory, *Elementos de Música,* published in 1823; founded the first music society, *Sociedad Filarmónica,* in 1824; established the first conservatory of music, the *Academia Filarmónica de Mexico,* in 1825; organized the first printing press for publication of secular music, in Mexico City in 1826; and assembled the first symphonic ensemble in Mexico, which he conducted on January 16, 1826, in a program that included his own Overture to the opera *La Italiana.* Elízaga's activities, as well as the general musical atmosphere of Mexico in the nineteenth century, are presented in great detail in the monograph on him by Jesús C. Romero (Mexico, 1934).

The *Conservatorio Nacional de Música,* the oldest music school now existing in Mexico, was founded in Mexico City on January 13, 1877. Melesio Morales was the guiding spirit in the early years of the *Conservatorio Nacional.* He inculcated the Italian style of composition almost to the exclusion of all others. This partiality led to an open rebellion among his disciples, six of whom, headed by Gustavo Campa, founded a rival music school in 1887 and championed the French operatic style of composition.

After the political revolution in Mexico, revolutionary changes also in the domain of the arts followed. In 1928, Carlos Chavez, then a youth of twenty-nine, was appointed Director of the *Conservatorio Nacional de Música*, a post that he held until 1934. In an article in *Modern Music* of March, 1936, he describes this period:

I launched a detailed program for the class in composition in the Conservatory of Music in 1931. We used no text. The students worked untiringly, writing melodies in all the diatonic modes, in a melodic scale of twelve tones, and in all the pentatonic scales. Hundreds of melodies were written, but not merely as exercises. We had instruments in the classroom, and the melodies were played on them. As a result, the young students wrote melodies with an amazingly acute instrumental sense.

In the same year that Chavez became the head of the *Conservatorio Nacional*, he founded the *Orquesta Sinfónica de Mexico*, presenting its first concert on September 2, 1928. Chavez was the conductor of the orchestra and Silvestre Revueltas the assistant conductor. Hernández Moncada became assistant conductor in 1936. The *Orquesta Sinfónica de Mexico* gives weekly concerts on Friday, repeating the same program on the following Sunday. The considered policy of the orchestra is to perform compositions by Mexican musicians. In the first fifteen years of its existence (1928–1943), the orchestra presented seventy works by thirty-one Mexican composers. Recently symphonic organizations have been formed in other cities and towns of Mexico, notably in Guadalajara, Morelia, and Merida.

Concert life in Mexico City includes recitals by visiting and native musicians. At the Palacio de Bellas Artes, concerts of chamber music are given. As yet, there are no permanent opera companies in Mexico. Perhaps for this reason, few modern Mexican composers write operas. In recent years, only one Mexican opera of consequence has been staged, *Tata Vasco* by Bernal Jiménez, not in Mexico City but in the provincial town of Patzcuaro. On the other hand ballet productions are numerous. Chavez, Revueltas, Ayala and other modern Mexicans have written ballets on Mexican subjects.

Otto Mayer-Serra, in his *Panorama de la Música Mexicana*, dates the modern phase of Mexican national music from 1912, when, on July 7,

Manuel Ponce, the author of the celebrated *Estrellita,* gave a concert of his compositions which included works in a purely national vein.

Mexican folklore, which had previously been regarded as exotic material to be treated in a European manner, received at the hands of Manuel Ponce an inner interpretation as a natural form of art. Chavez and Revueltas continued the cultivation of Mexican folklore in the harmonic and contrapuntal technique of ultra-modern music. The melo-rhythmic complex of Mexican folklore also serves as the foundation of works by a group of Chavez' disciples, Daniel Ayala, Salvador Contreras, Pablo Moncayo, and Blas Galindo. These four musicians banded together in 1935 into a *Grupo de los Cuatro,* and from the very beginning devoted their energies to native folklore interpreted in the contemporary technique.

In the meantime, Mexican musicology has made great progress. Numerous collections of Mexican folk songs have been published by the Secretariat of Public Education, among them *Musica Oaxaqueña,* which contains *Mañanitas* and other popular songs of the state of Oaxaca, three issues of *Sones, Canciones y Corridos Michoacanos,* etc. Rubén Campos has published one hundred Mexican melodies in his book, *El Folklore y la Música Mexicana* (351 pages, 1928). He also is the author of *El Folklore Musical de las Ciudades* (457 pages, 1930). Both these books were published by the Mexican Secretariat of Education. The National Museum of Mexico has sponsored the publication of the descriptive catalogue of pre-Cortezian instruments by Daniel Castañeda and Vicente T. Mendoza, *Instrumental Precortesiano* (1933), and the University of Mexico has published Mendoza's *Romance y Corrido* (833 pages, 1939). Since 1930 several histories of Mexican music have appeared in print. Of these, *Historia de la Música Mejicana* by Miguel Galindo (Colima, 1933) and *Historia de la Música en Mexico* by Gabriel Saldívar (Mexico, 1934) cover the period up to the nineteenth century and include a description of ancient instruments, whereas *Panorama de la Música Mexicana* by Otto Mayer-Serra (Mexico, 1941) deals with Mexican music from Independence down to the present day.

The contemporary school of Mexican music presents a wide variety of styles, from the academic to the ultra-modern. Virtually all composers make use of folklore, either by quoting from popular folk songs, or by re-creating the melodic and rhythmic character of native songs in original melodies. Chavez quotes Indian themes only in two of his works. Silvestre Revueltas (1899–1940) wrote music that was unmistakably Mexican without borrowing from folk songs at all. The composers of the

Grupo de los Cuatro make use of actual airs of the people only when making arrangements labeled as such, as for instance *Sones Mariachi* by Blas Galindo. More literal is the procedure applied by Luis Sandi, who leaves the Indian themes unadorned, adding nothing to the basic pentatonic melodies. Vicente T. Mendoza and Gerónimo Baqueiro Foster are primarily concerned with the authenticity of the melo-rhythmic structure of the airs and dances they use for instrumental arrangements.

Candelario Huizar records his childhood memories in a symphonic sketch, *Pueblerinas,* by quoting old Indian songs, and José Rolón follows the same procedure in his symphonic poem entitled *1895,* a year when he was a child. Manuel Ponce, in his symphonic triptych, *Chapultepec,* presents Mexican folklore in the Gallic dress of Impressionist writing. In varying degrees, Juan León Mariscal, Estanislao Mejía, Pedro Michaca, Bernal Jiménez, Miguel Meza, and Jiménez Mabarak resort to the natural music of the people for their inspiration. Alfonso de Elias sentimentalizes the Mexican themes, while Arnulfo Miramontes submits them to the process of formal counterpoint.

Rafael Tello makes use of folklore in order to lend an air of authenticity to his operas and symphonic poems based on historical subjects. José Vasquez makes occasional reference to Mexican folklore in his character pieces. Hernández Moncada, though professing to write absolute music, borrows native rhythms in the Finale of his Symphony. José Pomar, the Futurist of Mexican music, does not deem it unprofitable to make transcriptions of popular dances. Even Julian Carrillo, the redoubtable champion of quarter-tones, delves into folklore when writing in the tempered scale.

Such is the diversified panorama of Mexican music. Carlos Chavez has summarized this diversity in a terse statement: "The music of the Indians is Mexican music; but also Mexican is the music of Spanish origin. It is quite proper to regard even the native Italianized operas or the Germanized symphonies as Mexican. However, the state of being Mexican does not necessarily imply high merit. Only when Mexican music attains quality, does it become true national art."

MUSICIANS OF MEXICO

Rafael ADAME (1906——) studied the guitar and the violoncello. Adame was the first Latin American musician to write a concerto for the guitar and orchestra. He performed this concerto in Mexico City, as a soloist with a symphonic ensemble, on February 5, 1933. On July 28,

1939, he played the violoncello part in his Concertino for Violoncello and Orchestra, performed by the *Orquesta Sinfónica de Mexico*. These works are constructed in the form of a classical suite. In the native vein, Adame has written *Sinfónia Folklórica* for military band, and a Concertino for Guitar and Orchestra, based on Mexican popular themes of the *Mariachi* type. The manuscript scores of his Concerto and Concertino for violoncello and orchestra, as well as the Concerto and Concertino for Guitar and Orchestra, are in the Fleisher Collection in Philadelphia.

Daniel AYALA, Mexican composer of Indian blood, is a native of Yucatán. He studied violin and composition in Mexico City with Silvestre Revueltas. For a time he was compelled to earn his living by playing in the night club Salon Mexico. Later he was a violinist in the *Orquesta Sinfónica de Mexico*. In 1940, when he was thirty-two years old, he was appointed conductor of the *Banda de Policía* in Mérida, Yucatán. As a composer, Ayala consistently utilizes the ancestral modes and rhythms of the Mayan civilization as a basis for original works. Ayala applies the modern technique of composition to these indigenous subjects. His music has been described as *"alma nueva de la cosas viejas"* (the new soul of things old). Ayala's first important work in the native vein was *Uchben X'Coholte* (Ancient Cemetery), a symphonic poem based on a Mayan legend. It was performed in Mexico City on October 13, 1933, with the orchestra of the *Conservatorio Nacional de Mexico*, and later, in ballet form, on March 6, 1936, at the *Palacio de Bellas Artes* in Mexico City. Ayala's vocal composition *U Kayil Chaac*, an incantation for rain, to the text in the Mayan language, scored for soprano with a chamber orchestra and Mexican percussion instruments, was presented in Mexico City on July 24, 1934. Then followed a symphonic poem, *Tribu*, performed by the *Orquesta Sinfónica de Mexico*, Chavez conducting, on October 18, 1935. It is in three movements: *En la Llanura* (In the Valley), *La Serpiente Negra* (The Black Serpent), and *La Danza del Fuego* (Dance of Fire). The themes of *Tribu* are pentatonic, and there are polyrhythmic combinations in the percussion section, which includes native instruments. To the same category of Mexican works belong Ayala's orchestral suite *Paisaje* (Landscape), performed in Mexico City on June 2, 1936, and *Panoramas de Mexico* (in three sections, depicting the regions of Sonora, Veracruz, and Yucatán), which was presented by the Dallas, Texas, orchestra on December 1, 1940. Ayala's most ambitious work in the Mexican vein is the ballet *El Hombre Maya*, inspired by the legends of Mayan cosmogony. It was played in symphonic form by the orchestra of the

University of Mexico, on November 21, 1940, under the composer's direction. Ayala has furthermore arranged authentic Mayan themes in two suites for small orchestra, *Los Pescadores Seris* (Fishermen of the Seris Tribe), and *Los Danzantes Yaquis* (Yaqui Dancers), performed at a concert of Ayala's music given in Mérida, Yucatán, on July 31, 1942. In non-Mexican forms, Ayala has written a piano piece entitled *Radiogram*, which imitates the radio code signals; *El Grillo* (Cricket) for soprano and a chamber group; *Vidrios Rotos* (Broken Windows) for oboe, clarinet, bassoon, and piano; *Suite Infantil*, in five movements, for soprano and chamber orchestra; *Cinco Piezas Infantiles* for string quartet; and songs. In 1934, Ayala, together with Pablo Moncayo, Salvador Contreras, and Blas Galindo, formed the *Grupo de los Cuatro* (Group of the Four). The orchestral scores of *Tribu, Paisaje,* and *Panoramas de Mexico* are in the Fleisher Collection in Philadelphia.

Gerónimo BAQUEIRO FOSTER, musicographer and composer, studied music in Mérida, Yucatán, and played flute and oboe in military bands. Subsequently he took a course in composition with Julian Carrillo at the *Conservatorio Nacional* in Mexico City. For a number of years, Baqueira Foster wrote on music for newspapers. In 1942, at the age of forty-four, he founded an important music magazine, *Revista Musical Mexicana*. Baqueira Foster is chiefly interested in folklore, and his own compositions are stylizations or arrangements of Mexican dances and songs. His orchestral suite, *Huapangos*, arranged from Mexican dances of the last three centuries, was included in the program of Mexican music conducted by Chavez at the Museum of Modern Art in New York City, in May, 1940, and was recorded in Columbia's album of Mexican music. The score of *Huapango* No. 3 is in the Fleisher Collection in Philadelphia.

Miguel BERNAL JIMÉNEZ, born in Morelia, sang as a child in the choir at the Cathedral of Morelia. In 1928 he was sent to Rome to study at the Pontifical Institute of Sacred Music, where he received the master's degree in organ and church music. He returned to Mexico in 1933, when he was twenty-three years old, and was appointed director of the School of Sacred Music of Morelia. He married a descendant of the Mexican Emperor Iturbide. In his music, Bernal Jiménez uses liturgical chants as religious folklore. His most ambitious work of this nature is the symphonic drama in five acts, *Tata Vasco*, which is the people's name for the first bishop of Michoacan, who was famous in Mexican history for his charity work among the Indians. The thematic material of *Tata Vasco* contains both Gregorian and primitive Indian elements. The concluding act is designed in the form of a symphony. The musical treatment of these materials is eclectic, suggesting such diverse styles as Puccini, Palestrina, and Tchaikovsky. *Tata Vasco* was to be performed in 1940 at the *Palacio de Bellas Artes* in Mexico City, but at the last moment the government canceled the performance on the ground that the opera promoted religious fanaticism, which was contrary to the spirit of the Mexican Constitution. The opera was finally performed in the provincial town of Patzcuaro. In addition to *Tata Vasco*, Bernal Jiménez has written a symphonic poem, *Noche en Morelia* (Night in Morelia), which depicts a scene at the church, with the contrasting sounds of a cabaret orchestra mingling with the solemnity of the church bells. *Noche en Morelia* was performed on August 1, 1941, by the *Orquesta Sinfónica de Mexico*, Chavez conducting. The orchestral scores of *Noche en Morelia* and a suite, *Michoacan*, are in the Fleisher Collection in Philadelphia.

The composer and music educator, Gustavo CAMPA, was a native of Mexico City, where he died, on October 29, 1934, at the age of seventy-one. He studied music with Melesio Morales. Dissatisfied with Morales' method of teaching, Campa banded together with five other disciples of Morales and formed in 1887 a rival music school in Mexico City, in which he championed French music, to combat the Italian tradition inculcated by Morales. From 1898 to 1914, Campa edited a progressive music magazine, *Gaceta Musical*. Campa wrote an opera, *El Rey Poeta*, a Mass, and numerous piano pieces and songs, all of them unpublished.

Julian CARRILLO, the ultra-modernist of Mexican music, is of Indian extraction. He was born in 1875, in Ahualulco, and studied violin at the *Conservatorio Nacional* in Mexico City. In 1899 Carrillo won a special prize offered by the Dictator-President Porfirio Diaz for music study in Europe, and went to Leipzig, where he studied composition and played the violin. Later he took courses at the Conservatory of Ghent in Belgium. Returning to Mexico in 1905, he gave numerous violin recitals, and also appeared as conductor. He was for several years Director of the *Conservatorio Nacional*. In 1926 he visited the United States.

Carrillo's career as a composer falls into three phases, the first entirely academic in style, the second distinctly Mexican in its inspiration and romantic in treatment, and the third of the revolutionary character, marked principally by the development of his theory of fractional tones, *Sonido 13*. The academic period had its inception during his studies at

Leipzig, where he composed his First Symphony in D major, his Second Symphony in C major, a Requiem for voices and orchestra, two Masses, four violin sonatas, a Sonata for Violoncello and Piano, two orchestral suites, a Piano Quintet, a String Quartet in E flat, and a String Sextet. To the same period belong his two early operas, *Mathilda* in four acts and *Ossian* in one act. The second period of Carrillo's creative work comprises his three-act opera *Xulitl*, to the subject of ancient Mexico; an opera in four acts, entitled *Mexico in 1810*; a Fantasy for piano and orchestra; the orchestral overture *8 de Septiembre;* and a symphonic poem, *Xochimilco* (name of a pueblo in Mexico). His suite *Impresiones de la Habana* for orchestra may also be added to this group.

The third phase overlaps the first two and is characterized by an earnest inquiry into musical potentialities outside the framework of traditional harmony and scale structure. These experiments in the new tonal relationships are exemplified by his two atonal string quartets. Often Carrillo applies new scales to music of distinctly native inspiration, as, for instance, *Xochimilco* (1935), based on the progression C, D flat, E flat, F flat, G, A flat, B double flat, C. In his Concerto for Violin, Flute, and Violoncello (1942), Carrillo uses a six-tone scale, C, D flat, E, F sharp, G, B flat, C. But his most far-reaching innovation is undoubtedly the theory which he has named *Sonido 13*, symbolizing the field of sounds smaller than the twelve semitones of the tempered scale. The first formulation of this theory dates back to 1895, which should establish Carrillo's place as a pioneer. He has also developed a special number notation for fractional intervals, comprising ninety-six divisions to an octave, the unit being one-sixteenth of a tone. The notes of the scale are marked by a number from O, corresponding to C, up to 95, which corresponds to the sound one-sixteenth of a tone lower than the octave C. The octave register is indicated by lines above or below the numbers. In order to clarify the nature of fractional tones, Carrillo made transpositions into the quarter-tone system of Bach's and Beethoven's music, by virtue of which the octave is compressed into a tritone, with other intervals similarly halved. Carrillo has written at least forty works for quarter-tones, eighth-tones and sixteenth-tones, and has constructed special instruments for their performance. Carrillo's works in fractional tones are *5 Primeras Composiciones*, which include *Preludio a Cristóbal Colón* for soprano, violin, flute, and guitar in quarter-tones, piccolo in eighth-tones, and harp in sixteenth-tones; *Ave Maria* for mixed choirs in quarter-tones and accompanying instruments in fractional tones; *Tepepán*, a pastoral scene for voices in quarter-tones and harp in sixteenth-tones; Prelude for violoncello in quarter-tones, accompanied by an ensemble of instruments in fractional tones; and *Hoja de Album* (Album Leaf) for violin, flute, clarinet, and guitar in quarter-tones, piccolo in eighth-tones, and harp in sixteenth-tones; Capriccio for French horn in sixteenth-tones; and *Fantasia Sonido 13* for a chamber orchestra in fractional tones. Carrillo conducted this *Fantasia* with a group of specially trained players in Mexico City on May 18, 1930.

His Concertino for violin and guitar in quarter-tones, piccolo in eighth-tones, violoncello in quarter-tones and eighth-tones, French horn and harp in sixteenth-tones, with the accompaniment of a normal symphony orchestra, was performed on May 4, 1927, by the Philadelphia Orchestra under Stokowski, who wrote to Carrillo: "With sixteenths of tone you are starting a new musical epoch. I want to be of service to this beautiful idea." During Carrillo's stay in the United States he published a magazine in English and Spanish, *The Thirteenth Sound*, of which a few issues appeared on the thirteenth day of the month. He has also written a song in English, "I Think of You," for a soprano singing in quarter-tones to the accompaniment of instruments in quarter-, eighth-, and sixteenth-tones. In Mexico Carrillo published explanatory pamphlets, *Pre-Sonido 13* (1930) and *Génesis de la Revolución Musical del Sonido 13* (1940). *Preludio a Cristóbal Colón*, in the original number notation, was published by *New Music* in its issue of April 1944. The following orchestral scores are in the Fleisher Collection in Philadelphia: Symphony No. 1, Symphony No. 2, Suite No. 1, *Impresiones de Habana*, orchestral suite *Los Naranjos* (Oranges), *Penumbras, Xochimilco, and 5 Primeras Composiciones* in quarter-tones, eighth-tones, and sixteenth-tones, in the number notation.

The foremost Mexican composer and conductor is Carlos CHAVEZ, born on June 13, 1899, in Mexico City, as the seventh child in a Mestizo family (his mother was Indian). He studied the elements of music with his older brother, Manuel, and later took lessons with Manuel Ponce in piano and composition. As early as 1914, when Chavez was only fifteen years old, he composed piano pieces in the manner of salon music. His piano piece *Extase*, marked Op. 7, after a poem of Victor Hugo, shows attempts at dramatic expression. More interesting are the piano pieces *Cantos Mexicanos*, Op. 16, composed in 1914, which include arrangements of revolutionary Mexican songs, among them the famous *Cucaracha*. In 1919 Chavez wrote a full-fledged symphony, in C minor, academic in structure, but displaying a mature technique. In 1921 Chavez composed his first

Mexican work, a ballet entitled *El Fuego Nuevo* (The New Fire), scored for a large orchestra, with the use of indigenous instruments of percussion. The writing follows procedures of Debussy and the Impressionists. The ballet was not produced until November 4, 1928, when Chavez conducted it with the *Orquesta Sinfónica de Mexico*.

Related in spirit to *El Fuego Nuevo* is Chavez's indigenous ballet *Los Cuatro Soles*, symbolic of four "suns," or ages of earth, air, fire, and water. Chavez conducted this work with the *Orquesta Sinfónica de Mexico* on July 22, 1930. *Tierra Mojada* (Humid Soil), a short work for oboe, English horn, and chorus, composed in 1932, was performed on September 6, 1932, at a Conservatory concert in Mexico City. *Tierra Mojada* is written after an impressionistic poem, but the music possesses elements that are Mexican in character.

In 1921 Manuel Ponce wrote about Chavez as a composer: "Carlos Chavez is a rare example of fecund studiousness which stands out in our environment of secular laziness. . . . The most striking feature of Chavez's music is an aspiration for modernism and originality, which is perfectly justified in so young a man. For Chavez is still very young, despite his appearance of earnestness, and a little melancholy. He has talent. He finds himself under the double influence of romanticism of the type of Schumann and Chopin, and of modernism which attracts him with its glamor of novelty and exoticism."

In 1922 Chavez went to Europe, and later spent several years in New York. During these peregrinations, Chavez acquired a taste for the type of abstract and quasi-scientific music that was the fashion of the day. His compositions written between 1923 and 1934 reflect these influences. Sometimes he emphasizes the abstraction of his music in titles from geometry and physics, as evidenced in *Polígonos* (Polygons) for piano (1923), *Exágonos* (Hexagons) for voice and piano (1924), *36* for piano (1925), *Energía* for nine instruments (1925, first performed by Slonimsky in Paris on June 11, 1931), *Soli* for oboe, clarinet, bassoon, and trumpet (1933), *Espiral* (Spiral) for piano and violin (1934), and the unfinished orchestral score entitled *Pyramids*. This period culminated in the ballet *H. P.* (Horsepower, 1931).

His compositions in absolute forms, a Piano Sonata (1928), Sonatina for Violin and Piano (1928), and *Unidad* (Unity) for piano (1930), are characterized by a style deliberately angular, sparse, unprepossessing, and almost dialectic in its uncompromising brevity and compactness. Paul Rosenfeld describes Chavez's piano music of this period in an article published in *Modern Music* of May, 1932, as "a marvel of contraction and astringency . . . austere, flinty, foreshortened . . . partial to hollow octaves and single unsupported voices." In the same spirit of absolute music, but with some concessions to classic tradition, is the Concerto for Four Horns. Written originally in 1930, the Concerto was later orchestrated, and Chavez conducted it in Washington on April 11, 1937.

The ballet *H. P.* is the apotheosis of the machine age. The Mexican painter, Diego Rivera, who collaborated in the production of *H. P.*, wrote: "It is the unfolding of plastic and musical deeds, whose connotations are in accord with the rhythm of the aspirations, interests, and necessities of our social existence." Chavez himself describes *H. P.* "as a symphony of the sounds around us, a revue of our times." As to musical material, Chavez states: "Some melodies and dances of the people may be encountered in my music. However, they do not represent the constructive basis of the work but simply happen to coincide with my form of self-expréssion." The program note of the ballet further elucidates the action: "The ballet *H. P.* symbolizes the relationship existing between the North and the Tropics. The Tropics produce raw materials, pineapples, coconuts, bananas. The North transforms these raw materials into daily consumers' goods." The ballet is in four movements. The first, *Danza del Hombre* (The Dance of Man), symbolizes Man as the creator of things. The second, *El Barco* (The Ship), depicts the commerce flourishing between North and South America. There is a mariner's dance, followed by a tango, expressive of the lure of the South. The third movement, *El Tropico*, pictures the ship's stay in a Southern port. Two native dances, the *Sandunga* and *Huapango*, are included in this movement. The last movement, *Danza de los Hombres y las Máquinas*, portrays a North American city with its skyscrapers. The workers rebel against the despotism of the machine, and panic seizes the capitalists. Finally the workers conquer the machines and convert them to their own use.

H: P., composed between 1926 and 1931, embodies elements of Chavez's "geometric" music, as well as his Mexican characteristics. The sections depicting the machine age are almost brutal in their dissonance, while the tropical music is rhythmically sensuous. *H. P.* was performed as a symphonic suite on December 4, 1931, in Mexico, under Chavez's direction. It was staged as a ballet by the Philadelphia Grand Opera Company, under the direction of Leopold Stokowski, on March 31, 1932. Olin Downes, writing in *The New York Times*, ridiculed the ballet as "a confounding mixture of Mexican folk tunes, with sounds that suggest the whirring, clicking, and roaring of machines." He added: "The audience listened and laughed. Perhaps the composer laughed too. . . . Just two words in behalf of Chavez. Mr. Chavez is a very serious man that never laughs or makes jokes. He is always sad, very sad indeed!"

In 1928, at the age of only twenty-nine, Chavez was appointed director of the *Conservatorio Nacional de Música* in Mexico City. He introduced new methods of instruction, putting emphasis on the importance of writing melody and melodic counterpoint in all styles: diatonic, chromatic, and pentatonic. Among his pupils were Daniel Ayala, Salvador Contreras, Pablo Moncayo, and Blas Galindo. In 1933 Chavez relinquished the direction of the *Conservatorio*, and was appointed on February 21, 1933, Chief of the Department of Fine Arts, a post which he held for one year. In 1928 Chavez founded the *Orquesta Sinfónica de Mexico*, of which he became the permanent conductor. In 1930 he launched a new series of concerts, *Conciertos para Trabajadores* (Concerts for Workers), at which he featured music of social consciousness.

The conviction that music should reflect the life of society as a whole is already noticeable in *H. P.* It is made emphatic in Chavez's *Sinfonía Proletaria* or *Llamadas* (Calls), which opens with these words from a revolutionary ballad: "This is how the proletarian revolution will come." Chavez conducted the first performance of the *Sinfonía Proletaria* in Mexico City on September 29, 1934.

In his *Obertura Republicana*, first performed under the composer's direction on October 18, 1935, he quotes several popular tunes of the Mexican revolutionary period. His rebellion against tradition is expressed in a semi-facetious note attached to the score of the *Obertura Republicana:* "In naming this piece an overture I did not intend to convey the meaning of formal construction. I chose this title merely because the sound of the word is pleasant." To the same period belongs *El Sol,* for chorus, based on an original Mexican *Corrido.* Chavez conducted this work with the *Orquesta Sinfónica de Mexico* on July 17, 1934.

The two most significant orchestral works of Chavez are *Sinfonía de Antigona* and *Sinfonía India.* They are contrasted in spirit and treatment. *Sinfonía de Antigona* was designed as incidental music to a performance of Sophocles' *Antigone* in the version by Jean Cocteau, produced at the *Palacio de Bellas Artes* in Mexico City in 1932. Later Chavez amalgamated this music into symphonic form and reorchestrated it. Chavez supplied the following explanatory note for the first performance of *Sinfonía de Antigona* given under his direction in Mexico City on December 15, 1933: "This is a piece of music suggested by the Greek tragedy. It is a symphony, not a symphonic poem, which is to say that the music is not subordinated to any program. Only the most rudimentary materials are made use of in the score. Stark and elemental, this music can be made expressive only by laconic strength, just as primitive art can be exalted only by power that is also primitive." The orchestration is unusual, requiring diversified wind instruments, including a bass flute and a heckelphone, as well as eight horns, percussion, and two harps. The work is impressive for its very static quality, and the eloquent absence of dynamic or rhythmic effects.

Quite different in design and execution is the *Sinfonía India,* written by Chavez during his first tour in the United States as conductor, in December, 1935. The world première took place in a broadcast performance on January 23, 1936. Chavez subsequently conducted a concert performance of *Sinfonía India* with the Boston Symphony Orchestra on April 10, 1936, and later in Mexico City on July 31, 1936. As the title implies, *Sinfonía India* is an expression of the Indian's soul, and specifically that of the Mexican Indian. In *Sinfonía India,* Chavez uses three Indian melodies in such a way as to provide three basic musical ideas for three movements played without pause. Indigenous Mexican instruments, such as *jícara de agua, güiro,* and *cascabeles* are included in the score, as a supplement to the normal symphony orchestra. A large assortment of Mexican instruments is also used in Chavez's Aztec composition, *Xochipili-Macuilxochitl* (the name of the Aztec god of music), which he conducted with an especially assembled group of Mexican players at the Museum of Modern Art in New York City on May 16, 1940. To approximate the sound of the ancient Mexican snail's shell, Chavez used a trombone.

In 1937 Chavez returned to composition for piano. He wrote ten Preludes for piano solo, quite different in treatment from his piano compositions of an earlier period. Both in form and in the natural pianism of the Preludes, Chavez renounced his former combativeness, and created instead the modern counterparts, terse, linear, and percussive, of Bach's Preludes. In 1938, Chavez embarked on the composition of a Piano Concerto, which he completed on the last day of the year 1940. The Concerto was first performed on January 1, 1942, by the Philharmonic Orchestra of New York. It is in three movements, of which the first is the most extensive. Rather than use the traditional sonata form, Chavez gives to the piano and the orchestra two separate sets of themes, developed antiphonally until the concluding section, when both are united. The second movement is lyric in character, and the third is a scherzo. The writing for the instrument is in the modern percussive manner, which, however, does not exclude real virtuosity of technique.

Most of Chavez's music has been published in the United States. *New Music* has published the following: Sonatina for Violin and Piano (July, 1928), Piano Sonata (January, 1933), *Spiral* for violin and piano (April, 1935), *Polygons, Solo, 36, Blues, Fox, Paisaje, Unidad* (October, 1936). Sonatina for Piano was published by Cos Cob Press in 1930. Schirmer has published the Preludes for piano and a reduction for two pianos of the Piano Concerto. Chavez's orchestral scores are also available through Schirmer. The scores *Energía* and *Soli* are in the Fleisher Collection in Philadelphia. In Mexico, Chavez's early pieces—*Extase, Vals Intimo,* and *Cantos Mexicanos* for piano—were published in 1921 by Wagner and Levien. The piano score of *Sinfonía Proletaria* was published with illustrations by Diego Rivera by the Mexican Ministry of Fine Arts in 1934.

A book by Chavez, *Toward a New Music,* in the English translation by Herbert Weinstock, was published in New York by Norton (1937). In this book Chavez reiterates his faith in music as a fluid art capable of progress. Much of the contents of the book is given to the discussion of the potentialities of electrical instruments and the radio.

In 1944, the Pan American Union published a comprehensive brochure, *Carlos Chavez,* in English and Spanish, with a complete catalogue of his works, recordings, bibliography, and a biographical article by Weinstock.

Salvador CONTRERAS (1912———), who belongs to the vanguard of Mexico's musicians, studied violin with Silvestre Revueltas. He played in the cabarets of Mexico City and subsequently entered the *Orquesta Sinfónica de Mexico,* and took lessons in composition with Carlos Chavez. In 1935 Contreras, then twenty-three, joined Daniel Ayala, Pablo Moncayo, and Blas Galindo to form a *Grupo de Jovenes Compositores,* later renamed *Grupo de los Cuatro.* At the first concert of this group given in Mexico City on November 25, 1935, Contreras presented his Sonata for Violin and Violoncello, and *Danza* for piano; at another concert, on October 15, 1936, he presented a String Quartet and *Tres Poemas* for soprano and chamber orchestra, descriptive of three geographical Mexican scenes. In larger forms, Contreras has written *Música para Orquesta Sinfónica,* performed by the *Orquesta Sinfónica de Mexico* on August 16, 1940, and *Corridos* in four sections, for orchestra and chorus, performed on August 15, 1941. The latter work is based on Mexican ballads, from melodies in the book *El Romance Español y el Corrido*

Mexicano, by Vicente Mendoza. The music of Contreras is markedly contrapuntal in texture, and the treatment is that of modern neoclassicism. In 1942, Contreras composed *Obertura en Tiempo de Danza*, in 7/8 and 5/8 time, alternating with 2/4 and 3/4. The scores of *Tres Movimientos Sinfónicos*, Suite for chamber orchestra, and *Música para Orquesta Sinfónica* are in the Fleisher Collection in Philadelphia.

Alfonso de ELIAS, of Mexico City, studied piano, and took a course in composition with Gustavo Campa and Rafael Tello. A very prolific composer, Alfonso de Elias has adopted a romantic style reminiscent of Brahms and Tchaikovsky, without a trace of contemporary influence. Among his works are two symphonies, several symphonic poems, string quartets, pieces for piano, violin, and violoncello, as well as vocal compositions. His "symphonic triptych," *El Jardín Encantado* (1924), and the First Symphony (1926) were performed by the orchestra of the Conservatory of Mexico, on October 9, 1927. The same orchestra presented his *Variaciones sobre un Tema Mexicano*, on March 4, 1928, and the Second Symphony, on July 1, 1935. His symphonic poem on Mexican themes, *Cacahuamilpa*, was performed by the *Orquesta Sinfónica de Mexico*, Carlos Chavez conducting, on August 12, 1930. Elias' ballet *Las Biniguendas de Plata* (1933) was performed in symphonic form by the orchestra of the University of Mexico, under the composer's direction, on November 21, 1940. His Mexican suite *Tlalmanalco*, for strings, clarinet, bassoon, trumpet, and piano, was given at the *Palacio de Bellas Artes* in Mexico City, on January 22, 1937. The program note described Elias as "still fascinated by the sirens of romanticism," but held out the hope that "the sincerity of the composer, the solidity of his technique, and his youth are propitious for a desirable change." The following orchestral scores by Alfonso de Elias are in the Fleisher Collection in Philadelphia: *El Jardín Encantado*, *Variaciones sobre un Tema Mexicano*, Symphony No. 1, *Las Biniguendas de Plata*, *Cacahuamilpa*, and *Tlalmanalco*.

Juan B. FUENTES (1869——) was born in Guadalajara. Although largely self-taught, Fuentes has developed a technique of composition based on the French nineteenth-century musical tradition. He has published several manuals on harmony and solfeggi. He has written *Sinfonia Mexicana* for orchestra, in which folk themes are used as thematic material. He has also composed for piano and voice. His music remains unpublished.

Blas GALINDO, who is of Indian blood, studied composition at the Conservatory of Mexico with Chavez, Rolón, and Huizar. In the summer of 1941, when he was thirty years of age, he enrolled in the Berkshire Academy, Massachusetts, where he took lessons with Aaron Copland. In 1935, together with Ayala, Contreras, and Moncayo, he formed a group of young composers known as the *Grupo de los Cuatro*. His Quartet for Violoncellos was performed at the concert of the *Grupo de los Cuatro* in Mexico City on October 15, 1936. Two of his ballets, *Entre Sombras Anda el Fuego* (Among Shadows Walks Fire) and *Danza de las Fuerzas Nuevas* (Dance of the New Forces), were staged in Mexico City in 1940. *Sones Mariachi*, for orchestra, illustrative of the type of music played by the Mexican *Mariachi* bands, was introduced by Chavez at the festival of Mexican music at the Museum of Modern Art in New York City, on May 16, 1940, and was also recorded in the Columbia album of Mexican music. Galindo has also written a piece scored exclusively for indigenous Mexican instruments, which was performed under the title *Obra para Orquesta Mexicana* on October 28, 1938, by the specially assembled orchestra. All these works are characterized by an almost literal interpretation of Mexican folklore, in somewhat crude diatonic harmonies. After his studies at the Berkshire Academy in 1941, Blas Galindo moderated his style in the direction of dignified neoclassicism, without, however, relinquishing the characteristic Mexican flavor. To this period belongs his Sextet for flute, clarinet, bassoon, horn, trumpet, and trombone. His Piano Concerto in three movements, written in 1942 from the material of an earlier Concertino for Two Pianos, is Mexican in thematic content, while adhering structurally to the general outline of classical sonata form. It was performed for the first time by the *Orquesta Sinfónica de Mexico*, Chavez conducting, on July 24, 1942. In 1944 Galindo wrote a symphony and a piano sonata. The orchestral scores of Galindo's *Preludios* and *Danza de las Fuerzas Nuevas* are in the Fleisher Collection in Philadelphia.

Son of a German father and a Spanish mother, Rodolfo HALFFTER, composer now resident in Mexico, is a native of Madrid. His brother, Ernest Halffter, is a well-known Spanish composer. Both Ernesto and Rodolfo Halffter were self-taught in composition, and both were influenced by Manuel de Falla and Stravinsky. Rodolfo Halffter, at the age of twenty-four, began to compose in 1924, when he wrote an orchestral suite. In 1931 he composed a choreographic divertissement, *Don Lindo de Almería,* which was performed at the Barcelona Festival on April 22, 1936. He has also written *Obertura Concertante* for piano and orchestra (1932), some piano music, and songs. After the outbreak of civil war in Spain, Rodolfo Halffter became a member of the Central Musical Council of the Spanish Republic, and Chief of the Music Section of the Ministry of Propaganda. When the Republic fell, he crossed on foot to France. Several of his musical manuscripts, among them *Impromptu* for orchestra and a one-act opera after Cervantes, were lost when a bomb hit the house where he stayed at the Spanish frontier. Halffter arrived in Mexico in 1939, and became naturalized as a Mexican citizen. In Mexico he wrote a ballet, *La Madrugada del Panadero* (The Baker's Morning), and Concerto for Violin and Orchestra in A major, in four classical movements. The Concerto was performed by Samuel Dushkin, the violinist, who commissioned the composition of the work, and the *Orquesta Sinfónica de Mexico,* Carlos Chavez conducting, on June 26, 1942. The style of Halffter's music is marked by terseness of expression and compactness of musical development. His melos is rooted in Spanish folklore, and his rhythmic invention adds impetus to the thematic material. His harmonic texture is basically tonal, with chordal agglomerations at dynamically climactic points, and his counterpoint is free from formal restraint. Halffter's piano pieces were published in Spain. His *Danza de Avila* for piano is included in the series *Masters of Our Day,* issued by Carl Fischer (New York, 1941). Halffter has also compiled a collection of Spanish Melodies, *Cancionero Musical Español,* published in Mexico in 1939.

Eduardo HERNÁNDEZ MONCADA (1899——) began to study music at an early age, and earned his living as a boy playing in theaters and cinemas. Later he went to Mexico City, and entered the *Conservatorio Nacional de Música,* where he studied composition with Rafael Tello. At the same time he was engaged in numerous other pursuits, as an electrician, book salesman, and farmer. Hernández Moncada, then thirty-seven, was appointed assistant conductor of the *Orquesta Sinfónica de Mexico* in 1936. He began to compose late in life, and wrote education pieces for music schools. His first work of importance was a symphony in four movements, which was performed for the first time by the *Orquesta Sinfónica de Mexico,* on July 31, 1942. Entirely academic in structure and technical treatment, the symphony has the merit of being an effective and well-orchestrated composition. The last movement contains some Mexican rhythms.

A very significant Mexican composer is Candelario HUIZAR, of Indian origin, who was born at Jerez in 1888. He learned the rudiments of music largely by instinct, and as a youth played in military bands. In 1918 he went to Mexico City, where he studied with Gustavo Campa. Huizar began to compose late in life, and has written exclusively for orchestra. His music is imbued with the spirit of Indian folklore. For his themes, he uses both actual folk songs and his original melodies. He often combines an Indian theme in free counterpoint with its own variation, in contrasting instrumental colors. His harmonic texture is strong and compact. His orchestration, never opulent, is individual and sensitive. Huizar's first orchestral work, *Imagenes,* written at the age of forty-one, was performed by the *Orquesta Sinfónica de Mexico,* Chavez conducting, on December 13, 1929. His second symphonic poem, *Pueblerinas,* reflects the memories of an Indian village. It is one of Huizar's most typically Mexican scores. Its three sections are based on authentic themes, one of which is a popular *Jarabe,* danced usually at harvest time in Huizar's native region. *Pueblerinas* was performed by Chavez on November 6, 1931. His third symphonic poem, *Surco* (literally, plow), depicts a village fiesta, beginning with a pastoral song and ending in a parade. *Surco* was given its first performance by Chavez on October 25, 1935.

Huizar has written four symphonies, all inspired by Mexican folklore, but not textually derivative from it. The form of Huizar's symphonies is cyclic, with the initial theme often recapitulated in the finale. The First Symphony, performed by Chavez on November 14, 1930, is in three movements: *Vivo, Adagio, Allegro Vivo.* The Second Symphony bears the subtitle *Oxpaniztli,* which is the Aztec name for the month of October. There are imitations of bird calls in the wood-wind instruments, and the ancient Aztec drums, *teponaxtle* and *huehuetl,* are included in the score. *Oxpaniztli* was performed on September 4, 1936, by the *Orquesta Sinfónica de Mexico,* Chavez conducting. Huizar's Third Symphony, performed by Chavez on July 29, 1938, is in the traditional four movements. The writing is diatonic without being confined to a definite key, and the rhythmic element is very strong. The Fourth Symphony, presented by the *Orquesta Sinfónica de Mexico* under Mitropoulos on August 7, 1942, is also in four movements, with the melodic material taken from folk songs and dance airs of Jalisco. The principal theme of the slow movement is a pentatonic *Ave Maria* of the Mexican Indians. The orchestral scores of Huizar's first three symphonies, three symphonic poems, and an orchestral fantasy on the Mexican waltz *Sobre las Olas* are in the Fleisher Collection in Philadelphia. There is a detailed analysis of Huizar's music in *Panorama de la Música Mexicana* by Otto Mayer-Serra (Mexico, 1941).

The composer, Carlos JIMÉNEZ MABARAK, was educated in Belgium. He studied music in Brussels, and upon his return to Mexico in 1937 began to compose. At that time Jiménez Mabarak was twenty-one years old. His preference is for Mexican subjects, which he stylizes in the manner of Manuel de Falla. He has written a monodrama for radio, *Erigona*, a Concerto for Piano and Orchestra, and several ballet suites, among them *La Muñeca Pastillita* (The Doll Pastillita). The orchestral scores of two works by Jiménez Mabarak, *El Sastrecillo y el Dueño* (Little Tailor and the Landlord) and a Rondo, are in the Fleisher Collection in Philadelphia.

Jacobo KOSTAKOWSKY, a naturalized Mexican musician, was born in Russia in 1893 and settled in Mexico in 1925. Kostakowsky studied violin in Russia; in 1908 he went to Vienna, where he took lessons in composition with Schoenberg. Later he spent some time in Paris, where he attended classes of Vincent d'Indy. Kostakowsky began to compose late in life; all his major works date since 1935. His style is basically Russian, reflecting the lyricism of Tchaikovsky. His harmonic writing is opulent, somewhat in the Mahler manner. Kostakowsky has written numerous works for orchestra. In recent years he has adopted Mexican folklore as thematic material for programmatic music and ballets. Several of his works for chamber orchestra have been performed by the *Orquesta de Cámara* of the Secretariat of Public Education, at the *Palacio de Bellas Artes* in Mexico City, namely: *Clarín* and *Barricada*, two ballets with chorus, on the subject of the Mexican Revolution, in which Kostakowsky quotes five revolutionary songs (August 26, 1935); *Estampas Callejeras* (Street Sketches, January 22, 1937, Revueltas conducting); *Triangulo*, a ballet suite in four movements (December 9, 1937); *Marimba*, a capriccio for piano and orchestra (September 6, 1939); and *Sinfonietta Tropical* in four movements (November 6, 1941). Kostakowsky has also written three symphonic poems, *Taxco* (1937), *Juventud* (1937), *Lascas* (1938); a ballet, *La Creación del Hombre* (1939); a symphonic suite in four movements, *El Romancero Gitano* (1938); *Suite Neo-Romantica* (1941); Serenata (1941); Concertino for Violin and Orchestra (1940); and Concerto for Violin and Orchestra (1942); as well as two string quartets, piano pieces, and songs. All symphonic works by Kostakowsky. are in the Fleisher Collection in Philadelphia.

Juan León Mariscal, whose birthplace was Oaxaca, studied at the *Conservatorio Nacional* in Mexico City with Julian Carrillo. In 1923, when Mariscal was twenty-four years old, he received a government prize for a symphonic work and was given a fellowship for study in Germany. Upon his return to Mexico he was appointed instructor of composition at the *Conservatorio Nacional*. Mariscal has written two symphonies, *Fantasia Mexicana* for large orchestra, Sinfonietta, a Septet, a String Quartet, piano pieces, and songs. His most characteristic work is an orchestral suite, *Tres Estampas Oaxaqueñas*, in three movements, depicting landmarks of the composer's native region. Under the title *Guelaguetza* this suite was performed by the *Orquesta Sinfónica Nacional*, Revueltas conducting, at the *Palacio de Bellas Artes* in Mexico on June 9, 1936. His First Symphony was performed by the *Orquesta Sinfónica de Mexico* on February 3, 1929. The orchestral scores of *Guelaguetza* and *Fantasia Mexicana* are in the Fleisher Collection in Philadelphia.

Estanislao Mejía was born in Tlaxcala in 1882 and studied at the *Conservatorio Nacional* in Mexico City. His first important work, the opera, *Edith*, was written in 1918, when he was thirty-six years of age. A symphony was written in 1921, and a ballet, *Schadani*, in 1934. In a purely Mexican manner he has composed *Suite Mexicana* for orchestra, which was performed in Mexico City on May 1, 1919. Mejía has also published a manual of counterpoint, canon and fugue. Between 1934 and 1938 he was the director of the *Conservatorio Nacional* in Mexico City. In that capacity, he continued the nationalist tradition established by Chavez, and urged his students to use Mexican folk themes as prime sources in their music. Mejía's compositions have not been published. The score of his ballet *Schadani* and two *Trozos Mexicanos* are in the Fleisher Collection in Philadelphia.

Vicente T. Mendoza, born in Cholula, specializes in Mexican folklore. In 1907, when he was thirteen years old, he went to Mexico City, where he studied piano and composition at the *Conservatorio Nacional de Música*. At the same time he studied drawing, and between 1912 and 1930 occupied the post of a topographer at the Department of Forestry. Later he taught solfeggio at the *Conservatorio Nacional*. Mendoza's chief interest, however, lies in Mexican folklore and in musical paleography. In collaboration with Daniel Castañeda he has compiled a valuable treatise on pre-Cortezian instruments, which was published in 1937 under the title *Instrumental Precortesiano*. He has also published a comparative study, *El Romance Español y El Corrido Mexicano* (Mexico City, 1939). As a composer he confines himself to arrangements of Mexican folk songs and dances. His orchestral *Danza Tarahumara* was performed by the *Orquesta Sinfónica de Mexico* on July 22, 1930, Chavez conducting. This score and also *Jalisco, Suite Indigena, Impresiones de Estio,* and *Tierras Solares* are in the Fleisher Collection in Philadelphia.

Miguel C. MEZA is a native of San Luis Potosí. He studied piano and composition at the *Conservatorio Nacional* in Mexico City, and upon graduation in 1932, when he was twenty-nine years of age, he dedicated himself to teaching, choral conducting, and composition. Meza has written several orchestral works, among them *Sinfonía en Estilo Mexicano* (Symphony in a Mexican Style), a symphonic poem entitled *Revolución,* an orchestral suite, *Impresiones,* and a ballet, *Las Biniguendas de Plata,* performed by the *Orquesta Sinfónica de Mexico* on October 4, 1935.

Pedro MICHACA, a composer who specializes in theoretical research and musical pedagogy, comes from Canatlán. Michaca studied with Gustavo Campa and Manuel Ponce at the *Conservatorio Nacional* in Mexico City. In 1925 he was appointed instructor at the Conservatory. In 1942 Michaco, then forty-five years old, compiled an analytical manual of harmony, *La Evolución de la Armonía a Través del Principio Cíclico-Musical,* in which he traces the evolution of the diatonic, pentatonic, and chromatic scales, with a supplementary chapter on musical systems based on the division of the octave into equal intervals. Michaca has composed little. The orchestral score of his symphonic poem *El Zarco* (nickname of a romantic Mexican bandit) is in the Fleisher Collection in Philadelphia.

Arnulfo MIRAMONTES (1882———), one of Mexico's most prolific composers, is a native of Tala. He studied organ at Aguas Calientes, and in 1907, at the age of twenty-five, went to Berlin, where he took courses in piano and composition, returning to Mexico in 1911. Miramontes has written two operas, two cantatas, twelve orchestral compositions, eighteen religious works, eleven pieces for organ, forty-nine piano pieces, and thirteen songs. The subjects of his operas and symphonic poems usually relate to pre-Cortezian Mexico. His technique of composition is contrapuntal, and often reaches a considerable degree of linear complexity, while keeping well within the traditional precepts of European harmony. His opera *Anáhuac* was produced in Mexico on January 28, 1918; his second opera, *Cihuatl,* has not been performed. Among his orchestral works, the following have been performed by various ensembles in Mexico City: *Obertura Primavera* (September 26, 1910), First Symphony (July 14, 1916), *Suite Sinfónica Mexicana* (May 15, 1918), *Revolución* (August 23, 1936), and a ballet suite, *Iris* (November 21, 1940). The following works by Miramontes are in the Fleisher Collection in Philadelphia: two symphonies, *Suite Sinfónica Mexicana, Iris, La Leyenda de los Volcanes* (Legend of the Volcanoes, from the opera *Anahuac),* *Jarabe* (Mexican dance), *Theme and Variations,* and a symphonic Prelude.

A Mexican composer of the vanguard, Pablo MONCAYO began to study piano at the age of seventeen with Hernández Moncada, and later studied composition with Chavez. To earn his living he played in jazz orchestras and cabarets in Mexico City, and later joined the percussion section of the *Orquesta Sinfónica de Mexico.* In his compositions, Moncayo follows the precepts established by Chavez, using indigenous melodic material in his music. In 1935 Moncayo, who was then twenty-three, together with Ayala, Contreras, and Galindo, formed the *Grupo de los Cuatro,* dedicated to the cause of Mexican modern music. Moncayo's piece for flute·and string quartet, to an Aztec subject, entitled *Amatzinac,* was presented at the first concert of the *Grupo de los Cuatro,* on November 25, 1935, in Mexico City. His Sonatina for Violin and Piano and *Romanza* for piano trio were performed at the second concert of the group, on October 15, 1936. His first orchestral work, a Mexican dance *Huapango,* was performed by Chavez and the *Orquesta Sinfónica de Mexico* on August 15, 1941. The orchestral scores of Moncayo's symphonic dance *Hueyapán* and of *Amatzinac* are in the Fleisher Collection in Philadelphia.

A composer who was a firm believer in the superiority of the Italian style, and who inculcated the Italian tradition in his teaching, was Melesio MORALES (1838–1908), who died at San Pedro de los Pinos at the age of seventy. As a boy, he showed talent for composition. After a few years' study in Italy, he was appointed professor of composition at the newly established *Conservatorio Nacional* (1877) in Mexico City. He wrote eight operas, of which four were produced in Mexico City: *Romeo and Juliet* (January 27, 1863), *Ildegonda* (January 27, 1866), *Gino Corsini* (July 14, 1877), and *Cleopatra* (November 14, 1891). He also composed a curious orchestral piece, *La Locomotiva,* performed on November 16, 1869, on the occasion of the opening of a new railroad in Mexico. Morales' piano music, in a somewhat Chopinesque style, enjoyed a certain degree of popularity in Mexico. See the bibliographical note on Melesio Morales by Jesús Romero, in *Revista Musical Mexicana* of November 7, 1943.

Jaime NUNÓ (1824–1908), author of the Mexican National Anthem, was born in Spain, lived in Mexico, and died in the United States. His body was exhumed and transferred to Mexico in November, 1942. The first performance of the Anthem took place at the *Teatro Santa Ana* in Mexico, on September 15, 1854.

Perhaps, the most unconventional composer of Mexico is José POMAR. He did not begin to compose seriously until the age of forty-eight (in 1928), when he embarked at once on experimental and modernistic procedures. He also took part in leftist political manifestations. Pomar has written two ballets: *Ocho Horas*, in which he gave an orchestral interpretation of a newspaper plant at work, and *Bestia Parda* (Brown Beast), an anti-Hitler pantomime composed in 1937. He has also written *Prelude and Fugue* for instruments of percussion only, performed by Chavez and the *Orquesta Sinfónica de Mexico* on November 11, 1932. His Mexican dance for orchestra, *Huapango*, was performed by Chavez on November 27, 1931. The scores of *Huapango*, *Prelude and Fugue* and *Ocho Horas* are in the Fleisher Collection in Philadelphia.

Manuel PONCE (1886–1948) is the first Mexican composer to have written in a pronounced native style. He was born in Fresnillo and learned rudiments of music from his sister. He made first attempts to compose at the age of seven, when he wrote a little piece entitled *La Marcha del Sarampión*. At the age of twelve, Ponce played the organ at the Cathedral in Aguas Calientes, and at fourteen composed a *Gavotte*, made famous subsequently by the dancer Argentina, who used it for her programs all over the world. In 1901 Ponce, then fifteen, entered the *Conservatorio Nacional* in Mexico City, and three years later was given an opportunity to go to Europe for further study. He took a course in composition with Enrico Bossi in Bologna, and in 1906 studied piano with Martin Krause in Berlin. In 1908 he returned to Mexico and was appointed a professor of the *Conservatorio Nacional*. Among his piano pupils was Carlos Chavez. On July 7, 1912, Manuel Ponce gave a concert of his compositions, the major work on the program being his Concerto for Piano and Orchestra. The Concerto reveals Ponce's admiration for Chopin's pianistic style; in the second movement, *Andantino Amoroso*, there are themes distinctly Mexican in character. The occasion marked, according to the opinion of

Otto Mayer-Serra (*Panorama de la Música Mexicana*, page 95), the opening phase of musical nationalism in Mexico. Shortly afterwards, Ponce wrote two Mexican Rhapsodies for piano, in which Mexican themes were explicitly represented. In February, 1914, Ponce published an album of songs, one of which was *Estrellita*, destined to become one of the most celebrated Latin American melodies. Because of a technical oversight in the copyright arrangement, *Estrellita* has been widely reprinted without payment of royalties to the composer. During this period of his career Ponce published a number of piano pieces in the style of refined salon music, waltzes, mazurkas, preludes, serenades, barcarolles, and berceuses, as well as romantic pieces with such titles as *Desire, Album Leaf, Souvenir, Melancholy*, etc. Between 1915 and 1918 Ponce lived in Havana. In 1916 he visited New York, where he gave a recital of his works. After a few years in Mexico, where he was active as a teacher, he decided to go to Paris in order to perfect his technique of composition, particularly in the field of counterpoint and orchestration. In 1926, at the age of forty, he joined the class of Paul Dukas at the *École Normale de Musique*. He was profoundly impressed by Dukas' ideas on free thematic development and orchestral color. Ponce was now resolved to apply the new technique to Mexican themes. The product of this attempt was *Chapultepec*, a symphonic triptych, named after the suburb of Mexico City, where Ponce himself made his home. The separate movements of the triptych are entitled *Primavera, Nocturno Romantico*, and *Canto y Danza*. The scoring is characteristically Gallic, with subtle dynamics, and prominence given to solo instruments, particularly in the wood-wind section. Dissatisfied with the first version of the score (which was in the meantime performed by Chavez and the *Orquesta Sinfónica de Mexico* on August 25, 1929), Ponce rewrote the work. The second version, completed in France in July, 1934, was performed by Chavez on August 24, 1934, soon after Ponce's return to Mexico. Among Ponce's other works of the same period were *Canto y Danza de los Antiguos Mexicanos*, performed by the *Orquesta del Conservatorio Nacional*, Revueltas conducting, on October 13, 1933; *Poema Elegiaco*, written in memory of a friend, and performed by the *Orquesta Sinfónica de Mexico* on June 28, 1935; and *Tres Cantos de Tagore* for voice and orchestra, performed at the same concert, with Ponce's wife, the French singer Clema Ponce, as soloist.

Still another aspect of Ponce's career as a composer is revealed in his *Suite en Estilo Antiguo*, in four movements, *Preludio, Canon, Pavane*, and *Fughetta*, performed by Chavez on September 6, 1935. In this suite

Ponce reverts to the classical mode of expression. The theme of the *Fughetta* is taken from the subject of Bach's E major fugue. Ponce has arranged this suite for a string trio (violin, viola, and violoncello). In the same neoclassical manner is his *Sonate en Duo* for violin and viola (1938). Ponce returns to Mexican themes in his "symphonic divertissement" *Ferial* (1940). Characteristically, the score bears the dedication "A Mexico." *Ferial* is an orchestral picture of the Mexican popular festival, beginning with a scene at the church entrance, and culminating in a fiesta with dancing, whistling, and playing upon the guitar. The themes are original, with the exception of an old Mexican song, which is played in the orchestra by two oboes in parallel thirds, in imitation of the Mexican wood instrument *chirimía. Ferial* was first performed by the *Orquesta Sinfónica de Mexico*, Chavez conducting, on August 9, 1940. In 1941, by a special arrangement between the Mexican government and the governments of several South American republics, Manuel Ponce made a tour by plane of Argentina, Uruguay, Chile, and Peru, conducting concerts of his works with the local symphony orchestras. During this tour, André Segovia, the Spanish guitarist, played the solo part in Ponce's *Concierto del Sur* (Concerto of the South), for guitar and small orchestra. The world premiere of this Concerto took place in Montevideo on October 4, 1941.

In 1942 Ponce wrote a Concerto for Violin and Orchestra, which he orchestrated in June, 1943. The first movement, *Allegro non troppo*, is in a soberly classical vein. The second movement, *Andante*, is lyrical, and contains undisguised allusions to the melody of *Estrellita*. The last movement is a free rondo, bearing the imprint of *Mañanitas*, a type of popular Mexican song. The Concerto was performed by the Polish violinist Henryk Szeryng with the *Orquesta Sinfónica de Mexico*, Chavez conducting, on August 20, 1943.

Ponce's early piano pieces and songs, numbering over seventy, were published in Mexico by Wagner and Levien, and are mostly out of print. Maurice Sénart in Paris has published several of Ponce's compositions written between 1930 and 1938: *Tres Poemas* for voice and piano, *Deux Poèmes de Tagore* for violin and piano, *Préludes* for violoncello and piano, *4 Pièces* for piano, *4 Miniatures* for string quartet, *Granada* and *La Mort* for voice and piano, and *Sonate en Duo* for violin and viola. Numerous compositions written by Ponce for guitar, and dedicated to Segovia, have been published by Schott in Germany, among them four sonatas, twenty-four Preludes, twenty-two Variations, and dances. Ponce's

Estrellita has been published in numerous arrangements, of which Jascha Heifetz' transcription for violin and piano is very popular. Ponce's *Dansas Mexicanas* for piano and *6 Canciones Arcaicos* have been published by the *Editorial Cooperativa Interamericana de Compositores* in Montevideo, and his two Études for piano are included in the Schirmer album *Latin-American Art Music for the Piano* (New York, 1942). His orchestral scores, two piano sonatas, a Violin Sonata, and some forty songs remain in manuscript. The scores of the following orchestral works by Ponce are in the Fleisher Collection in Philadelphia: *Gavotte, Danse des Anciens Mexicains, Instantaneas Mexicanas* (Mexican Snapshots), *Poema Elegiaco, Estampas Nocturnas, Balada Mexicana,* Concerto for Piano and Orchestra, *Chapultepec,* and a symphonic suite arranged by Ponce from Albéniz's opera *Merlin.*

Silvestre REVUELTAS, the modern Mexicanist of music, was born in Durango on the last day of the 1800's, December 31, 1899. He studied violin in Durango, and from 1913 to 1916 took a course in composition with Rafael Tello at the *Conservatorio Nacional de Música* in Mexico City. In 1916 he went to the United States, where he continued his studies at Austin, Texas, and later at the Chicago Musical College, under Felix Borowski. He gave violin recitals in Mexico in 1920, and returned to the United States in 1922 to study violin with Ševčik. From 1926 to 1928 Revueltas conducted theater orchestras in Texas and Alabama, and in 1929 was appointed assistant conductor of the *Orquesta Sinfónica de Mexico.* In 1931, at the urgent suggestion of Carlos Chavez, Revueltas began to compose. In 1933 he taught at the *Conservatorio Nacional,* and directed concerts of the Conservatory orchestra. In 1936, he left the *Orquesta Sinfónica de Mexico,* and organized a new group, the *Orquesta Sinfónica Nacional,* which had a brief existence. In 1937, during the Spanish civil war, Revueltas went to Spain, and participated in the cultural activities of the Music Section of the Loyalist Government. Returning to Mexico, he resumed his work as composer and conductor. Weakened by a reckless mode of life, Revueltas succumbed to an attack of pneumonia, on the night when his ballet *Renacuajo Paseador* was produced at the *Palacio de Bellas Artes,* in Mexico City, October 4–5, 1940.

In an autobiographical note to the author, written in 1932, Revueltas wrote: "I do not think I was a child prodigy, but I showed some inclination for music quite early, as the result of which I became a professional musician. Contributors to this were some teachers of mine from whom I fortunately did not learn much, due probably to the bad habit of independence. I play the violin, and I have given recitals all over the country, but I found of no interest posing as a virtuoso, so I have devoted myself to composition and conducting—perhaps, a better pose. I like all kinds of music. I can even stand some of the classics, and some of my own works, but I prefer the music of the people of ranchos and villages of my country."

During the decade 1930–1940, Revueltas composed prolifically. There are no symphonies or symphonic poems on the list of his works; rather they are sketches, evocations of moods, or musical pictures of Mexico. Revueltas could be sardonic to the point of nihilism, but when he was emotionally moved he showed a deep lyrical strain. The forms in which he cast his music do not fall into any traditional category; they are agglutinative, the ideas following one another in free succession, governed only by the laws of contrast and recurrence. The harmonic and contrapuntal texture of his music is based on free superposition of simple melodic phrases. His orchestration is often inspired by the type of Mexican popular orchestras composed of violins, trumpets, and drums, reinforced by a piano. His scoring is heterophonous, exploiting instrumental colors of contrasting qualities, against the background of multirhythmic percussion. The folkloric element is always present in Revueltas' melos, and part writing in characteristic Mexican progressions of parallel thirds enhances the sense of local color. But Revueltas never quotes popular tunes; he prefers to re-create the native rhythms and melodies in his individual manner. Revueltas summed up his code of esthetics in a program note for his "geometric dance," *Planos:* "My music is functional architecture, which does not exclude sentiment. Melodic fragments derive from the same impulse, the same emotion as in my other works; they sing in persistent rhythms, ever in motion; they produce sonorities that may seem strange because they are not common. My rhythms and sonorities are reminiscent of other rhythms and sonorities, just as building material in architecture is identical with any building material, but it serves for constructions that are different in meaning, form, and expression."

Revueltas decried the conventional idea of program music. In his explanatory note to *Ventanas* (Windows), he wrote: *"Ventanas* is a composition without a program. When I composed the music, I may have intended to convey a definite idea. Now that several months have elapsed, I no longer recall what it was." In the preface to his orchestral sketch *Cuanahuac* (ancient Indian name of the Mexican resort, Cuernavaca), Revueltas makes a burlesque of "musical tourists": "This is a music with-

G. Schirmer, Inc.

Carlos Chavez

Manuel M. Ponce

José Rolón

Candelario Huízar

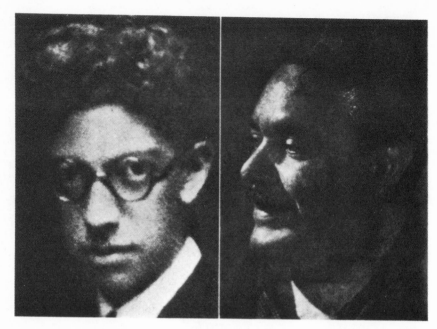

Luis Sandi   Silvestre Revueltas

The Mexican "Group of Four": Salvador Contreras,
Daniel Ayala, Pablo Moncayo, and Blas Galindo

out tourism. In the orchestra, the *huehuetl* (Indian drum) is used as a means of nationalist propaganda. Other instruments in the score are even more nationalistic, but no attention should be paid to them; it is all just anticapitalist agitation."

For his little orchestral piece entitled *Janitzio*, Revueltas supplied this note: "Janitzio is a fishermen's island in Lake Patzcuaro. Lake Patzcuaro is filthy. The romantic travelers have embellished it with verses and music of the picture postcard type. Not to be outdone, I too add my grain to the sandpile. Posterity will undoubtedly reward my contribution to national tourism."

In a note on a composition bearing the enigmatic title *8 x Radio* (which simply means, eight musicians playing over the radio, for the piece was written for a radio octet), Revueltas indulges in some clowning: "*8 x Radio* is an algebraic equation which cannot possibly be solved unless one possesses profound knowledge of mathematics. The composer has attempted to solve it by means of musical instruments." And with reference to his *Música para Charlar* (Music for Chatter), Revueltas declares: "Music that makes one think is intolerable, excruciating. There are people who like it; as to myself, I adore music that puts me to sleep."

Beneath this good-natured banter, a deep emotion is often felt. In lyric passages, such as the Cradle Song in *Homenaje a Federico García Lorca* (Homage to García Lorca, Spanish poet killed by the Fascists), Revueltas is capable of sublimity. There is no facetiousness in his music descriptive of Indian life, as *Colorines* (colored beads, worn by Indian women), and in his music of revolutionary content. There is profound sentiment in Revueltas' score *Esquinas* (Corners): "It would be amusing to find in this music the noise of taxi horns, street cars, and trucks," he wrote, "but unfortunately there is nothing of that in it. Rather it is the sound, or perhaps the silence of the inner traffic of the souls, passing by. Conventional analysis may discover in the music some definite form, binary, ternary, song-form, etc. That is of no consequence. The traffic of which I speak is multiform, without visible coherence. It is subordinated to the rhythm of life, not to the distance from one side of the street to the other."

Much of Revueltas' music was written for children, as *Renacuajo Paseador* (Pollywog Takes a Stroll), *Duo para Pato y Canario* (Duet for Duck and Canary), and *Alcancías* (Piggy Banks). The complete list of his works with dates of composition follows: String Quartet No. 1 (June, 1930), String Quartet No. 2 and No. 3 (March, 1931), *Cuanahuac* (version for small orchestra, June, 1931; for large orchestra, December

1932), *Esquinas* (for small orchestra, August, 1931; for large orchestra, October, 1933), *Duo para Pato y Canario* (for small orchestra and soprano, December, 1931), *Ventanas* (for orchestra, December, 1931), *Colorines* (small orchestra, May, 1932), *Alcancías* (small orchestra, July, 1932), Toccata (for violin and seven wind instruments, January, 1933), *El Renacuajo Paseador* (March, 1933), *8 x Radio* (1933), *Janitzio* (July, 1933; new version, December, 1936), *Caminos* (for orchestra, January, 1934), *Planos* (small orchestra, March, 1934; large orchestra, June, 1934), *Homenaje a Federico García Lorca* (for small orchestra, October, 1936), *Caminando* (voice with small orchestra, February, 1937), *Sensemaya,* an Afro-Cuban chant (voice with small orchestra, May, 1937; large orchestra, March, 1938), *Canto de Guerra de los Frontes Leales* (War Song of the Loyalist Fronts, for three trumpets, three trombones, two tubas, percussion, and piano, February, 1938), and *Siete Canciones* (Seven Songs, to poems of García Lorca, for voice and piano, 1938).

In 1940, Revueltas began the composition of a ballet, *La Coronela,* to the story of a girl colonel during the revolutionary movement against the dictatorship of Porfirio Diaz. The score, left unfinished at the death of Revueltas, was completed and orchestrated by Blas Galindo and Candelario Huizar.

The following works by Revueltas were performed for the first time by the *Orquesta Sinfónica de Mexico,* under the composer's direction: *Esquinas* (November 20, 1931), *Ventanas* (November 4, 1932), *Cuanahuac* (June 2, 1933), and *Planos* (November 5, 1934). *Caminos* was performed by Chavez on July 17, 1934. *Janitzio* and *8 x Radio* were conducted by Revueltas on October 13, 1933, at the *Palacio de Bellas Artes.* *Colorines* was performed by the Pan American Orchestra in New York, on November 4, 1933, Nicolas Slonimsky conducting. *Homenaje a Federico García Lorca* was given in Madrid on September 22, 1937, Revueltas conducting. *El Renacuajo Paseador* was performed on October 4, 1940. *La Coronela* was produced posthumously on November 20, 1941.

Revueltas wrote music for the following films: *Redes* (1935), *Vamos con Pancho Villa* (1936), *El Indio* (1938), *Ferrocarriles de Baja California* (Railroads of Lower California, 1938), *La Noche de los Mayas* (The Night of the Mayas, 1939), *Bajo el Signo de la Muerte* (Under the Sign of Death, 1939), and *Los de Abajo* (Those from the Lower Classes, 1940).

Redes was presented by Revueltas on October 7, 1937, at the meeting-concert of the Committee against War and Fascism in Barcelona, Spain. A suite from *Ferrocarriles de Baja California* was performed under the title *Música para Charlar*, in Mexico City on December 15, 1938.

Very little music by Revueltas has been published. *Canción* and *Allegro* for piano were published by C. Fischer, and several songs have been published by the *Editorial Cooperativa* in Montevideo. The lithographed orchestral score of *Homenaje a Federico García Lorca* is available through *New Music*. The Fleisher Collection in Philadelphia has the following scores by Revueltas: *Alcancías, Cuanahuac, Esquinas, Homenaje a Federico García Lorca, Música para Charlar, Planos, Redes, Sensemaya*, Toccata, and *8 x Radio*. See "Silvestre Revueltas and Musical Nationalism in Mexico" by Otto Mayer-Serra, in *The Musical Quarterly* (April, 1941).

José ROLÓN (1883–1945), composer of a number of symphonic works, studied music first under his father in Ciudad Guzmán, Jalisco, and at a local music school. Later he was sent to Paris, where he took lessons with Moszkowski. In France he acquired a taste for modern music, and was particularly impressed with Debussy. He returned to Mexico in 1907, and founded a music school in Guadalajara. In 1927, when he was forty-four years old, Rolón went once more to Paris, where he attended classes of Nadia Boulanger and Paul Dukas. His predilection for French impressionist technique of composition was further strengthened, but the diffuseness of his early style was now replaced by contrapuntal and harmonic compactness. His Symphony and Overture are in the academic tradition, but with his symphonic fairy tale, *El Festín de los Enanos* (Festival of the Dwarfs), Rolón adopted the modern French technique, in harmony as well as in orchestration. The thematic material of this work is taken from popular Mexican nursery songs. *El Festín de los Enanos*, composed in 1925, was performed by the *Orquesta del Conservatorio* in Mexico City on March 4, 1928, Revueltas conducting. Rolón's *Scherzo Sinfónico* was performed by the *Orquesta Sinfónica de Mexico*, Chavez conducting, on January 6, 1929, and the same orchestra gave the first performances of Rolón's *Cuauhtémoc* (January 10, 1930), *Baile Michoacano* (July 22, 1930), *Zapotlán* (subtitled *Suite Sinfónica 1895*, performed on November 4, 1932), and Piano Concerto (September 4, 1942). The *Baile Michoacano* is a stylization of popular rhythms of the Michoacan state. *Cuauhtémoc* (the name of the last Aztec Emperor) is in three movements, *Cortejo y Coronación, Defensa Heroica*, and *Finale*, and the melodic structure of the principal themes is pentatonic. *Zapotlán* is the realm of the Zapotec Indians of Mexico. The subtitle *1895* is an allusion to Rolón's childhood memories of that year. The Piano Concerto (which was originally performed under the composer's direction, with a local symphonic ensemble in Guadalajara, on January 31, 1936) is written in a greatly advanced idiom, and the piano part is cast in the modern virtuoso style. The Concerto is, however, in the definite key of E minor, and the feeling of tonality is maintained throughout. There are three movements, and the form is traditional. Some piano pieces, notably *Trois Danses Mexicaines*, were published in Paris. The orchestral scores of *El Festín de los Enanos, Zapotlán, Cuauhtémoc*, Piano Concerto, and a symphonic suite from *Ballet de los Gallos* are in the Fleisher Collection in Philadelphia.

Chiefly known for his essays on music, Adolfo SALAZAR (1890——) is a Spanish musicologist now resident in Mexico. Born in Madrid, Salazar's musical knowledge has been largely self-taught, although he did take a few lessons with Manuel de Falla. In 1916, Salazar published his first compositions, *Tres Preludios* for piano and *Tres Poemas* to the text by Verlaine. In larger forms, he has written three symphonic works—*Paisajes, Estampas*, and *Don Juan de los Infernos*. Salazar's book *Música y Músicos de Hoy* (1928) is widely read. After the civil war in Spain, Salazar settled in Mexico, where he published a survey of European music, under the title *La Rosa de los Vientos en la Música Europea* (1940).

Luis SANDI was born in 1905. He studied violin, voice and composition at the Conservatory of Mexico, and upon graduation became a choral conductor. Later he was appointed Chief of the Music Section of the Secretariat of Public Instruction. Sandi's own music is permeated with Mexican folklore, while the structural element of his works is on the classical side. The most ambitious of his folkloric compositions is *Norte*, a symphonic suite in three movements, based on indigenous melodies of northern Mexico. The scoring is marked by frequent solo passages, particularly in the wood-wind section, and the folk themes are combined in free counterpoint. *Norte* was performed by the *Orquesta Sinfónica de Mexico*, Chavez conducting, on August 15, 1941. To the same category belongs Sandi's symphonic poem, *Feria*, portraying a village fair. Even more literal in the application of popular melodies and rhythms is Sandi's composition for two guitars and chamber orchestra, *Las Guarecitas*

(Girls), which imitates the sonority of a popular band. *El Venado* (Venison), written for an ensemble of Mexican instruments, is based on themes of the Yaqui Indians. *El Venado* was conducted by Sandi with the *Orquesta Mexicana* on October 28, 1938, at the *Palacio de Bellas Artes* in Mexico City. In the spirit of caricature, Sandi wrote *Suite Banale* for small orchestra, which was performed by the Radio Orchestra on January 22, 1937. All these scores, and also a suite from Sandi's film music *La Hoja de Plata* (Silver Leaf) are in the Fleisher Collection in Philadelphia.

Rafael TELLO (1872——), composer and music educator, studied music with his mother in Mexico City, and gave his first piano recital at the age of thirteen. In 1896, at the age of twenty-four, he became an instructor at the *Conservatorio Nacional,* and from 1917 to 1930 was director of the new *Conservatorio Libre.* He then returned to the faculty of the *Conservatorio Nacional.* Tello began to compose at the age of nineteen, and became particularly interested in the problem of Mexican national opera. Accordingly, he selected a historic character as the central figure for his second opera, *Nicolas Bravo,* which was produced in Mexico City on August 27, 1910. His first opera, *Juno,* remains unperformed. Another opera, *Due Amori,* was produced on February 27, 1916. In 1942 Tello wrote a new operatic work, *El Oidor.* Tello conducted the first performance of his *Sonata Tragica* for violin and orchestra at the inaugural concert of the *Orquesta Sinfónica de Mexico,* on September 2, 1928. *Patria Heroica,* an epic poem, illustrating in four traditional movements the events of a heroic battle, was performed by the same orchestra, on May 16, 1930, under the direction of Carlos Chavez. Tello's *Fantasia* for two pianos and orchestra, written in a deliberately simple style, was performed by the *Orquesta Sinfónica de Mexico* on July 2, 1943. As a composer, Tello cultivates a rhapsodic and somewhat discursive style, often turbulently dynamic at climactic points. His music remains in manuscript. The orchestral scores of his *Sonata Tragica,* the Overture to the opera *Nicolas Bravo,* and two juvenilia (Minuet and Intermezzo) are in the Fleisher Collection in Philadelphia.

José VASQUEZ (1895——), a native of Guadalajara, is variously active as a composer, an orchestral conductor, and instructor at the University of Mexico. He studied at the *Conservatorio Nacional de Música,* graduating in 1914, when he was nineteen years old. Vasquez then took a correspondence course in composition with the *École Univèrselle* in Paris. An exceptionally prolific composer, he has written five operas, three symphonies, a ballet, four piano concertos, a Violin Concerto, a symphonic triptych, six piano sonatas, a Violin Sonata, a Violoncello Sonata, a Trio, two string quartets, and eighty songs. The following operas by Vasquez have been performed: *Citlalli* (on an Aztec subject, November, 1922), *El Mandarín* (June, 1934), *El Rajah* (September 15, 1934), and an opera-ballet, *El Último Sueño* (April, 1935). His Symphony No. 1 was performed in Mexico City, under the composer's direction, on August 17, 1915; Symphony No. 2, in December, 1922; three piano concertos on October 11, 18, and 25, 1939, respectively; and the *Tríptico Sinfónico* on May 5, 1930, by the University orchestra, Vasquez conducting. He conducted his *Poema Sinfónico* for soprano, chorus, and orchestra, with the *Orquesta Sinfónica de Mexico* on November 4, 1928. Vasquez's music is distinguished by a quasi-impressionist manner of writing, with programmatic connotations. His works remain in manuscript. The orchestral scores of the three piano concertos, the Violin Concerto, *Poema Sinfónico,* and a suite of three sketches, *Acuarelas de Viaje,* are in the Fleisher Collection in Philadelphia.

Nicaragua

¡Nicaragua, divina Nicaragua!
[JUAN B. DELGADO]

Nicaragua, the country of volcanoes and lakes, lies between Costa Rica and Honduras. It is the largest nation of Central America in area. Its population numbers about 1,400,000, the majority being mestizos.

The folk music of Nicaragua is part of the musical heritage of the Maya and Quiché branches of Central American Indians. Little of this music has come down to us, but some melodies and rhythms peculiar to the ancient race still survive in remote villages on the coast.

The early travelers who had witnessed the native dance festivals of the Indians of Nicaragua describe them in contemptuous terms, stressing the fact that "wine was there as plentiful as were the songs and the dances."

In Lothrop's valuable treatise *Pottery of Costa Rica and Nicaragua*, we find the English translation of the accounts of these dances by the historiographer of Columbus, Gonzalo Fernandez de Oviedo y Valdes, quoted from *La Historia Natural y General de las Indias*, lib. XLII, cap. XI:

One Saturday, on the twenty-ninth day of August, 1528, in the *plaza* of *Nicoya*, under the *cacique* of that province, Don Alonso, known by another name as *Nambi*, which in his language means dog, two hours before nightfall, about eighty or a hundred Indians began to sing and dance in an *Areito*, in one part of the *plaza*; they must have been of the vulgar and plebeian people, because in another part of the same *plaza*, the *cacique*, with much enjoyment and festivity, seated himself on a *duho*, or small bench, and his chief officials and about seventy or eighty other Indians on similar *duhos*. A girl began to bring them drink, in small gourds, like bowls or cups, of *chicha*, which is a very strong and rather acid wine which they make of maize, and which, in its color, resembles chicken broth into which the yolks of one or two eggs have been broken.

In the same section of Lothrop's volume, we find a description by Benzoni of a Nicaraguan native festival:

Two or three hundred, or even three or four thousand Indians assemble together, and having carefully swept the place where they are going to dance, one of them comes forward to lead the rest. He goes nearly always backward, turning himself occasionally, and so do all the others, by threes or fours, in regular order. Those who beat the drum begin to sing some of their songs, and the man who leads the dance is the first to answer. Then the rest do the same progressively. Some carry a fan in the hand, some a calabash with pebbles in it; some wear feathers on the head, others wear rows of sea-shells on their arms and legs; some raise their legs, others flourish their arms; some act the blind man, others pretend to be lame; some laugh, others cry; and thus with many other gestures, and frequent drinking of their wine, they dance all day, and sometimes part of the night also.

The mention of the "calabash with pebbles in it" is interesting, for it shows the antiquity of this Indian shaker, which is now universally known as the *Maracas*. The contemporary Nicaraguan Indians still use their ancient instruments, which they have in common with other Central American Indians. Among wind instruments, the *Chirimía*, which is a primitive clarinet, and the *Zul*, a primitive flute with five or six apertures, are used by the natives. Drums of all sizes and shapes and the *Marimba* are popular in Nicaragua as in all Central America. The Nicaraguan Indians also have a primitive monochord, called the *Quijongo*, in which a string supported by a movable bridge is attached on both ends to an oblong sound box. There is also the *Juco*, or a bull-roarer, which is made of a barrel covered with a drumhead, with a string passed through the membrane. When the string is pulled, a peculiar roaring or whining sound is made. Some other Nicaraguan instruments, such as the *Cacho*, which is a primitive trumpet made of an animal horn, and the *Chilchil*, a small bell, are in use among the natives.

Among Nicaraguans, native Indian customs and rituals are combined with the Catholic religious rites, resulting in an interesting amalgam of cultures. The Nicaraguan festival play known under the name *Güegüence* is celebrated on St. Jerome's day, the thirteenth of September. Its text represents a mixture of Spanish with the indigenous Nahuatl dialect. One of these plays is reproduced, in Spanish and Nahuatl, in a book entitled *Güegüence*, compiled by D. G. Brinton, and published in 1883 in Philadelphia.

Luis A. Delgadillo, the foremost musician of Nicaragua, contributes these specimens of native dance melodies: the *Yegüecita* (little mare, so named because the dancers hold a wooden model of a horse's head); *Los Caballitos* (little horses); and *El Zopilote* (buzzard, so named because the dancers dress in bird costumes).

La Yegüecita

Three Nicaraguan Melodies (*Delgadillo*)

Music culture in Nicaragua is little advanced. The chief purveyor of music is the *Banda de los Supremos Poderes* in Managua, organized in 1914. The annals of Nicaragua record the name of José de la Cruz Mena, a leper who lived in isolation and wrote religious music. His manuscripts were destroyed after his death.

Delgadillo paints a melancholy picture of the present status of music in Nicaragua in an article in *Música* (Bogotá, July 1941): "My compatriots have little desire to support the national arts; they are too preoccupied with politics. The people of Nicaragua are musical; what is needed is the establishment of music schools and conservatories. The ten plagues of Egypt reign in Nicaragua. We are the Quixotes of music, victims of the materialistic environment and general lassitude."

MUSICIANS OF NICARAGUA

Nicaragua's foremost composer is Luis A. DELGADILLO, whose birth in Managua took place on August 26, 1887. Delgadillo showed musical ability at an early age, and was sent by the Nicaraguan government to study in Italy at the Milan Conservatory. After five years in Europe, Delgadillo returned to Nicaragua, where he conducted the *Banda de los Supremos Poderes* in Managua and directed a music school. On September 14, 1921, Delgadillo conducted in Guatemala the first performance of his *Sinfonía Centroamerica*, based on native themes. After a South American tour, Delgadillo wrote a *Sinfonía Incaica*, which he conducted in Caracas, Venezuela, on May 20, 1927. There followed an orchestral suite, *Diciembre*, which Delgadillo performed for the first time on October 20, 1929, in Havana, Cuba. After a trip to Mexico, Delgadillo composed a suite on Mexican themes, *Teotihuacán*, performed by the orchestra of the University of Mexico on October 12, 1941. Inspired by Nicaraguan folklore are the orchestral suite in four movements, *Escenas Pastoriles*, and *Los Tincos*, which the composer presented with the *Orquesta Sinfónica de Nicaragua* on May 12, 1939. Of Incaic inspiration are *Invocation to the Moon, Dance to the Coca,* and *Yaravi Peruano. La Danza de Flechas* is based on the pentatonic scale, and reflects the ancient modes of Indian music. A symphonic poem, *Tramonto en la Cumbre* (1941), is of a religious character. The ballet *La Cabeza del Rawí* (1942), which received a prize from the Ministry of Public Instruction in Nicaragua, is orientalistic in treatment. Delgadillo's *Sinfonía Serrana* (1942) is in a pastoral mood. Of interest is his *Ballet Infantil*, which portrays Felix the Cat and Mickey Mouse. In addition, Delgadillo has written two operas, *Final de Norma* and *Mavaltayán,* four operettas, eight string quartets, three trios, twenty-four Preludes for piano, twenty-two melodies for violin and piano, over fifty songs, and fourteen "romanzas" to the texts of Rubén Darío, the great Nicaraguan poet. Delgadillo's orchestral manuscripts are in the Fleisher Collection in Philadelphia.

The few musicians in Nicaragua who possess some degree of professional competence are pupils of Delgadillo. In 1943 Delgadillo went to Panama where he taught at the National Conservatory of Panama City and edited the music magazine *Armonía.* In 1945 he resigned his position and returned to Managua.

Panama

> *¿De do viene el caballero?*
> *Viene de Panama.*
> [LOPE DE VEGA]

The Republic of Panama is situated on the neck of land connecting South America with Central America. Its position is of the greatest political importance because of the Panama Canal. In area, Panama is larger than Costa Rica or El Salvador, but smaller than the other Central American republics. Panama's population numbers about 600,000. There is a great variety of races, Indians living in the jungle, Negroes on the coasts, and Americans in the Panama Canal Zone.

In spite of the smallness of its territory, Panama has produced a considerable variety of distinctive dances and songs. Panama's music is racially differentiated, depending on the region. It is Indian in the jungle of the interior; it is Spanish-American on the coasts; and in Panama City it is as international as the port itself.

A wealth of information on the Indian music of Panama is provided in the exemplary treatise *Tradiciones y Cantares de Panama* by Panama's musician-diplomat, Narciso Garay. This volume contains numerous musical illustrations and photographs, which together give a graphic picture of the dances, songs, and instruments of the Panamanian Indians. Additional information on native music is found in a paper by Frances Densmore, *Music of the Tule Indians of Panama,* published by the Smithsonian Institution.

The most primitive Indian chants of Panama still retain the pentatonic structure of pre-Columbian America. Many of these songs are part of the ritual, and are invested with magical power by the natives. There is an authentic report that a native musician has charged, and collected, as much as fifteen dollars for teaching the Indians a song supposed to attract turtles to the catcher.

The musical instruments of Panama's Indians are rudimentary flutes and drums. European guitars and violins and Cuban shakers are in common use. The violins often have only three strings, and are known under the name *Rabel.* There are drums of three sizes: the *Tambor* (large), the *Pujador* (medium), and the *Repicador* (small). The Cuban *Güiro* is here called *Guáchara,* while the Cuban *Maracas* is sometimes referred to as *Güiro,* which is apt to create confusion.

The Panamanian guitar is called the *Mejoranera,* because it often accompanies the native dance *Mejorana.* It is so tuned that the harmony appears in the form of a six-four chord, which influences the character of the harmonization.

The *Mejorana,* the *Tamborito,* and the *Punto* are the typical dance forms of Panama. The *Tamborito* is an old air, dating as far back as the seventeenth century. In its present form, it is usually sung by a woman soloist, followed by a chorus singing the refrain. The singing, as distinct from the dance, is designated by the word *Tonada.* The dance is punctuated by hand-clapping and a rhythmical beat of the small drums. The *Tamborito* is written in a major key and in a lively two-four time. As the tempo increases, the syncopated drum accompaniment is smoothed into triplet rhythms. The choreography of the *Tamborito* is simple: the partners dance opposite each other, while the crowd forms a circle around them. The drummers are placed within the circle, next to the dancers.

The *Tamborito* has long been regarded as a licentious dance. A native poet describes it as "more enticing than the nudity of Venus." There is a special, more sedate type of the *Tamborito,* danced in private homes, which is called *Tambor de Orden,* or an orderly *Tambor* (*Tambor* is a frequent abbreviation for *Tamborito*).

The *Mejorana* is also an old air, probably of Spanish origin. In Panama, it is played as an improvisation "en contrapunto" on two guitars, which take the name of the dance, and are called *Mejoraneras.* Like the *Tamborito,* the *Mejorana* is usually written in the major key. When it is minor, it has a special name, the *Gallino*. The rhythm of the *Mejorana* is dual, and is determined by the singing line which is in two-four time, and an accompanying figure which is six-eight time. Narciso Garay, however, sets the meter of the *Mejorana* as three-eight, six-eight, or nine-eight. There is a vocal version of the *Mejorana*, called the *Socavón*, which is itself known under two different names, depending on whether it ends on the tonic (in which case it is called the *Zapatero*) or on the dominant (when it is called the *Mesano*). Furthermore, there exists a slow, Saraband-like type of *Mejorana*, which is called *Mejorana-Poncho*.

The *Mejorana* is a square dance, with the partners facing each other. Two different dancing steps are used: the *Zapateo* (literally, shoe dance), and the *Paseo* (the promenade).

The third characteristic dance form of Panama, the *Punto*, is a rapid dance maintaining a steady six-eight time, with a melody tending towards two-four time. In the villages engaged couples often dance the *Punto*, and the spectators throw coins at their feet. The *Punto*, in common with other airs of Panama, is usually in a major key. There exists also a *Punto* in minor, which is called the *Coco*.

Other popular dances of Panama are the *Tamborera* (which is probably of Mexican origin), *Curacha, Pindin, Papelón, Sueste, Chiriqui*, and the *Tono*. Most of these dances adhere to the rhythmic formula of the *Punto*. Narciso Garay cites a specimen of *Chiriqui* in three-four time, played on a three-stringed violin with the accompaniment of a drum.

A group of Panamanian dances are of Negro origin. Of these, the *Cumbia* is characteristic. It has been described as "the representation of the erotic struggle between the male and the female."

Panama's composers are mostly amateurs who write popular songs and dances for local bands. Among the better known native musicians are Alberto Galimany and Ricardo Fábrega.

In recent years, steps have been taken by the Government of Panama to promote native music culture. In 1940, a National Conservatory was established in Panama City, under the direction of the Panamanian violinist Alfredo de Saint-Malo, with a capable faculty including foreign musicians. Since 1943 the Conservatory of Panama has published a music monthly, *Armonía*.

In Panama City there is a symphonic ensemble conducted by Herbert de Castro, a highly trained musician who is also a composer. Several military bands furnish open-air music in all towns and villages of Panama. A piece originally composed for the *Banda Republicana* by its conductor,

Santos Jorge, and entitled *Himno Istmeño*, has become the National Anthem of the Republic of Panama.

MUSICIANS OF PANAMA

The Panamanian musician and conductor, Herbert de CASTRO (1906——), studied in Paris with Albert Roussel. In 1942, when de Castro was thirty-six years of age, he was appointed conductor of the newly founded symphony orchestra in Panama. He has written some atmospheric piano pieces.

Roque CORDERO (1917——) is a young Panamanian Negro. His orchestral movement on native themes, *Capricho Interiorano*, was first performed by the *Orquesta Sinfónica* in Panama on August 10, 1942. This work is included in the Fleisher Collection in Philadelphia.

The Panamanian composer of popular music, Ricardo FÁBREGA (1905——), is a native of Santiago de Veraguas. Fábrega has composed dances in the native manner, bearing descriptive titles such as *Una Noche Tropical*, *Bajo el Palmar*, and *Panama Viejo*.

Alberto GALIMANY, composer of popular music, was born in Villafranca, Spain, in 1889. Galimany studied at the Barcelona Conservatory, and then went to Panama, where he was appointed conductor of the *Banda Republicana*, a post which he held until 1937. A theater arrangement of Galimany's patriotic piece *Panama* has been published in Barcelona, and is in the Fleisher Collection in Philadelphia.

Narciso GARAY (1876——), better known as a diplomat than as a musician, was born in Panama City. He studied music at the Musical Institute in Cartagena, and later in Bogotá. In 1897 he went to Brussels, where he attended the Royal Conservatory of Music. He graduated with a *Premier Prix*, and then took a course at the *Schola Cantorum* in Paris. In Paris he published a Violin Sonata. Later Garay abandoned music for a diplomatic career, and was at one time Minister of Foreign Affairs of the Republic of Panama. In 1930, he issued an important publication, *Tradiciones y Cantares de Panama*, which has become a source book for Panamanian folklore.

Santos JORGE (1870–1941), author of the National Anthem of Panama, was born in Peralta, Spain, and died in Panama City. He settled in

Panama in 1889. In 1897, he wrote the music to the *Himno Istmeño*, which was proclaimed the National Anthem of Panama after the separation of Panama from Colombia in 1903. A biographical sketch of Santos Jorge is published in the November, 1943, issue of *Armonía*, organ of the National Conservatory of Panama.

The violinist, Alfredo de SAINT-MALO (1898———) studied at the Paris Conservatory, and graduated in 1919, when he was twenty-one years old, with a *Premier Prix*. Saint-Malo has made concert tours in Europe and America, and in 1928 played with Ravel in the United States. In 1941, he was appointed director of the National Conservatory in Panama City.

Paraguay

¡Paraguay, tierra ideal,
Es tu suelo un jardín de poemas, amores y flores!
[FROM A POPULAR SONG]

Paraguay, an inland country, lying astride the tropic of Capricorn, has been called the Paradise of South America for its natural beauty and the serenity of its climate. Paraguay is the smallest South American nation in population, which numbers scarcely over one million inhabitants, most of them Indians of the Guarany branch.

The native musical culture of Paraguay is part of the tradition of the jungle country in the heart of the South American continent. The original music of the natives is based on the pentatonic scale, and, like all Indian music, it is slow in tempo and melancholy in mood. Contact with the Spanish elements has resulted in extension of the original scale to the European seven-tone scale, with the minor mode predominant. From the few extant specimens of the Guarany music of Paraguay, it appears that there was in it little variety of rhythm, and that each song was a succession of musical phrases separated by cadences. In many Latin American countries, the vivacious rhythmic lilt reflects the influence of the Negro element, introduced by the African slaves. There is virtually no Negro population in Paraguay, and consequently the Afro-American elements are not present in the music of the natives.

The primitive instruments of the Guarany Indians are still in use among the natives of Paraguay and in the adjoining provinces of Brazil. These are wind instruments, made of grooved pieces of wood and held together by strong hoops, or vertical flutes made of sugar cane. The generic name of these wind instruments is *Memby*. According to size and function, there are different types of the *Memby*, called *Memby-Apará*, *Memby-Chué*, *Memby-Guazú*, and *Memby-Tarará*. There is also a primitive war trumpet, the *Inubia*. Among the native drums, there is the *Trocano*, a burned-out trunk of a tree placed on wooden supports and struck with mallets. Other native drums are the *Matapú*, the *Muré-Muré* and the *Curugú*. The native name of the *Maracas* is *Mbaracá*. The Guarany Indians have made use of human bones for the manufacture of instruments. According to travelers' reports, there were cases of musical cannibalism, as when the Guarany Indians slew the missionaries and made scrapers from their bones. The native name for such striated bones, similar in function to the Cuban *Güiro*, is *Congoerá*.

Pioneers of musical education in Paraguay were the Jesuit missionaries, who settled in South America in the sixteenth century; they introduced church singing into the country which is now Paraguay. Among these Jesuit musicians was the celebrated Italian composer, Domenico Zipoli, who died in Córdoba, Argentina, in 1726. The annals of Paraguay also contain the name of one Luis Berger, a Jesuit missionary, who settled in Paraguay in 1616, and who was an accomplished violinist as well as a painter and a physician. Among the musicians of Indian origin was Julian Atirahu, who lived a century ago and who acquired considerable skill in composition. Among his pieces is a minuet which can be played simultaneously right side up and upside down, resulting in perfect harmony.

In the nineteenth century, the influx of European salon music, and the universal adoption of the guitar as the principal instrument of the people, led to the appearance in Paraguay of a hybrid type of popular music, European in structure and harmony, performed in a "tropical" manner. Under Paraguay's skies, the Waltz, the Polka, and the Galop acquire a new and peculiar inflection. The *Polka Paraguaya* follows the traditional oom-pah beat of the German prototype, but its accompaniment flows in lazy triplets, in three beats to a measure in two-four time. The Paraguayan Galop may have the bass in three-four time, and the melody in six-eight time, following the familiar formula of so many dances of Hispanic origin.

An interesting feature of this type of Paraguayan popular music is the text, which is often sung in the Guarany language, which is the second language of Paraguay. Thus, the Paraguayan *Canción* is also known as *Purajhei* in the Guarany language, which, in contrast to most Indian dialects, has a mellifluous cadence and abounds in vowels.

Recently a successful attempt was made by a Paraguayan musician, José Asunción Flores, to revive the spirit of the Guarany song and to create a new form of popular music that would draw on native melodic resources rather than on the European stock of music. In collaboration with the Paraguayan poet Ortiz Guerrero, José Asunción Flores initiated the *Guarania*, which is a ballad in slow waltz time and usually in a minor mode. The *Guaranías* soon became popular, and may now be regarded as part of Paraguayan musical folklore. Numerous other Paraguayan composers of popular music, among whom Herminio Giménez and Emilio Bigi are the best known, have followed the lead of José Asunción Flores and have written *Guaranías*.

The present state of music in Paraguay holds considerable promise for a bright future. There are now in Asunción two music schools, the *Escuela Normal de Música*, under the direction of Remberto Giménez, and the *Conservatorio de Música* at the Ateneo, headed by Juan Carlos Moreno González.

The Conservatory of Asunción maintains a student orchestra, which gives occasional performances of classical music. There is also a military band, the *Banda de Policía*. The only musician in Paraguay who has attempted to write music in larger forms is Juan Carlos Moreno González, the author of a symphony on native themes. Remberto Giménez, director of the Conservatory in Asunción, has written some semi-popular music.

MUSICIANS OF PARAGUAY

José Asunción FLORES was born in 1904 in Asunción, ran away from home as a child, and was placed in a reform school, where he began to study music. Later he played the cornet and the violin in the *Banda de Policía* in Asunción. The signal achievement of José Asunción Flores is the creation of a new type of native air, which he called *Guarania*, in allusion to the Guarany Indians of Paraguay. He has published several such *Guaranías* in Buenos Aires, where he now serves as an attaché at the Legation of Paraguay.

The composer and educator, Remberto GIMÉNEZ (1899——), is a native of Coronel Oviedo. He studied with Alberto Williams in Buenos Aires, and later went to Paris for further study at the *Schola Cantorum*. Upon his return to Paraguay, he became director of the *Escuela Normal de Música*. Giménez is also the conductor of the Asunción Symphony Orchestra. As a composer, he has written a *Rapsodia Paraguaya*, and has made an official arrangement of the National Anthem of Paraguay.

Juan Carlos MORENO (1912——) is a young Paraguayan who, at the age of thirteen, suffered a street-car accident, which resulted in the loss of both legs. Despite this grave handicap, Moreno began to study music, without a teacher. In 1938, when he was twenty-six, Moreno went to São Paulo, Brazil, for further study of piano and composition. Upon his return to Asunción, he was appointed director of the Conservatory of the Ateneo. Juan Carlos Moreno has written a piano Trio, a String Quartet, two piano sonatas, a Violin Sonata, a symphonic Suite on native themes, and several piano pieces. He possesses an instinctive melodic gift, but lacks an adequate technique. His music is interesting as the first attempt to use native Paraguayan themes in the established forms. Three of his pieces were published in 1939 by the Rotary Club of Asunción.

Peru

Dios en climas nos dió vario elemento
Con que a las producciones mas extrañas
El Perú ofrece hospitalario asiento.
[FELIPE PARDO Y ALIAGA]

Peru lies in the tropical zone, just south of the Equator, and enjoys a variety of climates, dry and moderate on the coast, torrid in the jungle, and bleak and cold in the high Andes. The population of Peru, the majority of whose members are Indian, numbers about seven million.

Peru is the cradle of pre-Columbian civilization. The El Dorado of the conquistadores, Peru reveals the existence of treasures more precious than gold; the pottery of the Chimu culture, the textiles of the Nazca and Tiahuanaco, the ivory-and-gold sculptures of the Incas, rank beside the great art of all time. The music of ancient Peru has come down to us in the oral tradition of the Indians, descendants of the Incas. We know that Peruvian music was essentially pentatonic, although the occasional use of passing diatonic and even chromatic tones is not excluded. Then came the Spanish, and out of the impact of the two cultures was generated a new hybrid product, the music of the mestizo, or *música chola* as it is called.

Carlos Raygada, the Peruvian writer on music, gives a picture of this process in his essay *Panorama Musical del Perú*, published in Volume II of the *Boletín Latino-Americano de Música:*

The musical system of the Peruvians, which is characterized by a vigorous originality within the limits of the pentatonic scale, came to acquire considerable emotional power in its various modalities, sufficient to serve the needs of the ritual music, love music, war music, and funeral music of our remote ancestors. The sudden appearance of the Spanish produced a general confusion, not only from the shock of the conquest itself, but also from the intrusion into everyday life of new human types, new arms, customs, habits, a new language, and even unknown animals, all of which must have dumbfounded the simple soul of the worshippers of the Sun. And in music, new scales and unusual rhythms, performed on strange and complex instruments, added to the bewilderment.

There was a clash of sensations. The conquistador, bold warrior that he was, avid for gold and power, could hardly be expected to take an interest in the music of the Incas, with its limited melodic resources. But soon the Spanish began to feel the attraction of this original native art. The result of the interpenetration of the esthetic notions of the two races was at first an unconscious and then a deliberate musical miscegenation. But it was not absolute, for the innate hereditary pride of the aborigines reserved, in the sacred intimacy of their private lives, an art peculiar to the race. This passive resistance made it possible to preserve the aboriginal musical expression, with its characteristic structural elements. It was a tactical retreat; the hybrid product remained for the mestizos, while the pure Indians kept their heritage through centuries of oral tradition.

André Sas, writing in Volume I of the *Boletín Latino-Americano de Música*, advances an interesting theory that Inca music was based on the fundamental triads, the minor tonic and major mediant.

A pioneer in collecting native songs was Daniel Alomias Robles (1871–1942). He left, at his death, about 650 melodies which he had gathered in the towns and villages of Peru. Only a few of these melodies

An Authentic Inca Melody as Harmonized by André Sas

have been published. The bulk of his material still remains in manuscript. A number of Incaic melodies from Peru, Bolivia and Ecuador are included in the monumental work *La Musique des Incas et ses Survivances* by M. and Mme. Raoul d'Harcourt, which also gives the most lucid exposition of the tonal foundations of Inca music.

The music of the Incas and their descendants has been classified into three categories: ceremonial music, pertaining to sun worship, war and public events, which was collectively designated by the word *Huanca;* music of intimate character, which went under the generic name *Harawi;* and dance music, known as *Huaiño.*

These types of music have evolved into contemporary forms, but on the whole have retained their original character. The ceremonial chants are exemplified in Hymns to the Sun, still heard at the Indian festivals in the highlands. The *Harawi* type resulted in the creation of the lyrical song *Yaravi;* and the *Huaiño* is no longer a generic term for dance music, but refers to one particular dance.

The *Yaravi* (which is but a transliteration of *Harawi,* all other ingenious etymologies of the word to the contrary notwithstanding) is performed on a flute, or sung without accompaniment to a text of nostalgic love. The authentic *Yaravi* does not follow any definite rhythmic pattern; it is rather a succession of musical phrases separated by long holds. The *Yaravies* were known in Peru under that name at least as early as 1791, for in that year the Lima publication *Mercurio Peruano* carried an article dealing with "music in general, and *Yaravies* in particular," in which the form was described as written in three-four time (which remains true for all *Yaravies* composed by Peruvian musicians in historic times), and the tonality of the song was said to be in minor, with transitions into major when required by the change of mood. The first native-born composer of *Yaravies* was Mariano Melgar (1791–1814), who treated this native form as a romantic *Lied*.

Some *Yaravies* are followed by a very short rapid movement, which is called *Fuga*, meaning flight. This *Fuga* is of course not connected in any way with the classical polyphonic form of the Fugue.

The following expressive *Yaravi* is quoted by d'Harcourt:

Peruvian Yaravi (*d'Harcourt*)

The *Huaiño* (which is spelled either with or without the *tilde* over the letter *n*) is identical with the Bolivian dance of the same name. It is in two-four time and is usually marked with syncopation.

The *Cachua* (also spelled *Kaswa* or *Kashwa*) is a round dance popular in the Peruvian highlands, danced by couples holding hands. Like most Peruvian dances, it is in two-four time, usually without syncopation, but in straight rhythm of one eighth-note and two sixteenth-notes, or two sixteenth-notes and one eighth-note.

A unique instance of an artificial name applied to a folk dance relates to the *Marinera*, a Peruvian dance of Hispanic extraction, in dual time of three-four and six-eight, and performed at a lively tempo, with the dancers waving handkerchiefs. The *Marinera* was originally called *Cueca Chilena*, or simply *Chilena*, because its popularity first spread into Peru from Chile. During the war between Chile and Peru in 1879–1883, a nationalist Peruvian writer, Abelardo Gamarra, proposed that the *Chilena* should be renamed *Marinera*, with the double purpose of striking off the reminder that the dance had come from the enemy country and at the same time honoring the gallant deeds of the Peruvian Navy. The suggestion was taken up, and the name of the dance has remained *Marinera*. Like the Chilean *Cueca*, it is danced and sung in a lively tempo, and its time-signature is three-four or six-eight, depending upon whether the first or the second of the two isochronic meters is predominant. The partners usually dance apart, waving handkerchiefs, but the choreography varies according to locality. In northern Peru, the *Marinera* appears in a form called *Tondero:* the *Marinera* is at times cast in a major mode but the *Tondero* is always in minor. A rustic form of the *Marinera*, notable for its suggestiveness, is known as *Mozamala*, literally "bad girl."

Among comparatively recent dance forms popular in Peru are the *Pasacalle* and the *Tanguino*. The *Pasacalle* (literally, passing through the street) has nothing in common with the classical *Passacaglia*, but is a carnival march, usually performed by a brass band. The *Tanguino* is a slow dance in four-four time and has no connection with the *Tango*.

Modern American dances are popular in Peru as in other South American republics. An attempt has been made by popular composers to link the ancient tradition with the modern popular dance in such hybrid creations as the *Inca Step*, which adapts the pentatonic melos of the Incas to the pace of an American Foxtrot.

The instruments used by native performers for their dances and songs have retained the chief characteristic of their Inca prototypes. The most expressive of these instruments is the *Quena*, or *Kena*, which is a vertical flute, made of reed or of the leg bone of the llama. This flute usually has five holes, corresponding to the five tones of the pentatonic scale. When, under the influence of Spanish music, the European seven-tone scale was introduced, the manufacture of *Quenas* capable of producing the diatonic scale was a natural consequence of the "hybridization" of Inca music. It must be stated in this connection that cultures more ancient than that of the Incas apparently possessed scales other than the pentatonic. André Sas has examined the musical instruments preserved in the National Museum of Archeology in Lima belonging to the Nazca culture which flourished some 1500 years ago, and has found that the scales playable on these instruments include semitones and even fractional intervals smaller than the semitone. But if so, what compelled the Incas to forego the more developed scales of the Nazca era in favor of the humble pentatonic? The suggestion presents itself that the Inca culture, superseding the Nazca, Chimu and Tiahuanaco civilizations, found these rich melodic resources unsuitable to the austere ideals of the race, and deliberately reduced the number of tones to five. Such a hypothesis has its attractions, for it would tend to prove that the Inca art of music was not merely the instinctive expression of an untutored mind, but a rational selection of a melodic medium best suited to the peculiar needs of the people's religious and ceremonial ritual. Besides, the number five, symbolic of the hand, may have had a special significance in the conceptual order of the Incas: the hand of Pachacamac, the Zeus of the Incas, appears in some of the extraordinary sculptures of gold and stone that are left as the heritage of Inca art.

The *Quena* is the most characteristic instrument of the Peruvian Indians. The panpipe, in use by the Indians of all South America, is known in Peru under the name *Antara*. It consists of a series of connected reeds of different sizes. The Peruvian ocarina, or *Ayariche* in the vernacular, should also be mentioned. The Peruvian Indians use primitive trumpets, capable of producing several harmonic sounds. They are called the *Aylli-Quepa* (also transliterated as *Hayllai-Quipac*), and the *Tock-Oro*. These trumpets are made of wood or baked clay. In the church at Pisac, conch shell trumpets are used in the Catholic Sunday service.

Of the drums, the Peruvians have the *Tinya*, which is a barrel with a membrane covering each end. Another drum, the *Huancar*, with one membrane, is capable of producing a definite pitch. The *Maracas*, a gourd filled with dry seeds, is known in Peru under the onomatopoeic name *Chil-Chil*. These primitive instruments are included in the score of the ballet suite *Suray-Surita* by the late Indian Peruvian composer Teodoro Valcárcel.

During the early centuries of the conquest, the native dances and instruments were regarded by the colonial administration as potentially dangerous. The Church combated the native arts on religious grounds. Thus in 1614, the Archbishop of Lima ordered all native musical instruments burned. Any Indian found in possession of such instruments was to be given three hundred lashes and paraded through the streets in a red shirt riding a llama. The Jesuit Arriaga, in his report *Extirpación de la Idolatría del Perú* (1621), boasted that he had punished 679 Indians and destroyed 603 large and 3418 small musical instruments in his personal punitive expedition across the land.

Parallel to the suppression of native music, attempts were made by some ecclesiastics in Peru to turn the native art to Christian use. Thus in 1551 the organist of the Cuzco Cathedral wrote a choral work in the pentatonic system of the Incas, with a text in the vernacular glorifying the Sun God, and had a group of natives sing it in the church. There were, in the course of the centuries, many other contacts between the Christian and native Indian ritual. A curious product of this musical osmosis is the *Guailichada,* originally an Inca chant, which is now sung at Christmas time as a carol.

During the colonial period, Peru, which then included the territory of Bolivia and Ecuador, was the cultural as well as the administrative center of Spanish America. Lima was the arbiter of fashion, and the phrase "al uso de Lima" was a mark of distinction.

The European court dances, such as the Minuet and the Gavot, penetrated into Spanish America through Lima. The French traveler Frézier, in his *Rélations du Voyage de la Mer du Sud* (Paris, 1716), makes the earliest references to a native dance form, the *Sapateado* or *Zapateo,* a "shoe dance." It is a lively movement in three-four time, with a rhythmic pattern composed of a dotted eighth-note, a sixteenth-note, and an eighth-note, with a semi-cadence, marked by an eighth-note and a quarter-note, in every fourth bar.

The pioneer among Peruvian composers was José Bernardo Alzedo (1798–1878), the author of the National Anthem of Peru. He also wrote a number of patriotic and sentimental songs under such titles as *The Parting of Chilean Maidens with the Peruvian Army of Liberation.* Alzedo was also the author of the first Peruvian manual of music theory, *Filosofía Elemental de Música.*

The first Peruvian composer who wrote music based on national themes was José María Valle-Riestra (1859–1925), the author of the first native opera, *Ollanta.* Luis Duncker Lavalle (1874–1922) was a composer of salon music in the popular urban style. Claudio Rebagliati (1843–1909), an Italian musician who settled in Peru, is remembered through his collection of South American dances published in Italy.

The most original Peruvian composer of the twentieth century was Teodoro Valcárcel (1900–1942), a full-blooded Indian, born near Lake Titicaca. His ballet music possesses unmistakable authenticity, although his lack of technique prevented the full development of his talent. The same defect is noticeable in the works of many other Peruvian composers. Most of their symphonic works are orchestrated by foreign musicians resident in Peru.

Lima possesses a National Conservatory and several private music schools. On December 11, 1938, was inaugurated the *Orquesta Sinfónica Nacional,* which performs the standard repertoire of orchestral literature. The permanent conductor of the new orchestra is the Austrian musician

Theo Buchwald. In the first five years of its existence, this orchestra gave 181 concerts in Lima, of which 117 were broadcast, and presented forty-four compositions by Peruvian composers.

MUSICIANS OF PERU

Rodolfo BARBACCI, the Argentine-Peruvian musicologist and composer, was born in Buenos Aires in 1911. He studied piano, harp, cello, and musical theory, first in Buenos Aires, and later in Milan, Italy. Upon return to Argentina, Barbacci published and edited three short-lived but informative magazines, *Revista Musical Argentina*, *America Musical*, and *Clave*. In 1937 he went to Peru, where he played the harp in the *Orquesta Sinfónica Nacional de Lima*, and issued a valuable bulletin, *Revista Musical Peruana*. Barbacci has published some of his short compositions for piano, written in a modernistic vein, and several pamphlets, *La Nervosidad de los Músicos* (1939), *Educación de la Memoria Musical* (1940), and *Anecdotas Musicales* (1942).

Theo BUCHWALD (1902———), the Austrian conductor naturalized in Peru, came originally from Vienna. He studied piano and conducting. In 1935, he went to South America to conduct operatic and symphonic concerts. Buchwald was appointed the first conductor of the newly organized *Orquesta Sinfónica Nacional* in Lima in 1938. His basic policy as conductor is the constant encouragement of native Peruvian composers, whose works figure on most of his programs.

The musician and collector of musical folklore, Policarpio CABALLERO (1894———) now lives in Buenos Aires, but was born in Cuzco, Peru. Caballero has traveled extensively in Peru, Bolivia, and Argentina, and has compiled three volumes of material dealing with the melody and rhythm of Inca music.

Roberto CARPIO VALDES (1900———), a native of Arequipa, studied piano with his father. He began to compose experimentally in 1921 when he was twenty-one years old. His Suite in three movements for piano, written in a somewhat modernistic manner, was published in 1942 by the *Editorial Cooperativa Interamericana de Compositores* in Montevideo. The score of his Prelude, in the orchestration of Rudolph Holzmann, is in the Fleisher Collection in Philadelphia.

Pablo CHAVEZ AGUILAR (1898———), whose reputation rests chiefly in the field of religious composing, left his native city of Lima to study in

Rome, Italy. Returning to Lima, Chavez Aguilar, then twenty-five years old, presented his Mass for voices and orchestra, on December 9, 1924. Outside his religious works, he has written six *Inca Preludes,* and Variations on an Inca theme. Several of his compositions have been published.

Alfonso DE SILVA's brief life of not quite thirty-four years began in Callao on December 22, 1903, and ended in Lima on May 7, 1937. Without benefit of a systematic musical education, de Silva evolved his own method of composition. His songs, on the model of the German *Lied,* possess lyrical charm. He also wrote piano and violin pieces. His music remains in manuscript. See *Catálogo de las Obras de Alfonso de Silva* by Rudolph Holzmann, in *Boletín Bibliográfico* of the University of San Marcos in Lima, December, 1943.

Federico GERDES (1873——) was born in Tacna, Peru. As a boy he was sent to Germany, where he attended classes in piano and composition at the Leipzig Conservatory. In 1908 he returned to Peru and was appointed director of the National Academy of Music, a position he held until 1944. Gerdes is the author of a *Festive March* for orchestra (the score of which is deposited in the Fleisher Collection in Philadelphia), and some songs, all in a traditional European manner.

A Peruvian who is a painter as well as an amateur musician is Francisco GONZÁLEZ GAMARRA (1890——). Both in his paintings and in his music, González Gamarra is a Peruanist, and his art bears the imprint of the Inca tradition. On the occasion of the quadricentennial of Lima in 1935, he published an album of "musical essays" for piano with chorus, each of which depicted a scene of life or ritual in Cuzco, the ancient capital of the Inca empire. González Gamarra has designed two postage stamps for the government of Peru. Several of his dance movements have been orchestrated by Rudolph Holzmann, and the scores are included in the Fleisher Collection in Philadelphia.

Rudolph HOLZMANN, German-born composer resident in Peru, was born in 1910 in Breslau. He studied violin and composition in Germany, and in 1933 went to Paris, where he took lessons with Nadia Boulanger. On April 3, 1934, his Suite for trumpet, bass clarinet, saxophone, and piano was performed at the Florence Festival of Contemporary Music. After a brief stay in Switzerland, he went to South America, and settled in Lima as a violinist in the *Orquesta Sinfónica Nacional.* His *Divertimento* for piano and wood-wind instruments was performed by that orchestra on July 14, 1943. Holzmann cultivates a neoclassical style in his music, strongly contrapuntal in texture. Of his works written in Peru, *Passage Perpetuel*, for wood-winds and percussion, and *Due Movimenti*, for orchestra, are available in the Fleisher Collection in Philadelphia. Holzmann has rendered a signal service to Peruvian music by orchestrating a number of native compositions by Peruvians who do not possess the requisite technique of instrumentation.

Among native-born Peruvian musicians of the younger generation is Ulises LANAO, born in Callao in 1913. He plays the violin in the *Orquesta Sinfónica Nacional* in Lima. Lanao has written short pieces in conventional style. His symphonic sketch, *Estampas del Cuzco* was performed by the *Orquesta Sinfónica Nacional* on April 19, 1942. The score is included in the Fleisher Collection in Philadelphia.

Ernesto Lopez MINDREAU (1890———), originally from Chiclayo, first studied engineering in Lima. In 1920, when he was thirty years old, he went to Berlin to study music. He remained in Germany for ten years. Mindreau has written an opera, *Nueva Castilla*, based on the colonial history of South America. His piano pieces, mostly dances and airs in the native manner, have been published. While not possessing a technical mastery, Mindreau's music shows a genuine feeling for native rhythms and melodic inflections.

Enrique Fava NINCI (1883–1948) was a naturalized Peruvian musician. Born in Italy, he studied flute and composition. He went to Buenos Aires in 1908, and later settled in Lima where he became the first flutist in the Lima Symphony Orchestra. He is the author of a ballet on Inca themes written in a fluent Italianate style.

Luis PACHECO DE CESPEDES, born in Lima in 1893, had the benefit of a European musical training. As a youth he went to Paris where he studied with Gabriel Fauré and Reynaldo Hahn. Later, he conducted theater orchestras in Monte Carlo, Cannes, and other spas. He returned to Lima in 1940. Although his entire musical career evolved in France, Pacheco de Cespedes cultivates Peruvian themes in his music. Among his orchestral works of native inspiration are *Danza Sobre un Tema Indio*, performed by the *Orquesta Sinfónica Nacional* in Lima on August 7, 1940; *La Selva* (The Jungle), performed in Lima on November 26, 1942; *Suite Limeña* (Lima Suite), produced as a ballet on January 17, 1942; and *Himno al Sol*. His operetta *La Mariscala* was presented in

Lima on May 16, 1942. In his technical treatment, Pacheco de Cespedes applies some devices of modern music, as for instance whole-tone scales.

The musical folklorist, Daniel Alomia ROBLES (1871–1942), was of Indian blood. He dedicated his entire life to collecting indigenous songs of Peru and Bolivia, often traveling from village to village on foot. Before his death, he had collected 650 melodies of the Inca and colonial periods, including the *Himno al Sol* that Robles first heard sung by a 117-year-old Indian. Robles spent fifteen years (1919–1934) in the United States. He lacked formal knowledge, and most of his music had to be arranged by professional musicians. Thus, Vicente Stea has arranged, from material supplied by Robles, a symphonic poem *El Resurgimiento de los Andes*, which illustrates the historical events of the Inca Empire. It was performed by the *Orquesta Sinfónica Nacional* of Lima on July 29, 1940. Rudolph Holzmann arranged the orchestral suite *El Indio*, which was performed in Lima on July 29, 1941. Holzmann's orchestration of Robles' *Danza Huanca* was played in Lima on October 16, 1939. Five melodies from Robles' collection of native songs are quoted in d'Harcourt's *La Musique des Incas et ses Survivances* (Paris, 1925). The orchestral scores of *El Indio, Himno al Sol, El Resurgimiento de los Andes*, and orchestrations of dances by Robles are available in the Fleisher Collection in Philadelphia. The *Inca Dance* from an operetta by Robles, *El Condor Pasa*, is included in the album *Collection Espagnole* (New York, 1936). A complete catalogue of Robles' music, compiled by Rudolph Holzmann, is published in the July, 1943, issue of *Boletín Bibliográfico* of the University of San Marcos in Lima. A special memorial issue of the Argentine magazine *Eco Musical* of July, 1943, contains a detailed biography of Robles.

Carlos SÁNCHEZ MÁLAGA (1904——) of Arequipa studied music at La Paz, Bolivia. He returned to Peru in 1929, and went to Lima. Here, at the age of twenty-five, he founded the *Conservatorio Bach*. Sánchez Málaga composes mostly in smaller forms. His piano pieces, with such impressionistic titles as *Crepúsculo* or *Visperas*, show a lyrical talent. In 1944, Sánchez Málaga won a prize at the National Culture Contest in Peru for his song *Palomita de Nieve*. A detailed biographical sketch of Sánchez Málaga is found in *Who's Who in Latin America*.

The foremost composer of Peru is André SAS who was born in Paris (of a Belgian father and a French mother) on April 6, 1900, and studied music and chemical engineering in Brussels. In 1924 he was engaged by the

Peruvian government as a violin instructor at the National Academy of Music in Lima. In 1929, Sas and his wife, the Peruvian pianist Lily Rosay, founded a private music school in Lima. As a composer, Sas has written comparatively little, but his mastery of the technique of composition makes his pieces an important contribution to Peruvian music, for most of his music is based on native Peruvian melodies and rhythms. His harmonic structure is terse and his melorhythmic design finely proportioned. In his harmonizations of indigenous melodies, Sas consistently applies only two chords, the minor tonic and the major mediant, which he believes to be inherent in Inca music. Several of his instrumental suites of pieces in the native Peruvian manner have been published in Paris and Brussels, among them the following works for violin and piano: *Recuerdos* (1931), *Cantos del Perú* (1935); and for piano: *Aires y Danzas Indios del Perú* (1934), *Suite Peruana* (1935). His *Himno y Danza* is included in the album *Latin American Art Music for the Piano*, published by Schirmer in 1942. Four of his songs are published by the *Editorial Cooperativa Interamericana de Compositores*, in Montevideo (1941); *Quenas* for voice, flute, and harp is included in the music supplement to Volume IV of the *Boletín Latino-Americano de Música*. In larger forms, Sas has written a *Rapsodia Peruana* for violin and orchestra (the score of which is deposited in the Fleisher Collection in Philadelphia), *Himno al Sol* and *Himno y Danza* for orchestra, and a *Poema Indio* for orchestra. Of importance also is his *Sonatina India* for flute and piano, based on the pentatonic modes. *Cantos del Perú* for violin and piano has been recorded by Columbia in the album of *South American Chamber Music* (1941). In the field of native musicology, Sas has contributed papers on ancient Peruvian music and instruments, published in the *Boletín Latino-Americano de Música*.

Vicente STEA (1884–1943) was a native of Gioia del Colle in Italy. He studied in Naples, and after graduation conducted operas in Italy. He went to South America with an Italian opera company in 1917, and settled in Lima, where he founded a private Conservatory bearing his name. Stea's music is distinguished by lyricism and technical mastery, while the style of his compositions is Italianate, with some Wagnerian echoes. In Peru, Vicente Stea wrote a *Sinfonía Autóctona*, based on pentatonic themes of the Inca type, and received for it a gold medal at the music competition on the occasion of the Quadricentennial of Lima in 1935. He conducted this symphony on June 30, 1939, on the same program with his early Symphony in G, at a concert of the *Orquesta*

Sinfónica Nacional in Lima. On November 13, 1940, Stea conducted two of his early works for small orchestra, *Burlesca* and *Notturno,* and his two *Peruvian Dances* for full orchestra. Stea has also arranged and orchestrated, from the material supplied by the Peruvian folklorist Robles, a symphonic poem *El Resurgimiento de los Andes.* The scores of all these works are in the Fleisher Collection in Philadelphia. A complete catalogue of Stea's compositions is published by Rudolph Holzmann in the *Boletín Bibliográfico* of San Marcos University in Lima, December, 1943.

Eduardo Walter STUBBS du Perron (1891——) is a Peruvian composer of mixed heredity. His father was an American of German descent, and his mother French. In 1909, he went to Buenos Aires where he studied with Alberto Williams. He went to Paris in 1926, and returned to Lima in 1940. As composer, Stubbs cultivates Peruvian themes. His harmony and orchestration are influenced by Russian music; one of his Inca dances is subtitled "Rimsky-Korsakov before the Inca ruins." Stubbs is the author of a ballet, *Atahualpa,* based on the story of the last Emperor of the Incas. Its score is included in the Fleisher Collection in Philadelphia. In a traditional manner, Stubbs has written three symphonies and some chamber music.

A Peruvian composer of Indian parentage was Teodoro VALCÁRCEL (1900–1942). He was sent to Europe at the age of fifteen, and took lessons with Felipe Pedrell in Spain. His early pieces are imitations of Chopin, with touches of Debussy. Upon his return to Peru in 1920, Valcárcel turned for inspiration to the native folklore. In 1929 he made another trip to Europe, and took part in the Ibero-American Music Festival in Barcelona. On April 12, 1930, he presented his piano works and songs at a special concert in Paris. Despite Valcárcel's lack of formal technique (until the end he failed to master orchestration, and possessed little contrapuntal skill), he succeeded in forming a style which is genuinely Peruvian. He also attempted, in his unpublished collection of thirty *Cantos de Alma Vernacular,* to create a native art form in the nature of a *Lied,* based on the pentatonic melos of the Incas. His suite of dances, *Suray-Surita,* published in Paris in 1939, is an important contribution to Peruvian music. Several movements from *Suray-Surita* were performed in the orchestration of Rudolph Holzmann by the *Orquesta Sinfónica Nacional* in Lima on October 9, 1939, and August 15, 1940. Rudolph Holzmann has also orchestrated Valcárcel's symphonic poem *En las Ruinas del Templo del Sol* (1940), which was performed in Lima on July 28, 1942. The complete catalogue of Valcárcel's works, prepared by Holzmann, was published in the December, 1942, issue of the *Boletín Bibliográfico* of the San Marcos University in Lima. Holzmann has also compiled a detailed analysis of Valcárcel's music for the memorial issue of the Argentine magazine *Eco Musical*, of March, 1943. The score of Valcárcel's *Concierto Indio* for violin and orchestra, and Holzmann's orchestrations of eight of Valcárcel's ballet movements are included in the Fleisher Collection in Philadelphia.

Carlos VALDERRAMA (1887———) is best known as a composer of popular music. Self-taught, he has never succeeded in mastering the requisite technique of composition. In 1925, at the age of thirty-five, he went to New York, where he played his Peruvian dances based on the pentatonic scale. His appearances aroused interest because of the novelty of the idiom. Seven of Valderrama's piano pieces and songs in the popular vein have been published by Brandes in Lima.

The first Peruvian composer to receive a thorough European education was José María VALLÉ-RIESTRA (1858–1925). His opera *Ollanta*, produced in Lima on December 26, 1900, was the first native theatrical work based on a well-known South American epic. Another opera, *Atahualpa*, based on the life of the last Inca Emperor, remained unfinished. The orchestral score of the *Coronation March* from *Atahualpa* and a symphonic fragment *En Oriente* have been published, and are included in the Fleisher Collection in Philadelphia. The style of Valle-Riestra's music is European in essence, but native pentatonic themes are used in his operatic scores.

Raoul de VERNEUIL (1901———), of French extraction on his father's side, left Lima to study music in Paris, where he lived from 1925 to 1939. He returned to Peru via New York in 1940, and on November 21, 1940, presented in Lima a concert of his works, which included a String Quartet, a Quintet for wind instruments, piano pieces, and songs. In his music, Verneuil strives for modernistic effects, along polytonal lines, while his melodic material is often of native inspiration. His two Dances for piano are published in Paris. He has also written an *Inca Legend* for voice and eight instruments, and a *Danza Peruana* for orchestra. The score of the *Danza Peruana* is included in the Fleisher Collection in Philadelphia.

El Salvador

Siempre noble sonó El Salvador . . .
[FROM THE NATIONAL ANTHEM]

El Salvador is the smallest of the Central American Republics, and the most thickly populated one. The population of El Salvador numbers about 1,800,000, of which the majority are mestizos.

The dances and songs popular in El Salvador are common to all Central America. They are the *Danza,* the *Pasillo* and the *Marcha.* The *Danza* is an offspring of the Spanish *Contradànza* and is ultimately traced to the English Country Dance. The *Pasillo* is a dance of Spanish origin and is written in the dual time signature three-four and six-eight. The *Marcha* is a lively Latin American version of the German military march.

The native instruments of the Indians of El Salvador are also common to all Central America. The *Tun* of El Salvador is identical with the Mexican *Teponaxtle,* and is made of a section of burned-out tree trunk, with a quadrangular aperture in the middle. It is capable of producing two tones, struck to the right or to the left of the central aperture. Another percussion instrument, the *Zambumbia,* is a snare drum.

The wind instruments used by the Indians of El Salvador are vertical flutes and primitive clarinets, the latter known under the generic name of *Chirimía.* The *Marimba* is popular in El Salvador, as it is all over Central America. Then there is the *Caramba* or *Carimba.* It is a curious instrument, which consists of a bow with a metal string attached at both ends to a wooden box, in the manner of a monochord. The same instrument is known in Nicaragua, where it is called the *Quijongo.*

The Indians of El Salvador still celebrate their traditional fiestas, some of which date back to early centuries. One of these fiestas is known as *Historia de Moros y Cristianos.* This *Historia* depicts the conflict between the Moors and the Christians; it is a sort of mystery play borrowed by the natives from their Spanish conquerors. The Moors wear elaborate costumes and gaudy ornaments. The Christians wear simple dress, with floral wreaths for headgear. Both camps wear masks, blue for the infidels, red for the Christians. They also carry all kinds of handy objects, including umbrellas. The music of the *Historia* is represented by a single melody, but this melody changes in rhythm and tempo according to the action of the play, and is alternately gay or sad, martial or peaceful.

The "Father of Salvadoran Music" was a native of Guatemala named José Escolástico Andrino, an educated musician and also a composer of sorts. He settled in San Salvador in 1845. Later in the nineteenth century, several Italian musicians emigrated to El Salvador, among them the pianist Goré, the teacher of a generation of native musicians, and Juan Aberle, the future author of the National Anthem. There was at one time a *Sociedad Orquestal Salvadoreña*, which numbered a hundred players. The director was an Italian musician, Antonio Gianoli. This orchestra soon disbanded, and in its place was organized the *Orquesta Sinfónica de los Supremos Poderes*, which was succeeded in its turn by the *Banda de los Supremos Poderes*. Its present conductor, Alejandro Muñoz, has done good work in promoting native music. He has also orchestrated numerous compositions by María de Baratta and other Salvadoran composers. There is another good band, in the town of Santa Ana, which is led by Domingo Santos, a musician educated in Europe.

The first Salvadoran to make use of native themes was Wenceslao García, the author of an opera entitled *Adela*. The vocal score of this opera has been published, but copies are extremely rare. Among contemporary composers, Jesús Alas, Domingo Santos, and María de Baratta make use of native melos in their works.

The music of El Salvador is summarized in a valuable compilation by Dr. Rafael González Sol, entitled *Historia del Arte de la Música en El Salvador* (San Salvador, 1940). A hopeful augury for the future of musical research in El Salvador was the formation, on November 20, 1941, of the Committee for the Study of Salvadoran Folklore under the direction of María de Baratta, who has already collected numerous native melodies.

MUSICIANS OF EL SALVADOR

Jesús ALAS (1866——) studied music with Juan Aberle, and has acquired a solid technique in composition, in a traditional academic manner. The bulk of his output consists of music for military band, and there are also violin pieces. On June 18, 1929, Alas was awarded the order of

Guillermo Uribe-Holguin

André Sas

Teodoro Valcárcel on
Lake Titicaca

Segundo Luis Moreno

Luis A. Delgadillo   María de Baratta

Enrique de Marchena   Ricardo Castillo

Merito Artistico by the National Assembly of El Salvador. Alas has acted for many years as conductor of the *Banda de los Supremos Poderes* in San Salvador. The score of his *Obertura Patriotica* is included in the Fleisher Collection in Philadelphia.

María de BARATTA (1894——) is a composer and specialist in folklore. Her great-grandfather was the last Indian chief of the tribe of the Lencas, and her mother was Spanish. María de Baratta studied at the Conservatory of Bologna, Italy, and later in San Francisco. Her major work is the ballet *Nahualismo,* based on the themes of the Indian ritual relating to *Nahual,* a powerful spirit incarnated in a serpent, or a tiger. In the orchestration by Ricardo Hüttenrauch, the ballet was performed by the *Banda de los Supremos Poderes* in San Salvador on April 19, 1936. *Ofrenda de la Elegida,* a short ritual dance for piano, was performed in the orchestration by A. Muñoz, with the same orchestra, on September 22, 1931; *Danza del Incienso,* also orchestrated by A. Muñoz, was presented on August 3, 1937. All these orchestrations are included in the Fleisher Collection in Philadelphia. *Nahualismo, Ofrenda de la Elegida,* and two songs, *Can-Calagui-Tunal* (Incantation to the Sun) and *Los Tecomatillos,* are published by the composer, with decorative covers designed by her husband, the Italian architect Augusto Baratta.

Alejandro MUÑOZ (1902——), the band leader and arranger, went to Mexico in 1921, and took lessons with José Vasquez. Upon his return to San Salvador, he was appointed conductor of the *Banda de los Supremos Poderes.* He has made numerous arrangements of compositions by María de Baratta and other Salvadoran composers.

Domingo SANTOS (1892——) studied in Italy. In 1928 he was appointed conductor of the military band in the town of Santa Ana in El Salvador. He has written three piano sonatas, six Requiems, six Funeral Marches, a Heroic March, and two overtures entitled *Martita* and *Dorita. Martita* was performed in San Salvador on December 7, 1924. Santos' Suite of four short pieces for piano has been printed in Paris. The scores of the overtures are included in the Fleisher Collection in Philadelphia.

Uruguay

La República del Uruguay es un país per-
fectamente civilizado.
[FROM *El Uruguay a través de un Siglo*]

Uruguay is the smallest nation of South America, but by European geographic standards, it is not so small: its area is larger than that of England. The name Uruguay means "the river of birds." The country is flat, and ideally suited for agriculture and cattle breeding. Uruguay's population numbers over two million, of which fully one-third lives in Montevideo, the capital. The aboriginal Indians of Uruguay are all but extinct.

In terms of racial geography, Uruguay is a white man's land, and its culture has little of either the Indian or the Negro. As in Argentina, the people's musician of Uruguay is the Gaucho, the wandering minstrel of the pampas, who roves the plains on horseback with his faithful guitar slung over his shoulder. The subject of the Gaucho songs is usually romantic love, but often these songs are ballads and narratives of personal adventure, similar to the cowboy songs of the North American West.

Musically speaking, Uruguay is a dependency of Argentina. The songs and dances of Argentina are the folklore of Uruguay. The only musical form that may be said to be Uruguay's own product is the *Pericón,* an old round dance in triple time, which was revived in 1889 by a Montevideo theatrical company and has since regained its popularity.

In a useful booklet *La Música en Iberoamérica* by Raúl A. Buccino and Luis Benvenuto (Buenos Aires, 1939), the common origin of Uruguayan and Argentine music is traced to Spain: "Uruguay's dances and songs are taken from the wealth of Spain's music treasury. This music became acclimatized in the coastal provinces of the old state of Rio de la Plata, and gave birth to the popular music of Uruguay and Argentina. The *Triste, Cielito, Triunfo, Milonga, Tango, Vidala, Pericón* and other airs and dances of Uruguay are intimately connected with the Argentine airs of the same name. Yet this affinity is not that of complete identity: to an attentive ear, a characteristic inflection distinguishes the Uruguayan song from its Argentine counterpart."

The accessibility of Uruguay to the sea, and its long coast line, made the nation a natural receptacle for European influences. Italian musicians began to settle in Uruguay early in the nineteenth century. On May 14, 1830, Rossini's opera *L'Inganno Felice* was presented in Montevideo, with three members of an Italian family of singers, Angelita, Marcello, and Pasquale Tanni taking the leading parts. In his interesting book *Crónica de una Temporada Musical en el Montevideo de 1830*, published in 1943, the Uruguayan musicologist Lauro Ayestarán gives a circumstantial account of the flourishing musical life of the period.

The National Anthem of Uruguay, adopted by the government on July 27, 1848, and composed by one Fernando Quijano, bears testimony to the strength of Italian influence. Its melody has a striking resemblance to the Gondoliers' Chorus from Donizetti's *Lucrezia Borgia*. To honor the operatic art of Verdi, a *Conservatorio Verdi* was founded in Montevideo in 1890. The first native-born composers of symphonic and operatic music, Luis Sambucetti (1860–1926) and León Ribeiro (1854–1931), also did homage to Italy in their compositions, which are entirely in the Italian tradition.

The founders of the modern school of composition in Uruguay are Carlos Pedrell and Alfonso Broqua. Although they spent most of their adult years in France, they never lost the feeling for Uruguayan folklore, which colors much of their vocal music.

Of the present-day composers now living in Uruguay, the name of Eduardo Fabini comes first. His music is imbued with native folklore, even though his harmonic style is European. Vicente Ascone and Luis Cluzeau Mortet are composers of music in the romantic vein. Of the younger set, the names of Carlos Estrada, Luis Pedro Mondino, and Guido Santórsola should be mentioned. The child prodigy of Uruguayan music is Hector Tosar Errecart, born in 1923, whose precocious talent has attracted considerable attention. Benone Calcavecchia is an Italian conductor-composer, now living in Uruguay. Ramón Rodriguez Socas is the author of numerous operas in the Italian tradition.

Thanks to a German scholar naturalized in Uruguay, Francisco Curt Lange, Montevideo has become a center of Latin American musicology. As part of his multifarious activities in behalf of Latin American music, Lange publishes the *Boletín Latino-Americano de Música*, and heads a cooperative music publishing firm, *Editorial Cooperativa Interamericana de Compositores.* Lange is also the founder and director of the *Discoteca Nacional de Uruguay,* which possesses one of the richest collections of phonograph records in Latin America.

Montevideo has become a symphonic capital of the first rank with the establishment of the radio orchestra, *Orquesta Sinfónica del Servicio Oficial de Difusión Radio-Electrica* (OSSODRE, or SODRE). Inaugurated on June 20, 1931, under the direction of its permanent conductor Lamberto Baldi, the SODRE has presented in its regular programs a number of first performances of symphonic works by Uruguayan composers.

MUSICIANS OF URUGUAY

Vicente Ascone (1897——) studied trumpet and composition at the Montevideo Conservatory. When the radio orchestra OSSODRE was founded in 1931, he was engaged as the first trumpet player. The OSSODRE has given performances of all of Ascone's major works: *Suite Uruguaya* (July 11, 1931); *Paraná Guazú* (July 25, 1931); *Farsa Sentimental y Grotesca* (September 5, 1931); *Cantos del Atardecer* (October 14, 1933); *Nocturno Nativo* (November 23, 1935); and *Tres Danzas* (April 4, 1936). His *Montes de mi Queguay,* poems for voice and string quartet, are published by the *Editorial Cooperativa,* and his violin piece, *La Carreta,* is included in the supplement to Volume III of the *Boletín Latino-Americano de Música.* The score of Ascone's *Cantos del Atardecer* is in the Fleisher Collection in Philadelphia. The style and technique of Ascone's music are entirely within the bounds of the European tradition.

A Uruguayan composer who spent virtually all his life in France, Alfonso Broqua (1876–1946) studied with Vincent d'Indy at the *Schola Cantorum* in Paris. His first important work was a lyric opera, *Tabaré.* There followed *Poema de las Lomas,* a triptych for piano, reflecting the folkloric motives of his native country. In 1918, Broqua composed an opera, *The Southern Cross,* on the subject of the Spanish conquest. Broqua is the author of two ballets, *Thelen et Nagoüe,* based on Inca themes (1934), and *Isabelle* (1936). In 1938 he completed the orchestral version of *Preludes of the Pampas.* In 1940 Broqua suffered a mental collapse and was confined to a sanitarium. Several of his songs, *Trois Chants de l'Uruguay, Chants du Parana,* and *Evocaciones Criollas* for guitar, have been published in Paris. Also published is his Piano Quintet in G minor. Broqua's Tango from the collection *Trois Chants de l'Uruguay* is recorded in the album, *South American Chamber Music* (Columbia, 1941).

Benone CALCAVECCHIA (1886——), the Uruguayan composer and conductor, was born in Caronia, Sicily. In 1907 he went to South America, and for a time played the trombone in the military band of Montevideo. He began composing in 1922, and has since written numerous orchestral compositions, of which the following were performed by the radio orchestra OSSODRE in Montevideo: *Uruguay* (July 18, 1931), *Impresiones de 1930* (July 25, 1931), and *Preludio* (August 15, 1931). He has also written a *Hymn to Football*, which was awarded first prize at the contest of the Football Association of Uruguay in 1927.

Luis CLUZEAU MORTET (1893——) studied piano and violin with his grandfather in Montevideo. In 1931 he joined the radio orchestra OSSODRE in Montevideo as a viola player. As a composer, Cluzeau Mortet leans towards romanticism, and his unaffected piano pieces, songs, and short symphonic poems are melodic, without pretensions at modernism. His *Poema Nativo* for orchestra was performed by the OSSODRE on July 25, 1931, and *Llanuras*, inspired by the folklore of the pampas, on October 14, 1933. His Concerto for String Orchestra, in a classical manner, was performed by the OSSODRE on August 20, 1936. The orchestral score of *Llanuras*, which was privately published, is in the Fleisher Collection in Philadelphia. Two piano Preludes by Cluzeau Mortet are included in the musical supplement to Volume III of the *Boletín Latino-Americano de Música*, and his song *Mar de Luna* has been published by the *Editorial Cooperativa Interamericana de Compositores* in Montevideo.

Carlos ESTR\DA (1909——) studied in Uruguay and later went to Paris where he completed his musical education in composition with Roger-Ducasse and Henri Busser. In 1936, he founded a chamber orchestra in Montevideo. His song *Caminos Tristes* is published by the *Editorial Cooperativa Interamericana de Compositores*. Estrada's musical style is in the romantic tradition, conventional as to harmony.

Eduardo FABINI (1883——) was born in Solis. In 1900 he went to Brussels, where he studied violin with César Thomson. Returning to Uruguay in 1905, he dedicated himself to teaching and composition. His first important work was a symphonic poem, *Campo*, which was composed in 1909, and performed in Montevideo on April 29, 1922. It was also included in the program that Richard Strauss conducted in 1923 on his South American tour. Fabini's symphonic poem, *Isla de los Ceibos* (the title means a clump of silk-cotton trees), reflects native themes. His ballet *Mburucuyá* (the name is the Guarany word for a luxuriant native plant) is also permeated with native melos. In the score of *Melga Sinfónica* (*Melga* means a tilled soil), Fabini pays tribute to Montevideo by spelling its name in Morse code rhythm. The following compositions by Fabini have been performed by the Montevideo radio orchestra OSSODRE: *Isla de los Ceibos* (June 20, 1931); *Melga Sinfónica, Patria Vieja* (both on October 11, 1931); and *Tristes* (August 8, 1931). The scores of *Isla de los Ceibos, Campo,* and *Mburucuyá* are published by Ricordi, and are also available in the Fleisher Collection of Philadelphia. *Isla de los Ceibos* is recorded by Victor. Fabini's song *El Tala* is included in the supplement to Volume I of the *Boletín Latino-Americano de Música,* and his *Triste* for piano is published in the album *Latin-American Art Music for the Piano* (Schirmer, 1942). In a prefatory note to this collection, Francisco Curt Lange writes: "Eduardo Fabini embodies the sentiments of the people of Uruguay. Without being a 'folkloristic' composer, he knows how to express in his music the very essence of his native land. It should be noted that most of the folk-like themes used in his works are original, and present a product of his complete assimilation with the life of the nation." See also "Eduardo Fabini, Músico," *Boletín Latino-Americano de Música,* Volume III.

Francisco Curt LANGE (1903——) is the foremost Latin American musicologist; he was born in Eilenburg, Germany. In Germany he studied music, architecture, sociology, and philosophy, and among his teachers were Arthur Nikisch and Hermann Abert. Lange emigrated to Uruguay in 1923, rapidly acquired a mastery of the Spanish language, and in 1933 launched a movement which he christened *Americanismo Musical.* The most important product of his labors is the publication of five voluminous issues of the *Boletín Latino-Americano de Música,* which constitutes a veritable archive of Latin American musicology. In 1940, Lange launched a cooperative music publishing enterprise, *Editorial Cooperativa Interamericana de Compositores,* which publishes works by Latin American composers. In conjunction with the Radio Service of Montevideo, he has organized a *Discoteca,* a collection of phonograph records. He has traveled widely in Latin America, and he visited the United States in 1939. Apart from his extensive monographs in the *Boletín,* Lange has published a number of books on music, literature, and philosophy.

Luis Pedro MONDINO (1903——), born in Montevideo, studied in Paris with Nadia Boulanger. He has written a symphonic poem, *Fiesta Vasca,* as well as piano pieces and songs.

Carlos PEDRELL (1878–1941) studied in Madrid with his uncle Felipe Pedrell, and in Paris with Vincent d'Indy. He spent most of his life in Paris, and it was there he died. In his music, Pedrell adopts an impressionist technique. Many of his songs (*Hispaniques, As Orillas del Duero, Cantigas del Buen Amador*) and the six vocal poems *De Castilla* are stylizations of Spanish rhythms and melodies. But he has also written some music in the South American vein, as for instance *Quatre Chansons Argentines*. In his *Montmartre,* for voice and orchestra, he stylizes the tango. Pedrell's only opera, *Ardid de Amor,* was produced at the *Teatro Colón* in Buenos Aires on June 7, 1917. His song *Caballitos* is recorded in the album *South American Chamber Music* (Columbia, 1941).

Ramón RODRIGUEZ SOCAS (1890——), the composer and pedagogue, studied at the Conservatory "La Lira," in Montevideo, of which he is now director. At the age of eighteen he wrote an opera, *Alda*. He went to Italy, to perfect his technique, and there composed several more operas, among them *Yeba, Amor Marinaro, Morte di Amore, Antony Griette, Murinedda, Sor Tofano,* and numerous operettas. Several of these operas were produced in Milan. His other works are a choral symphonic poem, *El Grito de Asencio;* for orchestra, *Undinas, Afrodita, Bolero,* and *Obertura Andina* (on an Inca theme).

Guido SANTÓRSOLA (1904——) was born in Canosa di Puglia, Italy. He was taken to Brazil at the age of five, where he studied violin and gave a recital at the age of nine. He studied composition in São Paulo with Agostino Cantù, and later with Lamberto Baldi. In 1931 he joined the radio orchestra OSSODRE in Montevideo as first viola player. Santórsola has written a Concerto for chorus without words and viola d'amore, an Oratorio, and a Brazilian dance for orchestra. In chamber music, he affects unusual combinations: two double basses and piano; violin, two violas, and cello; ten capriccios for violin unaccompanied. His expressionistic vocal composition, *Agonía,* is published by the *Editorial Cooperativa Interamericana de Compositores*.

Hector TOSAR ERRECART (1923——) studied with Lamberto Baldi. He began to compose very early, and at the age of nineteen had already accumulated a long list of works: an orchestral Toccata, a Sonatina, and two Études for piano; *Nocturne* and *Scherzo* for violin, clarinet, and piano; and a String Quartet. Tosar Errecart writes in a neoclassical manner, but recently he has begun to use native themes in his music, as in his *Danza Criolla* for piano.

Venezuela

¡*Cuna del gran Bolívar!* ¡*Venezuela!*
[OLEGARIO V. ANDRADE]

Venezuela means "little Venice," and was thus named by the early colonists because of the resemblance of the cluster of islands off the coast to the Italian city of the canals. Venezuela has now about 3,500,000 inhabitants, including some 100,000 Indians. The capital is Caracas, named after the Indian tribe of Caracas.

The racial ingredients of Venezuela's musical folklore are the aboriginal Indian, the Negro, and the colonial Spanish. The Indian strain is strongest in the Orinoco region, where the Indians have lived virtually isolated from the rest of the country and so have conserved the arts and crafts of pre-Columbian times almost without change. Their songs are scarcely more than monotonous chants, intoned to the accompaniment of primitive flutes and drums, but to the Indians they have a variety of meanings. In a paper on the musical folklore of the Taurepan Indians of Venezuela, published in Volume IV of the *Boletín Latino-Americano de Música*, Baltasar de Matallana characterizes the native chants as possessing "the unmistakable racial spirit of the South American aborigines, a melancholy which finds its expression in mournful inflections and wistful monotonous rhythms."

This Indian music still retains its religious character. José Antonio Calcaño, in *Contribución al Estudio de la Música en Venezuela*, tells of mysterious jungle rites in which "men gather together in darkness, ululating lugubriously, and flagellating themselves to the accompaniment of horrisonant instruments."

Much mystery has been attached to the existence of these "horrisonant instruments," which no traveler is allowed to see or touch. In all probability, these instruments are jungle drums, capable of carrying sound to great distances. The generic name of these drums is spelled variously as

Botutó, Bututó, Bututú, Bototó, Fotutó, Fututú, Fototó, Potutó or
Pututú. Drums of African origin are used by the natives of Negro extraction. These drums are called *Cumaco* and *Curveta*. An instrument *sui
generis* is the *Furruco*, which makes a grunting sound when a rosined cord
is drawn through an aperture in the drumhead. The *Mine* is a squatting
drum, with a drumhead measuring up to three feet in diameter and a low
body. The curious *Culo-en-tierra* (literally, buttock in the earth) should
be mentioned. It consists of half of a coconut, which is covered with parchment and placed in a small hole in the ground.

The wind instruments used by the Indians of Venezuela are mostly of
the flute family. These flutes are made of animal bones or bamboo reeds.

The popular music of Venezuela is Spanish in essence, with the Negro
influence revealed in the occasionally syncopated rhythms and in the free
use of percussion instruments. In an article on Venezuelan folklore by
Juan Liscano, originally published in the *Boletín del Instituto Cultural
Venezolano-Britanico* of August 6, 1942, and reproduced in the *Revista
Musical Mexicana* of May 7, 1943, the interdependence of the Indian,
Spanish, and Negro influences in Venezuelan music is summed up in the
following words: "Between the Negro and the Indian there was a history
of blood and extermination. Between the Negro and the Spaniard there ex-
isted a renaissance of artistic and social forms. Our music is the daughter of
Spain and Africa. Like our soil, it is rich and dark. It stems from the
Spanish guitar and the Negro drum."

The purest type of native folklore is exemplified by the *Tono Llanero*,
"the melody of the plains." It is a dancing song, cast in a major or
a minor mode. Its rhythm is characteristically Spanish, within the alternating six-eight and three-four time. We quote from such a *Tono* (it is
sometimes called *Tonada*), from the collection *Pequeñas Canturias y
Danzas Venezolanas*, published by the Radio Caracas in 1942.

Venezuelan Tono Llanero

The typical dance of Venezuela is the *Joropo,* usually performed in a lively jig-like movement, in six-eight time. The Venezuelan *Pasillo* is to all intents and purposes identical with the Colombian *Pasillo.* It alternates three-four time and six-eight time, with resultant cross-accents. The *Merengue* from Santo Domingo is also popular in Venezuela, as is the Mexican topical ballad, the *Corrido.* The Argentine *Tango* is known in Venezuela under a diminutive name, *Tanguito.* A peculiar humorous song in changing rhythms of two and three notes to a beat, *La Guasa* is Venezuela's own contribution to the treasury of Latin American airs.

Music history in Venezuela dates back to the eighteenth century. The following events, illustrating the development of musical culture in Venezuela, are listed in *Primer Libro Venezolano de Literatura, Ciencias y Bellas Artes,* published in Caracas in 1895:

1711. The first organ is installed in the Cathedral of Caracas.

1725. Music courses are inaugurated at Caracas University.

1790. Several Austrian musicians settle in Venezuela.

1796. The first pianoforte is imported into Caracas.

1810. A French opera company gives performances in Caracas.

1811. On April 19, on the occasion of the first anniversary of the Revolution, five orchestras composed of thirty players each give concerts in Caracas.

1859. The first military band is organized in Caracas.

1868. The first Conservatory of Music is opened in Caracas.

1873. On May 4, the first native opera, *Virginia,* by José Angel Montero, is produced in Caracas.

1880. On October 28, the *Teatro Municipal* is opened in Caracas.

Robert Semple, an English traveler who made a journey to Venezuela in the nineteenth century, gives some sidelights on early musical life in Caracas in a book entitled *Sketch of the Present State of Caracas; Including a Journey from Caracas through La Victoria and Valencia to Puerto Cabello* (London, 1812). "The audiences are not difficult to please. Patriotic songs are occasionally brought forward, and the singer is frequently not only applauded, but is rewarded by pieces of money cast upon the stage. This circumstance is sometimes attended by inconvenience; and I have seen a hero obliged to stoop to avoid a friendly dollar thrown at his head."

The existence of a surprisingly flourishing school of native composition in the latter part of the eighteenth century was revealed to the world when some three hundred orchestral and choral manuscripts of the colonial period were discovered in a wooden box in the cellar of the *Escuela de Música* in Caracas. The full scores of eight ecclesiastical compositions for chorus and orchestra from this collection were published in 1943 by the Ministry of National Education of Venezuela, in collaboration with the Institute of Interamerican Musicology of Montevideo, Uruguay.

The pioneer of Venezuelan music was Pedro Palacios y Sojo, a priest who made a trip to Rome and Madrid in order to collect music and instruments. Upon his return to Caracas in 1770, he founded a society in which the members were encouraged "to play the game of ball and give concerts." A younger contemporary of Sojo, Juan Manuel Olivares, who was a mulatto, composed religious music in the style of Haydn. Other composers of the same period were José Francisco Velásquez and José Antonio Caro de Boesi.

A list of nineteenth century Venezuelan musicians comprises the following names: José Angel Lamas, Cayetano Carreño, Juan José Landaeta, Lino Gallardo, Pedro Nolasco Colón, and José Francisco Velásquez, Jr., the son of the elder Velásquez. Of these, Lamas (1775–1814) was the most prolific; forty of his compositions have been preserved. Carreño (1774–1836), the grandfather of the famous Venezuelan pianist Teresa Carreño, was Chapel Master at the Cathedral of Caracas. Juan José Landaeta occupies an historic place in Venezuelan history as the composer of the patriotic hymn *Gloria al Bravo Pueblo*, which was proclaimed the national anthem of Venezuela on May 25, 1881. Landaeta perished during the earthquake of 1812.

The following Venezuelan musicians were active in the nineteenth century as performers and composers: José Angel Montero (1839–1881), chorus master at the Cathedral of Caracas, and the author of the first native opera *Virginia* (1873); Felipe Larrázabal (1816–1873), pianist and composer of chamber music; and Federico Villena (1835–1900), a composer of piano pieces.

Juan Bautista Plaza, in a paper read at the American Musicological Society on March 27, 1942, and subsequently published in *The Musical Quarterly* of July 1942, sums up the significance of the composers of the colonial period in these words:

It would seem as though these men, having one fine day discovered music, devoted themselves earnestly to its cultivation; for surely it opened fresh vistas to them—another New World. In reality, however, what they discovered was but one phase of music—that is, sacred music. In this field they felt happy and at home. As true descendants of the Spaniards, they preserved the ardent faith of their ancestors. The Church, of course, welcomed them and utilized their services; furthermore, the society in which they lived delighted in their works, which could be understood by all and spoke straight to the heart. The first performance of a new Mass by Lamas or Carreño must undoubtedly have been an important event to that provincial society, which, under the influence of the Catholic clergy, lived primarily in the Church and for the Church. The music of these composers, therefore, was closely related to their environment, time, and race.

The cause of musical education in Venezuela has made important strides in the last few years. Caracas possesses one of the finest choral ensembles on the continent, the *Orfeon Lamas,* which is led by Vicente Emilio Sojo. In contrast to the Venezuelan composers of the old school, native musicians of the new generation are cultivating a national tradition and using indigenous melodies and rhythms. Vicente Emilio Sojo, María Luisa Escobar, Moises Moleiro, Juan Bautista Plaza and Juan Lecuna have all contributed to the formation of a national school.

The symphony orchestra of Caracas is the *Sinfónica Venezuela,* conducted by Vicente Emilio Sojo. Its members are recruited from the graduates of the *Escuela de Música* of Caracas.

The Ministry of National Education has inaugurated a plan for the publication of native airs and dances in a collection entitled *Biblioteca Venezolana de Cultura.* Three albums of songs suitable for schools were published in 1940. In 1942, Radio Caracas published three albums of national songs and dances. Choruses and songs by Vicente Emilio Sojo have been published by the *Asociación Venezolana de Conciertos.* María Luisa Escobar has published some songs of her own.

Two Venezuelan-born musicians have made a mark for themselves in the music world, but neither lived in Venezuela during adult life. Reynaldo Hahn, the opera composer of considerable renown, went to Paris with his family at the age of three. Teresa Carreño, the "Valkyrie of the piano," was taken to New York at the age of eight.

MUSICIANS OF VENEZUELA

María Luisa Escobar (1903——) founded the *Ateneo* of Caracas, an institution dedicated to the cultivation of the native arts, in 1932. As a composer, she has written songs and piano pieces, and a symphony-ballet,

Orquídeas Azules (1941), based on Venezuelan folklore. Her work as collector of Venezuelan songs is described in the article "Ritmo y Melodia Nativos de Venezuela," in Volume III of the *Boletín Latino-Americano de Música*. In 1937, María Luisa Escobar was a delegate at the International Congress of Music Education in Paris. Her songs, *Ternura* and *Naranjas de Valencia,* are published in Caracas.

Juan LECUNA (1898——) was born in Valencia. After a study of the rudiments of music in Caracas, he went to the United States, where he took lessons with Gustave Strube. Lecuna is the only Venezuelan composer who has achieved a mastery of contemporary technique of composition. His four pieces for piano, *Vals, Criolla, Joropo,* and *Danza,* published in Paris in 1938, are written in a native manner. Lecuna has also written a *Suite Venezolana* for four guitars, a String Quartet, and a Piano Concerto.

Moisés MOLEIRO (1905——) studied in Caracas with Vicente Emilio Sojo. In 1936, he was appointed instructor in piano at the *Escuela de Música* in Caracas. Moleiro's music, chiefly songs and short piano pieces in rudimentary harmony, is reflective of native rhythms, which led a critic to remark: "En Moleiro palpita Venezuela."

Juan Bautista PLAZA (1898——), the composer and educator, was born in Caracas and received his primary education in the French College there. For a while he studied medicine. Owing to the efforts of the Archbishop of Caracas, he was sent to Rome in 1920, to study at the Pontifical Institute of Sacred Music. He completed his education in 1923, and upon returning to Venezuela became organist of the Cathedral of Caracas. In 1924 he was appointed professor of composition at the *Escuela de Música.* In 1936 he took charge of the valuable archive of the *Escuela de Música,* which contains manuscripts of music of the colonial period. In 1942 he made a trip to the United States. Plaza has written three Masses, a Requiem, several Motets, and other religious works; three symphonic poems, *El Picacho Abrupto, Vigilia, Campanas de Pascua;* and a tone poem for orchestra with chorus, *Las Horas,* in commemoration of the Centenary of Bolívar's death. In the native manner, Plaza has composed a *Fuga Criolla,* the score of which is in the Fleisher Collection in Philadelphia, and a *Sonatina Venezolana,* which is included in the collection *Latin-American Art Music for the Piano* (Schirmer, 1942). Also published are his *Seven Venezuelan Songs.* Regarding his style of composition, Plaza writes: "My music is very uneven, for I have never preoccupied myself with the problem of enlarging my technical resources, or of creating a personal style."

Vicente Emilio Sojo (1887——) is the conductor of the *Orfeon Lamas* of Caracas, which is one of the finest choral organizations in Latin America. Sojo is also the conductor of the Caracas symphony orchestra, *Sinfónica Venezuela*. He is the author of a cantata, a Requiem, three Masses, and numerous vocal works. His choruses, *La Nube, La Coca, Rondel Matinal, Gárgaro Malojo,* and five songs are published in Caracas.

PART III

DICTIONARY OF LATIN AMERICAN MUSICIANS, SONGS AND DANCES, AND MUSICAL INSTRUMENTS

GUIDE TO PRONUNCIATION

Spanish

h : always silent.
j : like a strong English *h*, as in "Navajo."
ll : like *y*, as in "yes."
ñ : like *ny*, as in "canyon."

Indian

Transliterations; pronounced as written.

Portuguese

ã : much like French *an* or *en*, as in "Jean" or "entente."
ç : like French *ç* or English *s*, as in "say."
lh : much like *lli*, as in "million."
nh : much like *ny*, as in "canyon."
x : generally like *sh*, as in "fashion."

A

aboio. A Brazilian shepherd's call.

abuelito (little grandpa). An obsolete dance once popular in Chile.

acalanto. A Brazilian cradle song.

Adame, Rafael. Mexican guitarist and composer of competently academic music. Born in Jalisco, September 11, 1906. *See* pp. 225-226.

adjá. An Afro-Brazilian metal bell.

adjulona. A primitive wind instrument with a corrugated leaf for a reed; used by Brazilian Indians.

adoración. A Bolivian Christmas carol.

adufé (from Moorish). A Brazilian tambourine.

afofié. A small Afro-Brazilian flute.

agidavi. An Afro-Brazilian drumstick.

agogó. An iron anvil used as a percussion instrument by the Brazilian Negroes.

aguinaldo. A Puerto Rican Christmas carol.

Aguirre, Julian. Argentine composer of songs and piano music in native vein. Born in Buenos Aires, January 28, 1868; died there, August 13, 1924. *See* p. 82.

aiapá. A species of the Brazilian shaker **chocalho.**

aidjé (hippopotamus). A bull-roarer, or **thunder-stick,** of the Bororó Indians of Brazil.

aire Indio. An Indian air, characteristic of Bolivia, and free in rhythm and form.

alabado. A Mexican regional air.

Alas, Jesús. Salvadoran composer of band music. Born in Santa Tecla, April 7, 1866. *See* pp. 280-281.

alfandoque. A Colombian name for the **maracas.**

Allende, Adolfo. Chilean music critic and composer, brother of Humberto Allende. Born in Santiago, August 29, 1890. *See* p. 154.

Allende, Humberto. Chilean composer, pioneer of native modern music. Born in

Santiago, June 29, 1885. *See* pp. 154-157.

almirez. A brass mortar; used in Panama as a percussion instrument.

amelé. A Brazilian rattle, similar to the chequeré.

Amengual Astaburuaga, René. Chilean composer of the modern school. Born in Santiago, September 2, 1911. *See* p. 157.

amorfino. A popular song of Ecuador, in ⅝ time.

anata. A vertical flute of Bolivia.

Andrade, Mario de. Brazilian musicologist and modernistic poet. Born in São Paulo, October 9, 1893; died there, February 25, 1945. *See* p. 123.

André, José. Argentine composer of songs in a romantic vein. Born in Buenos Aires, January 17, 1881; died there, July 13, 1944. *See* p. 82.

angelito. An Argentine song of condolences for a dead child.

angogó. A Brazilian flute.

anguá. The mortar water drum of the Guarany Indians.

anguarai. *See* anguá.

antara. A Peruvian panpipe, made of reeds of different sizes tied together; called sicu in Bolivia, rondador in Ecuador, and capador in Colombia.

apanha-o-bago. An Afro-Brazilian dance.

arabicus. A distorted Spanish colonial name for yaravi.

Araujo, João Gomes de. Brazilian composer of Italianate operas. Born in Pindamonhangaba, August 5, 1846; died in São Paulo, September 8, 1942, at the age of ninety-six. *See* p. 123.

Ardévol, José. Spanish-Cuban composer of neoclassical chamber music. Born in Barcelona, Spain, March 13, 1911, resident in Havana since 1930. *See* pp. 183-184.

areito. A pre-Columbian air of the West Indies.

Aretz-Thiele, Isabel. Argentine composer and specialist in musical folklore. Born in Buenos Aires, April 13, 1909. *See* p. 82.

Arias, Luis Felipe. Guatemalan composer of character pieces. Born in Guatemala City August 23, 1870; assassinated there, March 24, 1908. *See* p. 204.

aribú. A Brazilian air similar to the lundú.

arpa-ché. A Guatemalan musical bow.

Arrau, Claudio. Foremost Chilean pianist. Born in Chillan, February 6, 1904. *See* p. 157.

Arredondo-Miura, Clodomiro. Dominican composer of popular music. Born in Santo Domingo, March 3, 1864; died there, March 24, 1908. *See* p. 204.

Arredondo-Sosa, Horacio, son of Clodomiro Arredondo-Miura. Dominican composer of dance music. Born in Santo Domingo, June 5, 1912. *See* p. 192.

arrullo. The generic Spanish word for a lullaby.

Ascone, Vicente. Uruguayan composer of melodious music on native themes. Born in Montevideo, August 16, 1897. *See* p. 284.

asson. A Haitian rattle, similar to the maracas.

assotor. A Haitian drum; *also*, a Haitian dance named after the drum.

atabal. A small drum, used by the natives of Central America and the West Indies.

atabaqué. *See* tabaqué.

atecocolli. The Aztec name for the caracol marino.

auto. Generic designation for religious plays with music introduced into South America by the missionaries.

ayacaztli. The ancient Aztec name for the maracas.

Ayala, Daniel. Mexican Indian composer of the modern national school. Born in Abalá, Yucatán, July 21, 1908. *See* pp. 226-227.

ayariché. A Peruvian ocarina.

aykhori. A long twin flute with the two reeds tied at one end, used by the Indians of the central plateau in South America.

aylli-quepa. A primitive Peruvian trumpet made of a conch shell, capable of producing two different tones.

ayochicahuaztli. *See* chicahuaztli.

ayotl. An ancient Mexican tortoise-shell drum, played upon with a stag's antler.

azucena. An ornamented tree with which the Peruvian Indians stamp the rhythm of Christmas songs.

B

babacué. An Afro-Brazilian fetish song.

baboule. A Haitian dance similar to the juba.

baby drum. The smallest of Haitian drums.

baguala. An Argentine song similar to the vidala.

baile. A generic Spanish word for dance, sometimes specifically salon dances, as opposed to danza.

bailecito. A song-dance of Argentina and Bolivia in 6/8 time, consisting of two sections in different keys and usually sung to the accompaniment of a guitar.

bajón. A very large type of sicus gigantes, consisting of graduated tubes made of palm-tree leaves and sugar reeds, reaching two meters in length.

balsié tumbado. A low flat drum used by the natives of Santo Domingo, similar to the timbal.

bamba. An old Mexican air from the province of Veracruz, recently modernized as a ballroom dance.

bamboche. A Haitian dance.

bambuco. The national dance of Colombia, in 3/4 or 6/8 meter, characterized by cross accents, in moderate tempo.

bambula. A primitive drum of the Antillean Negroes; also an Afro-Antillean dance in 2/4 time and syncopated rhythm, named after the drum.

bandalón. An ancient Mexican string instrument, similar to the mandolin.

bandola. A small bandurria.

bandolin. A four-string guitar.

bandoneón. Argentine accordion.

bandurria. A guitar with twelve strings.

bansá. An Afro-Brazilian musical bow, consisting of an arched bow with a cord rubbed by a piece of wood or a bone.

bapó. The maracas of the Bororó Indians of Brazil.

Baqueiro Foster, Gerónimo. Mexican musicologist specializing in native folk-lore. Born in Hopelchen, state of Campeche, January 7, 1898. See p. 227.

Baratta, María de. Salvadoran folklore specialist and composer. Born in San Salvador, February 27, 1894. See p. 281.

Barbacci, Rodolfo. Argentine-Peruvian musicologist and composer of modernistic piano pieces. Born in Buenos Aires, February 28, 1911. See p. 272.

batá. An Afro-Brazilian drum.

batá-cotó. A war drum of the Brazilian Negroes.

baté-baú. An Afro-Brazilian dance popular in the region of Bahia, similar to the samba.

baté-pé. An Afro-Brazilian dance of the samba type.

batucada. See batuque.

batuque. An Afro-Brazilian dance, characterized by sharply syncopated rhythm in duple meter.

Bautista, Julian. Spanish composer of the modern school, resident in Argentina since 1940. Born in Madrid, April 21, 1901. See pp. 82-83.

béguine. A popular dance of the islands of St. Lucia and Martinique, resembling a rumba.

bendengue. See jongo.

benta. A musical bow of the West Indian Negroes.

berimbau. A musical bow of the Brazilian Indians; also, a jungle incantation of the fetishist ritual.

Bermudez Silva, Jesús. Colombian composer of orchestral and other music. Born in Bogotá, December 24, 1884. See pp. 169-170.

Bernal Jiménez, Miguel. Mexican composer of operatic and orchestral music on native themes. Born in Morelia, February 16, 1910. See pp. 227-228.

berra-boi. A primitive Brazilian thunder-stick

Berutti, Arturo. Argentine composer of Italianate operas. Born in San Juan, March 27, 1862; died in Buenos Aires, January 3, 1938. See pp. 82-83.

Berutti, Pablo. Argentine composer of piano music and an opera, brother of

Arturo Berutti. Born in San Juan, September 24, 1870; died in Buenos Aires, 1916. *See* p. 83.

bexelac. A local Mexican name for the ayotl.

birimbau. *See* **berimbau.**

Bisquertt Prado, Prospero. Chilean composer of orchestral music on native themes. Born in Santiago, June 8, 1881. *See* pp. 157-158.

blocos. Brazilian religious plays connected with Christmas.

boali. *See* **noari.**

bocana. A native guitar of Panama, larger than the **mejoranera.**

bocina. An animal horn with an embouchure made of wood; used by the Indians of equatorial America.

bocina huanca. A Venezuelan wind instrument with a tube of sugar cane and the mouthpiece of animal horn.

Boero, Felipe. Argentine composer of Italianate operas. Born in Buenos Aires, May 1, 1884. *See* p. 83.

bolé-bolé. An Afro-Brazilian dance popular near Bahia.

bolero. A Cuban dance in ¾ time, in contrast to the Spanish **bolero** in ¾ time.

bolero-son. A Cuban air, combining elements of the Cuban **bolero** with those of the **son.**

bomba. A dance of the Haitian Negroes.

bombo. The generic Spanish American name for a bass drum.

bongó (commonly used in plural, **bongós**). Cuban twin drums, held on the knees and played with fingers.

bordonua. A Puerto Rican guitar with supernumerary strings.

boré. *See* **toré.**

boseró. A small flute of the Brazilian Indians.

bototó. *See* **bututú.**

botutó. *See* **bututú.**

Braga, Francisco. Brazilian composer of the romantic school. Born in Rio de Janeiro, April 15, 1868; died there March 14, 1945. *See* pp. 123-124.

Brandão, José Vieira. Brazilian composer of native-inspired songs and piano

pieces. Born in Cambuquira, September 26, 1911. *See* p. 124.

Bravo, Antonio González. *See* **González Bravo, Antonio.**

Broqua, Alfonso. Uruguayan composer. Born in Montevideo, Dec. 11, 1876; died in Paris, Nov. 24, 1946. *See* p. 284.

buá. A small Brazilian flute of the species yapurutú.

Buchardo, Carlos Lopez. Argentine composer of native-inspired music. Born in Buenos Aires, October 12, 1881; died there, April 21, 1948. *See* p. 83.

Buchwald, Theo. Austrian conductor of the *Orquesta Sinfónica Nacional* in Lima. Born in Vienna, September 27, 1902. *See* p. 272.

bula. A small Haitian drum.

bull-roarer. *See* **thunder-stick.**

bumba. *See* **bomba.**

bumbum. A musical bow with a bowstring drawn inward by a cord passed through a small gourd to the back of the bow; used by the Lenca Indians of Honduras.

buré. A Brazilian hunting whistle that imitates bird calls; made of wood, palm trees, or animal skulls.

Burle Marx, Walter. Brazilian conductor and composer. Born in São Paulo, July 23, 1902. *See* pp. 124-125.

Bustamente, Bienvenido. Dominican musician. Born in San Pedro de Macoris, February 27, 1924. *See* p. 192.

butori. *See* **buttori.**

buttori. A rattle of the Bororó Indians of Brazil, made of deer hoofs strung on a lace.

bututó. *See* **bututú.**

bututú. A primitive flute of the South American Indians; *also*, a stamping tube struck rhythmically in a hole in the ground; *also*, a war trumpet consisting of several superposed clay jars. *See also* **pututú.**

C

Caba, Eduardo. Bolivian composer of folkloric music. Born in Potosi, October 13, 1890. *See* p. 107.

cabaça (calabash). *See* **chequeré.**

Caballero, Policarpio. Peruvian collector of musical folklore. Born in Cuzco, January 26, 1894. *See* p. 272.

caboclinho (little **caboclo**). A Brazilian carnival dance-song of a rustic character.

caboclo (peasant). A Brazilian country dance, nostalgic or gay according to mood.

cachampa. *See* **kachampa.**

cacharpaya. A Bolivian carnival dance of Indian origin.

cacho. A Nicaraguan trumpet made of an animal horn.

cachua. A Peruvian song-dance in persistent ¾ time without syncopation, in rapid tempo.

cachullapi. An Ecuadorian song of Indian inspiration, in ⁶⁄₈ time and a rather rapid tempo.

cadacada. Shell castanets used by the Araucanian Indians in Chile.

cairé. A primitive Brazilian rattle in the form of a cross.

caixa (box). The Portuguese name for a snare-drum.

caixinha (little box). A Brazilian box rattle.

caja. A generic Spanish name for all kinds of drums.

calabash. A gourd.

Calcavecchia, Benone. Italian-Uruguayan composer of competently conventional music. Born in Caronia, Sicily, June 27, 1886. *See* p. 285.

calenda. A pre-Columbian South American dance.

callejera (street dance). A popular air of Costa Rica, usually in ⁶⁄₈ time, with occasional cross accents.

calypso. Topical ballads in English, sung by the natives of Trinidad.

camalião. A Brazilian country dance.

Cámara, Juan Antonio. Cuban composer of the modern school. Born in Havana, September 28, 1917. *See* p. 184.

camisão (literally, a shirt). Brazilian box-like square drum, struck with the hand.

Campa, Gustavo. Mexican music educator and composer. Born in Mexico City, September 8, 1863; died there, October 29, 1934. *See* p. 228.

caña (circle). A choreographic figure in which the dancers describe a complete circle holding hands. A half-circle is called **media caña.**

cana verde. A Brazilian dance of Portuguese origin, in ¾ time.

canción. A generic Spanish word for song.

candeia (luminosity). A Brazilian country air in slow ¾ time.

candieiro (candlestick). A Brazilian air similar to the **candeia.**

candombe. An old Argentine dance in mildly syncopated rhythm; now coalesced with the **Tango.**

candomblé. Afro-Brazilian fetishist dance.

canoa (canoe). A Brazilian barcarolla.

cantaletas. Nineteenth century ballads on topical subjects once popular in Santo Domingo.

Cantillano, Roberto. Costa Rican composer of semi-classical band pieces. Born in Santo Domingo de Heredia, March 2, 1887. *See* p. 176.

Cantù, Agostino. Italian-Brazilian composer of romantically colored pieces. Born in Milan, April 24, 1880. *See* p. 125.

capador. A panpipe of Colombian Indians, made of reeds of different sizes tied together; called **antara** in Peru, **sicu** in Bolivia, and **rondador** in Ecuador.

capoeira. A Brazilian rustic dance.

caqueltrún. An Araucanian drum, related to the **cultrún.**

carabiné (from carabiner, a cavalry soldier). A military march once popular in Santo Domingo.

caracalho. A primitive Brazilian scratcher.

caracará. A primitive Brazilian trumpet.

caracaxá. A Brazilian shaker of the **maracas** type.

caracol marino. A conch shell of Mexico and Central America.

caramba. *See* **carimba.**

carángano. A Colombian name for the **maracas.**

carangueijo. A Brazilian dance in fast ¾ time.

carao. An Argentine song-dance of the **milonga** type.

Cárdona, Ismael. Costa Rican composer of salon music. Born in San Ramón, December 5, 1877. *See* p. 176.

carimba. The musical bow of the Indians of El Salvador, consisting of a long, thick reed, strung with a metal wire, which is drawn inward at one-third of its length by a cord attached to an inverted calabash shell.

carimbó. A drum of the Brazilian Negroes.

carioca (abbreviation of samba carioca). A samba played and danced in the style of Rio de Janeiro.

carnavalito (little carnival). Argentine round dance suggesting a village carnival.

Carpio Valdes, Roberto. Peruvian composer of piano pieces. Born in Arequipa, February 23, 1900. *See* p. 272.

carraca. The native Colombian güiro.

carracas, Mexican jingle bells, worn by the dancers on the belt.

carrasca. *See* guacharaca.

carretilha. A type of the Brazilian desafio, usually in rapid tempo and duple time.

Carrillo, Julian. Mexican composer of quarter-tone music. Born in Ahualulco, January 28, 1875. *See* pp. 228-230.

Carrillo, Manuel Gomez. Argentine composer of native-inspired music in traditional style. Born in Santiago del Estero, March 8, 1883. *See* p. 83.

carrizo (reed-grass). A generic name for a reed, fife, or a flute.

Carvajal, Armando. Chilean conductor of the *Orquesta Sinfónica de Chile*. Born in Santiago, June 7, 1893. *See* p. 158.

Carvalho, Dinorá de. Brazilian composer of piano pieces in native vein. Born in Uberaba, June 1, 1905. *See* p. 125.

Carvalho, Eleazar de. Brazilian composer and brilliant conductor. Born in Fortaleza, July 28, 1912. *See* p. 125.

Casabona, Francisco. Brazilian composer of competent music in the Italian style. Born in São Paulo, October 16, 1894. *See* pp. 125-126.

Casal Chapí, Enrique. *See* Chapí, Enrique Casal.

Casanova Vicuña, Juan. Chilean conductor and composer. Born in Santiago, December 27, 1895. *See* p. 159.

Casas, Gabriel Escobar. *See* Escobar Casas, Gabriel.

cascabeles. Small jingle rattles or beads made of dried fruit shells, clay, or beaten metal with pellets inside; in use among Mexican Indians.

Casella, Enrique M. Uruguayan-Argentine composer of vocal music in the native manner. Born in Montevideo, Uruguay, August 1, 1891. *See* p. 84.

Castañeda, José. Guatemalan music theorist and critic. Born in Guatemala City, May 24, 1898. *See* pp. 204-205.

Castillo, Jesús. Guatemalan musical folklorist. Born and died in Quezaltenango, Sept. 9, 1877–April 23, 1946. *See* p. 205.

Castillo, Ricardo. Half-brother of Jesús Castillo. Guatemalan composer of music of native inspiration. Born in Quezaltenango, October 1, 1891. *See* p. 205.

Castro, Herbert de. Panamanian conductor. Born in Panama, January 18, 1906. *See* pp. 260-261.

Castro, José María. Argentine composer of neo-romantic orchestral and vocal music. Born in Avellaneda, November 17, 1892. *See* pp. 84-85.

Castro, Juan José. Brother of José María Castro. Argentine composer-conductor, writing in the neo-classical style. Born in Buenos Aires, March 7, 1895. *See* pp. 85-86.

Castro, Sergio de. Argentine composer of romantic piano pieces. Born in Buenos Aires, September 15, 1922. *See* p. 87.

Castro, Washington. Brother of José María and Juan José Castro. Argentine composer of neo-classical pieces. Born in Buenos Aires, July 13, 1909. *See* p. 87.

castruera. A Colombian flute.

catacá. Brazilian wooden blocks, one striated and one plain, that are rubbed together to produce a rasping sound similar to that of the reco-reco.

cateretê. A Brazilian rustic air, in ⅝ or ¾ time, with steady rhythm and moderate tempo.

catimbau. *See* catimbó.

catimbó. An Indo-Brazilian air, in rapid ¾ time, often of fetishistic connotations, popular in the Brazilian Northwest.

catira. A regional variant of the cateretê.

catuquinarú drum. The earth drum of the Catuquinarú Indians of Rio Jurua;

a pit in the ground, in which a hollow trunk of a palm tree is placed on end, is filled in with rubber, hide, powdered mica, bone fragments, etc., on which the performers stamp to produce a rumbling hollow sound.

Caturla, Alejandro García. Cuban composer of ultra-modern music in Afro-Cuban vein. Born in Remedios, March 7, 1906; assassinated there, November 12, 1940. *See* pp. 184-185.

cavaquinho. A small Brazilian guitar, usually with four strings, popular in Carnival music.

caxambú. A Brazilian drum; in orchestral works of Villa-Lobos, **caxambú** is described as a bottle filled with gravel and shaken to produce a rattling noise.

cencerro. A piece of metal used in Cuban popular orchestras as a bell.

Cerón, José Dolores. A Negro Dominican composer of band music. Born in Santo Domingo, June 29, 1897. *See* p. 192.

chacarera. A popular Argentine air in alternating ⅜ and ¾ time and lively tempo.

cha-cha. *See* **Tcha-tcha.**

chamamé. A popular dance of Argentina in ¾ time and moderate tempo, with a peculiar rhythm of a triplet on the first beat, followed by two groups of eighth notes.

chamarra. An Argentine air similar to the **milonga.**

chamarrita. *See* **chamarra.**

chanrará. An Andean rattle of the species **zacapá.**

Chapí, Enrique Casal. Spanish conductor and composer, resident in the Dominican Republic since 1940. Born in Madrid, February 15, 1909. *See* p. 193.

charango. An armadillo-shell guitar having from two to five strings; used throughout Latin America.

charca. A Bolivian wooden flute of the same type as the **pinquillo.**

Chavez, Carlos. Foremost composer of Mexico and conductor of the *Orquesta Sinfónica de Mexico.* Born in Mexico City, June 13, 1899. *See* pp. 230-235.

Chavez Aguilar, Pablo. Peruvian composer of religious music. Born in Lima, March 3, 1899. *See* pp. 272-273.

chayna. A large **quena.**

chequeré. A Brazilian rattle usually made of two metal octohedrons connected by a tube and encased in two rotating metal hoops.

cherqué. A primitive flute used by Bolivian and Peruvian aborigines.

chiapaneca (from the province of Chiapas in Southern Mexico), a regional variant of the Mexican **huapango.**

chiba. An Afro-Brazilian dance.

chicahuaztli. A metal rattle of the ancient Mexicans.

chil-chil. In Nicaragua, a small bell; in Ecuador and Peru, a shaker similar to the **maracas.**

chilena. An abbreviation for **cueca chilena.**

chililihtli. An Aztec flute of baked clay.

chinchin. The Guatemalan name for the **maracas.**

chirimía. A clarinet-like wind instrument used by the Indians of Central America, Colombia, and Venezuela.

chiriqui. A Panamanian air of the **punto** type, in ¾ time and usually in a major key.

chirisuya. A Peruvian wind instrument similar to the **chirimía.**

chispa. A Colombian rustic air in alternating rhythms of three and four beats to a bar, and usually in a minor mode.

chiuka. A primitive flute of the Incas still in use among the Peruvian and Bolivian Indians.

chocalho. A Brazilian shaker, consisting of a metal sphere, a double cone filled with pellets of metal, or a gourd with dried seeds inside.

choquela. A primitive flute used among the Peruvian and Bolivian Indians; *also* an air played on the flute.

chôro (or **chôros**). A Brazilian air characterized by free improvisation, a flowing melody and incisive rhythm; Villa-Lobos uses the word *chôros* to denote any musical form in a Brazilian folk manner.

chotis. A South American variant of the European Schottische, assuming the rhythm of a slightly syncopated Polka.

chucalho. *See* **chocalho.**

chuchas. *See* **chucho.**

chucho. The name in the Colombian province of Cundinamarca for the **maracas.**

chula. A Brazilian dance song of Portuguese origin, in ¾ time and a major key.

chulado. *See* **chula.**

chuli. A small twin flute of Bolivia.

chulo-phusaña. A small trumpet made of snails' shells; used by the Indians of Bolivia and Peru.

churú. A jingle rattle similar to the **zacapá.**

cielito (little heaven). An old Argentine air in lively waltz time.

cielo. *See* **cielito.**

cifra. A song of the Argentine Gauchos, in ¾ or ⅜ time.

ciranda. A Brazilian children's round dance, in ¾ time and rapid tempo.

cirandinha. A short **ciranda.**

ciriri. A dance of the Brazilian jungle.

clarín. A long reed fife of Central and South America.

claves. Cuban cylindrical blocks made of hard wood; when they are struck together, the cupped palm of the hand provides resonance.

Cluzeau Mortet, Luis. Uruguayan composer of romantic pieces in the native style. Born in Montevideo, November 18, 1893. *See p. 285.*

cobo. A conch shell in use among the natives of the island of Santo Domingo.

coco. A Panamanian **punto** in a minor key.

côco. A Brazilian dance in ¾ time, with even rapid notes.

côco de embolada. *See* **embolada.**

colcheia. A Brazilian six-line air in ¾ time and lively tempo.

colo. *See* **kohlo.**

comparsa. Afro-Cuban ritual dance play.

conchas de tortuga. Tortoise shells used by the ancient Mexicans as drums.

condición. A dance of northern Argentina with two sections, the first in slow ¾

time and the second in lively ⅜ time.

conga. A large Cuban drum; *also* an Afro-Cuban dance named after the drum, and characterized by the extreme violence of accents on the strong beats in ¾ meter, with a rhythmic anticipation of the second beat in every other bar of a basic two-measure phrase.

congada. An Afro-Brazilian dance derived from the ritual play of the Negro slaves, characterized by highly syncopated rhythm.

congo. A number of Haitian dances, the various forms of which are known, according to the locality, as *congo mazonne, congo loangue,* etc.

congoerá. A notched scraper often made of human shinbones; used by the Guarany Indians of Paraguay.

contracanto. In Brazilian popular usage, a second voice sung in counterpoint to the principal melody.

contrapunto. A term used in Argentina and other South American countries to designate a musical dialogue improvised by two singers to the accompaniment of a guitar.

Contreras, Salvador. Mexican composer of the modern school. Born in Cueramaro, November 10, 1912. *See pp. 235-236.*

conyvi. A small **quena.**

coplas (couplets). An improvised song to a given tune, popular throughout Latin America.

cordão. A Brazilian pantomime, danced at carnivals.

Cordero, Roque. Panamanian Negro composer. Born in Panama City, August 16, 1917. *See p. 261.*

corrido. A folk ballad on topical subjects, cultivated in Mexico and other Latin American countries.

corta-jaca. A Brazilian dance-song in ¾ time, of the **samba** type, usually with the rhythmic background of rapid even notes.

Cosme, Luiz. Brazilian composer of the modern school. Born in Porto Alegre, March 9, 1908. *See p. 126.*

Costa, Pedro Valenti. Argentine composer of choral music. Born in Buenos

Aires, November 13, 1905. *See* p. 87.

Cotapos, Acario. Chilean composer of music in an advanced modern style. Born in Valdivia, April 30, 1889. *See* p. 159.

coyoli. *See* **chil-chil.**

criolla. A generic term denoting musical forms in a creole or white native style, as in **barcarola criolla.**

cuando. An Argentine parlor dance resembling a minuet.

cuatro. A four-string guitar.

Cuban bolero. *See* **bolero.**

cubarro. A species of the Venezuelan flute **turá.**

cucumbí. A Brazilian Negro drum; *also,* an Afro-Brazilian song-pantomime similar to the **congada.**

cueca. An abbreviation for **cueca chilena** and **zamacueca**; in Argentina, the **cueca** is a lively dance in ¾ time, with occasional syncopation.

cueca chilena. The Bolivian and Argentine name for the Chilean **zamacueca.**

cuica. A Brazilian lion-roarer, consisting of a drum with a rosined string extending through the membrane, producing a raucous noise when pulled by the hand.

cullcull. *See* **küllküll.**

culo-en-tierra (buttock-in-the-earth). A tiny drum of the Venezuelan Indians, made of a cocoanut covered with a membrane, and played with two sticks.

cultrún. *See* **kultrún.**

cumaco. A large jungle drum of the Venezuelan Negroes.

cumbia. A dance of the Panamanian Negroes.

cumbiamba. A Colombian rustic dance in lively ¾ time.

cununú. A large Colombian jungle drum, made of a burned-out, hollow tree trunk covered with a monkey hide.

curacha. A Panamanian air resembling the **punto.**

currulao. A Colombian country dance.

curugú. A drum of the Brazilian Indians.

curuqué. A primitive Brazilian trumpet.

cururú. A Brazilian jungle dance in ¾ time.

curveta. A small drum of the Venezuelan Negroes.

cuyana. A song of the Argentine province of Cuyo, similar to the **zamacueca.**

cuyvi. *See* **conyvi.**

D

Da Cunha, João Itiberé. Brazilian music critic and composer. Born in Rio de Janeiro, August 8, 1870. *See* p. 126.

dadoo. A Venezuelan shaker of the **maracas** type.

danza. A generic Spanish word for dance, sometimes specifically a rustic dance, as opposed to **baile.**

danzante. A melancholy song of Ecuador in ⅝ or ¾ time.

danzón. An Afro-Cuban dance in syncopated rhythm.

decima. A song-poem in ten lines of verse.

Delgadillo, Luis A. Nicaraguan composer of orchestral and theatrical music on native themes. Born in Managua, August 26, 1887. *See* pp. 256-258.

Del Orbe, Gabriel. Dominican composer of popular music. Born in Moca, March 18, 1888. *See* p. 193.

desafio. A freely improvised Brazilian musical dialogue, in three different types, generally in ¾ time: **ligeira,** in short phrases and rapid tempo; **martelo,** in recitative style; **carretilha,** in vigorous rhythmic movement; and **parcela,** in moderate tempo.

De Silva, Alfonso. Peruvian composer of lyrically inspired songs. Born in Callao, December 22, 1903; died in Lima, May 7, 1937. *See* p. 273.

Diaz Zelaya, Francisco. Honduran band leader and composer of popular music. Born in Ojojana, October 6, 1898. *See* p. 213.

Dos Santos, Ernesto. Brazilian Negro composer of popular music. Born in Rio de Janeiro, April 5, 1891. *See* p. 126.

Drangosch, Ernesto. Argentine composer of instrumental music in romantic vein. Born in Buenos Aires, January 22, 1882; died there, June 26, 1925. *See* p. 87.

Dublanc, Emilio. Argentine composer of instrumental pieces in a lyrical manner.

Born in La Plata, July 15, 1911. *See* p. 87.

Duncker Lavalle, Luis. Peruvian composer of semi-classical songs. Born in Arequipa, July 15, 1874; died there, October 29, 1922. *See* p. 271.

dyadiko. A South American foot drum, representing a large hollow slab placed with its convex side up, on which the dancers stamp.

E

Elias, Alfonso de. Mexican composer of romantic music in different genres. Born in Mexico City, August 30, 1902. *See* p. 236.

Elie, Justin. Haitian composer of salon music. Born in Cap Haitien, September 1, 1883; died in New York City, December 3, 1931. *See* p. 211.

embolada (rolling ball). A Brazilian air sung and danced in rapid ⅔ time, in moderately syncopated rhythm.

enkómo. A small Cuban drum.

erque. A horn with a movable tube; used among the Indians of the central Andean plateau.

erquencho. *See* **erque.**

Escobar, María Luisa. Venezuelan composer of vocal music in native manner. Born in Valencia, December 5, 1903. *See* pp. 292-293.

Escobar Casas, Gabriel. Colombian composer of songs in native rhythms. Born in Barranquilla, April 6, 1900. *See* p. 170.

esçondido (hidden). An Argentine dance in ⅔ time and lively tempo, similar to the **gato**; the partners hide from each other, hence the name.

Espinola y Reyes, Juan Bautista. Dominican composer of popular music. Born in La Vega, June 24, 1894; died there, September 29, 1923. *See* p. 193.

Espinosa, Guillermo. Colombian conductor of the *Orquesta Sinfónica Nacional* in Bogotá. Born in Cartagena, January 9, 1905. *See* p. 170.

Espoile, Raúl. Argentine composer of Italianate operas. Born in Mercedes, January 25, 1888. *See* pp. 87-88.

Esposito, Arnaldo d'. Argentine composer of theater music. Born in Buenos Aires, August 30, 1897; died there, August 22, 1945. *See* p. 88.

esquinazo (from *esquina*, corner). A Chilean serenade in ⅔ time and moderate tempo.

esquipado. A Brazilian round dance.

estilo. A lyrical Argentine air, usually with two sections, the first in slow tempo and ¾ time, the second in a lively movement and in ¾ or ⅔ time.

Estrada, Carlos. Uruguayan composer of lyrical songs. Born in Montevideo, September 15, 1909. *See* p. 285.

Estrada, Juan A. García. Argentine composer of songs and instrumental pieces. Born in Buenos Aires, November 8, 1895. *See* p. 88.

estribillo (Spanish). A refrain.

F

Fabini, Eduardo. Uruguayan composer of orchestral music of native inspiration. Born in Solis, May 18, 1883. *See* pp. 285-286.

Fábrega, Ricardo. Panamanian composer of popular songs and dances. Born in Santiago de Veraguas, January 28, 1905. *See* p. 261.

fado. A Portuguese song popular in Brazil, similar to the **modinha.**

federal. A nineteenth-century Argentinian variant of the European minuet.

Fernandez, Oscar Lorenzo. Brazilian composer of thematically native-inspired music. Born in Rio de Janeiro, November 4, 1897; died there, August 26, 1948. *See* pp. 126-129.

Ficher, Jacobo. Russian-Argentine composer of neoromantic music in a pronounced modern idiom. Born in Odessa, January 14, 1896, resident in Buenos Aires since 1923. *See* pp. 88-89.

firmeza (firmness). An Argentine air in ⅔ time and lively tempo, consisting of a four-bar phrase repeated many times.

Fleites, Virginia. Cuban composer of the young vanguard group. Born in Melena del Sur, July 10, 1916. *See* p. 185.

Flores, José Asunción. Paraguayan composer of folkloric ballads. Born in Asunción, August 27, 1904. *See* p. 264.

Fonseca, Julio. Costa Rican composer of semi-classical music on native themes. Born in San José, May 22, 1885. *See* p. 176.

Foster, Gerónimo Baqueiro. *See* **Baqueiro Foster, Gerónimo.**

fotutó. *See* **bututú.**

França, Agnelo. Brazilian composer of choral music. Born in Valença, December 14, 1875. *See* p. 129.

frêvo (from mispronounced *fervura*, fervor). A Brazilian march-polka characterized by insistent unsyncopated rhythm and strident instrumentation.

Fuentes, Juan B. Mexican composer of vocal and piano music in traditional manner. Born in Guadalajara, March 16, 1869. *See* p. 236.

fuga. The concluding section of a **yaraví.**

fungador. A drum of the Brazilian Negroes.

furruco. A bull-roarer of the Venezuelan natives, made of a barrel, with a cord pulled through the drumhead.

fututó. *See* **bututú.**

fututú. *See* **bututú.**

G

gadalovi. A Haitian dance.

gaita. A Colombian vertical flute.

gaita costeña. A Colombian reed flute used by the Indians of the coast.

gaita de foles. A Brazilian accordion.

Gaito, Constantino. Argentine composer of theater music in Italian tradition. Born in Buenos Aires, Aug. 3, 1878; died there, Dec. 14, 1945. *See* pp. 89-90.

Galeano, Ignacio Villanueva. *See* **Villanueva Galeano, Ignacio.**

galerón. A Colombian folk ballad.

Galimany, Alberto. Spanish-Panamanian composer of popular music. Born in Villafranca, Spain, December 31, 1889. *See* p. 261.

Galindo, Blas. Mexican Indian composer of the modern school. Born in Mexico City, February 3, 1911. *See* p. 237.

Gallet, Luciano. Brazilian musicologist and composer of folkloric music. Born in Rio de Janeiro, June 28, 1893; died there, October 29, 1931. *See* p. 129.

gallino. A **mejorana** in a minor key.

gallumba. *See* **gayumba.**

galopa. The Paraguayan version of a European galop, in which the ¾ meter in the melody is combined with a ¾ rhythm in the bass.

ganzá. A Brazilian scraper, similar to the **reco-reco.**

Garay, Narciso. Panamanian folklore collector and composer. Born in Panama City, June 12, 1876. *See* p. 261.

García, Juan Francisco. Dominican composer of music on native themes. Born in Santiago de los Caballeros, June 16, 1892. *See* p. 193.

Garrido, Pablo. Chilean investigator of native folklore and composer. Born in Valparaiso, March 26, 1905. *See* pp. 159-160.

gato. An Argentine song-dance in rapid ¾ time and steady rhythm.

gato con relaciones. A special type of gato in which the male partner recites *relaciones*, or improvised dialogues.

gayumba. A musical bow of Santo Domingo, made of a flexible piece of wood with a cord attached to a plank covering a hole in the ground; *also*, an old Indian dance of the island.

Gerdes, Federico. German-educated Peruvian musician and pedagogue. Born in Tacna, Peru, May 19, 1873. *See* p. 273.

Gianneo, Luis. Argentine composer of folkloric pieces in a modern idiom. Born in Buenos Aires, January 9, 1897. *See* pp. 90-91.

Gil, José. Argentine composer and pedagogue. Born in Spain, May 29, 1886. *See* p. 91.

Gilardi, Gilardo. Argentine composer of operas and ballets in native manner. Born in San Fernando, May 25, 1889. *See* p. 91.

Giménez, Remberto. Paraguayan composer and educator. Born in Coronel Oviedo, February 4, 1899. *See* p. 265.

Ginastera, Alberto. Argentine composer of the modern school. Born in Buenos Aires, April 11, 1916. *See* p. 92.

Gnattali, Radames. Brazilian composer of native-inspired music in a neoromantic style. Born in Porto Alegre, January 27, 1906. *See* p. 129.

Gomes, Carlos. Brazilian opera composer. Born in Campinas, July 11, 1836; died in Belem, September 16, 1896. *See* pp. 130–131.

gongon. An Afro-Brazilian drum.

González Bravo, Antonio. Bolivian music educator and composer of choral pieces. Born in La Paz, September 2, 1885. *See* p. 107.

González Gamarra, Francisco. Peruvian painter and composer of folkloric piano pieces. Born in Cuzco, June 4, 1890. *See* p. 273.

González Iñiguez, Hilario. Cuban composer of folkloric piano pieces and songs. Born in Havana, January 24, 1920. *See* p. 185.

goyom. The Guatemalan Indian name for the marimba.

Graetzer, Guillermo. Austrian-Argentine composer of neoclassical music. Born in Vienna, September 5, 1914. *See* p. 92.

Gramatges, Harold. Cuban composer of the vanguard group. Born in Santiago de Cuba, September 26, 1918. *See* p. 185.

granbo. A Haitian stamping tube, made of a bamboo reed and stamped rhythmically against a hole in the ground, covered with wooden planks.

Grisolia, Pascual. Argentine composer of lyrical pieces. Born in Buenos Aires, February 4, 1904. *See* p. 92.

grijutians. Mexican jingles.

guabina. A Colombian song in ¾ meter and quick tempo.

guáchara. A primitive scraper in the form of a notched gourd; used by the Indians of Panama.

guacharaca. A Colombian scraper, similar to the güiro.

guaché. A hollow pipe of hard wood, filled with seeds which make a rattling sound; used among the Colombian Indians.

guaiño. *See* huaiño.

guajey. A gourd filled with pebbles, used by the natives of Santo Domingo as a shaker, identical with the maracas.

guajira. A Cuban country dance, usually in ¾ or ⁶⁄₈ time, sometimes performed in the conga manner.

gualambo. A musical bow of the central lowlands of South America.

gualichada. A Peruvian Christmas carol.

guamó. *See* cobo.

guaracha. A lively Cuban song-dance of Spanish origin in ⁶⁄₈ time, sometimes performed with rumba rhythms in duple meter.

guaranda. A type of danzante popular in the Guaranda region of Ecuador.

guaranía (from Guarany Indian). A Paraguayan dance, usually in slow waltz time, created by José Asunción Flores.

guarapo. A folk ballad once popular in Santo Domingo.

guarará. An Indo-Brazilian species of the shaker chocalho.

Guarnieri, Camargo. Brazilian composer of folklore-inspired music in a distinct modern idiom. Born in Tieté, February 1, 1907. *See* pp. 131–133.

guasa. A satirical Venezuelan ballad in ⁶⁄₈ or ¾ time, with a basic rhythm of a triplet followed by a duplet.

Guastavino, Carlos. Argentine composer of instrumental and vocal music in a neoromantic manner. Born in Santa Fé, April 5, 1914. *See* pp. 92–93.

guayo. A ratchet of the Indians of Santo Domingo.

guazá. A Colombian name for the maracas.

guella. *See* hueya.

güiro. A notched gourd played by rubbing a stick on the surface; used in Cuba and elsewhere.

guitarra. The guitar of the Spanish type, usually with six strings; a four-string guitarra is called cuatro; a three-string type is the tiple.

guitarrón. A large guitar.

Guzmán, Rafael Petitón. *See* Petitón Guzmán, Rafael.

H

habanera. A Cuban air in ¾ time marked by a characteristic swaying rhythm of a dotted eighth-note, a sixteenth-note, and two eighth-notes.

hait-teataçu. A nasal disc flute. *See* tsinhali.

Halffter, Rodolfo. Spanish composer of instrumental music in the modern idiom, resident in Mexico since 1939. Born in Madrid, October 30, 1900. *See* pp. 237-238.

harawi. Peruvian song; *also*, generic term embracing the lyric type of ancient Inca music; identical with yaravi.

harpa. The Mexican monochord with a tuning peg; similar to a musical bow except that the rod is straight.

hayllai-quipac. *See* aylli-quepa.

herá-herajun. A transverse flute of the Indians of Brazil.

Hernández, Gisela. Cuban composer of neoclassical chamber music. Born in Cárdenas, September 15, 1910. *See* p. 185.

Hernández, Julio Alberto. Dominican composer of popular music. Born in Santiago de los Caballeros, September 27, 1900. *See* p. 194.

Hernández Moncada, Eduardo. Mexican composer of symphonic music in the academic style. Born in Jalapa, Veracruz, September 24, 1899. *See* p. 238.

hezó-hezó. A large trumpet with a calabash bell; used by the Amazon Indians of Brazil.

Holzmann, Rudolph. German-Peruvian composer of instrumental music in the neoclassical genre. Born in Breslau, November 27, 1910; resident in Peru since 1937. *See* pp. 273-274.

hool. *See* jul.

horesomoi. *See* matabó.

hororó-até. A musical bow of the Amazon Indians.

hountor. A ritual dance of Haiti.

hu. A large Afro-Brazilian drum.

huacatocori (bull fight). A Bolivian carnival dance imitating the bull fight.

huada. The name of the Araucanian Indians of Chile for the maracas.

huaiñito (diminutive from huaiño). A short Peruvian dance derived from the Bolivian huaiño.

huaiño. A lively air or dance in ¾ time popular in the Andean region of South America; in Ecuador it is called sanjuanito.

huájira. Bull horn used by northern Argentine Indians at festivals; also native dance performed at such festivals.

huanamigi. A musical bow of the Amazon region.

huanara. A Bolivian drum.

huancar. A flat drum of Bolivia and Peru, covered with membrane on both ends.

huapango. A popular Mexican dance in polyrhythmically combined ⅔, ¾, and ⅝ time, and lively tempo.

huaylla-quepa. A Peruvian panpipe made of baked clay.

huayra-puhura. A panpipe of the Indians of equatorial America.

huehuetl. A Mexican vertical drum made of a segment of hollowed-out tree, about 50 centimeters in diameter and 90 centimeters in height, and covered with a hide of a tiger or other animal; played with sticks or fingers.

huella. *See* hueya.

hueya. An Argentine air in ⅝ time and lively tempo.

Huizar, Candelario. Mexican composer of folklore-inspired symphonic works in an advanced harmonic idiom. Born in Jerez, February 2, 1888. *See* pp. 239-240.

hulero. The musical bow of the Mosquito Indians of Central America, identical with the carimba.

Hunac, Iwan. The *nom de plume* (formed by anagram) of Da Cunha, João Itiberé.

hunpri. A medium-sized Brazilian drum.

I

Iberé de Lemos, Arthur. Brazilian composer of lyrical songs in native vein. Born in Belem, June 9, 1901. *See* p. 133.

ibigumbiri. A South American musical bow.

ieumai. A Venezuelan name for the maracas.

Iglesias Villoud, Hector. Argentine composer of ballet music. Born in San Nicolas, January 31, 1913. *See* p. 93.

Ignacio, Rafael. Dominican composer of folkloric dances and songs. Born in San Francisco de Macorís, June 15, 1897. *See* p. 194.

ika. A primitive trumpet consisting of a long wooden tube and emitting a low funereal sound; used by the Bororó Indians of Brazil.

ilu. A large wooden drum of the Brazilian Negroes.

inubia. A war trumpet of the Guarany Indians of Paraguay.

Ippisch, Franz. Austrian-Guatemalan composer of orchestral and chamber music in the academic style, resident in Guatemala since 1938. Born in Vienna, July 18, 1883. *See* pp. 205-206.

ireré. A war trumpet of the Amazon Indians, made of bamboo and furnished with a vibrating reed.

Isamitt, Carlos. Chilean composer of neo-romantic music based on native Indian themes. Born in Rengo, March 13, 1885. *See* p. 160.

Itiberé, Brasilio. Brazilian composer of instrumental and vocal music of folkloric derivation. Born in Paraná, May 17, 1896. *See* p. 133.

Itiberé da Cunha, João. *See* **Da Cunha, João Itiberé.**

iuké. A Brazilian Indian "rhythm baton" with a chocalho tied to it.

J

jacarandá. A Brazilian country dance.

jaleo. A Spanish air in ⅜ time, used in Latin American dances as an introduction.

janubia. *See* **inubia.**

jarabe. A characteristic Mexican dance in combined ¾ and ⅝ time, sometimes played in the rhythm of a mazurka.

jarana. A typical dance of Yucatán, Mexico, in combined ⅝ and ¾ time.

jaranita. A Mexican five-string guitar, used to accompany the jarana.

jararacá. *See* **yararacá.**

Jeanty, Occide. Haitian composer of military marches. Born in Port-au-Prince, March 16, 1860; died there, January 28, 1936. *See* p. 211.

jicara de agua. A water drum used in Mexican street bands, consisting of an inverted half-gourd placed in a basin of water and struck with a stick.

Jiménez Mabarak, Carlos. Mexican composer of ballet music in the native style. Born in Mexico City, January 31, 1916. *See* p. 240.

Jiménez, Miguel Bernal. *See* **Bernal Jiménez, Miguel.**

jiruquias. A Mexican percussion instrument.

jongo. An Afro-Brazilian air in ¾ time accompanied by drums.

Jorge, Santos. Spanish-born composer of the Panamanian National Anthem. Born in Peralta, Spain, November 1, 1870; died in Panama City, December 22, 1941. *See* pp. 261-262.

joropo. The typical dance of Venezuela, in ¾ or ⅝ time with steady rhythm.

juba. A small pear-shaped Haitian drum; *also*, a social dance of Haitian Negroes, named after the drum.

juco. A Central American lion-roarer, consisting of a barrel covered with a membrane through which a rosined string is passed; pulling and rubbing the string produces sound.

jul. A musical bow of Central America.

jula-jula. A Bolivian panpipe.

Julião, João Batista. Brazilian composer of choral music. Born in Silveiras, September 19, 1886. *See* p. 133.

juque. *See* **juco.**

jurupari. *See* **yurupari.**

K

ka. A Brazilian drum made of an animal hide stretched over a high wooden barrel; *also*, a Haitian dance.

kachampa. A Peruvian war dance, in vigorously accented ¾ time.

kahuis. A long stamping staff of the Chaco Indians.

kala. The flute of the Cuna Indians of Panama.

kallu (child, from Aymará Indian). A small flute of the **pusi-ppia** type, and sounding an octave higher than the **taica** of the same family.

kaluyo. A Bolivian shoe-tapping dance, similar to the Chilean **zamacueca**.

kambaua (condor bone). A **musical bow** of the Andean region.

kammu. *See* **kamu**.

kamu. A native flute of the San Blas district in Panama.

kandiroé. A **musical bow** of the Amazon Indians.

kanutitsunanikora. A **musical bow**; in use among the aborigines of the Amazon basin.

karutaná. *See* **taquará**.

kashwa. *See* **cachua**.

kaspichaqui. A primitive flute used by the Indians of the central plateau of South America.

kaswa. *See* **cachua**.

katiwu. A local Brazilian species of the **toré**.

kayab. The Mayan name for **ayotl**.

ken. A species of **toré**.

kena. *See* **quena**.

keppa. *See* **quepa**.

khayna. *See* **chayna**.

khoana. A flute of the **pinquillo** type used by the Indians of the central Andean plateau.

kjaswa. *See* **cachua**.

kkepa. *See* **quepa**.

Koellreutter, Hans-Joachim. German composer of atonal music, resident in Brazil since 1937. Born in Freiburg, September 2, 1915. *See* p. 133.

kohlo. The **musical bow** of the Pata-gonian Indians, made of a horse's rib bone, bent by a horsehair string, and played upon with a piece of bone.

kolo. *See* **kohlo**.

korki-kala. The flute of the Cuna Indians of Panama, made of a pelican wing.

Kostakowsky, Jacobo. Russian-Mexican composer of instrumental music in an advanced neoromantic style. Born in Odessa, February 5, 1893; resident in Mexico since 1925. *See* pp. 240-241.

küllküll. An animal horn used by the Araucanian Indians of Chile.

kultrún. A low flat drum used by the Araucanian Indians of Chile.

kulurina. A primitive trumpet of the Amazon Indians.

künkülkawe. An Araucanian twin bow, consisting of two interlocking bows with strings rubbed one against the other, producing a rasping sound.

L

Lamothe, Ludovic. Haitian Negro composer of lyric songs in the native manner. Born in Port-au-Prince, May 12, 1882. *See* pp. 211-212.

Lamuraglia, Nicolas. Argentine composer of instrumental music in a competently academic manner. Born in Buenos Aires, February 19, 1896. *See* p. 93.

Lanao, Ulises. Peruvian composer of miscellaneous pieces on native themes. Born in Callao, October 30, 1913. *See* p. 274.

Lange, Francisco Curt. Foremost Latin American musicologist. Born in Eilenburg, Germany, December 12, 1903; resident of Uruguay since 1923. *See* p. 286.

laquitas. *See* **sicuris**.

Lavin, Carlos. Chilean specialist in musical folklore and composer. Born in Santiago, August 10, 1883. *See* p. 160.

lé. A small Afro-Brazilian drum of the **tabaqué** type.

Lecuna, Juan. Venezuelan composer of native-inspired pieces in a modern idiom.

Born in Valencia, Venezuela, November 20, 1898. *See* p. 293.

Lecuona, Ernesto. Cuban composer of popular songs and dances. Born in Guanabacoa, Cuba, August 7, 1896. *See* pp. 185-186.

lenda (*legend* in Portuguese). A Brazilian art form corresponding to the European ballade.

Leng, Alfonso. Chilean composer of romantically colored symphonic music and songs. Born in Santiago, February 11, 1884. *See* pp. 160-161.

Letelier Llona, Alfonso. Chilean composer of vocal and instrumental music. Born in Santiago, October 4, 1912. *See* p. 161.

Ley, Salvador (real name, **Levy**). Guatemalan composer of piano music in a neoromantic manner. Born in Guatemala City, January 2, 1907. *See* p. 206.

licu. A medium-sized twin flute of Bolivia.

ligueira. A type of **desafio**, characterized by a succession of short rhythmic phrases in rapid tempo.

Lima, Emirto de. Colombian investigator of musical folklore. Born in Barranquilla, January 25, 1892. *See* p. 170.

Lima, Souza. Brazilian pianist and composer of piano pieces. Born in São Paulo, March 21, 1898. *See* p. 133-134.

limba. A Haitian dance.

llamada (call). A generic term for a composition of a proclamatory nature.

llamador (caller). The solo drum, or the principal drum in the ensemble.

llanto (crying). An Argentine air in ¾ time; the name derives from a figure in the dance where the partners press a handkerchief to the eyes.

llaqui-aru. The Indian name for a Bolivian **yaravi.**

loku. A primitive Brazilian flute similar to the **adjulona.**

lolkin. An Araucanian cane pipe, on which sound is produced by violent inhalation of air.

loncomeo. A melancholy song of the Araucanian Indians of Patagonia.

Lopez Buchardo, Carlos. *See* **Buchardo, Carlos Lopez.**

Lopez Mindreau, Ernesto. Peruvian composer of piano pieces in the native vein. Born in Chiclayo, June 17, 1890. *See* p. 274.

los aires (airs). An old Argentine dance in rapid ⅜ time.

louvor. A slow Brazilian air.

Lovelace, Manuel de Jesús. Dominican composer of popular music. Born in Santo Domingo, June 8, 1871. *See* p. 194.

lucumi. An Afro-Cuban mass dance.

lundú. An Afro-Brazilian air in ¾ time, greatly varied in style, from a melancholy slow type to a vigorous rhythmic movement, with occasional syncopation.

Luzzatti, Arturo. Italian-Argentine composer of orchestral music in a romantic manner. Born in Turin, Italy, May 24, 1875. *See* p. 93.

M

machete. A Brazilian small guitar, similar to the **cavaquinho.**

Mackenna, Carmela. Chilean composer of polyphonic chamber music. Born in Santiago, July 31, 1879. *See* pp. 161-162.

macumba. An Afro-Brazilian ritual, or the music played at such a ritual.

magüey. Ancient slit drum made of a hollow tree trunk, once in use among the Indians in Santo Domingo.

mahalta. A Bolivian twin flute.

mala (medium-sized). A Peruvian flute, one-third smaller than the average **quena.**

malambo. An old Argentine dance in a lively ⅜ time.

mama drum. A large Haitian ritual drum.

mana-chica. A Brazilian song of Portuguese origin, similar to the **modinha.**

mañanita. Mexican salon piece, in the style of a serenade.

manchai-puito. A native flute of equatorial South America.

mandola. A species of the **mandolin.**

mandolin. An oval-shaped string instrument of the guitar family, played with a plectrum, and usually having four strings.

mandura. A species of **pandura.**

manguaré. A large Colombian drum,

similar to the Mexican **teponaxtle**, made of a hollowed-out tree trunk with a hole in the center.

mangulina. A once-popular air of Santo Domingo, usually of an amorous nature.

manuba. A Haitian dance, reputedly danced only by homosexual men.

mapachera. A regional Mexican drum.

mapalé. A Colombian rustic dance-song.

maracá. The Brazilian name for **maracas**.

maracas. A pair of gourds or calabash shells filled with dry seeds and rhythmically shaken with both hands; in use all over Latin America and the islands since pre-Columbian times.

maracatú. An Afro-Brazilian air in ¾ time, played by an ensemble of trumpets and percussion.

marcha. The Latin American counterpart of the military march, characterized by a faster tempo and occasional syncopation.

Marchena, Enrique de. Dominican composer of atmospheric pieces in the native manner. Born in Santo Domingo, October 13, 1908. *See* p. 194.

marchinha (little march). Brazilian short march played at carnival time.

mare. A primitive Caribbean trumpet.

mariachi. A Mexican band consisting of guitars, violins, and trumpets; *also*, the music played by such a band.

mariandá. A Puerto Rican song of Spanish origin, usually in ⁶⁄₈ time.

maricuba. A nickname for the guitar among the natives of the island of Santo Domingo.

marimacho. A twin flute of the Andean region, similar to the **aykhori** and **sicuris**.

marimba. A popular keyboard instrument played with mallets; similar to a xylophone.

marinera. A lively Peruvian dance in ⁶⁄₈ time, identical with the Chilean **cueca**, and renamed **marinera** in honor of the Peruvian Navy.

mariquita (diminutive of Maria). An obsolete Argentine air in ⁶⁄₈ time and lively tempo.

Mariscal, Juan Leon. Mexican composer of symphonic music with native subject matter. Born in Oaxaca, August 29, 1899. *See* p. 241.

marote. An Argentine air in vigorous ¾ and ⁶⁄₈ time.

martelo. A Brazilian air in ¾ time and moderate tempo, often performed as part of the **desafio**.

Martín, Edgardo. Cuban composer of the vanguard group. Born in Cienfuegos, October 6, 1915. *See* p. 186.

maruga. The name sometimes used in Cuba for **maracas**.

marujada (marine adventure). Brazilian festive play with dancing and singing.

Marx, Burle. *See* **Burle Marx, Walter.**

Massa, Juan Bautista. Argentine composer of operas in the Italian tradition. Born in Buenos Aires, October 29, 1885; died in Rosario, March 7, 1938. *See* pp. 93-94.

Mata, Julio. Costa Rican composer of theater music of folkloric derivation. Born in Cartago, December 9, 1899. *See* pp. 176-177.

matabó. The primitive bamboo trumpet of the Amazon Indians.

matapú. A native Paraguayan drum.

matraca. A Brazilian wooden rattle.

matti-phusaña. A war trumpet used by the Aymará Indians in the central Andean plateau.

matungo. A set of iron bars used for bells by the Brazilian Negroes.

maxixe. A Brazilian dance of urban character, in ¾ time and rapid tempo with slight syncopation.

maychil. *See* **chil-chil.**

mayoyo. A Haitian dance.

mazonne. *See* **congo.**

mbaracá ("divine calabash"). A Guarany Indian name for **maracas**.

meçapaqueña. A lively dance of the Bolivian province of Meçapaca.

media caña. An obsolete Argentine dance of urban origin, containing elements of the **gato**, **pericón**, and **zamacueca**, and written in ⅜ time with a syncopated figure in every other bar.

media tuna. An old country dance of the

Dominican Republic, essentially Spanish in derivation, and usually in ⅝ time; also a laborers' song.

megaló. A Brazilian bull-roarer or **thunder-stick.**

Mejía, Adolfo. Colombian composer of instrumental pieces in a native genre. Born in Cartagena de Indias, February 5, 1909. *See* p. 170.

Mejía, Estanislao. Mexican composer of symphonic music based on indigenous themes. Born in Hueyotlipa, November 13, 1882. *See* p. 241.

Mejia-Arredondo, Enrique. Dominican symphonic composer. Born in Santo Domingo, December 24, 1901. *See* pp. 194-195.

mejorana. A traditional air of Panama, written in a major key, with the melody in ¾ time and the accompanying figure in ⅝ time.

mejorana-poncho. A slow **mejorana.**

mejoranera. A five-stringed guitar of Panama, so named because it is used to accompany the **mejorana,** Panama's native dance.

Melo Gorigoytía, Hector. Chilean composer of atmospheric piano pieces. Born in Santiago, October 30, 1899. *See* p. 162.

memby. A family of flutes used by Paraguayan and Brazilian Indians, subdivided according to size and pitch into several types: *memby-apará, memby-chué, memby-guazú,* and *memby-tarará.*

memby-apará. *See* **memby.**

memby-chué. *See* **memby.**

memby-guazú. *See* **memby.**

memby-tarará. *See* **memby.**

Mena, Luis E. Dominican composer of music in various genres. Born in Santo Domingo, November 12, 1895. *See* p. 195.

Menchaca, Angel. Argentine musical theorist, inventor of a sloping piano keyboard. Born in Asunción, Paraguay, March 1, 1855; died in Buenos Aires, May 8, 1924. *See* p. 94.

Mendoza, Alberto. Guatemalan music educator and composer. Born in Guatemala City, March 30, 1889. *See* p. 206.

Mendoza, Vicente T. Mexican folklore investigator and composer. Born in Cholula, January 27, 1894. *See* pp. 241-242.

mento. A native dance of Jamaica, similar to the **rumba.**

merengue. The characteristic national dance of the Dominican Republic, in ¾ time with a syncopation of the first beat.

meringue. The Haitian name for the **merengue.**

mesano. A special form of the Panamanian air **socavón,** in which the melody ends on the dominant.

Meza, Miguel C. Mexican composer of symphonic poems in the national style. Born in San Luis Potosí, September 29, 1903. *See* p. 242.

Michaca, Pedro. Mexican composer and musical theorist. Born in Canatlán, November 26, 1897. *See* p. 242.

Mignone, Francisco. Brazilian composer of numerous works of native inspiration, in a modernistic neoromantic idiom. Born in São Paulo, September 3, 1897. *See* pp. 134-136.

Miguez, Leopoldo. Brazilian composer of operas. Born in Rio de Janeiro, September 7, 1850; died there, July 6, 1902. *See* pp. 136-137.

milonga. An Argentine dance in ¾ time, once popular in Buenos Aires but now coalesced with the **tango** in the form of a **milonga-tango.**

Mindreau, Ernesto Lopez. *See* **Lopez Mindreau, Ernesto.**

mine. A low flat drum of the Venezuelan Negroes, played with two sticks.

mini. The generic name for wind instruments of the **yurupari** ritual of the Amazon Indians.

Miramontes, Arnulfo. Mexican composer of theatrical music with native subject matter, in a Germanic contrapuntal idiom. Born in Tala, July 18, 1882. *See* pp. 242-243.

mitote. A generic name for a native air or dance of Central America.

miudinho. A lively Brazilian dance in ¾ time, resembling the **polka.**

moda. A Brazilian lyrical air of Portuguese derivation, usually in a minor key and moderately slow ⅔ time.

modinha (diminutive of moda). A Brazilian urban song of sentimental character, mostly in a minor key.

Moleiro, Moisés. Venezuelan composer of piano pieces and songs with native flavor. Born in Zaraza, March 28, 1905. *See* p. 293.

Molina Pinillo. José. Guatemalan composer of chromomusical pieces on native themes. Born in Guatemala City, August 28, 1889. *See* p. 206.

Moncada, Eduardo Hernández. *See* Hernández Moncada, Eduardo.

Moncayo, Pablo. Mexican composer of the vanguard school. Born in Guadalajara, June 29, 1912. *See* p. 243.

Mondino, Luis Pedro. Uruguayan composer of lyric pieces. Born in Montevideo, November 19, 1903. *See* p. 286.

Monestel, Alejandro. Costa Rican composer of religious music and band pieces on native subjects. Born in San José, April 26, 1865. *See* p. 177.

monos (monkeys). A Colombian dance in which the partners hold hands.

montuno. In Cuban music, a short instrumental refrain after the vocal part.

Morales, Melesio. Mexican operatic composer. Born in Mexico City, December 4, 1838; died in San Pedro de los Pinos, May 12, 1908. *See* pp. 243-244.

morão. A Brazilian air in slow waltz time.

Moreno, Juan Carlos. Paraguayan composer of lyrical piano pieces. Born in Asunción, February 19, 1912. *See* p. 265.

Moreno, Segundo Luis. Ecuadorian composer of folkloric music. Born in Cotacachi, August 3, 1882. *See* p. 199.

Morillo, Roberto García. Argentine composer of instrumental music in an advanced modern idiom. Born in Buenos Aires, January 22, 1911. *See* pp. 94-95.

Mosca, Radames. Brazilian composer of piano pieces and songs. Born in São Paulo, March 8, 1908. *See* p. 137.

moundongue. A ritual dance of· the Haitian Negroes.

mozamala (bad girl). A variant of the Peruvian marinera.

mulungú. An Afro-Brazilian drum.

Muñoz, Alejandro. Salvadoran band leader and arranger. Born in San Salvador, February 3, 1902. *See* p. 281.

muré-muré. A native drum of the Guarany Indians of Paraguay.

Murillo, Emilio. Colombian composer of folkloric dances. Born in Bogotá, April 9, 1880; died there, August 8, 1942. *See* p. 170.

musical bow. The generic name for an indigenous monochord consisting of a pliable rod strung by a wire and played upon with a bone stick (South America); or with the string divided into two unequal parts by a cord attached to the rod, with a gourd for a resonator (Central America).

N

náñiga. Afro-Cuban carnival dance.

Napoleão, Arthur. Portuguese-Brazilian pianist and music publisher. Born in Oporto, Portugal, March 6, 1843; died in Rio de Janeiro, May 12, 1925. *See* p. 137.

Napolitano, Emilio. Argentine composer of songs in a native vein. Born in Buenos Aires, November 12, 1907. *See* p. 95.

nasal flutes. Disc-shaped wind instruments with perforations, played by blowing air through the nostrils; in use among the Indians in Brazil and Paraguay.

nasisi. The Panamanian maracas.

natapú. A primitive trumpet of the Brazilian Indians.

nau catarineta (ship *Catarineta*). Brazilian folk pageant of the marujada type depicting incidents of the time of discovery.

Nazareth, Ernesto. Brazilian composer of popular music. Born in Branco, March 20, 1863; died there, February 1, 1937. *See* p. 137.

Negrete Woolcock, Samuel. Chilean composer of symphonic pieces with Chilean rhythms. Born in Santiago, December 18, 1893. *See* p. 162.

Nepomuceno, Alberto. Brazilian composer, pioneer of modern musical nationalism. Born in Fortaleza, July 6, 1864; died in Rio de Janeiro, October 16, 1920. *See* p. 137.

Netto, Barrozo. Prolific Brazilian composer of lyrical pieces in native manner. Born in Rio de Janeiro, January 30, 1881; died there, September 1, 1941. *See* p. 138.

Nieto, Cesar. Spanish-born composer of chromomusical pieces. Born in Barcelona, October 31, 1892. *See* p. 177.

Ninci, Enrique Fava. Italian-Peruvian flutist and composer. Born in Spezia, Italy, October 4, 1883; died in Lima, December 5, 1948. *See* p. 274.

Nin y Castellanos, Joaquín. Cuban composer of colorful Hispanic pieces in Gallic manner. Born in Havana, September 29, 1879. *See* p. 186.

Nin-Culmell, Joaquín. Son of **Nin y Castellanos**; composer of chamber music in the modern idiom. Born in Berlin, Germany, September 5, 1908. *See* p. 186.

Nito, José de. Argentine composer of choral music. Born in Rosario, November 12, 1887; died there, August 26, 1945. *See* p. 95.

noari. The primitive trumpet of the Bororó Indians of Brazil, consisting of a reed tube slit longitudinally and stuck into a gourd with four holes in its side.

nora. A Panamanian vertical flute.

nose-flutes. *See* **nasal flutes.**

Nuñez Navarrete, Pedro. Chilean composer of symphonic pieces. Born in Constitución, August 3, 1906. *See* p. 162.

Nunó,. Jaime. Author of the National Anthem of Mexico. Born in San Juan de las Abadesas, Spain, September 8, 1824; died in Auburndale, New York, July 18, 1908; body transferred to Mexico in October 1942. *See* p. 244.

O

ocarina. A conch shell or a clay jar with holes, capable of producing several sounds.

Octaviano, João. Brazilian composer of instrumental and vocal music of native inspiration. Born in Porto Alegre, April 22, 1896. *See* pp. 138-139.

ogan. A metal block used in Haiti as a bell.

omichicahuaztli (bone noise). An ancient Mexican scraper, made of a serrated human bone, usually the femur, and rubbed with a conch shell to produce a rasping sound.

omitzicahuastli. *See* **omichicahuaztli.**

ondú. The Argentine form of the Brazilian **lundú.**

Orbón, Julian. Spanish-Cuban composer of neoclassical chamber music. Born in Avilés, Spain, August 7, 1925; resident in Havana since childhood. *See* p. 186.

Oswald, Henrique. Brazilian composer of theatrical music in a romantic tradition. Born in Rio de Janeiro in 1852; died there, June 10, 1931. *See* p. 139.

ouay. *See* **chocalho.**

oufuá. *See* **ufuá.**

Ovalle, Jaime. Brazilian composer of piano pieces and songs in Afro-Brazilian rhythms. Born in Belem, August 5, 1894. *See* p. 139.

oyualli. A Mexican jingle rattle made of snail shells.

P

Pacheco de Cespedes, Luis. Peruvian composer of theater music on Inca subjects. Born in Lima, November 25, 1893. *See* pp. 274-275.

Padua, Newton. Brazilian composer of orchestral music on native themes. Born in Rio de Janeiro, November 3, 1894. *See* p. 140.

pagelança. A Brazilian folk pageant of mixed Christian and fetishist derivation.

Pahissa, Jaime. Spanish-Argentine composer of ultra-modernist and innovating music. Born in Barcelona, October 7, 1880; resident in Argentina since 1935. *See* pp. 95-96.

pala-pala. A Bolivian carnival dance.

palito. An old Argentine air in ¾ or ⅜ time, related to the **gato.**

Palma, Athos. Argentine composer of theater music in the Italian tradition. Born in Buenos Aires, June 7, 1891. *See* p. 96.

palmas. The clapping of hands to accentuate the rhythm.

pamo. *See* pamy.

pamy. A primitive cornet of the Brazilian Indians, made of two segments of grooved-out wood, hooped together so as to form a tube.

pandeiro (Portuguese). A tambourine.

pandero (Spanish). A tambourine.

pandura. A species of bandurria.

panhuehuetl. A medium-sized huehuetl.

Paniagua, Raúl. Guatemalan composer of symphonic music in a competent modern idiom. Born in Guatemala City, February 17, 1898. *See* pp. 206-207.

Paniagua Martinez, Julian. Guatemalan composer of popular marches and songs; uncle of Raúl Paniagua. Born in Guatemala City, September 5, 1856. *See* p. 207.

Panizza, Hector. Argentine composer of operatic music in an Italianate manner. Born in Buenos Aires, August 12, 1875. *See* p. 96.

panna. A multiple trumpet of the Bororó Indians of Brazil, consisting of three or four gourds impaled on a hollow tube.

papa drum. The medium-sized Haitian drum, smaller than the mama drum.

papelón. A Panamanian song-dance of the punto type.

parabién. A Chilean salon dance, in vogue during the nineteenth century.

parcela. A form of Brazilian desafio, sung in rhythmic recitative.

pasacalle. A Bolivian serenade in ¾ or 2/4 time; *also* in Peru, a carnival march.

paseo (promenade). The more stately section of the dance, contrasted with the zapateo.

pasillo. A Latin American dance of Spanish derivation in combined 6/8 and ¾ time, popular in Colombia (where it is also called *vals del pais*), Venezuela, Ecuador, and Costa Rica.

pasillo-mazurka. A pasillo performed in the rhythm of a mazurka, with a slight accent on the second beat.

pasodoble. A Latin American one-step or march.

pastorel. A ritual dance of the Haitian Negroes.

pastoris (the shepherds). A Brazilian Christmas pageant.

payada. An improvised song or a duet sung by the Argentine *payadores*, itinerant singers.

Paz, Juan Carlos. Argentine composer of atonal music. Born in Buenos Aires, August 5, 1897. *See* pp. 96-97.

Pedrell, Carlos. Uruguayan composer of vocal music in a modern Gallic idiom. Born in Minas, Uruguay, October 16, 1878; died in Paris, March 9, 1941. *See* p. 287.

Peña Morell, Esteban. Dominican Negro musician and folklorist. Born in Santo Domingo in 1894; died in Barcelona, Spain, March 6, 1939. *See* p. 196.

pendejo. A Venezuelan drum of the culo-en-tierra type.

Peralta, Ramón Emilio. Dominican musician of popular music. Born in Santiago de los Caballeros, February 1, 1868; died there, September 7, 1941. *See* p. 195.

Perceval, Julio. Belgian-Argentine composer of chamber music in neoclassical vein. Born in Brussels, July 17, 1903; resident in Argentina since 1925. *See* pp. 97-98.

Pereira, Arthur. Brazilian composer of piano pieces. Born in São Paulo, September 12, 1904. *See* p. 140.

pererenga. An Afro-Brazilian drum.

pericón. A lively Uruguayan and Argentine dance in 3/8 time and steady rhythm.

Petitón Guzmán, Rafael. Dominican composer of light music in the native tradition. Born in Salcedo, December 18, 1894. *See* p. 195.

petro. A ritual dance of Haiti, named after the legendary character Don Pedro; *also*, a Haitian drum.

pézinho. A Brazilian country dance.

pfucullu. A Peruvian whistling jar.

pfutu-huancar. A species of the Peruvian drum huancar.

phala. A wooden transverse flute used by the Indians of the central plateau of South America.

phuna. A long twin wooden flute made of two reeds tied together at one end; used by the Andean Indians.

phusaña-matti. See matti-phusaña.

phutuca. A drum used by the Aymará Indians in the central Andean plateau.

Piaggio, Celestino. Argentine composer of academically competent music. Born in Concordia, December 20, 1886; died in Buenos Aires, October 28, 1931. See p. 98.

piano de cuia. See chequeré.

pifano. A Peruvian flute.

pifulka. An Araucanian Indian primitive flute.

pimpím. A wooden kettledrum of the Chaco Indians consisting of a mortar half-filled with water and covered with a goat skin.

pincollo. See pinquillo.

pincullu. See pinquillo.

pindín. A Panamanian song-dance of the punto type.

pingullo. See pinquillo.

pinkülwe. An Araucanian flute of the pinquillo type.

pinpín. See pimpím.

pinquillo. The vertical flute of the central plateau of South America, similar to, and sometimes identical with, the quena.

pinquillo mohoceño. A long flute of the pinquillo family.

Pinto, Alfredo. Italian-Argentine composer of romantically colored character pieces. Born in Mantua, Italy, October 22, 1891; resident in Argentina since 1915. See p. 98.

pinyque. A Haitian dance.

pio. A Brazilian friction instrument consisting of a wooden stick producing a whistling noise when rubbed with a piece of folded cloth.

pito. The generic name for a vertical flute used by the Central American Indians.

piuta. See cuica.

pivillca. An Araucanian wind instrument.

Plaza, Juan Bautista. Venezuelan composer of musical pieces based on native rhythms. Born in Caracas, July 19, 1898. See pp. 293-294.

plena. A Puerto Rican folk ballad, similar to the calypso songs of Trinidad.

poari. See noari.

polca brasileira. A Brazilian polka, differing from the European by accents on the weak beats.

polka paraguaya. A Paraguayan version of the European polka, characterized by a ¾ melody against an accompanying figure of triplets.

Pomar, José. Mexican composer of modernistic theater scores. Born in Mexico City, June 18, 1880. See p. 244.

Ponce, Manuel. Mexican composer, Mexican musical nationalism pioneer. Born in Fresnillo, Dec. 8, 1886; died in Mexico City, April 24, 1948. See pp. 244-247.

ponteio. A lively Brazilian air in an emphatic, rhythmic style.

porfías. An improvised instrumental or vocal dialogue of Venezuela, similar to the Brazilian desafio and the Argentine contrapunto.

porro. Colombian dance-song usually performed in foxtrot time, with lyrics on topical matters.

Posada-Amador, Carlos. Colombian composer of orchestral and choral music. Born in Medellín, April 25, 1908. See pp. 170-171.

potutó. See pututú.

ppakochi. A small vertical flute, usually with only three apertures; used in Peru and Bolivia.

Prado, Prospero Bisquertt. See Bisquertt Prado, Prospero.

pregón. The street vendor's cry.

puicullu. See pinquillo.

puita. See cuica.

puja. The common abbreviation for pujador.

pujador. A medium-sized drum of Panama.

pululú. A primitive fife used by the Indians of the central plateau in South America.

pungacuquá. A primitive Mexican trumpet made of wood or baked clay.

punto. In Cuba, Santo Domingo, and

Puerto Rico, a song of Spanish flavor in either ¾, ⅜, or ⅝ time and free as to rhythm; *also*, a popular air of Panama and other Caribbean countries, written in a major key and ⅝ time and danced in a rapid tempo.

punto cibaeño. A provincial Dominican dance in ¾ time, resembling the Panamanian **punto**.

purajhei. The Guarany word for song, descriptive of the Paraguayan type of romantic ballad.

pusi-ppia. A primitive flute capable of producing four different notes; used by the Indians of the South American altiplano.

putuca. A large drum used by the Indians of the South American altiplano.

pututó. *See* **pututú**.

pututú. The primitive trumpet of the Bolivian Indians; *also* synonymous with **bututú**, a drum of South American aborigines.

puya. Colombian popular dance, in the genre of **pasillo**.

Q

qquena. *See* **quena**.

Quaratino, Pascual. Argentine composer of songs and piano pieces in the native genre. Born in Buenos Aires, June 13, 1904. *See* pp. 98-99.

quena. The generic name for a vertical flute made of bamboo, baked clay, or even gold, usually capable of producing the five notes of the pentatonic scale; of the type used by the Incas.

quenacho. A species of **quena**.

quenali. A species of **quena**.

quena-quena. A native dance of the Andean Indians accompanied by the **quena** flutes.

quepa. The Peruvian ocarina made of baked clay; sometimes used synonymously for **quena**.

Quesada, José. Costa Rican composer of popular songs. Born in San Rafael, October 6, 1894. *See* p. 177.

quijada del burro. The jawbone of an ass, varnished and ornamented with bells; used as a shaker in Cuban orchestras.

quijongo. A musical bow of the Central American Indians, made of a long, thick hollow reed bent by a wire attached to the ends, and drawn inward by a string connected with a gourd on the back of the bow.

quilombo. A popular Brazilian ballad.

quimbeté. An Afro-Brazilian dance of the **batuque** type.

quinan. *See* **salongo**.

quinquecahué. *See* **kohlo**.

quiquiztli. A Mexican conch shell.

quissangé. An Afro-Brazilian drum.

quita. Magic dances of Haiti, of which the best known are: *quita-chéché*, danced to stop the rains; and *quita-moyé*, danced to stop the dry spell.

R

rabeca. A primitive Brazilian violin.

rabel. A primitive violin, usually with three strings.

Raco, Antonio de. Argentine composer of neoclassical music. Born in Buenos Aires, August 21, 1915. *See* p. 99.

rada. A ritual dance of Haiti.

ramada. A rustic Chilean air.

ranchera. An Argentine country dance of the ranches, in ¾ time accompanied by a uniform eighth-note rhythm in ⅝.

rancho dos reis (place of kings). A Brazilian folk pageant with music, performed at Christmas time.

rara. A Haitian dance.

raspador (from Spanish). The generic name for a scraper, applied to the **güiro** and similar instruments.

Ravelo, José de Jesús. Dominican composer of religious music. Born in Santo Domingo, March 21, 1876. *See* p. 195.

realéjo. A Brazilian carnival accordion.

reco-reco. A Brazilian scraper, consisting of a notched hollow tube that is scraped with a stick.

recortado. A lively Brazilian air similar to the **cateveté**.

refalosa. An Argentine dance of Peruvian origin, in ⅜ or ¾ time and a lively tempo.

reisados (from **reis**, kings). Brazilian Christmas pageant depicting the Adoration of the Magi.

relación. In Gaucho songs, a refrain added to the principal verse and addressed to the female partner, as in **gato con relaciones.**

remedio (remedy). An Argentine song-dance, similar to the **pericón,** in steady ⅜ meter and usually in a minor key, with humorous verses offering cure from love and drink.

repicador. A drum which carries the principal rhythm in a street band.

Republicano, Assis. Negro Brazilian composer of operas with native subjects. Born in Porto Alegre, November 15, 1897. *See* p. 140.

requinto. A small clarinet; in Bolivia a small panpipe; and in the province of Cuyo, Argentina, a small twelve-stringed guitar.

resbalosa. *See* **refalosa.**

Revueltas, Silvestre. Mexican composer of instrumental music in a distinctive modern idiom with native rhythms. Born in Santiago Papasquiaro, Durango, December 31, 1899; died in Mexico City, October 5, 1940. *See* pp. 247-251.

rhythm batons. Long bamboo sticks used by Amazon Indians to stamp the rhythm in time with the dance.

Rivera, Camilo. Honduran composer of band music. Born in Jesús de Otoro, July 21, 1878. *See* p. 213.

Rivera, Luis. Dominican composer of band music. Born in Monte Cristi, June 22, 1902. *See* p. 195.

Robles, Daniel Alomia. Peruvian folklore collector. Born in Huánuco, January 3, 1871; died at Chosica, near Lima, July 17, 1942. *See* p. 275.

roda (wheel). A Brazilian round, especially a children's song in square time and plain unsyncopated rhythm.

Rodriguez, Esther. Cuban composer of neoclassical music. Born in Manzanillo, November 29, 1920. *See* p. 186.

Rodriguez Socas, Ramón. Uruguayan

composer of Italianate operas. Born in Montevideo, August 31, 1890. *See* p. 287.

Rogatis, Pascual de. Italian-Argentine composer of operatic and symphonic music. Born in Teora, Italy, May 17, 1881; went to Argentina as a child. *See* p. 99.

Roig, Gonzalo. Cuban conductor and composer of vocal music. Born in Havana, July 20, 1890. *See* p. 186.

Roldán, Amadeo. Cuban mulatto composer of orchestral and vocal music inspired by Afro-Cuban folklore. Born in Paris, July 12, 1900; died in Havana, March 2, 1939. *See* p. 187.

Rolón, José. Mexican composer of orchestral music in a considerably advanced modern style. Born in Ciudad Guzmán, Jalisco, June 22, 1883; died in Mexico City, February 3, 1945. *See* pp. 251-252.

romance. The generic designation of the old-fashioned Spanish ballad, the prototype of the Latin American **corrido.**

roncador. An Afro-Brazilian drum.

Roncal, Simeón. Bolivian composer of dances and songs in the native manner. Born in Sucre, April 21, 1872. *See* pp. 107-108.

rondador. A panpipe of Ecuadorian Indians, made of baked clay or of reeds tied together; called **antara** in Peru, **capador** in Colombia, **sicu** in Bolivia.

Rozo Contreras, José. Colombian band conductor and composer. Born in Bochalema, January 7, 1894. *See* p. 171.

Rueda, Fernando. Dominican composer of band music. Born in Santo Domingo, May 22, 1859; died there, May 25, 1939. *See* pp. 195-196.

Ruiz, Ramón. Nicaraguan-Honduran amateur musician. Born in Somota, Nicaragua, February 28, 1894; settled in Honduras as a boy. *See* p. 213.

rum. A large Afro-Brazilian drum of the **tabaqué** family.

rumba. A greatly popular Cuban dance of African antecedents, in ¾ time, diversified with polyrhythmic counterpoint.

rumpi. A medium-sized Afro-Brazilian drum of the **tabaqué** family.

S

sacabuche. A sackbut, primitive form of the slide trombone.

saccapá. *See* zacapá.

Saint-Malo, Alfredo de. Panamanian violinist. Born in Panama City, December 13, 1898. *See* p. 262.

sajuriana. *See* zajuriana.

Salazar, Adolfo. Spanish musicologist resident in Mexico since 1939. Born in Madrid, March 6, 1890. *See* p. 252.

Salgado, Luis H. Ecuadorian composer of symphonic music with native themes. Born in Cayambé, December 10, 1903. *See* pp. 199-200.

salla. The Incan flute, of the quena family.

salliva. A large salla.

salongo. A ritual dance of the Haitian Negroes.

samba. A popular Brazilian dance characterized by a rolling rhythm in 2/4 time with rapid notes; loosely, any Brazilian dance in fast tempo.

samba-batucada. A Brazilian dance which combines the characteristics of a samba with the explosive rhythms of a batuque.

samba-canção. A song in the samba manner, with long sustained notes in the melody against the rapid rhythm of the accompaniment.

Sammartino, Luis R. Argentine composer of instrumental music in conventional forms. Born in Buenos Aires, April 8, 1890. *See* p. 99.

Sanchez de Fuentes, Eduardo. Cuban composer of operas and songs in characteristically native rhythms. Born in Havana, April 3, 1874; died there, September 7, 1944. *See* pp. 187-188.

Sánchez Málaga, Carlos. Peruvian composer of piano .pieces and songs. Born in Arequipa, September 8, 1904. *See* p. 275.

Sandi, Luis. Mexican composer of folklorically colored orchestral and choral music. Born in Mexico City, February 22, 1905. *See* pp. 252-253.

sandunga. *See* zandunga.

sanfona. A popular Brazilian name for the accordion.

sanjuanito (named after St. John). The national dance of Ecuador, in 2/4 time and a minor key, similar to the Bolivian huaiño.

Santa Cruz Wilson, Domingo. Chilean composer of the national vanguard movement. Born in La Cruz, July 5, 1899. *See* pp. 162-164.

Santoro, Claudio. Brazilian composer of atonal music. Born in Manaos, November 23, 1919. *See* p. 140.

Santórsola, Guido. Italian-born Uruguayan composer. Born in Canosa di Puglia, November 18, 1904. *See* p. 287.

Santos, Domingo. Salvadoran composer of instrumental music in an academic manner. Born in San Esteban, August 4, 1892. *See* p. 281.

sarambo. A characteristic dance of the interior of Santo Domingo, similar to the zapateado montuno.

Sas, André. French-Peruvian composer of orchestral and chamber music in a distinctive modern style. Born in Paris, April 6, 1900; resident in Peru since 1924. *See* p. 276.

saudade. A Portuguese word meaning nostalgic memory, and used as a title for evocative pieces by Brazilian composers.

Schianca, Arturo. Argentine musicologist and composer. Born in Carmen de Areco, December 26, 1889. *See* p. 99.

Schiuma, Alfredo. Argentine composer of Italianate operas. Born in Buenos Aires, June 25, 1885. *See* pp. 99-100.

schote. The Brazilian version of the schottische, in 2/4 time and steady rhythm, without syncopation.

seis. A Puerto Rican ballad in a Spanish manner.

senka tankana. A large Bolivian vertical flute.

seresta. A Brazilian serenade sung to the accompaniment of a small instrumental ensemble.

serrote. A Brazilian country dance.

Siccardi, Honorio. Argentine composer of instrumental music in a complex modern idiom. Born in Buenos Aires, September 13, 1897. *See* p. 100.

sicu. A Bolivian panpipe; called antara

in Peru, **capador** in Colombia, **ronda-dor** in Ecuador.

sicuris. Twin flutes of the Andean region.

sicus gigantes. Bolivian panpipes made of several reeds of enormous length, emitting a low, lugubrious sound.

sihuenta. A large twin panpipe of Bolivia.

Siliézar, Felipe. Guatemalan composer of colorful musical pieces. Born in Guatemala City, May 1, 1903. *See* p. 207.

Silva, Jesús Bermudez. *See* **Bermudez Silva, Jesús.**

Simó, Manuel. Dominican composer of chamber music in a competent manner. Born in San Francisco de Macorís, June 30, 1916. *See* p. 196.

Siqueira, José. Brazilian composer of numerous orchestral works in a nativistic manner. Born in Conceição, June 24, 1907. *See* pp. 140-141.

siquimiriqui. An Araucanian Chilean dance, now extant only on the island of Chiloé.

siringa aymará (Aymará syrinx). *See* **sicu.**

socador. An Afro-Brazilian drum.

socavón. The vocal variant of the **mejorana.**

Sojo, Vicente Emilio. Venezuelan choral conductor and composer of vocal music. Born in Guatine, December 8, 1887. *See* p. 294.

sombrerito (little hat). A dance of northern Argentina in ¾ time; the name derives from a figure in the dance where the partners deposit their hats.

son (sound). The generic name of native airs of Cuba and Central America, denoting variable melo-rhythmic patterns according to locality.

son afro-cubano. A Cuban **son** with strong syncopation and percussive instrumentation typical of Negro songs and dances.

sonajas. The Mexican name for the **maracas.**

son chapín. See **son guatemalteco.**

sones mariachi. The generic name for airs and dances performed by the Mexican **mariachi** bands.

son guatemalteco (Guatemalan **son**). The typical dance of Guatemala in the rhythm of a rapid waltz or mazurka.

Soro, Enrique. Chilean composer of numerous works of all genres in an academic harmonic idiom. Born in Concepción, July 15, 1884. *See* pp. 164-165.

Spena, Lorenzo. Italian-Argentine composer of operas. Born in Naples, April 29, 1874; resident in Argentina since 1901. *See* p. 100.

Stea, Vicente. Italian-Peruvian composer of neoromantic orchestral music. Born in Gioia del Colle, April 19, 1884; died in Lima, July 10, 1943. *See* pp. 276-277.

Stubbs du Perron, Eduardo Walter. Peruvian composer of colorful musical theater pieces. Born in Lima, December 31, 1891. *See* p. 277.

sueste. A Panamanian air of the **punto** type.

Suffern, Carlos. Argentine composer of neoimpressionistic piano pieces and chamber music. Born in Luján, September 25, 1905. *See* p. 100.

sambacueca. *See* **zamacueca.**

sukcha. A percussion instrument of the Peruvian Indians consisting of the skull of a llama.

suribi. A wooden trumpet of the Amazon Indians consisting of a tube enclosed in a cylindrical resonance box.

T

tabaqué. An Afro-Brazilian drum made of a segment of a hollowed-out tree covered with animal hide.

tacapú. *See* **taquará.**

taica (Aymará Indian word for mother). A long Bolivian flute.

taica-hirpa. A species of **taica.**

tamaracá. A primitive Brazilian drum of the **tabaqué** type.

tambô de criolo (drum of the native). An Afro-Brazilian song of the fetishist ritual.

tambor. The abbreviation for **tamborito.**

tambor (from Spanish). A generic name for drums of all kinds and sizes.

tambora. A variant of tambor.

tambor de orden. A parlor form of the rural tamborito in Panama.

tamborera. A Panamanian dance of Mexican origin, of the huapango type.

tamborito. A Panamanian dance of Spanish origin, usually written in a major key and in ¾ time.

tambor surdo (Portuguese). A muted drum.

tambour meringouin. A Haitian "earth bow," consisting of a string attached to a stick buried in the earth, which serves as the resonance body; used to play for the meringue.

tambour-travaille. The "work drum" of Haiti.

tambú. A drum of the Brazilian Negroes.

tango. The most popular Argentine parlor dance characterized by the swinging rhythm of a habanera in ¾ time; usually in two sections, the first in minor, the second in major.

tango brasileiro. A Brazilian tango, characterized by a greater syncopation and chromatic ornamentation in the melody than in the Argentine prototype.

tango-milonga. The Argentine song-dance combining the sentiment of the old-fashioned rural milonga with the rhythm of the modern urban tango.

tanguinho (diminutive of tango). A short tango Brasileiro.

tanguino. A Peruvian dance having little in common with the Argentine tango, and usually written in 4⁄4 time.

tanguito. A Venezuelan variant of the tango.

taquará. A Brazilian Indian "rhythm baton" or stamping tube, made of a long tube of sugar cane or of wood, which is struck on the ground.

tarca. See charca.

tarka. See charca.

tartaruga. A Brazilian medium-size drum.

Tavares, Hekel. Brazilian composer of numerous songs and piano pieces in native rhythms. Born in Satuba in 1896. See pp. 141-142.

tayca. See taica.

tcha-tcha. A Haitian rattle, similar to the maracas.

tecsiztli. A Mexican conch shell.

tede. A Peruvian flute made of an armadillo skull and a bird bone.

teirú. A medium-sized transverse flute of the Amazon Indians of Brazil.

Tello, Rafael. Mexican composer of academically competent instrumental and vocal music. Born in Mexico City, September 5, 1872. See p. 253.

ténabari. A Mexican rattle made of a butterfly cocoon, worn on the ankles.

teponahuaste. The Salvadoran Indian name for teponaxtle.

teponaxtle (teponacao, to grow). A horizontal Mexican slit drum made of a hollowed-out tree trunk, with two distinct sounds produced by striking a wooden mallet on either side of a large aperture in the middle of the trunk.

teponaztli. See teponaxtle.

ternos. Christmas pageant in Brazil.

tetl. The "sonorous stone" of the Mayas, usually with a perforation in the center for better resonance.

tetzilacatl. A metal gong of the ancient Mexicans.

thumb piano. The West Indian name for the marimba.

thunder-stick. A thin flat piece of wood, swung on a cord to produce a whirring noise.

timbal. In West Indies, a horizontal drum covered with animal hide on one end, and open on the other.

timbirimba. A Colombian musical bow played by rubbing the string so as to produce a distinct sound.

tintaya. A form of tambourine used by the Indians of the South American altiplano.

tinya. A small flat Peruvian drum with one membrane.

tiple (treble). A high-pitched guitar without the lower strings.

tirana. A song of the Azores imported into Brazil, characterized by a steady ¾ rhythm.

tlapanhuehuetl. A large huehuetl.

tlapitzali. An Aztec ocarina, or whistling jar, made of baked clay.

toada (Portuguese word for the Spanish tonada). A Brazilian air of flexible form and rhythm, expressing pensive or wistful moods.

toboinha sonante (sounding box). The thunder-stick of the Amazon Indians of Brazil.

tock-oro. A primitive Peruvian trumpet made of wood or baked clay, which produces a sound resembling the bass clarinet.

tolero. A Panamanian vertical flute, usually with five apertures.

tolo. A fife of the Panamanian Indians with a double-reed mouthpiece.

tomangú. A Central American musical bow.

tonada (that which is sounded). A generic Spanish word for a folk song of a meditative character.

tonada maguanera. A rustic air of the province La Maguana of Santo Domingo.

tondero. A north Peruvian form of the marinera.

tono. A Panamanian air of the punto type.

tono llanero (song of the plains). The Venezuelan song of the flatlands, characterized by a meditative nostalgia.

torbellino. A Colombian dance in ¾ time, with heavy accents on the strong beat.

toré. A primitive trumpet of the Brazilian and Paraguayan Indians, made of sugar cane or baked clay, and producing a raucous, lugubrious sound.

tori. See toré.

torito negro. A Bolivian carnival dance, imitating a bullfight.

torokaná. See trocano.

Torra, Celia. Argentine composer of atmospheric pieces in native manner. Born in Concepción, Uruguay, September 18, 1889. See pp. 100-101.

Torre Bertucci, José. Argentine composer of piano pieces and songs. Born in Buenos Aires, July 8, 1888. See p. 101.

Tosar Errecart, Hector. Uruguayan composer of precociously expert chamber music in a neoclassical idiom. Born in Montevideo, July 18, 1923. See p. 287.

tot. An incrustated conch shell used by the Guatemalan Indians as an ocarina.

tototlapitzali. An ancient Mexican bird-shaped whistle.

tratripuli. A species of the vertical flute quena; also a dance performed to the sound of the flute.

Traversari, Pedro. Ecuadorian composer of chromomusical pieces with native subjects. Born in Quito, July 28, 1874. See p. 200.

tres. A Cuban guitar with three double strings.

triste. A melancholy love song of northern Argentina, of Peruvian origin, similar to the yaraví.

triunfo (triumph). An Argentine dance in lively ⅜ time once popular in the rural regions.

trocano. A horizontal drum of Paraguay and Brazil, consisting of a burned-out tree trunk set on two wooden tripods.

Troiani, Gaetano. Italian-Argentine composer of stylized native dances. Born in Chieti, Italy, October 20, 1873; died in Buenos Aires, September 3, 1942. See p. 101.

trote. The Bolivian version of "trot," or "foxtrot."

trumpa. A species of musical bow.

trutruca. A long reed pipe used by the Araucanian Indians of Chile.

tsin-hali. A nasal ocarina of the Brazilian Indians, made of two discs of a gourd and sounded by the pressure of the air from only one nostril, the other being closed with a finger.

tumba. A once-popular dance of Santo Domingo, in the genre of a tarantella.

tun. The Central American name for the teponaxtle.

tuna. A social form of the rustic tamborito of Panama.

tuncul. The Mayan name for the teponaxtle.

turá. The Venezuelan native flute, similar to the quena.

turá-maracá. A Brazilian stamping tube, consisting of a long reed with a maracá tied to it, which is struck on the ground to keep time.

turumba. A species of musical bow.

tu-ti. A nickname for castanets among the natives of the island of Santo Domingo.

tuto. A small panpipe of the Bolivian Indians.

tzicahuaztli (strong noise). A Mexican notched ratchet.

tzijolaj. A Guatemalan Indian vertical flute with four apertures.

U

ualalocé. A transverse flute of the Amazon Indians of Brazil.

uapí. A vertical Indo-Brazilian drum, consisting of a hollow tree trunk covered on top with animal hide.

uarangá. The rhythm baton or a stamping tube of the Amazon Indians.

uaraperú. An Indio-Brazilian transverse flute.

uatapí. See uapí.

ubatá. An Afro-Brazilian drum.

ufuá. A species of the trumpet toré.

Ugarte, Florio M. Argentine composer of theatrical music. Born in Buenos Aires, September 15, 1884. See p. 101.

umcungá. A musical bow of central Brazil with a string stopped at one-third of its length by a cord attached to the rod, and played by beating with a stick.

upa. A primitive dance of the West Indian aborigines.

Uribe-Holguin, Guillermo. Foremost composer of Colombia, writing orchestral and chamber music in a neoimpressionist idiom with native rhythms. Born in Bogotá, March 17, 1880. See pp. 171-172.

Urrutia Blondel, Jorge. Chilean composer of choral and theatrical music on native subjects. Born in La Serana, September 17, 1905. See p. 166.

urucá. An Indo-Brazilian conch shell used as an ocarina.

V

vaccine. The Haitian bamboo trumpet.

Valcárcel, Teodoro. Peruvian Indian composer of native-inspired original music. Born in Puno, October 18, 1900; died in Lima, March 20, 1942. See pp. 277-278.

Valderrama, Carlos. Peruvian amateur composer of dances and songs with native flavor. Born in Trujillo, September 4, 1890. See p. 278.

Valencia, Antonio María. Colombian composer of chamber music in an impressionist vein. Born in Cali, November 10, 1903. See p. 172.

Valle-Riestra, José María. Peruvian composer of operatic music. Born in Lima, November 9, 1859; died there, January 25, 1925. See p. 278.

vals. A waltz.

vals del pais. See pasillo.

vals tropical. A tropical variety of the European waltz, characterized by a faster tempo.

Valverde, Mariano. Guatemalan amateur composer of popular dances. Born in Quezaltenango, November 20, 1884. See p. 207.

vapí. See uapí.

Vargas, Teófilo. Bolivian folklore collector and composer of dances in popular vein. Born in Cochabamba, November 3, 1868. See p. 108.

Vasquez, José. Mexican composer of orchestral and chamber music in neoromantic manner. Born in Guadalajara, October 4, 1895. See pp. 253-254.

vatapí. The same as vapí and uapí.

Vega, Augusto. Dominican composer of folkloric music for orchestra. Born in Puerto Plata, October 10, 1885. See p. 196.

Velasco Maidana, José María. Bolivian composer of vocal and instrumental music with native themes. Born in La Paz, July 4, 1899. See p. 108.

Verneuil, Raoul de. Peruvian composer of modernistic piano pieces. Born in Lima, April 9, 1901. See p. 278.

Vianna, Fructuoso. Brazilian composer of folksong-flavored piano pieces. Born in Itajuba, September 6, 1896. See p. 142.

vidala. A popular Argentine air in ¾ or ⅜ time, and in moderate tempo.

vidalita. An Argentine air in ⅜ or ⁶⁄₈ time, differing from the **vidala** as to rhythm; the name comes from the repetition of the word *vidalita* (little life) in every other line of the verse.

Villalba-Muñoz,. Alberto. Spanish-Argentine composer of theatrical music on Spanish-American subjects. Born in Valladolid, November 10, 1878. *See* pp. 101-102.

Villa-Lobos, Heitor. Foremost composer of Brazil, writing prolifically in all genres, with native-inspired material elaborated in an individualized modern style. Born in Rio de Janeiro, March 5, 1887. *See* pp. 142-150.

Villanueva Galeano, Ignacio. Honduran amateur musician. Born in La Esperanza, February 1, 1885. *See* p. 213.

violão. A Brazilian guitar.

Viscarra Monje, Humberto. Bolivian composer of piano pieces. Born in Sotaya, March 30, 1898. *See* p. 108.

vodoun drums. *See* **voodoo drums.**

voodoo drums. The ritual drums of Haiti.

vú. *See* **vuvú.**

vudu. *See* **voodoo.**

vuvú. An Afro-Brazilian drum.

W

wada. *See* **huada.**

wainyo. *See* **huaiño.**

wankar. *See* **huancar.**

wayno. *See* **huaiño.**

wewetl. *See* **huehuetl.**

Williams, Alberto. Argentine composer of nine symphonies and numerous other works in the spirit of native folklore. Born in Buenos Aires, November 23, 1862. *See* pp. 102-104.

X

xácara. A type of popular Brazilian ballad.

xangó. A dance of the **macumba** ritual, in honor of the Afro-Brazilian deity **Xangó.**

xaqué-xaqué. *See* **chequeré.**

xocalho. *See* **chocalho.**

xôro. *See* **chôro.**

xu. *See* **zul.**

xucalho. *See* **chocalho.**

Y

yapurutú. A vertical flute of the Amazon Indians of Brazil, with one aperture near the mouthpiece and closed at the end by the natural knot of a bamboo reed.

yararacá. A Brazilian trumpet made of a bamboo tube with jingles affixed at both ends.

yaravi. Spanish spelling of **harawi**; a slow melancholy song of the Andean Indians, in short phrases, and in a minor mode.

yegüecita (little mare). A Nicaraguan folk dance in which the dancers hold a wooden horse's head.

yoeri. A **musical bow** of the central lowlands of South America.

yupururó. A species of the flute **turá.**

yurupari. A long wooden trumpet used in the Amazon region; named after the tribal god of the Amazon Indians.

yüullu. The **cascabeles** of the Araucanian Indians.

Z

zacapá. An Andean jingle rattle made of dried fruit shells.

zacatán. The Mayan name for the **huehuetl.**

zajuriana. A variant of the **zamacueca**, as danced in the province of Chiloé in Chile.

zamacueca. The national air of Chile, in a major key and in ⁶⁄₈ time alternating with ¾ in rapid tempo.

zamba. An Argentine dance, derived from the **zamacueca**, in ⁶⁄₈ time and moderate tempo.

zambacueca. *See* **zamacueca.**

zamba cuyana. *See* **cuyana.**

zambé. An Afro-Brazilian drum.

zambumbia. A Central American drum.

zamponã. The generic name for panpipes; called **antara** in Peru, **capador** in Colombia, **rondador** in Ecuador, **sicu** in Bolivia.

zandunga (graceful woman). An old-fashioned Mexican air in waltz time.

zapateado. *See* zapateo.

zapateado montuno. A country dance of Santo Domingo in which the partners perform a tap dance.

zapateo (shoe dance). A tap dance, often used as a section of another dance.

zapatero. A special type of the Panamanian **socavón,** in which the melody ends on the tonic and not on the dominant.

zapotecano. *See* **marimba.**

zopilote (buzzard). A Nicaraguan folk dance in which the dancers dress like birds.

zorataló. A large transverse flute of the Amazon Indians of Brazil.

zu. *See* **zul.**

zubak (sounding bone, from Maya). *See* **zul.**

zuholocé. *See* **ualalocé.**

zul. A primitive Central American flute.

zumbidor. A Brazilian bull-roarer, or **thunder-stick,** consisting of a cord and a small perforated box which is swung in the air, producing a rumbling noise.

zuzá. The **chocalho** of the Amazon Indians of Brazil.

Addenda: 1972

Allende, Adolfo. Died in Santiago in 1966.

Allende, Humberto. Died in Santiago, August 16, 1959.

Bautista, Julian. Died in Buenos Aires, July 8, 1961.

Bernal Jiménez, Miguel. Died in León, Mexico, July 26, 1956.

Bisquertt Prado, Prospero. Died in Santiago, August 2, 1959.

Boero, Felipe. Died in Buenos Aires, August 9, 1958.

Caba, Eduardo. Died in La Paz, March 3, 1953.

Carrillo, Julian. Died in Mexico City, September 9, 1965.

Casella, Enrique M. Died in Tucumán, December 10, 1948.

Castillo, Ricardo. Died in Guatemala City in 1967.

Castro, Herbert de. Died in Panama City, July 23, 1969.

Castro, José María. Died in Buenos Aires, August 10, 1964.

Castro, Juan José. Died in Buenos Aires, September 3, 1968.

Cluzeau Mortet, Luis. Died in Montevideo, September 28, 1957. Date of birth, November 16, 1889, *not* November 18, 1893.

Cosme, Luiz. Died in Rio de Janeiro, July 17, 1965.

Cotapos, Acario. Died in Santiago, November 22, 1969.

Da Cunha, João Itiberé. Died in Rio de Janeiro, February 25, 1953.

Delgadillo, Luis A. Died in Managua in 1965.

Espoile, Raúl. Died in Buenos Aires, April 13, 1958.

Fabini, Eduardo. Died in Montevideo, May 17, 1950.

Fonseca, Julio. Died in San José, June 22, 1950.

França, Agnelo. Died in Rio de Janeiro, August 8, 1964.

Fuentes, Juan. Died in León, Mexico, February 11, 1955.

Garay, Narciso. Died in Panama City, March 27, 1953.

Gilardi, Gilardo. Died in Buenos Aires, January 16, 1963.

Ippisch, Franz. Died in Vienna, February 20, 1958.

Kostakowsky, Jacobo. Died in Mexico City in 1953.

Lavin, Carlos. Died in Barcelona, August 27, 1962.

Lecuna, Juan. Died in Rome, April 15, 1954. Date of birth, November 20, 1894, *not* 1898.

Lecuona, Ernesto. Died in Santa Cruz de Tenerife, Canary Islands, November 29, 1963.

Luzzatti, Arturo. Died in Buenos Aires in 1959.

Mendoza, Vicente. Died in Mexico City, October 27, 1964.

Moncayo, Pablo. Died in Mexico City, June 16, 1958.

Nin y Castellanos. Joaquín. Died in Havana, October 24, 1949.

Ovalle, Jaime. Died in Rio de Janeiro, September 9, 1955.

Pahissa, Jaime. Died in Buenos Aires, October 18, 1968.

Palma, Athos. Died in Miramar, Argentina, January 10, 1951.

Panizza, Hector. Died in Buenos Aires, November 27, 1967.

Perceval, Julio. Died in Santiago, September 7, 1963.

Pinto, Alfredo. Died in Buenos Aires, May 26, 1968.

Plaza, Juan Bautista. Died in Caracas, January 1, 1964.

Roig,. Gonzalo. Died in Havana, June 13, 1970.

Salazar, Adolfo. Died in Mexico City, September 27, 1958.

Sás, André. Died in Lima, July 26, 1967.

Schiuma, Alfredo. Died in Buenos Aires in 1963.

Soro, Enrique. Died in Santiago, December 2, 1954.

Tavares, Hekel. Died in Brazil, August 1969.

Tello, Rafael. Died in Mexico City, December 17, 1946.

Torre Bertucci, José. Died in Buenos Aires, August 31, 1970.

Traversari, Pedro. Died in Quito in 1956.

Valderrama, Carlos. Died in Lima, August 1, 1950.

Valencia, Antonio María. Died in Cali, July 22, 1952.

Villa-Lobos, Heitor. Died in Rio de Janeiro, November 17, 1959.

Williams, Alberto. Died in Buenos Aires, June 17, 1952.

INDEX

327

INDEX